THE
Reflective
Leader

Implementing a
Multidimensional
Leadership Performance System

THE
Reflective
Leader

Implementing a
Multidimensional
Leadership Performance System

▲ Raymond Smith ▲ Karen Brofft ▲
▲ Nicole Law ▲ Julie Smith ▲

LEAD+
LEARN
PRESS

ENGLEWOOD, COLORADO

The Leadership and Learning Center
317 Inverness Way South, Suite 150
Englewood, Colorado 80112
Phone 1.866.399.6019 | Fax 303.504.9417
www.LeadandLearn.com

ISBN 978-1-935588-33-7
Printed in the United States of America

16 15 14 13 12   01 02 03 04 05 06 07

Contents

About the Authors

Dr. Raymond L. Smith is a Senior Professional Development Associate with The Leadership and Learning Center. Additionally, he recently served as an adjunct professor for the University of Colorado in Denver within the Principal Preparation Program, where he co-taught an 18-month integrated principal preparation course.

Dr. Smith has served as Director of High School Education for Douglas County School District in Castle Rock, Colorado, where his primary responsibility was leadership for and educational oversight of seven high schools and two alternative high schools—approximately 10,000 students in grades 9–12.

Dr. Smith has been a classroom teacher (elementary and secondary) and high school principal in two Colorado school districts. He has provided building leadership for three high schools, one of which involved the opening of a new 2,000-student high school in the Jefferson County Public Schools in Golden, Colorado.

Dr. Smith has presented, at both the district and state levels, seminars about "School Improvement Planning," "Leadership Development," "Leadership Assessment," "Cognitive Coaching," "Effective Teaching Strategies," and "Data Teams" to central office and building principals. He has authored several articles for the Ohio Department of Education and coauthored a book titled *School Improvement for the Next Generation* (2010). Most recently, he rewrote a seminar and training manual on the topic of *Advanced Decision Making for Results* (2011).

Additionally, Dr. Smith has served as one of the primary researchers on a team that conducted the original Planning, Implementation, and Monitoring (PIM™) Study for The Leadership and Learning Center. The PIM™ Study was initially highlighted in Dr. Douglas Reeves' book *The Learning Leader: How to Focus School Improvement for Better Results* (2006), with a more complete discussion in his book *Finding Your Leadership Focus: What Matters Most for Student Results* (2011). Dr. Smith holds a doctorate in educational leadership and innovation from the University of Colorado in Denver and Health Sciences Center, a master's degree in educational administration, and a bachelor's degree from the University of Northern Colorado at Greeley.

Dr. Smith lives with his wife, Julie, in Pacific City, a small fishing village in the Pacific Northwest on the Oregon Coast.

Karen Brofft is a Professional Development Associate with The Leadership and Learning Center. Karen's work with The Center integrates her years of school improvement experience with The Center's data and assessment processes and leadership performance models.

Currently, Karen serves as the Assistant Superintendent of Learning Services and Communications for Englewood Schools in Colorado, where Data Teams are in place district-wide. In addition to more than 20 years in education, Karen also worked in the public relations and technology fields for 7 years prior to entering education. She spent more than 20 years in Douglas County School District serving in a variety of teaching, administrative, and leadership roles. As a principal and later as the Director of Curriculum, Instruction, and Assessment, Karen implemented successful building and system-wide Professional Learning Communities using data and results as the cornerstone for measuring success.

In addition to her Ed. S. in administrative leadership and policy studies, Karen holds a master's degree in curriculum and instruction and a bachelor's degree in communications. Through her commitment to her own professional development as well as her extensive professional learning work with adults, Karen has developed a passion for delivering engaging, practical, professional development experiences that result in immediate application to student learning. Her experiences range from school and district-wide professional development to conference presentations and principal licensure cohorts with the University of Northern Colorado.

Karen is well grounded in the nature of effective professional development through ongoing coaching and mentoring. As a former instructional coach in Douglas County, she received extensive training in cognitive coaching, adaptive schools, and facilitation of group processes. These experiences, combined with her studies in communications, have provided Karen with a strong framework for working with a variety of adult learners in both individual and group settings. Karen is passionate about her work in education, and strives to ignite this passion in others.

Her commitment to her work keeps her busy. However, Karen still makes time on a daily basis to engage in yoga and reading. She has two older daughters. One recently graduated from Colorado State University and is working as an environmental planner, while Karen's younger daughter is currently pursuing a degree in business.

Nicole Law is a Professional Development Associate with The Leadership and Learning Center. Nicole uses her experience to present instruction on decision making for results, Data Teams, case studies for the 90/90/90 Schools Summit, and accelerating academic achievement of English learners.

Nicole has served as Curriculum Coordinator for English Language Learners, Cultural Responsibility, Advancement via Individual Determination (AVID), Mathematics, and Science in the Metropolitan School District of Wayne Township in Indianapolis, Indiana. In this position, Nicole created multi-layered and -faceted professional development for teachers and administrators, covering all aspects of directed programs and curricular areas. Nicole has written curriculum in the areas of science, mathematics, and English language development. Nicole trained and supported administrators, teacher leaders, site coordinators, and school improvement teams in the decision making for results and Data Teams processes.

Nicole has an array of educational experiences. During her 15 years in education, Nicole has been a junior high school science teacher, an elementary school teacher, an elementary school assistant principal, and an elementary school principal. As a former elementary school principal, Nicole led her school through a transformation in both school culture and instructional practice; she is now committed to doing the same for her district. Facing a growing student enrollment in English as a New Language (ENL), Nicole now leads her district in consistent implementation of highly effective, research-based instructional practices that apply to all learners.

Nicole is described as not living in the world of standardized tests and No Child Left Behind, but rather living in the world of learning and achievement for all. Nicole thrives on gaining new knowledge and pouring her energy and passion into her work of developing others. By this, Nicole seeks to help educators to understand the factors that allow all students to achieve academic success.

Nicole is a skilled trainer, presenter, and group facilitator. She thoroughly plans by prioritizing learning needs, organizing content, creating a learning environment, and designing learning experiences to deliver information in an interesting way to diverse audiences.

Nicole has received various recognitions throughout her career. She received a 2008 Milken Educator Award from the state of Indiana, Indiana's Keepers of the Village Award in 2010, and was a recipient of The Center for Leadership Development's award for Excellence in Education in 2009. She resides in Indianapolis, Indiana, with her husband, Stan, and son, Kyle. Nicole and her family enjoy cruising, skiing, and spending lazy summer days at many of Florida's beaches.

Dr. Julie Smith is a Professional Development Associate with The Leadership and Learning Center. Julie's work with The Center integrates her years of school improvement experience with the decision making for results, Data Teams, and leadership development processes.

With her unique and varied background, it is easy to see that Julie is a lifelong learner who truly believes in building leadership capacity at all levels of the organization. Julie maintains a clear focus on improving the practices of educators in order to improve student achievement, from district-level to building-level leaders and teachers.

Julie's most recent public school position was Executive Director of Elementary Schools for Cherry Creek School District in Greenwood Village, Colorado. Her primary responsibility was providing leadership and educational support to 40 elementary schools. As principal, she was selected to open two new 800-student, year-round K–6 elementary schools in Douglas County, Colorado. In addition to more than 30 years in education as a staff developer, principal, building resource teacher, and coach, Julie also worked five years as an adjunct professor for the University of Colorado at Denver in the Principal Preparation Program.

Julie has presented at both the district and state levels. She has demonstrated her strong professional development in her ability to work with large and small groups to establish rapport and trust quickly to ensure a safe and successful learning environment. She has been a Baldridge Continuous Quality Improvement and Integrated Management Models

(CQI) trainer, worked with Dr. Madeline Hunter as a trainer for Essential Elements of Instruction, served as a senior consultant for the International Center for Leadership in Education, chaired the Cherry Creek School District Standards-Based Report Card Committee, and was a member of the Douglas County Pay for Performance Council.

Prior to joining The Leadership and Learning Center, Julie served in a corporate position as Vice President of District Development for the Learning Together Company. In this position, she was responsible for the induction of her sales team and worked closely with superintendents and their district and school administration to understand and implement cross-age peer tutoring, reading, and math interventions.

In addition to receiving her Ph.D. in leadership and innovation from the University of Colorado Denver Health Sciences Center, she holds a master of arts in gifted and talented education from the University of Northern Colorado at Greeley, as well as a bachelor of arts from the University of Arizona in Tempe, Arizona.

Julie was selected to receive the University of Colorado at Denver's Wright Way Award for outstanding principal leadership. The innovative practices of one of her elementary schools was featured in the summer 1999 "Noteworthy" edition, published by McREL (Mid-continent Regional Educational Laboratory).

Julie lives with her husband on the west coast in Pacific City, Oregon. While her work keeps her busy, in her spare time she enjoys reading, treasure hunting on the beach, kayaking, and time with family and friends. The Smiths have two grown children and three grandchildren who all love to visit and explore the coast.

Preface

Donald Schön, a university professor, philosopher, researcher, consultant, and an accomplished pianist and clarinetist, playing in both jazz and chamber groups, made a number of significant contributions to the field of education (Schön, 1983; 1987). Some of these include studies of learning systems (and learning societies and institutions), double-loop and organizational learning (arising out of his collaboration with Chris Argyris), and the relationship of reflection-in-action to professional activity. It was, however, his contribution of "reflection" on practice that helped educators understand what professionals do that is most important to the topic of this book—*The Reflective Leader.*

Schön's (1987) notions of reflection-in-action and reflection-on-action were central to his efforts to help aspiring practitioners "meet the heightened societal expectations for their performance in an environment that combines increasing turbulence with increasing regulation of professional activity" (p. 7). The former is sometimes described as "thinking on our feet." It involves looking to our experiences, connecting with our feelings, and attending to our theories in use to apply just-in-time solutions to some of the most complex problems we face in education today. It entails building new understandings to inform our leadership actions in a situation that is unfolding. In a similar manner, Doug Reeves (2004) supports Schön's emphasis on the importance of reflection in leadership practice by observing that "the greater your responsibility and authority in an organization, the less likely you receive systematic and constructive evaluation … the greater the need for the reflection, coaching, midcourse corrections, and continuous improvement that are the hallmarks of effective evaluation" (p. ix).

A reflective leader allows herself to experience surprise, puzzlement, or confusion in a situation that she finds uncertain or unique. She reflects on the phenomenon before her (various problems of practice), and on the prior understandings that have been implicit in her behavior. She carries out an experiment (e.g., action research that monitors and measures a hypothesized high-leverage leadership strategy against key organizational indicators), which serves to generate both a new understanding of the phenomenon and a change in the situation (leadership practices) (Schön, 1983, p. 68).

Reflective leaders test out their theories or, as John Dewey might have put it, "leading ideas," and this allows them to evolve their responses and actions (adjustments to planned leadership strategies). More importantly, to do this, they do not closely follow established ideas and techniques—textbook schemes. Rather, they have to think things through, for every improvement opportunity is unique. However, they can draw on what has gone before.

This process of thinking on our feet is linked with reflection-on-action and occurs after implementing the professional growth plan and working (i.e., implementing, monitoring, measuring, and applying the results of) a couple of high-leverage strategies-in-action. Leaders may write up results of their improvement efforts, talk things through with a supervisor, and so on. The act of reflecting-on-action enables them to spend time exploring why they acted as they did, what was happening as a result, and more. By reflecting deeply on their actions and on the relationship between their actions and the impact they had on the core of their business (e.g., teaching and learning), leaders can determine, among other things, which actions should be eliminated or modified and which actions should be replicated. More importantly, the process of reflecting-on-action is not just a benefit to the school administrator; it is equally as beneficial to the school administrator's supervisor. As Viviane Robinson (2011) states, "When we understand a person's theory of action, we understand why he behaved as he did and we can work with him to evaluate whether or not the theory *in* his action matches his intentions" (p. 115). In so doing, reflective leaders and leaders of reflective leaders develop sets of questions and ideas about how best to spend their time or how not to spend their time, which practices seem to be more related to their most important results, thus inspiring the title of this book, *The Reflective Leader.*

Introduction

In his seminal book entitled *Leadership,* James MacGregor Burns (1978), a university professor, presidential biographer, authority on leadership studies, and a Pulitzer Prize–winning author, lamented that "If we know all too much about our leaders, we know far too little about *leadership*" (p.1). Burns went on to conclude that "Leadership is one of the most observed and least understood phenomena on earth" (p. 2). While Burns's comments may have accurately reflected views on leadership in the late 1970s, if we advance forward to today and the research conducted on the same topic by an impressive array of leaders in education, we can easily say that we have a very clear picture of what effective leaders must know and be able to do to address the challenges of transformational change (Kouzes and Posner, 1987, 1993, 2010; Fullan, 1997, 2005; Fullan, Hill, and Crévola, 2006; Leithwood, Jantzi, and Steinbach, 1999; Marzano, Waters, and McNulty, 2005; Heifetz, 1994; Heifetz and Linsky, 2002; Peters and Waterman, 1982; Peters, 1985; Reeves, 2002, 2006; Robinson, 2011; Hattie, 2009; Wahlstrom, et al., 2010).

As a result of the work of these authors and many others, we have come to understand clearly that highly effective leaders must be able to create schools as organizations that can learn and change quickly if they are to improve both individual and collective performance. School districts and schools need leaders who are adept at creating systems for change and who weave a web of connectivity, collaboration, and coordinated effort. By establishing powerful relationships with and across staff, such leaders awaken educators' passions for their work with those children entrusted to their care. These systems help everyone within the organization to easily access the organization's knowledge base, its collective brain. For the purpose of the work of the district and school, reflective leaders must create a shared understanding among staff of the internal, bone-deep beliefs that inform and direct external actions. Such commitment and ownership of a set of practices focuses everyone's decision making. This common understanding of the district's and school's identity empowers leaders to build strong partnerships with students, parents, and community stakeholders and thereby enhances their ability to produce increased student achievement.

The Reflective Leader: Implementing a Multidimensional Leadership Performance (MLP) System incorporates this contemporary view of highly effective reflective leaders and extends the thinking and writing of Dr. Douglas Reeves (2009) in his book *Assessing Educational Leaders*, as well as that of the content presented within The Leadership and Learning Center's seminar of the same title. That is, the present publication describes a professional development process that targets central office and building leaders and guides them through the successful creation and implementation of a multidimensional leadership assessment system.

The Purposes of the Evaluation

The ultimate purpose of the Multidimensional Leadership Performance (MLP) System is to improve leadership performance, thereby increasing the likelihood that teacher and student performance will also improve. The appraisal process acknowledges the growing demands on as well as the complexity of leadership in the 21st century. To become an exemplary leader, one must have a commitment to continuous improvement. The MLP System process will:

- Focus leaders on the leadership practices that are strongly related to increases in staff and student performance;

- Stimulate continuous growth of leaders by encouraging self-reflection, goal setting, data-driven decision making, collaborative learning processes, openness to change, and an informed view of educational needs;

- Inform higher education programs in developing the content and requirements of degree programs that prepare future leaders;

- Clarify the goals and objectives of districts and schools as they support, monitor, and evaluate leaders;

- Guide professional development for leaders; and

- Serve as a tool in developing coaching and mentoring programs for leaders throughout the organization.

1 Multidimensional Leadership Performance: System Overview

In his most recent edition of *Assessing Educational Leaders,* Douglas Reeves (2009) offers a compelling argument to support his contention that leadership evaluation at present is broken. Specifically, Reeves' research findings on this critically important issue conclude that most leadership evaluation systems simultaneously discourage effective leaders, fail to sanction ineffective leaders, and rarely consider their purpose to be the improvement of leadership performance. To improve leadership performance, Reeves believes that educators need to address three issues. First, educators must define effective leadership by creating "jargon-free" leadership standards. Second, these clearly expressed leadership standards must be translated into standards of performance that provide a continuum of evaluation to consistently differentiate adequate performance from performance that shows progress and performance that is exemplary. The third issue educators must address is ensuring these standards of leadership performance hold leaders accountable for matters directly within their control and/or influence. The alternative to leadership evaluation systems that don't address these three issues is Multidimensional Leadership Performance (MLP). In this system, the fundamental purpose of leadership assessment is to improve teaching and learning through enhancing the knowledge and skills of current and prospective educational leaders.

To build this knowledge and these skills, it is vital to consider the specific actions of educational leaders that are most linked to improving student achievement. The Planning, Implementation, and Monitoring (PIM™) studies conducted by The Leadership and Learning Center, as cited in Douglas Reeves' (2011) book *Finding Your Leadership Focus: What Matters Most for Student Results,* help leaders zero in on "clusters of effective leadership practice" (p. 26). The PIM™ studies were based on work with more than 2,000 schools in the United States and Canada, involving more than 1.5 million students comprising high- and low-poverty schools; high- and low-second-language schools; and schools from urban, suburban, and rural environments.

The Center found three vital clusters of leadership practices that positively impact student achievement: focus, monitoring, and efficacy. To begin with, The Center interprets "focus" to mean that leaders identify and monitor no more than six, but preferably two to three, priority instructional initiatives, which are connected clearly to specific student needs. Next, "monitoring" refers to the systematic observation of adult actions (at least five to six times per year)—that is, what teachers and leaders do in order to improve student learning. Last, "efficacy" refers to teachers and administrators believing that their actions are the primary influences on the academic success of students.

Robinson (2011) and Hattie (2012) support Reeves' (2011) findings that it is "clusters" of leadership practices, rather than leadership practices implemented in isolation, which will, in combination, have a strong probability of improving student results. Specifically, Robinson's (2011) analysis of 30 studies, mostly conducted in the United States, enabled her to categorize different leadership practices into five broad categories, or "leadership dimensions" (p. 9). It appears from her research that these five leadership dimensions, when practiced together, have a unique interrelationship to one another and positively impact student achievement. In other words, when these leadership practices are implemented with fidelity they, like Douglas Reeves' "clusters of leadership practices," produce a "moderate"

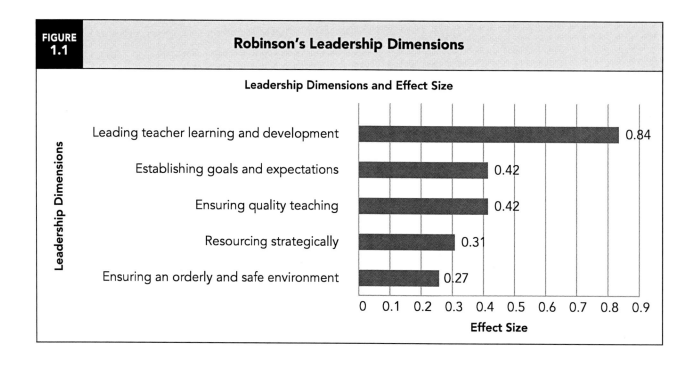

FIGURE 1.1 — **Robinson's Leadership Dimensions**

Leadership Dimensions and Effect Size

Leading teacher learning and development — 0.84
Establishing goals and expectations — 0.42
Ensuring quality teaching — 0.42
Resourcing strategically — 0.31
Ensuring an orderly and safe environment — 0.27

Leadership Dimensions (y-axis)
Effect Size (x-axis): 0 0.1 0.2 0.3 0.4 0.5 0.6 0.7 0.8 0.9

(i.e., an effect size of 0.40) to a "large" (i.e., 0.60 effect size and above) impact on student achievement as illustrated in Figure 1.1.

More importantly, this pattern among educational researchers of looking for "clusters" or "dimensions" of leadership practices that, when skillfully executed together, produce a significant impact on student achievement is not limited to these authors. For example, Marzano, Waters, and McNulty (2005) identified 21 leadership responsibilities all of which have a statistically significant relationship to student achievement. Louis, Leithwood, Wahlstrom, and Anderson (2010) found three leadership practices considered instructionally helpful, and Kouzes and Posner (2010) describe 10 "enduring truths" about leadership that hold consistent regardless of context or circumstance.

In *Assessing Educational Leaders,* Douglas Reeves (2004) states, "Effective leadership assessment depends on the candid acknowledgement of every leader's success and mistakes and the clear association of those leadership practices with organizational results" (p. 17). To assess effective leadership practices, it is essential to consider a complex set of variables through a protocol referred to as the *Multidimensional Leadership Performance (MLP) System.* In subscribing to this assessment protocol, school systems make a commitment to establish clear, coherent, and fair expectations for leaders. Reeves notes six essential criteria for MLP:

- **Proactive:** Starts before the job begins. Human resource departments can use the domain descriptions within their posting of open principal positions to help applicants understand the role as well as the qualifications required. Principal interview teams can use the descriptions of "Proficient" and "Exemplary" leadership practices as "look fors" in principal interviews. A newly hired principal can engage in a self-assessment at the beginning of her contract to determine areas of strength and areas of needed growth and support. The results from the principal's self-assessment then form the basis for developing a professional growth plan.

- **Reciprocal:** Gives leaders the opportunity to provide feedback to the organization. While many principal evaluation systems provide one-way feedback to the principal from her supervisor, few principal evaluation systems solicit a principal's thoughts as to how the organization can provide further support to the principal to work toward continuous improvement.

- **Empowering:** Provides leaders with the authority to make decisions that will improve their effectiveness. Frequent self-assessment (quarterly), along with the opportunity to make "just-in-time" changes to leadership strategies within their growth plan, puts leaders in charge of continuously improving their practices so they can be active rather than passive participants in the process.

- **Standards Based:** Includes clear standards for "Proficient" and "Exemplary" performance. Key to effective leadership evaluation is developing a mutual understanding between the organization and the leader about the specific behaviors and professional practices that constitute "Proficient" and "Exemplary" performance—as well as performance that, if demonstrated, would be considered non-proficient.

- **Truthful:** Leads to honest and accurate feedback. The dictionary defines truthful as "Telling or expressing the truth; honest." While this may seem obvious, Reeves (2009) discovered in his research that the demand for accuracy and honesty is absent in many leadership evaluations. We need to be as factual with our leaders as we are with our students when we are discussing their performance measured against a set of standards.

- **Objective:** Describes specific behaviors. Leaders at every level need to know what the expectations are in order to meet those expectations.

The MLP Matrix includes the following 10 leadership domains: resilience; personal behavior and professional ethics; student achievement; decision making; communication; faculty development; leadership development; time, task, and project management; use of technology; personal professional learning. The 10 leadership domains, along with related subdomains, are strongly connected to contemporary research on leadership. The relationship of the domains to current research in leadership is documented in Appendix A, as we have taken the domains and cross-referenced each to the related research on effective leadership practices.

The matrix that follows (Figure 1.2) provides descriptions for each domain on a performance continuum: exemplary, proficient, progressing, and not meeting standards. These domains are described in clear, objective terms to ensure equity and excellence.

FIGURE 1.2	Multidimensional Leadership Performance Generic Performance Scale		
Generic Scale			
Exemplary (System-wide Impact)	**Proficient (Local Impact)**	**Progressing (Leadership Potential)**	**Not Meeting Standards**
Leadership performance at this level is dramatically superior to "Proficient" or "Effective" in its impact on students, staff members, parents, and the school district. The leader helps every other element within the organization become as good as she is.	Leadership performance at this level has local impact (i.e., within the school) and meets organizational needs. The leader understands that her performance is adequate, necessary, and clearly makes a significant contribution to the school.	Leadership performance at this level shows potential, but lacks sufficient proficiencies to improve student learning, instructional practice, and/or other responsibilities. The leader understands what is required for success, is willing to work toward that goal, and, with coaching and support, can become proficient within a reasonable time.	Leadership performance at this level is inadequate. The leader does not demonstrate understanding of what is required for proficiency, or she has demonstrated unsatisfactory proficiency through both actions and inactions.

The "Proficient" level describes leadership performance that has local impact (i.e., within a department or within the school) and meets organizational needs. It is adequate, necessary, and clearly makes a significant contribution to the department or school. The "Exemplary" level is reserved for truly outstanding leadership as described by very demanding criteria. Performance at this level is dramatically superior to "Proficient" in its impact on students, staff members, parents, and the school district. In brief, the "Exemplary" leader helps every other element within the organization become as good as she. In other words, the "Exemplary" leader has system-wide impact or impact beyond what is normally in her control or influence. The "Progressing" level describes leaders who understand what is required for success, are willing to work toward that goal, and, with coaching and support, can become proficient within a reasonable time frame. Performance at the "Not Meeting Standards" level describes leaders who do not understand what is required for proficiency or who have demonstrated unsatisfactory proficiency through both actions and inactions. This capacity-building continuum gives leaders a deeper understanding of exactly where they need to focus their goals for continuous improvement. It also provides clear evidence for a school district as to where there might be a need for continuing professional development focused on specific domains of leadership.

To establish a system of leadership evaluation that guides and supports leadership growth at the central office and building levels, a Multidimensional Leadership Performance (MLP) System must include the following foundational components:

MLP Matrix: The matrix contains 10 domains of leadership and several sub-domains that further delineate each domain. Descriptions are included along a performance continuum for each domain and sub-domain. This document anchors the multidimensional leadership analysis process and guides the appraisal of each leader's strengths and areas for growth.

MLP Scoring Guide: The scoring guide is an instructional tool designed to help leaders and supervisors understand how to score individual sub-domains within the matrix, both on a formative as well as on a summative basis.

MLP Matrix Self-Reflection Guide: The self-reflection guide parallels the MLP Matrix and is designed to give leaders a formative assessment of where they stand in all or selected leadership performance areas, together with detailed guidance on how to improve. While the guide's checklists aren't intended for review by the leader's supervisor, they do reflect the key behaviors about which supervisors and leaders should be conversing frequently throughout the year. Moreover, these behavioral leadership descriptions will form the basis for leader and supervisor coaching sessions.

MLP Questionnaire: The MLP Questionnaire is a tool that allows leaders to get an accurate understanding of a leader's strengths and areas for growth. It is suggested that they survey members of their staff, student groups, parents, and other stakeholders within the community. This instrument uses a five-point Likert scale (i.e., an ordered, one-dimensional scale from which respondents choose one option that best aligns with their view; there are typically between four and seven options; for our purposes, we use a five-point scale; in scoring, numbers have been assigned to each option) and is designed to parallel the domains and sub-domains on the MLP Matrix. Leaders use this information to select and monitor areas for growth on which they will focus their leadership actions or to validate the impact their leadership practices have had on the perceptions of these representative groups within the district or school.

MLP Coaching Protocol: The coaching tool is designed to aid both leaders and supervisors as they guide a leader's thinking, problem solving, and goal achievement along the performance continuum on the selected domains and sub-domains of the MLP Matrix.

MLP Professional Growth Plan: The professional growth plan is designed to help leaders focus deeply on their selected areas for improvement. The plan includes a problem of practice that is based on district and/or school-wide areas needing improvement. In response, leaders establish a theory of action that also aligns with the domain and sub-domains for improvement selected from the MLP Matrix. To determine progress, leaders frequently (monthly) monitor their own actions in addition to student results indicators.

MLP Summative Evaluation Rating Form: The summative evaluation rating form is to be used after leaders have had the opportunity to implement their professional growth plans. They will meet with their supervisors to discuss their progress. Following this discussion, the supervisor will complete the Summative Evaluation Rating Form and place it in the leader's human resource file.

Multidimensional Leadership Performance Glossary of Terms

For purposes of the MLP System, the terms are defined as follows:

1. Artifact—A product resulting from a leader's work (practices). Artifacts are natural by-products of work and are not created for the purpose of satisfying evaluation requirements. Leaders may use artifacts as illustrative examples of their work only when the evaluator and the leader disagree on the final rating.

Examples of artifacts include:

- *School Improvement Plan*—A plan that includes problems of practice; hypothesized theories of action; SMART Goals; observable, measurable adult strategies; the formative student assessments against which the strategies of action are measured; data sources to monitor; and so forth. Plans remain in effect for no more than three years.

- *Results from the Implementation of a Professional Growth Plan*—A plan that demonstrates clear alignment with the school improvement plan (including many of the same plan features as referenced above for the school improvement plan) and one to two specific observable and measurable leadership strategies (related to a specific domain or sub-domain) compared to anticipated gains in student achievement on a locally developed and scored formative student assessment.

- *MLP Questionnaire*—The results from a survey of stakeholder groups that allows the leader to get an accurate understanding of her strengths and areas for growth based on stakeholder perceptions.

- *Student Achievement Data*—Student achievement/testing data available from district and statewide testing. Also, results from locally developed student formative assessment data.

- *Professional Development and Implementation Results*—Staff development practices based on research the leader has applied to her own practice, accompanied by measurable results and self-reflection that focuses on deepening knowledge and pedagogical skills in a collegial and collaborative environment.

2. Data—Factual information used as the basis for reasoning, discussion, or planning.

3. Evidence—Documents that demonstrate or confirm the work of the person being evaluated and support the rating on a given domain.

4. Feedback—Information provided by a supervisor, peer, book, rubric, self, or experience regarding qualities of the supervisee's performance or understanding.

5. MLP Matrix—A composite matrix of the domains and sub-domains of the Multidimensional Leadership Performance Matrix:

- *Domain*—The distinct aspect of leadership or realm of practices that forms the basis for the evaluation of the department or school leader.

- *Sub-domain*—The sub-categories of performance embedded within the leadership domain.

6. Performance Rating Scale—The following rating scale will be used for evaluating department and school leaders:

- *Exemplary*—Leadership performance at this level is dramatically superior to "Proficient" in its impact on students, staff members, parents, and the school district (i.e., system-wide impact). The leader helps every other element within the organization become as good as she is.

- *Proficient*—Leadership performance at this level has local impact (i.e., within the department or school) and meets organizational needs. The leader demonstrates her performance is adequate, necessary, and clearly makes a significant contribution to the department or school.

- *Progressing*—Leadership performance at this level shows potential, but lacks sufficient proficiencies to improve student learning, instructional practice, and/or other responsibilities. The leader understands what is required for success, is willing to work toward that goal, and, with coaching and support, can become proficient within a reasonable time.

- *Not Meeting Standards*—Leadership performance at this level is inadequate. The leader does not demonstrate understanding of what is required for proficiency, or has demonstrated unsatisfactory proficiency through action and inaction.

7. Self-Assessment—Personal reflection about one's professional practice, conducted with or without input from others, to identify strengths and areas for improvement.

8. Summative Evaluation—A composite assessment of the leader's performance based on the evaluation rubric and supporting evidence.

Evaluation Process Responsibilities

Evaluatee Responsibilities:

- Know and understand the state standards for school leaders;
- Understand the MLP System Evaluation Process;
- Prepare for the Pre-Evaluation Conference, including a self-evaluation, identifying performance goals, and identifying change initiatives under way at her school;

- Frequently (i.e., monthly) gather data, artifacts, evidence to support performance in relation to standards and progress in attaining goals;

- Develop and implement a professional growth plan that includes one to two specific observable and measurable strategies to improve personal performance and/or attain goals in areas individually or collaboratively identified; and

- Participate in the Midyear and Final Evaluation Conference.

Evaluator Responsibilities:

- Know and understand the state standards for school leaders;

- Participate in training to understand and implement the MLP System Evaluation Process;

- Supervise the MLP System Evaluation Process and ensure that all steps are conducted according to the approved process;

- Identify the principal's/assistant principal's strengths and areas for improvement and make recommendations for improving performance; and

- Ensure that the contents of the Principal/Assistant Principal Summative Evaluation Rating Form contains accurate information and accurately reflects the principal's/assistant principal's performance.

2 Instructions for the Multidimensional Leadership Performance System: Evaluation Process

The purpose of the evaluation process is to improve both the leader's as well as the organization's collective performance in relation to the MLP System Standards in a collegial and nonthreatening manner. The individual being evaluated will take the lead in conducting the evaluation process through the use of self-assessment, a personal growth plan, reflection, and input from the various stakeholders with an interest in the leadership in the district or school. The input and evidence gathered by the leader is not intended to become part of the portfolio. Rather, it should provide a basis for self-assessment, goal setting, growth plan development, professional development, and demonstration of performance on specific standards. The following steps in Figure 2.1 outline the required elements of the evaluation process.

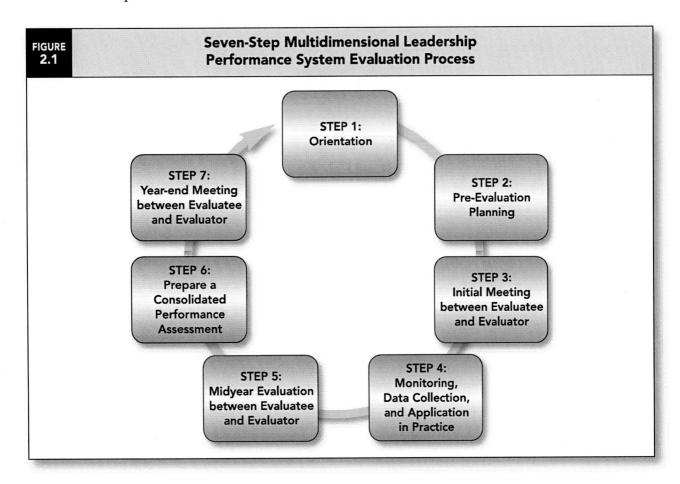

FIGURE 2.1

Seven-Step Multidimensional Leadership Performance System Evaluation Process

STEP 1: Orientation

STEP 2: Pre-Evaluation Planning

STEP 3: Initial Meeting between Evaluatee and Evaluator

STEP 4: Monitoring, Data Collection, and Application in Practice

STEP 5: Midyear Evaluation between Evaluatee and Evaluator

STEP 6: Prepare a Consolidated Performance Assessment

STEP 7: Year-end Meeting between Evaluatee and Evaluator

STEP 1: Orientation

The orientation step can occur at the start of a new work year, at the start of a new school year, or at the start of assignment (or new assignment) as a principal. The depth and detail of orientation may vary based on prior training and whether changes in evaluation model have occurred, but an annual orientation or refresher orientation should occur. The orientation step should include:

- District-provided orientation and training on the evaluation model that includes district expectations that are subject to the evaluation system.

- All leaders and evaluators should have access to the content and processes that are subject to the evaluation system. All leaders and evaluators should have access to the same information and expectations. This may be provided by the leader's review of district evaluation documents, mentor sessions, or face-to-face training where awareness of district processes and expectations are identified.

- At the orientation step, each school leader is expected to engage in personal reflection on the connection between her practice and the domains and sub-domains in the evaluation system. This is a "what do I know and what do I need to know" self-check aligned with the leadership domains (standards) and sub-domains.

STEP 2: Pre-Evaluation Planning

After the orientation process, the leader and the evaluator prepare for a formal conference to address evaluation processes and expectations. Three things occur:

- Leader's self-assessment of all domains and sub-domains from the orientation step moves to more specific identification of improvement priorities or leadership practice priorities. These may be instructional practice and/or leadership practice priorities.

- The leader will complete a self-assessment of all sub-domains and domains using the MLP Reflection Guide (worksheets), consider the results of the prior year evaluation process, and, if collected, reflect on perception data from staff, students, and parents (e.g., using the MLP Questionnaire). From this analysis of available data, the leader will prioritize these to three to five high-leverage areas (sub-domains) of focus. This self-assessment will serve as the basis for creating the preliminary professional growth plan, which should be completed prior to Step 3.

- Once the self-assessment is complete, the leader sends the self-assessment to the supervisor so that the supervisor may, prior to the initial meeting with the supervisee, compare the supervisee's self-assessment against the supervisor's assessment.

STEP 3: Initial Meeting between Evaluatee and Evaluator

The evaluatee will meet individually with her evaluator, who is responsible for discussing the results of the self-evaluation, rating levels, supporting documentation and/or artifacts, the three to five high-leverage areas of focus, the preliminary professional growth plan, and the evidence as well as data (evidence) to be gathered for the evaluation process. The evaluatee and the evaluator will agree on the data, evidence, and artifacts necessary to complete the evaluation process and confirm the evaluatee's level of performance. That is, for all practical purposes, the evaluator and the evaluatee agree upon the initial assessment of the evaluatee's level of performance for a majority (i.e., all but the three to five prioritized sub-domains) of the performance measures. In so doing, they commit to focusing their time, energy, and resources on those leadership performance areas that offer the greatest opportunity for the leader to have an impact on targeted improvement efforts.

STEP 4: Monitoring, Data Collection, and Application to Practice

During the span of time between the initial meeting with the evaluator and the midyear evaluation, and between the midyear evaluation and the year-end evaluation meeting, the leader will collect the data agreed upon in Step 3 as well as any additional data resulting from the midyear evaluation conference by utilizing a rich array of feedback mechanisms (e.g., information obtained from educational articles, books, peers, the MLP Rubric, supervisor, self, or experience regarding qualities of the supervisee's performance or understanding). These data may include the artifacts listed for each domain on the matrix; routine measures of implemented leadership strategies; feedback from staff, parents, students, and the school community; documentation of professional development completed and applied during the year; and other data to document achievement of performance goals. The leader's supervisor will interact with the leader (either face-to-face or electronically) during this period in order to determine progress to date on the leader's professional growth plan. Also, the supervisor will engage the leader in reflective dialogue using the Coaching Protocol (e.g., the elements and coaching moves) to support the leader's thinking, problem solving, and goal achievement within the MLP System.

STEP 5: Midyear Evaluation between Evaluatee & Evaluator

Leaders will meet individually with their respective evaluator to discuss the leader's formative progress toward achieving annual goals. This midyear dialogue will focus on the goal status and midyear adjustments to the professional growth plans that must be made in order to achieve goals by the end of the leader's contractual year. More importantly, this formal formative assessment meeting with the leader's evaluator provides the leader an opportunity to share the connections, or not, of her targeted leadership actions, the deliberate practice identified within her professional growth plan, and the impact of her actions on student achievement.

STEP 6: Prepare a Consolidated Performance Assessment

The leader will synthesize the information obtained in Steps 4 and 5 in order to prepare a consolidated assessment, or comprehensive view, of performance throughout the year. This summary of the data and artifacts will be used to judge the overall performance of the evaluatee on not only the three to five priority sub-domains but the rest of the sub-domains as well and should be provided to the evaluatee's evaluator well in advance of the meeting at which final performance levels will be discussed.

STEP 7: Year-End Evaluation Meeting between Evaluatee & Evaluator

The leader will meet with the evaluator at the end of the year to discuss progress in completing the evaluation process. They will discuss the self-assessment, consolidated assessment, and summary evaluation of the leader, which the evaluatee will have prepared in advance of the meeting. Should additional data or artifacts need to be brought into the discussion, the leader will have them readily available to share at that time. At this meeting, the leader and the evaluator will agree upon performance levels, degree of goal attainment, and recommendations for the professional growth plan.

3 Multidimensional Leadership Performance: Matrix

As Douglas Reeves (2009) argues, "The challenge in leadership evaluation is to identify those characteristics that are essential for leadership success and then to associate those characteristics with specific behaviors" (p. 37). In *Assessing Educational Leaders* (2nd ed.), Reeves identifies 10 domains of leadership:

- Resilience

- Personal Behavior and Professional Ethics

- Student Achievement

- Decision Making

- Communication

- Faculty Development

- Leadership Development

- Time, Task, and Project Management

- Technology

- Personal Professional Learning

The Multidimensional Leadership Performance (MLP) System is a matrix in which these 10 leadership domains contain continuum descriptions across four levels of performance, ranging from "Exemplary" to "Not Meeting Standards," with the performance levels of "Proficient" and "Progressing" in between. The MLP Matrix is an evidenced-based rubric that clearly articulates and defines the essential leadership practices. Some of the domains are universal and applicable to all leaders in every organization.

These 10 domains reflect leadership best practices (see Appendix A) that are well documented in three of the most recent studies on leadership (Louis, et al., 2010; Hattie, 2009, 2012; Robinson, 2011) and that have been validated by multiple studies and methodologies (i.e., those of Marzano, Waters, McNulty, Hattie, Reeves). Additionally, the 10 leadership domains align nicely with several national organizations' leadership standards (i.e., The National Board for Professional Teaching Standards—National Board Certification for Principals Standards, Interstate School

Leaders Licensure Consortium [ISLLC] Standards, and the New Leaders for New Schools [NLNS] Standards). Moreover, as of this writing, in testament to the strong alignment between research and practice, the Reeves MLP Matrix has been competitively selected by two states, Florida and New York, to serve as one of their approved statewide models for principal evaluation.

While The Center encourages each organization to establish its own domains of leadership based on its cultural environment and unique needs, this matrix can serve to jump-start that process. If you determine that it is in your best interests to establish your own leadership domains, The Center strongly recommends that when considering potential leadership domains for your evaluation system, you ask these questions to filter your list:

- Is this domain within the control or direct influence of the leader?

- Is this domain directly related to our mission and vision?

- Is this domain subject to objective description so that the people evaluating the leader have a clear and consistent understanding of what successful leadership in this domain "looks like"?

Only if the answers to all three of these questions are "yes" should a leadership domain be included in your final set of domains. As Douglas Reeves emphatically states (2009):

There are many lofty goals that appear as leadership standards, expectations, criteria, or other components of leadership evaluation, but if they do not pass through these filters, they waste time and divert attention. If the dimension is important, but not subject to the influence or control of the leader, then evaluation on such a dimension is a prescription for frustration on all sides. If the domain is popular with a vocal segment of stakeholders, but not part of the vision and mission of the entire system, then evaluation on this dimension will risk diverting time, energy, and resources away from the most essential priorities of the organization. If the dimension is full of rhetorical flourish and fine-sounding phrases, but is not subject to objective description, then a group of evaluators may have wildly different opinions about what the dimension really means. If such differences occurred in the evaluation of student performance, we would recognize it as an unreliable assessment and distrust the results. We should apply the same high standard of objectivity and consistency to leadership evaluation. (p. 40)

Figure 3.1 provides a worksheet for a group that wishes to establish its own domains of leadership based on its cultural environment and unique needs. Applying the ratings to the filter questions for evaluating prospective leadership domains will test the validity of each. Following Figure 3.1 is the MLP Matrix used in this book.

FIGURE 3.1 Worksheet for Prospective Leadership Domains

Leadership Domain	Leader's Impact? 4 = Direct control 3 = Direct influence 2 = Indirect influence 1 = Beyond leader's control	Relationship to Mission and Vision? 4 = Essential relationship 3 = Clear relationship 2 = Indirect relationship 1 = No relationship	Subject to Objective Description? 4 = Obvious distinctions between exemplary, proficient, progressing, and not meeting standards levels 3 = Distinction between proficient and non-proficient performance can be specified with clarity and consistency 2 = Performance distinctions can be clarified, but are inconsistent from one evaluator to the next 1 = Subjective and not amenable to objective description	Comments

The Multidimensional Leadership Performance Matrix

1.0 Resilience: Resilience is the ability of the leader to overcome setbacks and absorb any learning offered by those setbacks quickly and at the minimum cost. Resilience includes coping well with high levels of ongoing disruptive change, sustaining energy when under constant pressure, bouncing back easily from disappointment and setbacks, overcoming adversity, changing ways of working to incorporate learning when old ways are no longer possible, and doing all of this without acting in dysfunctional or harmful ways to others within the organization. More importantly, when leaders are practicing resilient behaviors, their actions are contagious as they model the way for others to act similarly.

	Exemplary (System-wide Impact) In addition to "Effective"…	Proficient (Local Impact)	Progressing (Leadership Potential)	Not Meeting Standards
1.1 Constructive Reactions The leader reacts to disappointment and barriers to success constructively.	• The leader acknowledges prior personal and organizational failures frankly and offers clear suggestions for system-wide learning resulting from those lessons.	• The leader acknowledges personal and organizational failures readily and offers clear suggestions for personal learning.	• The leader acknowledges personal and organizational failures when confronted with evidence.	• The leader is defensive and resists acknowledging error.
1.2 Willingness to Admit Error The leader demonstrates willingness to admit error and learn from it.	• The leader shares case studies of personal and organizational errors in a way that is used to guide, inspire, and teach colleagues throughout the organization. • The leader builds resilience in colleagues and throughout the organization by habitually highlighting and praising "good mistakes" where risks were taken, mistakes were made, lessons were learned, and both the individual and the organization learned for the future.	• The leader admits failures quickly, honestly, and openly with direct supervisor and immediate colleagues. • There is evidence of learning from past errors. • Has a nondefensive attitude toward accepting feedback and discussing errors and failures.	• The leader accepts evidence of mistakes when offered by others. • Some evidence of learning from mistakes is present.	• The leader is unwilling to acknowledge errors. • When confronted with evidence of mistakes, the leader is defensive and resistant to learning from mistakes.
1.3 Disagreement The leader handles disagreement with leadership and policy decisions constructively.	• The leader shows willingness to challenge executive authority and policy leaders appropriately with evidence and constructive criticism; but once a decision is made, the leader fully supports and enthusiastically implements organizational policy and leadership decisions.	• The leader accepts and implements leadership and policy with fidelity. • The leader represents initiatives in a way that advocates for policies as if they were the leader's idea. • The leader proactively brings concerns to the immediate supervisor by articulating disagreements and points of view in the interest of the organization.	• The leader sometimes challenges executive and policy leadership without bringing those concerns to appropriate executive and policy authorities. • The leader sometimes implements unpopular policies unenthusiastically or in a perfunctory manner.	• The leader ignores or subverts executive and policy decisions that are unpopular or difficult.

The Multidimensional Leadership Performance Matrix (continued)

1.0 Resilience: Resilience is the ability of the leader to overcome setbacks and absorb any learning offered by those setbacks quickly and at the minimum cost. Resilience includes coping well with high levels of ongoing disruptive change, sustaining energy when under constant pressure, bouncing back easily from disappointment and setbacks, overcoming adversity, changing ways of working to incorporate learning when old ways are no longer possible, and doing all of this without acting in dysfunctional or harmful ways to others within the organization. More importantly, when leaders are practicing resilient behaviors, their actions are contagious as they model the way for others to act similarly.

	Exemplary (System-wide Impact) In addition to "Effective"…	Proficient (Local Impact)	Progressing (Leadership Potential)	Not Meeting Standards
1.4 Dissent The leader handles dissent from subordinates constructively.	• The leader creates constructive contention, assigning roles (if necessary) to deliberately generate multiple perspectives and consider different sides of important issues. • The leader recognizes and rewards thoughtful dissent. • The leader uses dissenting voices to learn, grow, and, where appropriate, acknowledge the leader's own error. • The leader encourages constructive dissent in which multiple voices are supported and heard; as a result, the final decision is made better and more broadly supported.	• The leader uses dissent to inform final decisions, improve the quality of decision making, and broaden support for her final decision. • Defined structures and processes are in place for eliciting input.	• The leader tolerates dissent, but there is very little of it in public.	• Dissent is absent due to a climate of fear and intimidation.
1.5 Improvement of Specific Performance Areas The leader demonstrates explicit improvement in specific performance areas based on previous evaluations and formative feedback.	• The leader's previous evaluations are combined with personal reflection and 360-degree feedback to formulate an action plan that is reflected in the leader's daily choices of priorities, as well as in the organization's priorities. • The influence of previous evaluations has an impact not only on the leader, but on the entire organization.	• The leader's previous evaluations are explicitly reflected in projects, tasks, and priorities. • Performance on each evaluation reflects specific and measurable improvements along the performance continuum from unsatisfactory, to needs improvement, to effective, to highly effective.	• The leader is aware of previous evaluations, but has not translated them into an action plan.	• No evidence of reference to previous leadership evaluations is present in the leader's choices of tasks and priorities.

The Multidimensional Leadership Performance Matrix (continued)

2.0 Personal Behavior and Professional Ethics: Leaders in education demonstrate a high degree of personal and professional ethics characterized by integrity, emotional self-control, tolerance, and respect. These principals establish a culture in which all stakeholders practice exemplary ethical behavior.

	Exemplary (System-wide Impact) In addition to "Effective"…	Proficient (Local Impact)	Progressing (Leadership Potential)	Not Meeting Standards
2.1 Integrity The leader demonstrates integrity.	• The leader meets commitments—verbal, written, and implied—without exception. • Commitments to individuals, students, community members, and subordinates have the same weight as commitments to superiors, board members, or other people with visibility and authority. • The leader's commitment to integrity is clear throughout the organization, as any commitment from anyone who reports to this leader is as good as the leader's commitment.	• The leader meets commitments or negotiates exceptions where the commitment cannot be met. • Verbal commitments have the same weight as written commitments.	• The leader meets explicit written commitments. • The need to "get it in writing" does not allow subordinates or superiors to make assumptions that verbal statements have the weight of a commitment.	• The phrases "I'm working on it" or "I'm doing the best I can" are regarded as acceptable substitutes for commitments. • The leader does not follow through with tasks, budgets, and priorities critical to the performance of her site or responsibilities.
2.2 Emotional Self-Control The leader demonstrates emotional self-control.	• The leader possesses complete self-control, even in the most difficult and confrontational situations, but also provides assistance to colleagues on the techniques of emotional intelligence. • Not only is the leader an exemplar of emotional intelligence, but the entire organization reflects this commitment to self-control, empathy, and respect.	• The leader deals with sensitive subjects and personal attacks with dignity and self-control. • The leader never meets anger with anger, but instead defuses confrontational situations with emotional intelligence, empathy, and respect.	• The leader occasionally exhibits aggressive, dismissive, or demeaning behaviors, leading to a climate in which people are reluctant to raise sensitive issues.	• The leader loses her temper and is emotionally unstable. • Conversations on any sensitive topic are brief or nonexistent.
2.3 Ethical and Legal Compliance with Employees The leader demonstrates compliance with legal and ethical requirements in relationship to employees.	• The leader meets the letter and spirit of the law, avoiding both the fact and appearance of impropriety. • The leader inculcates the foundations of mutual respect for colleagues and for the law throughout the organization.	• There are no instances of illegal or unethical conduct with employees or prospective employees and no other conduct that crosses the line of policy or law.	• The leader's conduct does not support a school culture respectful of the legal and policy requirements for the relationship between leaders and employees.	• The leader violates (even just one time) the legal and policy requirements for the relationship between leaders and employees.

The Multidimensional Leadership Performance Matrix (continued)

2.0 Personal Behavior and Professional Ethics: Leaders in education demonstrate a high degree of personal and professional ethics characterized by integrity, emotional self-control, tolerance, and respect. These principals establish a culture in which all stakeholders practice exemplary ethical behavior.

	Exemplary (System-wide Impact) In addition to "Effective"…	Proficient (Local Impact)	Progressing (Leadership Potential)	Not Meeting Standards
2.4 Tolerance The leader demonstrates tolerance of different points of view within the boundaries of the values and mission of the organization.	• The leader actively seeks different perspectives, encouraging a variety of scenarios and curricula in the context of academic standards. • The leader explicitly differentiates divergent thinking when it is constructive and facilitates a transition to convergent thinking to support organizational goals.	• The leader focuses evaluation on the achievement of the mission and adherence to values without penalizing differences in points of view that are within the framework of organizational requirements.	• There is no punishment of alternative points of view, but there is also little or no development or encouragement of those views.	• The leader suppresses other points of view and discourages disagreement or divergent thinking.
2.5 Respect The leader honors the time and presence of others.	• The leader consistently demonstrates an ability to effectively manage time and meetings by engaging others in the process, achieving meeting objectives, and beginning and ending on time. • The leader models respect for others by arriving early to all meetings and has developed and shared a system to consistently encourage, welcome, and recognize diverse opinions—even when such opinions differ from those of the leader. • Colleagues can point to specific indicators of how they are afforded time, attention to their concerns, and respect during interactions with the leader.	• The leader arrives on time and is prepared, participates fully, and is ready to listen and respect others in planned and unplanned meetings. • The leader is fluent with agenda items (knowledge of each topic) and is prepared to offer ideas and engage others in meaningful dialogue. • Diverse opinions are consistently encouraged, welcomed, and recognized by the leader, even when such opinions differ from those of the leader. • Staff who report to the leader indicate that they are afforded time, attention to their concerns, and respect during interactions with the leader.	• The leader generally arrives on time and is prepared, participates fully, and is ready to listen and respect others in planned and unplanned meetings, with periodic exceptions (sidebar conversations, distractions during planned or unplanned meetings). • The leader is occasionally fluent with agenda items in terms of knowledge of each topic, but seldom offers ideas to engage others in meaningful dialogue. • Diverse opinions are sometimes welcomed by the leader, but this occurs inconsistently.	• The leader frequently arrives late and is not prepared, is often absent at key meetings, and tends to engage in disrespectful behaviors that do not honor others (sidebar conversations, distractions during planned or unplanned meetings). • The leader may be attentive, but generally only in the presence of supervisors, and rarely takes the time to be fluent and knowledgeable regarding agenda items and topics of interest to the organization.

3.0 Student Achievement: Leaders in education make student learning their top priority. They direct energy and resources toward data analysis for instructional improvement and the development and implementation of quality standards-based curricula, and evaluate, monitor, and provide feedback to staff on instructional delivery.

	Exemplary (System-wide Impact) In addition to "Effective"…	Proficient (Local Impact)	Progressing (Leadership Potential)	Not Meeting Standards
3.1 Planning and Goal Setting The leader demonstrates planning and goal setting aligned to the school/district improvement plan to upgrade student achievement.	• The leader routinely shares examples of specific leadership, teaching, and curriculum strategies that are linked to improved student achievement. • Other leaders credit this leader with sharing ideas, coaching, and providing technical assistance to implement successful new initiatives.	• Goals and strategies reflect a clear relationship between the actions of teachers and leaders aligned to the school/district improvement plan and the impact on student achievement. Results show steady improvements based on these leadership initiatives.	• Specific and measurable goals related to student achievement are established, but these efforts have yet to result in improved student achievement or planning for methods of monitoring improvements.	• Goals are neither measurable nor specific. The leader focuses more on student characteristics than on the actions of the teachers and leaders in the system.
3.2 Student Achievement Results The leader demonstrates evidence of student improvement through student achievement results.	• A consistent record of improved student achievement exists on multiple indicators of student success. • Student success occurs not only on the overall averages, but also in each group of historically disadvantaged students. • Explicit use of previous data indicates that the leader has focused on improving performance. In areas of previous success, the leader aggressively identifies new challenges, moving proficient performance to the exemplary level. Where new challenges emerge, the leader highlights the need to respond, creates effective interventions, and reports improved results.	• The leader reaches the required numbers, meeting performance goals for student achievement. • The average of the student population improves, as does the achievement of each group of students who have been identified previously as needing improvement.	• Some evidence of improvement exists, but there is insufficient evidence of changes in leadership, teaching, and curriculum that will create the improvements necessary to achieve student performance goals.	• Indifferent to the data, the leader blames students, families, and external factors. • The leader does not believe that student achievement can improve. • The leader has not taken decisive action to change time, teacher assignment, curriculum, leadership practices, or other variables in order to improve student achievement.

The Multidimensional Leadership Performance Matrix *(continued)*

3.0 Student Achievement: Leaders in education make student learning their top priority. They direct energy and resources toward data analysis for instructional improvement and the development and implementation of quality standards-based curricula, and evaluate, monitor, and provide feedback to staff on instructional delivery.

	Exemplary (System-wide Impact) In addition to "Effective"...	Proficient (Local Impact)	Progressing (Leadership Potential)	Not Meeting Standards
3.3 Instructional Leadership Decisions The leader demonstrates the use of student achievement data to make instructional leadership decisions.	• The leader can specifically document examples of decisions in teaching, assignment, curriculum, assessment, and intervention that have been made on the basis of data analysis. • The leader has coached school administrators in other schools to improve their data analysis skills.	• The leader uses multiple data sources, including state, district, school, and classroom assessments, and has at least three years of data. • The leader systematically examines data at the subscale level to deduce strengths and challenges. • The leader empowers teaching and administrative staff to determine priorities from data. • Data insights are regularly the subject of faculty meetings and professional development sessions.	• The leader is aware of state and district results and has discussed those results with staff, but has not linked specific decisions to the data.	• The leader is unaware of or indifferent to the data.
3.4 Student Requirements and Academic Standards The leader demonstrates understanding of student requirements and academic standards.	• Every faculty meeting and staff development forum is focused on student achievement, including periodic reviews of student work.	• The link between standards and student performance is evident from examples (exemplars) of proficient student work posted throughout the building.	• Standards are posted and required training has been conducted, but the link between standards and student performance is not readily apparent to faculty or students.	• Classroom curriculum is considered a matter of individual discretion. • The leader is hesitant to intrude or is indifferent to decisions in the classroom that are at variance with the requirements of academic standards.

The Multidimensional Leadership Performance Matrix (continued)

3.0 Student Achievement: Leaders in education make student learning their top priority. They direct energy and resources toward data analysis for instructional improvement and the development and implementation of quality standards-based curricula, and evaluate, monitor, and provide feedback to staff on instructional delivery.

3.5 Student Performance	Exemplary (System-wide Impact) In addition to "Effective"…	Proficient (Local Impact)	Progressing (Leadership Potential)	Not Meeting Standards
The leader demonstrates understanding of present levels of student performance based on consistent assessments that reflect local and state academic standards.	• Power Standards (i.e., prioritized standards) are used and shared with staff in other buildings. • Standards are viewed as essential building blocks because they provide enduring understanding and leverage across content areas, as well as provide a foundation for the next grade or course level. • Every faculty meeting and staff development forum is focused on student achievement, including reviews of individual student work compared to standards.	• Each academic standard has been analyzed and translated into student-accessible language. • Power Standards are widely shared by faculty members and are visible throughout the building. • The link between standards and student performance is in evidence from the posting of proficient student work throughout the building.	• Standards have been analyzed, but are not translated into student-accessible language. • Power Standards are developed, but not widely known or used by faculty. • Student work is posted throughout the building, but does not reflect proficient work.	• Power Standards have not been developed. • There is no student work posted.

The Multidimensional Leadership Performance Matrix *(continued)*

4.0 Decision Making: Leaders in education make decisions based on the vision and mission and using facts and data. They use a transparent process for making decisions and articulate who makes which decisions. The leader uses the process to empower others and distribute leadership when appropriate.

	Exemplary (System-wide Impact) In addition to "Effective"…	Proficient (Local Impact)	Progressing (Leadership Potential)	Not Meeting Standards
4.1 Factual Basis for Decisions The leader employs factual bases for decisions, including specific reference to internal and external data on student achievement and objective data on curriculum, teaching practices, and leadership practices.	• Decision making is neither by consensus nor by leadership mandate, but consistently based on the data. • Data is reflected in all decisions, ranging from course and classroom assignments to the discontinuance of programs. • The leader can cite specific examples of practices that have been changed, discontinued, and/or initiated based on data analysis. • A variety of data sources, including qualitative and quantitative, are used. • Data sources include state, district, school, and classroom assessments. • Inferences from data are shared widely outside the school community to identify and replicate the most effective practices.	• The pattern of decision making reflects a clear reliance on state and district student achievement data as well as on curriculum, instruction, and leadership practices data.	• Some decisions are based on data, but others are the result of personal preference and tradition.	• Data is rarely used for decisions. • The predominant decision-making methodology is mandated by the leader or based on popular theories.
4.2 Decision-Making Structure The leader demonstrates clear identificaiton of decision-making structure, including which decisions are made by consensus, or by the staff independently, which decisions are made by the leader after getting input from the staff, and which decisions are made by the leader alone.	• All stakeholders understand the difference between decision-making levels, including staff decisions made by consensus or majority, staff input that will significantly influence leadership decisions, and unilateral leadership decisions. • The leader uses data in such a compelling way that the vast majority of decisions achieve consensus or majority support. • Staff surveys reflect feelings of empowerment and personal responsibility for organizational success.	• The leader clarifies the decision-making method for major decisions and shares decisions with the staff, using data to the greatest extent possible to support those decisions.	• The leader uses both consensus and unilateral decision making, but the reason for changing decision-making structures is not consistently clear. • The leader's approach to decision making has no clear method and demoralizes or bewilders the staff.	• The leader's approach to decision making has no clear method and demoralizes or bewilders the staff.

THE REFLECTIVE LEADER: IMPLEMENTING A MULTIDIMENSIONAL LEADERSHIP PERFORMANCE SYSTEM

The Multidimensional Leadership Performance Matrix *(continued)*

4.0 Decision Making: Leaders in education make decisions based on the vision and mission and using facts and data. They use a transparent process for making decisions and articulate who makes which decisions. The leader uses the process to empower others and distribute leadership when appropriate.

	Exemplary (System-wide Impact) In addition to "Effective"…	Proficient (Local Impact)	Progressing (Leadership Potential)	Not Meeting Standards
4.3 Decisions Linked to Vision The leader links decisions to vision, mission, and strategic priorities reflected in the school/district improvement plans.	• The *current* vision, mission, and strategic priorities of the leader and the organization are visible, ingrained in the culture of the organization, and routinely used as a reference point for decisions. • The use of strategic guidelines for decision-making filters makes many decisions self-evident and avoids wasting time on unproductive arguments.	• The decisions of the leader are consistent with the vision, mission, and strategic priorities of the organization (as reflected in improvement planning documents).	• While the organization's vision, mission, and priorities may be visible, they are not consistently linked to the leader's decisions.	• The leader is unaware of or disconnected from the organization's vision, mission, and strategic priorities. • There is little or no evidence of the relationship of leadership decisions to these organizational guideposts.
4.4 Decisions Evaluated for Effectiveness The leader evaluates decisions for effectiveness and revises where necessary.	• The leader can provide clear and consistent evidence of decisions that have been changed based on new data. • The leader has a regular pattern of decision reviews and "sunsetting," in which previous decisions are reevaluated in light of the most current data. • There is a culture of "honest bad news" in which the leader and everyone in the organization can discuss what is not working without fear of embarrassment or reprisal.	• The leader has a record of evaluating and revising decisions based on new information.	• The leader has new information and appears to be willing to reconsider previous decisions, but does not have a clear record of making changes.	• There is little or no evidence of reflection and reevaluation of previous decisions.

The Multidimensional Leadership Performance Matrix *(continued)*

5.0 Communication: Leaders in education understand communication as a two-way street. They seek to listen and learn from students, staff, and community. They recognize individuals for good work and maintain high visibility at school and in the community. Regular communications to staff and community keep all stakeholders engaged in the work of the school.

	Exemplary (System-wide Impact) In addition to "Effective"…	Proficient (Local Impact)	Progressing (Leadership Potential)	Not Meeting Standards
5.1 Two-Way Communication with Students The leader engages in two-way communication with students.	• The leader goes to exceptional lengths to listen to students. The listening strategies may include focus groups, surveys, student advisory committees, and numerous one-on-one student conversations. • Discussions with students reveal that they know that the leader will listen to them and treat them with respect.	• The leader knows student names, regularly greets students by name, and is proactive in talking with and listening to students. • The leader is particularly visible at the beginning and end of the school day and during all other times when students are present.	• The leader knows most student names, is visible, often greets students by name, and talks with students frequently.	• The leader does not know student names, avoids student contact except where leadership presence is required, and retreats to the office during most occasions where students are likely to be present. • Many students do not know the leader's name or recognize the leader on sight.
5.2 Two-Way Communication with Faculty and Staff The leader engages in two-way communication with faculty and staff.	• The leader engages in "active listening" to the faculty and staff. • The leader's calendar reflects numerous individual and small-group meetings with staff at every level, not just with direct reports. Bus drivers, cafeteria workers, and first-year teachers all report confidence in their ability to gain a respectful hearing from the leader.	• Faculty meetings include open, two-way discussions. • Faculty members regularly have the opportunity for one-on-one meetings with the leader. • The leader knows all staff members and makes an effort to recognize the personal and individual contributions made by each one.	• The leader typically limits her listening to time during faculty meetings.	• Faculty meetings consist of the reading of announcements, with little or no interaction.

The Multidimensional Leadership Performance Matrix *(continued)*

5.0 Communication: Leaders in education understand communication as a two-way street. They seek to listen and learn from students, staff, and community. They recognize individuals for good work and maintain high visibility at school and in the community. Regular communications to staff and community keep all stakeholders engaged in the work of the school.

	Exemplary (System-wide Impact) In addition to "Effective" …	Proficient (Local Impact)	Progressing (Leadership Potential)	Not Meeting Standards
5.3 Two-Way Communication with Parents and Community The leader engages in two-way communication with parents and community.	• Clear evidence of parent-centered and community-centered communication is present, including open forums, focus groups, surveys, personal visits, and extensive use of technology. • Decisions in curriculum, leadership, staffing, assessment, and school appearance reflect parent and community involvement. • Survey data suggests that parents and community members feel empowered and supportive of educational objectives.	• The leader frequently interacts with parents and community members, including sending newsletters, giving briefings, and making visits and calls, as well as effectively using communication technology (e.g., voicemail, hotlines, email, Web sites). • There is clear evidence of input from parents and community members in decisions.	• Parents and community members receive a respectful hearing when they initiate the conversation.	• Parents and community members have little or no role to play in leadership decision making.
5.4 Analysis of Input and Feedback The leader listens actively and analyzes input and feedback.	• The leader models open communication by listening purposefully and actively. • The leader is able to read the situation and respond accordingly. • The leader maintains listening systems for major stakeholders (parents, teachers, students, patrons, and staff), explicitly plans analysis of and reflection on data, and establishes structures that facilitate action based on feedback and analysis.	• Observations and documentation provided by the leader demonstrate that the leader listens well, seeks mutual understanding, and welcomes the sharing of information. • The leader has established an effective communication plan, communicates openly, and is receptive to ideas from a variety of sources and perspectives.	• The leader appears to listen to others, but often relies on her interpretation of events rather than seeking out alternative perspectives and interpretations. • Analysis of listening data occurs rarely.	• The leader hears what others say, but relies on her personal interpretation. • The leader does not appear to communicate openly, omitting key details and attempting to resolve challenges without input or assistance.

The Multidimensional Leadership Performance Matrix (continued)

6.0 Faculty Development: Leaders recruit, hire, and retain proficient and exemplary teachers. In their efforts to retain proficient and exemplary teachers, leaders focus on evidence, research, and classroom realities faced by teachers. They link professional practice with student achievement to demonstrate the cause-and-effect relationship. Leaders also facilitate effective professional development, monitor implementation of critical initiatives, and provide timely feedback to teachers so that feedback can be used to increase teacher professional practice.

	Exemplary (System-wide Impact) In addition to "Effective"…	Proficient (Local Impact)	Progressing (Leadership Potential)	Not Meeting Standards
6.1 Faculty Proficiencies and Needs The leader understands faculty proficiencies and the needs for further development that will support and retain proficient and exemplary teachers.	• The leader has demonstrated a record of differentiated professional development for faculty based on student needs. • The leader has developed a system of job-embedded professional development that differentiates training and implementation based on teacher needs, which helps retain proficient and highly exemplary staff. • The leader routinely shares professional development opportunities with other schools, departments, districts, and organizations.	• Faculty development reflects the prioritized needs of the School Improvement Plan and some effort has been made to differentiate and embed professional development to meet the needs of all faculty (coaching, mentoring, collaborative teams, peer scoring). The leader uses data from evaluation of instructional personnel to assess proficiencies and identify priority needs to support and retain proficient and exemplary faculty members.	• The leader is aware of the differentiated needs of faculty and staff members, but professional development is only embedded in faculty meetings at this time, rather than incorporating the use of collaboration, study teams, and so forth.	• Professional development is typically "one size fits all," and there is little or no evidence of recognition of individual faculty needs or matching of faculty needs to student achievement needs. Consequently, retaining proficient and exemplary staff is problematic.
6.2 Leading Professional Development The leader personally participates in leading professional development.	• The leader is an active participant in teacher-led professional development, demonstrating with a commitment of time and intellect that the leader is a learner and is willing to learn regularly from colleagues. • The leader routinely shares learning experiences with other administrators and colleagues throughout the system.	• The leader devotes faculty meetings to professional development, not announcements. • The leader personally leads professional development at various times throughout the school year.	• The leader sometimes devotes faculty meetings to professional development and occasionally shares personal learning experiences with colleagues, but relies on others to lead each professional development opportunity.	• The leader displays little or no evidence of new learning or sharing that learning with colleagues.

The Multidimensional Leadership Performance Matrix (continued)

6.0 Faculty Development: Leaders recruit, hire, and retain proficient and exemplary teachers. In their efforts to retain proficient and exemplary teachers, leaders focus on evidence, research, and classroom realities faced by teachers. They link professional practice with student achievement to demonstrate the cause-and-effect relationship. Leaders also facilitate effective professional development, monitor implementation of critical initiatives, and provide timely feedback to teachers so that feedback can be used to increase teacher professional practice.

	Exemplary (System-wide Impact) In addition to "Effective"…	Proficient (Local Impact)	Progressing (Leadership Potential)	Not Meeting Standards
6.3 Formal and Informal Feedback The leader provides formal and informal feedback to colleagues with the exclusive purpose of improving individual and organizational performance.	• The leader uses a variety of creative ways to provide positive and corrective feedback. The entire organization reflects the leader's focus on accurate, timely, and specific recognition. • The leader balances individual recognition with team and organization-wide recognition.	• The leader provides formal feedback consistent with the district personnel policies and provides informal feedback to reinforce effective/highly effective performance and highlight the strengths of colleagues and staff. • The leader has effectively implemented a system for collecting feedback from teachers as to what they know, what they understand, where they make errors, and when they have misconceptions about use of instructional practices. • Corrective and positive feedback is linked to organizational goals, and both the leader and employees can cite examples of where feedback is used to improve individual and organizational performance.	• The leader adheres to the personnel policies in providing formal feedback, although the feedback is just beginning to provide details that improve teaching or organizational performance.	• Formal feedback is nonspecific. • Informal feedback is rare, nonspecific, and not constructive.

The Multidimensional Leadership Performance Matrix (continued)

6.0 Faculty Development: Leaders recruit, hire, and retain proficient and exemplary teachers. In their efforts to retain proficient and exemplary teachers, leaders focus on evidence, research, and classroom realities faced by teachers. They link professional practice with student achievement to demonstrate the cause-and-effect relationship. Leaders also facilitate effective professional development, monitor implementation of critical initiatives, and provide timely feedback to teachers so that feedback can be used to increase teacher professional practice.

6.4 Modeling, Coaching, and Mentoring The leader models coaching and mentoring.	Exemplary (System-wide Impact) In addition to "Effective" …	Proficient (Local Impact)	Progressing (Leadership Potential)	Not Meeting Standards
	• The leader is deliberate in establishing development structures that conform to the Learning Forward/ National Staff Development Council (NSDC) Standards. • The leader coaches other administrators on successful observation strategies, use of the educator standards to improve instruction and student learning, and communicating through a common language of instruction. • The leader is seen by staff as capable of coaching them to improve, yet willing to hold them accountable for performance that is not considered acceptable. • Multiple examples exist that verify a standards-based professional learning community, and action research is evident in context, process, and content.	• The leader engages in coaching to improve teaching and learning and is receptive to innovative teaching strategies and practices. The leader is also willing to facilitate new approaches to instruction through action research. • The leader monitors classroom visits in which the actual activity corresponds to the planned activity. • The leader actively coaches instructional staff in improving classroom practice by making effective use of a common language of instruction, the educator standards, and research-based instructional strategies linked to improvement of student learning and instructional practice. • A system has been developed that provides for regular observation of classrooms. • Observations are not just used for rating purposes; they are also used for coaching and professional development opportunities. • The leader has organized faculty into an effective learning/action research community, wherein coaching and mentoring occur formally and informally among the faculty.	• The leader is able to identify certain effective instructional strategies and complete observation processes, but needs to develop more prescriptive assistance related to strategies and practices to help teachers refine and improve their effectiveness.	• The leader views classroom observations as an obligation to make sure teachers are teaching and students are on task. • Evidence of coaching and mentoring, if any, does not specify effective teaching strategies or provide feedback that is either corrective or accurate.

The Multidimensional Leadership Performance Matrix (continued)

6.0 Faculty Development: Leaders recruit, hire, and retain proficient and exemplary teachers. In their efforts to retain proficient and exemplary teachers, leaders focus on evidence, research, and classroom realities faced by teachers. They link professional practice with student achievement to demonstrate the cause-and-effect relationship. Leaders also facilitate effective professional development, monitor implementation of critical initiatives, and provide timely feedback to teachers so that feedback can be used to increase teacher professional practice.

	Exemplary (System-wide Impact) In addition to "Effective"…	Proficient (Local Impact)	Progressing (Leadership Potential)	Not Meeting Standards
6.5 Recruitment and Hiring of Faculty The leader recruits and hires proficient and exemplary teachers.	• The leader tracks the success of recruitment and hiring strategies, learns from past experience, and revisits the process annually to improve the process continually. • The leader engages in a variety of traditional and non-traditional recruitment strategies then prioritizes based on where the most effective teachers have been found. • Effective recruiting and hiring practices are frequently shared with other administrators and colleagues throughout the system.	• The leader works collaboratively with the staff in the human resources office to define the ideal teacher, based upon the school's vision, culture, and performance expectations and on what type of teacher has been successful in the school. • The leader is sensitive to the various legal guidelines about the kind of data that can be sought in interviews. • Uses a hiring selection tool that helps interviewers focus on key success criteria aligned with Marzano's *Art and Science of Teaching*, compares findings with others more effectively, and develops more rigor in scoring and evaluating candidates. • A hiring process is established specifying the steps, which staff is included, who is responsible, and what the leader is looking for.	• The leader works with the staff in the human resources office to write and post a job description for the vacant teaching position. • Hiring processes are put into place, but may not be systematic or systemic in nature. Consequently, the process lacks standardization and improvement from year to year.	• The leader approaches the recruitment and hiring process from a reactive rather than a proactive standpoint. Consequently, the process may not be well thought out, is disjointed, and is not aligned with key success criteria embedded within the teacher evaluation documents essential to organizational success.

The Multidimensional Leadership Performance Matrix *(continued)*

7.0 Leadership Development: Leaders in education actively cultivate and grow other leaders within the organization. They also model trust, competency, and integrity, which positively impacts and inspires growth in other potential leaders

	Exemplary (System-wide Impact) In addition to "Effective"…	Proficient (Local Impact)	Progressing (Leadership Potential)	Not Meeting Standards
7.1 Mentoring Emerging Leaders The leader mentors emerging leaders to assume key leadership responsibilities.	• The leader has coached or mentored multiple administrators or instructional personnel, who have assumed administrative positions and responsibilities. • Multiple administrators throughout the system cite this leader as a mentor and contributor to their success.	• The leader has personally mentored at least one emerging leader to assume leadership responsibility in an instructional leadership or at an administrative level, with positive results.	• The leader provides some training to an emerging school leader or administrator who may, in time, be able to independently assume a leadership role.	• Persons under the leader's direction are unable or unwilling to assume added responsibilities; there is no evidence of effort to develop others.
7.2 Identification of Potential Future Leaders The leader consistently identifies potential future leaders.	• The leader routinely identifies and recruits new leaders. • The leader has specifically identified at least two new leaders in the past year and has entered them into the ranks of leadership training. • The leader is remarkable for identifying leaders from unexpected sources, including helping potential leaders find their own leadership strengths, even when they had not initially considered a leadership career. • The leader helps other leaders to identify and recruit potential leadership candidates.	• The leader has specifically identified and recruited new leaders.	• The leader follows personnel guidelines for accepting applications for new leaders, but has not implemented any systemic process for identifying emergent leaders.	• The leader does not recognize the need for leadership in the system.
7.3 Delegation and Trust The leader provides evidence of delegation and trust in subordinate leaders.	• Staff throughout the organization is empowered in formal and informal ways. • Faculty members participate in the facilitation of meetings and exercise leadership in committees and task forces; other employees, including noncertified staff, exercise appropriate authority and assume leadership roles where appropriate. • The climate of trust and delegation in this organization contributes directly to the identification and empowerment of the next generation of leadership.	• There is a clear pattern of delegated decisions, with authority to match responsibility at every level in the organization. • The relationship of authority and responsibility and delegation of authority is clear in personnel documents, such as evaluations, and also in the daily conduct of meetings and organizational business.	• The leader sometimes delegates, but also maintains decision-making authority that could be delegated to others.	• The leader does not afford subordinates the opportunity or support to develop or to exercise independent judgment.

The Multidimensional Leadership Performance Matrix *(continued)*

8.0 Time/Task/Project Management: Leaders in education manage the decision-making process, but not all decisions. They establish personal deadlines for themselves and the entire organization. Additionally, leaders understand the benefits of going deeper with fewer initiatives, as opposed to superficial coverage of everything. They also effectively manage and delegate tasks and consistently demonstrate fiscal efficiency.

	Exemplary (System-wide Impact) In addition to "Effective"…	Proficient (Local Impact)	Progressing (Leadership Potential)	Not Meeting Standards
8.1 Organization of Time and Projects The leader organizes time and projects for effective leadership.	• The leader maintains a daily prioritized task list. • Personal organization allows the leader to consider innovations and be available to engage in leadership activities and collaborate with people at all levels. • Calendar is free of conflicts and focused on the priorities of the leader and organization. • The leader applies project management to systems thinking throughout the organization.	• The leader provides supporting documentation of her use of organizational development tools. • Project/task accomplishments are publicly celebrated and project challenges are open for input from a wide variety of sources.	• Projects are managed using lists of milestones and deadlines, but are infrequently updated. • The impact of changes is rarely documented.	• Project management is haphazard or absent. • There is little or no evidence of lists of milestones and deadlines.
8.2 Fiscal Stewardship The leader provides fiscal stewardship by completing projects on schedule and within budget.	• The leader regularly saves time and money for the organization and proactively redeploys those resources to help the organization achieve its strategic priorities. Results indicate the positive impact of redeployed resources in achieving strategic priorities. • The leader has established processes to leverage existing limited funds and increase capacity through grants, donations, and community resourcefulness.	• The leader leverages knowledge of the budgeting process, categories, and funding sources to maximize all available dollars to achieve strategic priorities. • The leader has a documented history of managing complex projects, meeting deadlines, and keeping budget commitments. • The leader documents a process to direct funds to increase student achievement that is based on best practice and leveraging precedents of excellence in resources, time, and instructional strategies.	• The leader sometimes meets deadlines, but only at the expense of breaking the budget; or, the leader meets budgets, but fails to meet deadlines. • The leader lacks proficiency in using budget to focus resources on school improvement priorities.	• The leader has little or no record of keeping commitments for schedules and budgets.

The Multidimensional Leadership Performance Matrix *(continued)*

8.0 Time/Task/Project Management: Leaders in education manage the decision-making process, but not all decisions. They establish personal deadlines for themselves and the entire organization. Additionally, leaders understand the benefits of going deeper with fewer initiatives, as opposed to superficial coverage of everything. They also effectively manage and delegate tasks and consistently demonstrate fiscal efficiency.

	Exemplary (System-wide Impact) In addition to "Effective"…	Proficient (Local Impact)	Progressing (Leadership Potential)	Not Meeting Standards
8.3 Project Objectives and Plans The leader establishes clear objectives and coherent plans for complex projects.	• The leader uses project management as a teaching device, helping others understand the interrelationship of complex project milestones throughout the organization. • The leader uses complex project management to build systems thinking throughout the organization. • Project plans are displayed in heavily trafficked areas so that accomplishments are publicly celebrated and project challenges are open for input from a wide variety of sources. • Successful project results can be documented.	• Project management documents are revised and updated as milestones are achieved or deadlines are changed. • The leader understands the impact of a change in a milestone or deadline on the entire project and communicates those changes to the appropriate people in the organization. • The leader uses examples to differentiate between a task and a project.	• Project management methodologies are vague, or it is unclear how proposed project management tools will work together in order to help keep the project on time and within budget. • The impact of change in a milestone or deadline on the project is not clear or is rarely documented and communicated to people within the organization.	• There is little or no evidence of project management against goals, resources, timelines, and results.

The Multidimensional Leadership Performance Matrix *(continued)*

9.0 Technology: Leaders in education are technically savvy. They process changes and capture opportunities available through social-networking tools and access and process information through a variety of online resources. To analyze school results, they combine data-driven decision making with effective technology integration. Furthermore, leaders develop strategies for coaching staff as they integrate technology into teaching, learning, and assessment processes.

	Exemplary (System-wide Impact) In addition to "Effective"…	Proficient (Local Impact)	Progressing (Leadership Potential)	Not Meeting Standards
9.1 Use of Technology to Improve Teaching and Learning The leader demonstrates use of technology to improve teaching and learning.	• The leader serves as a model for technology implementation to other organizations. • The links between technology implementation and learning success are clear and public. • The leader provides evidence of greater efficiency, improved quality of information, and more responsive effective communication. • The leader coaches the entire staff on the results of the linkage between technology and organizational success, creating new ways to save resources and improve organizational effectiveness. • The leader pursues emerging best practices (e.g., Web-based lessons) relentlessly.	The leader can document adherence to the following: • Assists teachers in using technology to access, analyze, and interpret student performance data and in using results to appropriately design, assess, and modify student instruction. • Collaboratively designs, implements, supports, and participates in professional development for all instructional staff that institutionalizes effective integration of technology for improved student learning.	• The leader is personally proficient in required technology applications and appears to be an advocate for the use of instructional technology, but does not always show the link between technology implementation and a clear impact on teaching and learning.	• The leader does not display personal competence in the use of required technology applications. • The leader does not link the installation of technology to specific teaching and learning objectives.
9.2 Personal Proficiency In Electronic Communication The leader demonstrates personal proficiency in electronic communication.	• The leader creates new opportunities for learning and uses the organization as an example of effective technology implementation. • Leading by example, the leader provides a model of new learning.	• The leader personally uses email, word processing, spreadsheets, presentation software, databases, and district software. • Personal study and professional development reflect a commitment to continued learning.	• The leader has mastered some, but not all, software required for proficient performance. • The leader takes the initiative to learn new technology.	• The leader has limited literacy with technology. • There is little or no evidence of the leader taking a personal initiative to learn new technology.

MULTIDIMENSIONAL LEADERSHIP PERFORMANCE: MATRIX

The Multidimensional Leadership Performance Matrix (continued)

10.0 Personal and Professional Learning: Leaders in education stay informed on current research in education and demonstrate their understanding. They engage in professional development opportunities that improve their personal professional practice and align with the needs of the school system. In addition, leaders generate a professional development focus in their schools and districts that is clearly linked to the system-wide strategic objectives.

	Exemplary (System-wide Impact) In addition to "Effective" ...	Proficient (Local Impact)	Progressing (Leadership Potential)	Not Meeting Standards
10.1 Personal Understanding of Research Trends The leader demonstrates personal understanding of research trends in education and leadership.	• In addition to personal reading that is wide and deep in the fields of education research, the leader contributes directly to research, providing case studies, experimental results, and research questions to serve the interests of other leaders and educational organizations.	• Personal reading, learning, and teaching in education and leadership research trends are evident and documented.	• Some interest in education and leadership research trends is evident and documented. • The leader is able to link personal reading to some leadership actions.	• Little or no evidence of personal learning and research is present.
10.2 Personal Professional Focus The leader creates a personal professional focus.	• The leader approaches every professional development opportunity with a view toward multidimensional impact. • Knowledge and skills are shared throughout the organization and with other departments, schools, and districts. • Rather than merely adopting the tools of external professional development, this leader creates specific adaptations so that learning tools become part of the culture of the organization and are "homegrown" rather than externally generated.	• The leader engages in professional development that is directly linked to organizational needs. • Priority is given to building on personal leadership strengths. • The leader attends and actively participates in the professional development that is required of other leaders in the organization. • In the case of building principals, the leader attends and actively participates in the professional development required of teachers.	• The leader actively participates in professional development, but it relates to a personal agenda rather than the strategic needs of the organization. • The leader attends professional development for colleagues, but does not fully engage in it and set an example of active participation.	• The leader might introduce a professional development program, but does not participate in the learning activities along with the staff. • The leader is not strategic in planning a personal professional development focus aligned with the school or district goals.

The Multidimensional Leadership Performance Matrix *(continued)*

10.0 Personal and Professional Learning: Leaders in education stay informed on current research in education and demonstrate their understanding. They engage in professional development opportunities that improve their personal professional practice and align with the needs of the school system. In addition, leaders generate a professional development focus in their schools and districts that is clearly linked to the system-wide strategic objectives.

	Exemplary (System-wide Impact) In addition to "Effective"…	Proficient (Local Impact)	Progressing (Leadership Potential)	Not Meeting Standards
10.3 Professional Development Focus The leader creates a professional development focus.	• The leader has demonstrated the ability to integrate initiatives into one or two focus areas for professional development, with extensive time in faculty meetings, grade-level meetings, department meetings, and staff development meetings dedicated to intensive implementation of a few areas of learning. • The leader documents how professional development activities impact the closing of the learning gap for each sub-group.	• The leader's professional development plan has focused areas of emphasis and each of those areas is linked to the organization's strategic objectives. • The leader is able to identify specific professional development offerings from past years that have been systematically reviewed and terminated because they failed to support organizational goals. • The leader has a process for prior review of new professional development programs and rigorously applies it to applications for time and funding. • Professional development priorities are linked to the needs of the school, based on student and faculty achievement data.	• The leader's professional development opportunities are somewhat related to the organizational objectives, but no means of assessing their impact exists. • Participant evaluations are the primary criteria for selection, so programs that are popular but ineffective tend to be the norm.	• Faculty requests are routinely approved, whether or not they are related to student achievement. • The leader's personal professional development agenda is based on preference, not organizational needs.
10.4 Application of Learning The leader applies professional development learning.	• In addition to being proficient, this leader provides evidence of leverage, applying each learning opportunity throughout the organization. This leader creates forms, checklists, self-assessments, and other tools so that concepts learned in professional development are applied in the daily lives of teachers and leaders throughout the organization. In addition, this leader regularly shares these application tools with other schools, departments, or districts in order to maximize the impact of the leader's personal learning experience.	• There is clear evidence of the actual application of personal learning in the organization. Where learning has not been applied within the organization, this leader rigorously analyzes the cause for this and does not continue investing time and money in professional development programs that lack clear evidence of success when applied in the organization.	• The leader has given intellectual assent to some important learning experiences, but can give only a few specific examples of application to the organization.	• Even on those rare occasions when this leader engages in professional development, the purpose appears to be merely collecting information rather than reflecting on it and applying it to the organization. Professional development is an expense, not an investment in constructive improvements.

4 Multidimensional Leadership Performance: Scoring Guide

The Multidimensional Leadership Performance Matrix (rubric) is to be scored for each sub-domain within a domain. For example, "Domain 1.0: Resilience" has five sub-domains: 1.1) Constructive Reactions, 1.2) Willingness to Admit Error, 1.3) Disagreement, 1.4) Dissent, and 1.5) Improvement of Specific Performance Areas. The leader will complete a self-assessment by scoring each of the sub-domains. The evaluator also will score each of the sub-domains.

The MLP Rubrics are designed to give leaders a formative as well as a summative assessment of where they stand in all leadership performance areas and detailed guidance on how to improve. While these are not checklists for school visits by the leader's supervisor, they do reflect the key behaviors about which supervisors and those they are evaluating should be conversing frequently throughout the year. Moreover, these behavioral leadership descriptions will form the basis for leader and supervisor coaching sessions.

The "Proficient" level describes leadership performance that has local impact (i.e., within the school) and meets organizational needs. It is adequate, necessary, and clearly makes a significant contribution to the school. The "Exemplary" level is reserved for truly outstanding leadership as described by very demanding criteria. Performance at this level is dramatically superior to "Proficient" in its impact on students, staff members, parents, and the school district. In brief, the "Exemplary" leader helps every other element within the organization become as good as she is. The "Progressing" level describes leaders who understand what is required for success, are willing to work toward that goal, and, with coaching and support, can become proficient. Performance at the "Not Meeting Standards" level describes leaders who do not understand what is required for proficiency or who have demonstrated through their action and inaction that they choose not to become proficient.

When attempting to score a domain, the evaluatee and/or the evaluator should begin with the "Exemplary" level in each sub-domain of leadership behaviors and work progressively through "Proficient," "Progressing," and "Not Meeting Standards," highlighting (using a colored pen or highlighter) each description that best characterizes the leader's performance during the period for which she is being evaluated (e.g., beginning of the year, monthly, quarterly, semiannually, annually). This strategy creates a vivid graphic depiction of the leader's overall performance—areas for praise, as well as areas that require improvements. Generally speaking, the overall rating for each domain is the lowest rating for which all descriptors in each sub-domain are marked.

As illustrated in the example that follows, the principal in this hypothetical case would receive an overall rating of "Progressing" for the Domain 1.0: Resilience for this monitoring period, even though there are several descriptors for "Proficient" that were highlighted within the various sub-domains. This is because "Progressing" is the lowest rating for which all descriptors in each sub-domain were marked.

Example of How to Score the Multidimensional Leadership Performance Matrix

1.0 Resilience: Resilience is the ability of the leader to overcome setbacks and absorb any learning offered by those setbacks quickly and at the minimum cost. Resilience includes coping well with high levels of ongoing disruptive change, sustaining energy when under constant pressure, bouncing back easily from disappointment and setbacks, overcoming adversity, changing ways of working to incorporate learning when old ways are no longer possible, and doing all of this without acting in dysfunctional or harmful ways to others within the organization. More importantly, when leaders are practicing resilient behaviors their actions are contagious as they model the way for others to act in similar ways.

1.1 Constructive Reactions:
The leader reacts to disappointment and barriers to success constructively.

Exemplary (System-wide Impact)	Proficient (Local Impact)	Progressing (Leadership Potential)	Not Meeting Standards
• The leader acknowledges prior personal and organizational failures frankly and offers clear suggestions for system-wide learning resulting from those lessons.	• The leader acknowledges personal and organizational failures readily and offers clear suggestions for personal learning.	**• The leader acknowledges personal and organizational failures when confronted with evidence.**	• The leader is defensive and resists acknowledging error.

1.2 Willingness to Admit Error:
The leader demonstrates willingness to admit error and to learn from it.

• The leader shares case studies of personal and organizational errors in a way that is used to guide, inspire, and teach colleagues throughout the organization. • The leader builds resilience in colleagues and throughout the organization by habitually highlighting and praising "good mistakes" where risks were taken, mistakes were made, lessons were learned, and both the individual and the organization learned for the future.	• The leader admits failures quickly, honestly, and openly with direct supervisor and immediate colleagues. **• There is evidence of learning from past errors.** **• Has a nondefensive attitude toward accepting feedback and discussing errors and failures.**	**• The leader accepts evidence of mistakes when offered by others.** • Some evidence of learning from mistakes is present.	• The leader is unwilling to acknowledge errors. • When confronted with evidence of mistakes, the leader is defensive and resistant to learning from mistakes.

1.0 Resilience: Resilience is the ability of the leader to overcome setbacks and absorb any learning offered by those setbacks quickly and at the minimum cost. Resilience includes coping well with high levels of ongoing disruptive change, sustaining energy when under constant pressure, bouncing back easily from disappointment and setbacks, overcoming adversity, changing ways of working to incorporate learning when old ways are no longer possible, and doing all of this without acting in dysfunctional or harmful ways to others within the organization. More importantly, when leaders are practicing resilient behaviors their actions are contagious as they model the way for others to act in similar ways.

1.3 Disagreement:
The leader handles disagreement with leadership and policy decisions constructively.

Exemplary (System-wide Impact)	Proficient (Local Impact)	Progressing (Leadership Potential)	Not Meeting Standards
• The leader shows willingness to challenge executive authority and policy leaders appropriately with evidence and constructive criticism, but once a decision is made, the leader fully supports and enthusiastically implements organizational policy and leadership decisions.	• **The leader accepts and implements leadership and policy with fidelity.** • The leader represents initiatives in a way that advocates for policies as if they were the leader's ideas. • The leader proactively brings concerns to the immediate supervisor by articulating disagreements and points of view in the interest of the organization.	• The leader sometimes challenges executive and policy leadership without bringing those concerns to appropriate executive and policy authorities. • **The leader sometimes implements unpopular policies unenthusiastically or in a perfunctory manner.**	• The leader ignores or subverts executive and policy decisions that are unpopular or difficult.

1.4 Dissent:
The leader handles dissent from subordinates constructively.

Exemplary (System-wide Impact)	Proficient (Local Impact)	Progressing (Leadership Potential)	Not Meeting Standards
• The leader creates constructive contention, assigning roles (if necessary) to deliberately generate multiple perspectives and consider different sides of important issues. • The leader recognizes and rewards thoughtful dissent. • The leader uses dissenting voices to learn, grow, and, where appropriate, acknowledge the leader's own error. • The leader encourages constructive dissent, in which multiple voices are supported and heard; as a result, the final decision is made better and more broadly supported.	• The leader uses dissent to inform final decisions, improve the quality of decision making, and broaden support for her final decision. • Defined structures and processes are in place for eliciting input.	• **The leader tolerates dissent, but there is very little of it in public.**	• Dissent is absent due to a climate of fear and intimidation.

1.0 Resilience: Resilience is the ability of the leader to overcome setbacks and absorb any learning offered by those setbacks quickly and at the minimum cost. Resilience includes coping well with high levels of ongoing disruptive change, sustaining energy when under constant pressure, bouncing back easily from disappointment and setbacks, overcoming adversity, changing ways of working to incorporate learning when old ways are no longer possible, and doing all of this without acting in dysfunctional or harmful ways to others within the organization. More importantly, when leaders are practicing resilient behaviors their actions are contagious as they model the way for others to act in similar ways.

1.5 Improvement of Specific Performance Areas: The leader demonstrates explicit improvement in specific performance areas based on previous evaluations and formative feedback.

Exemplary (System-wide Impact)	Proficient (Local Impact)	Progressing (Leadership Potential)	Not Meeting Standards
• The leader's previous evaluations are combined with personal reflection and 360-degree feedback to formulate an action plan that is reflected in the leader's daily choices of priorities, as well as in the organization's priorities. • The influence of previous evaluations has an impact not only on the leader, but on the entire organization.	• The leader's previous evaluations are explicitly reflected in projects, tasks, and priorities. • Performance on each evaluation reflects specific and measureable improvements along the performance continuum from ineffective, to progressing, to proficient, to exemplary.	• **The leader is aware of previous evaluations, but has not translated them into an action plan.**	• No evidence of reference to previous leadership evaluations is present in the leader's choices of tasks and priorities.

We are not suggesting a purely mechanistic approach to this process, but rather endorse the leadership judgments of the superintendents and others evaluating the performance of administrators. This process is not designed to be an automated "administrator-proof" system, but rather a framework that attempts to add clarity, fairness, and consistency to the process, but does not replace human judgment. For instance, rating the fictitious principal's performance in Domain 1.0: Resilience as "Progressing" might be seen as very unfair if that determination had been made based on just a one-time assessment of "word picture" descriptions. However, if the principal's "Resilience" score were based on the following monitoring schedule, as depicted in Figure 4.1, and a preponderance of the data, what would be wrong with telling the administrator she needs improvement?

FIGURE 4.1	Sample Domain Monitoring Schedule					
Summative Assessment from Prior Year's Evaluation (Step 1)	Self-Assessment as Part of the Pre-Evaluation Planning (Step 2 & Step 3)	Self-Assessment from Monthly Monitoring of Applied Leadership Practices (Step 4)	Midyear Formative Evaluation (Step 5)	Consolidated Performance Assessment (Step 6)	Summative Evaluation (Step 7)	
Domain 1.0 Scored as Not Meeting Standards	Domain 1.0 Scored as Not Meeting Standards based on self-assessment and results of questionnaire	Domain 1.0 Scored as Not Meeting Standards based on results from Professional Growth Plan	Domain 1.0 Scored as Progressing based on results of Professional Growth Plan and self-assessment	Domain 1.0 Scored as Progressing based on results from self-assessment, questionnaire, and Professional Growth Plan	Domain 1.0 Scored as Progressing	

How to Determine an MLP System Score.

Generating a score for the Multidimensional Leadership Performance System has three steps:

STEP ONE: Rate Each Sub-domain.

Start with judgments on the sub-domains. Sub-domains in each domain are rated as E, P, Pr, or NMS based on accumulated evidence.

- The MLP System supports this sub-domain proficiency rating process with **rubrics** for distinguishing between the levels (E, P, Pr, and NMS) that are specific to the sub-domain.

- To guide the rating decision, **illustrative examples** of leadership actions are provided.

- The rubrics for sub-domains and the illustrative examples are found in the Matrix.

- Ratings can be recorded on the self-reflection guides.

Rating Labels: What do they mean?

The principal should complete a self-assessment by scoring each of the sub-domains. The evaluator also will score each of the sub-domains. In an end-of-the-year conference, their respective ratings are shared and discussed. The evaluator then determines a final rating for each sub-domain and, using the procedures in this scoring guide, calculates an MLP System score.

Sub-domain ratings:

When assigning ratings to sub-domains in the MLP System, the evaluator should begin by reviewing the sub-domain rubrics. These are "word-picture" descriptions of leadership behaviors in each of the four levels of leadership behavior—"Exemplary," "Proficient," "Progressing," and "Not Meeting Standards." The evaluator finds the level that best describes performance related to the sub-domain.

The rating rubrics provide criteria that distinguish among the proficiency levels on the sub-domain. The illustrative examples of Leadership Evidence for each sub-domain provide direction on the range of evidence to consider. The rating for each sub-domain is the lowest rating for which the "word picture" descriptors are appropriate and representative descriptions of what was observed about the leader's performance.

The ratings on the sub-domains aggregate to a rating on the domains using Tables 1 through 4 on the following pages in this guide. The ratings on the domains aggregate to an overall leadership performance rating, using tables and formulas in this scoring guide.

The MLP System rubrics are designed to give principals a formative as well as a summative assessment of where they stand in all leadership performance areas and detailed guidance on how to improve. While they are not checklists for school visits by the principal's supervisor, they do reflect the key behaviors about which supervisors and principals should be conversing frequently throughout the year. Moreover, these behavioral leadership descriptions will form the basis for principal and supervisor coaching and mentoring sessions. When you have a rating (E, P, Pr, or NMS) for each sub-domain in a domain, you then generate a domain rating.

STEP TWO: Rate Each Domain.

Ratings on the sub-domains in a domain are combined to assign a proficiency level (E, P, Pr, NMS) to a domain: The distribution of sub-domain ratings within a domain result in a Domain Rating. Since the number of sub-domains in a domain varies, the following formulas are applied to assign domain ratings. **For each domain, use the appropriate table.**

TABLE 1	
For Domains 4, 5, and 10 with **four Sub-domains**, each Domain is rated:	
Exemplary (E) if: three or more sub-domains are E and none are less than P.	
Examples: E+E+E+E= E	E+E+E+P=E
Proficient (P) if: at least three are P or higher and no more than one is Pr. None are NMS.	
Examples: P+P+P+E=P P+P+P+Pr=P P+P+P+P=P	
Progressing (Pr) if: criteria for P not met and no more than one is NMS.	
Examples: P+P+Pr+Pr=Pr E+E+Pr+Pr =Pr E+P+NMS+Pr=Pr	
Not Meeting Standards (NMS) if: two or more are NMS.	
Examples: E+NMS+NMS+E=NMS P+Pr+NMS+NMS=NMS P+P+NMS+NMS=NMS	

For the domains with fewer or more than four sub-domains, use the appropriate table below:

TABLE 2	
For Domains 1, 2, 3, and 6 with **five Sub-domains**, each Domain is rated:	
Exemplary (E) if: four or more sub-domains are E and none are less than P.	
Examples: E+E+E+E+E=E E+E+E+E+P=E	
Proficient (P) if: at least four are P or higher and no more than one is Pr. None are NMS.	
Examples: P+P+P+P+P=P E+E+P+P+P=P E+P+P+P+Pr=P E+E+E+E+Pr=E	
Progressing (Pr) if: criteria for P not met and no more than one is NMS.	
Examples: E+E+Pr+Pr+Pr=Pr P+P+Pr+Pr+NMS=Pr Pr+Pr+Pr+Pr+NMS=Pr	
Not Meeting Standards (NMS) if: two or more are NMS.	
Examples: E+E+E+NMS+NMS=NMS Pr+Pr+Pr+NMS+NMS=NMS	

TABLE 3			
For Domains 7 and 8 with **three Sub-domains**, each Domain is rated:			
Exemplary (E) if: two or more sub-domains are E and none are less than P.			
Examples: E+E+E=E	E+E+P=E		
Proficient (P) if: two or more are P or higher and no more than one is Pr. None are NMS.			
Examples: P+P+P=P	P+P+E=P	P+E+Pr=P	E+E+Pr=P
Progressing (Pr) if: criteria for P not met and no more than one is NMS.			
Examples: Pr+Pr+Pr=Pr	Pr+Pr+NMS=Pr	E+P+NMS=Pr	E+Pr+Pr=Pr
Not Meeting Standards (NMS) if: two or more are NMS.			
Examples: P+NMS+NMS=NMS	Pr+NMS+NMS=NMS		

TABLE 4			
For Domain 9 with **two Sub-domains**, each Domain is rated:			
Exemplary (E) if: both sub-domains are E.			
Examples: E+E=E			
Proficient (P) if: both are P or one is E and one is Pr. None are NMS.			
Examples: P+P=P	P+E=P	E+Pr=P	
Progressing (Pr) if: criteria for P not met and none are NMS.			
Examples: Pr+Pr=Pr	Pr+P+=Pr		
Not Meeting Standards (NMS) if: one or more are NMS.			
Examples: NMS+NMS=NMS	Pr+NMS=NMS	P+NMS=NMS	E+NMS=NMS

When you have determined domain ratings, you then combine those ratings to generate an MLP System score.

STEP THREE: Calculate the MLP System Score.

- In Step 1, ratings for sub-domains were made based on an assessment of available evidence and the rating rubrics.

- In Step 2, the apportionment of sub-domain ratings, using the tables provided, generated a rating for each domain.

- In Step 3, domain ratings are translated to a point scale using Table 5 below. All of these steps were based on evidence on the sub-domains and scoring tables.

At the MLP System scoring stage the model shifts to a weighted point system. Points are assigned to Domain ratings, direct weights are employed, and scores are converted to a numerical scale. The following point model is used:

TABLE 5	
Domain Rating	**Points Assigned**
A Domain rating of Exemplary	3 points
A Domain rating of Proficient	2 points
A Domain rating of Progressing	1 point
A Domain rating of Not Meeting Standards	0 points

TABLE 6 — The domain points are multiplied by the domain's direct weight: The rating is entered in column 2 ("Rating"), the points in column 3 ("Points"), and a weighted score calculated in column 5.

Domain	Rating	Points	Weight	Domain Weighted Score
Domain 1: Resilience			.05	
Domain 2: Personal Behavior and Professional Ethics			.05	
Domain 3: Student Achievement			.10	
Domain 4: Decision Making			.05	
Domain 5: Communication			.05	
Domain 6: Faculty Development			.30	
Domain 7: Leadership Development			.15	
Domain 8: Time/Task/Project Management			.05	
Domain 9: Technology			.05	
Domain 10: Personal and Professional Learning			.15	

TABLE 7	Example of Weighted Scores.				
Domain	**Rating**	**Points**	**Weight**	**Domain Weighted Score**
Domain I: Resilience	E	3	.05	.15
Domain 2: Personal Behavior and Professional Ethics	P	2	.05	.10
Domain 3: Student Achievement	P	2	.10	.20
Domain 4: Decision Making	P	2	.05	.10
Domain 5: Communication	E	3	.05	.15
Domain 6: Faculty Development	P	2	.30	.60
Domain 7: Leadership Development	P	2	.15	.30
Domain 8: Time/Task/Project Management	Pr	1	.05	.05
Domain 9: Technology	Pr	1	.05	.05
Domain 10: Personal and Professional Learning	P	2	.15	.30

TABLE 8	After a Domain Weighted Score is calculated, the scores are converted to a 100-point scale. This process results in an MLP System Score range of 0 to 300 points. This table illustrates the conversion of a Domain Weighted value to a 100-point scale.					
Domain	**Rating**	**Points**	**Weight**	**Weighted Value**	**Convert to 100 point scale**	**Domain Score**
Domain I: Resilience	E	3	.05	.15	x 100	15
Domain 2: Personal Behavior and Professional Ethics	P	2	.05	.10	x 100	10
Domain 3: Student Achievement	P	2	.10	.20	x 100	20
Domain 4: Decision Making	P	2	.05	.10	x 100	10
Domain 5: Communication	E	3	.05	.15	x 100	15
Domain 6: Faculty Development	P	2	.30	.60	x 100	60
Domain 7: Leadership Development	P	2	.15	.30	x 100	30
Domain 8: Time/Task/Project Management	Pr	1	.05	.05	x 100	05
Domain 9: Technology	Pr	1	.05	.05	x 100	05
Domain 10: Personal and Professional Learning	P	2	.15	.30	x 100	30
MLP System Score						**200**

TABLE 9	The domain scores are added up and an MLP System Score determined. The MLP System Score is converted to an MLP System rating of E, P, Pr, or NMS based on this scale:	
MLP System Score	**MLP System Proficiency Rating**	
240 to 300	Exemplary	
151 to 239	Proficient	
75 to 150	Progressing	
0 to 74	Not Meeting Standards	

5 Multidimensional Leadership Performance: Matrix Self-Reflection Guide and Midyear Evaluation Long and Short Forms

The personal process skill of self-reflection, as described in the preface of this book, is based on the work of Donald Schön (1987). We have expanded the concept and refined specific language patterns for operating within this process skill. Specifically, highly productive individuals rely upon expert inquiry to drive their individual practices. Toward that end, for leaders to continually grow in their capacity as individuals and thereby contribute to productive organizational work, they must engage in "reflection-in-action" (p. 29). In reflection-in-action, leaders compare their moment-by-moment practice to a standard of expected practice. As a result, such reflection gives rise to on-the-spot adjustments to their practice. As important as reflection-in-action is, it is even more important that this spirit of inquiry be extended to post-practice reflection, or "reflection on our past reflection-in-action" (p. 31) to help shape future practice. If leaders engage in present reflection on their earlier reflection-in-action, it initiates an internal dialogue of thinking and doing through which they become more skillful in their leadership practice.

The MLP Matrix Self-Reflection forms are a series of tools (worksheets) that both those being evaluated and those doing the evaluation can use jointly or individually during formative evaluation coaching sessions conducted throughout the year. Moreover, the leader's supervisor as well as the leader herself will use the results of this formative evaluation process as part of the documentation required to complete the MLP Summative Evaluation Form at the end of the year.

When a leader and/or supervisor is using this tool, it is assumed that they will ultimately be focusing on no more than three to five high-priority leadership sub-domains during an evaluation cycle, rather than attempting to engage in improvement efforts focused on all 10 domains and their related sub-domains. The reason for suggesting such a narrow versus a broad focus is that in our work at The Center, we have found that "by asking the right questions, focusing on the factors with the greatest leverage" (Reeves, 2011, p. 65), leaders can position themselves to focus on those leadership actions that will most likely have a direct and positive impact on key organizational goals. In other words, we understand that leaders are faced with a multitude of competing demands for their time. Given these complex and increasing time demands and the reality that there is almost always more to do than there is time in which to do those things, leaders must choose between one of two paths: the path of design or the path of default. Simply put, leaders can choose the path of "design" by prioritizing thoughtfully from the many to the vital few, well-focused actions they will pursue and rigorously monitor. Or they can select the less desirable route of "default" and allow the press of time along with the ever-increasing demands to determine which tasks they will not be able to accomplish. The risk leaders take when they pursue the latter path over the former is that some of the strategies that fall off of the "leadership plate" may be those that offer the greatest leverage and lead to lasting, significant improvement. The choice is yours. After careful consideration, which path offers the greatest opportunity to impact your most important targets positively?

Single-page worksheets (the Long Form) for each domain follow that provide leaders and supervisors a convenient way to capture the results of formative evaluation coaching sessions. Additionally, a Short Form also has been added should staff choose to use it rather than the Long Form.

Domain 1.0: Resilience				
Sub-Domains	**Exemplary**	**Proficient**	**Progressing**	**Not Meeting Standards**
SD 1.1 Constructive Reactions: The leader reacts to disappointment and barriers to success constructively.				
SD 1.2 Willingness to Admit Error: The leader demonstrates willingness to admit error and learn from it.				
SD 1.3 Disagreement: The leader handles disagreement with leadership and policy decisions constructively.				
SD 1.4 Dissent: The leader handles dissent from subordinates constructively.				
SD 1.5 Improvement of Specific Performance Areas: The leader demonstrates explicit improvement in specific performance areas based on previous evaluations and formative feedback.				
Overall Rating for Domain 1.0				

Comments (Leader and Evaluator):

Examples of evidence to support rating:

- Results of school-wide staff survey

- The leader cites examples where feedback has been used to enhance performance

- The leader cites examples where mistakes are acknowledged

- The leader offers evidence of learning from past errors

- Results of school-wide student survey

- Results of community survey

- Improvement plans reflect changes in leadership practices

Recommended actions for improvement, including needed support:

Domain 2.0: Personal Behavior and Professional Ethics

Sub-Domains	Exemplary	Proficient	Progressing	Not Meeting Standards
SD 2.1 Integrity: The leader demonstrates integrity.				
SD 2.2 Emotional Self-Control: The leader demonstrates emotional self-control.				
SD 2.3 Ethical and Legal Compliance with Employees: The leader demonstrates compliance with legal and ethical requirements in relationship to employees.				
SD 2.4 Tolerance: The leader demonstrates tolerance of different points of view within the boundaries of the values and mission of the organization.				
SD 2.5 Respect: The leader honors the time and presence of others.				
Overall Rating for Domain 2.0				

Comments (Leader and Evaluator):

Examples of evidence to support rating:

- Results of school-wide staff survey

- The leader can cite instances when confrontational situations were resolved through calm, thoughtful, and dignified problem solving

- Results of school-wide student survey

- Results of community survey

- Evidence of ability to confront ideological conflict and then reach consensus

- Dissemination of clear norms and ground rules

Recommended actions for improvement, including needed support:

Domain 3.0: Student Achievement

Sub-Domains	Exemplary	Proficient	Progressing	Not Meeting Standards
SD 3.1 Planning and Goal Setting: The leader demonstrates planning and goal setting to upgrade student achievement.				
SD 3.2 Student Achievement Results: The leader demonstrates evidence of student improvement through student achievement results.				
SD 3.3 Instructional Leadership Decisions: The leader demonstrates the use of student achievement data to make instructional leadership decisions.				
SD 3.4 Student Requirements and Academic Standards: The leader demonstrates understanding of student requirements and academic standards.				
SD 3.5 Students Performance: The leader demonstrates understanding of present levels of student performance based on consistent assessments that reflect local and state academic standards.				
Overall Rating for Domain 3.0				

Comments (Leader and Evaluator):	Examples of evidence to support rating:
	• Faculty meeting, department, grade-level agendas, professional development topics
	• School Improvement Plan goals and strategies reflect a clear relationship between the professional actions of teachers and leaders and student achievement
	• School Improvement Plan identifies quantifiable changes in professional practice (e.g., frequency of delivery, percentage of faculty delivering strategy, degree of implementation)
	• Annual state test results
	• School-wide progress monitoring of adult and student performance is documented, charted, and posted in high-traffic areas of the school
	• School Improvement Plan goals are achieved within a +/- 5 percent of SMART goal for school and/or targeted sub-group
	• Results of teacher-made common formative assessments to demonstrate proficiency on specific standards
	• "Power Standards" document
	• Report cards include detailed student performance in terms of demonstrating proficiency on specific standards as part of each reporting period

Recommended actions for improvement, including needed support:

Domain 4.0: Decision Making				
Sub-Domains	**Exemplary**	**Proficient**	**Progressing**	**Not Meeting Standards**
SD 4.1 Factual Basis for Decisions: The leader employs factual bases for decisions, including specific reference to internal and external data on student achievement and objective data on curriculum, teaching practices, and leadership practices.				
SD 4.2 Decision-Making Structure: The leader demonstrates clear identification of decision-making structure, including which decisions are made by consensus or by the staff independently, which decisions are made by the leader after getting input from the staff, and which decisions are made by the leader alone.				
SD 4.3 Decisions Linked to Vision: The leader links decisions to vision, mission, and strategic priorities.				
SD 4.4 Decisions Evaluated for Effectiveness: The leader evaluates decisions for effectiveness and revises where necessary.				
Overall Rating for Domain 4.0				

Comments (Leader and Evaluator):

Examples of evidence to support rating:

- Documented use of School Improvement Team in decision making

- Existence and work of Data Teams (e.g., professional learning communities)

- Recognition criteria and structure utilized

- Evidence that previous decisions are reevaluated in light of emerging data or trends

- School-wide student, staff, community survey results

- Evidence of shared decision making and distributed leadership

- Examples of previous decisions that have been reevaluated in light of emerging data or trends is evident

Recommended actions for improvement, including needed support:

Domain 5.0: Communication

Sub-Domains	Exemplary	Proficient	Progressing	Not Meeting Standards
SD 5.1 Two-Way Communication with Students: The leader engages in two-way communication with students.				
SD 5.2 Two-Way Communication with Faculty and Staff: The leader engages in two-way communication with faculty and staff.				
SD 5.3 Two-Way Communication with Parents and Community: The leader engages in two-way communication with parents and community.				
SD 5.4 Analysis of Input and Feedback: The leader listens actively and analyzes input and feedback.				
Overall Rating for Domain 5.0				

Comments (Leader and Evaluator):	Examples of evidence to support rating:
	• Evidence of formal and informal systems of communication
	• 360 feedback
	• The leader can share a personal strategy she is using to develop relationships with students
	• School safety and behavioral expectations
	• Examples of established expectations regarding teacher communication and relationship development with students
	• School-wide student, staff, parent, community survey results
	• Parent involvement in School Improvement Team
	• Evidence of business partners and projects involving business partners
	• Evidence of visibility and accessibility

Recommended actions for improvement, including needed support:

Domain 6.0: Faculty Development				
Sub-Domains	**Exemplary**	**Proficient**	**Progressing**	**Not Meeting Standards**
SD 6.1 Faculty Proficiencies and Needs: The leader understands faculty proficiencies and the needs for further development that will support and retain proficient and exemplary teachers.				
SD 6.2 Leading Professional Development: The leader personally leads professional development sessions.				
SD 6.3 Formal and Informal Feedback: The leader provides formal and informal feedback to colleagues with the exclusive purpose of improving individual and organizational performance.				
SD 6.4 Modeling Coaching and Mentoring: The leader models coaching and mentoring.				
SD 6.5 Recruitment and Hiring of Faculty: The leader recruits and hires proficient and exemplary teachers.				
Overall Rating for Domain 6.0				

Comments (Leader and Evaluator):	**Examples of evidence to support rating:**
	• Individualized teacher professional learning plans
	• Mentor records and beginning teacher feedback
	• Record of professional development provided to staff and the impact of professional development on student learning
	• School-wide teacher survey results
	• Documentation that professional development is determined on the basis of student achievement and teacher competency data
	• Evidence that the leader leads professional development for colleagues and faculty several times each year
	• The leader can cite multiple examples where she has provided professional development by modeling, guiding, and facilitating independent practice with a specific strategy
	• Classroom walk-through feedback provided to teachers
	• Recruitment and hiring process documents

Recommended actions for improvement, including needed support:

Domain 7.0: Leadership Development

Sub-Domains	Exemplary	Proficient	Progressing	Not Meeting Standards
SD 7.1 Mentoring Emerging Leaders: The leader mentors emerging leaders to assume key leadership responsibilities.				
SD 7.2 Identification of Potential Future Leaders: The leader consistently identifies potential future leaders.				
SD 7.3 Delegation and Trust: The leader provides evidence of delegation and trust in subordinate leaders.				
Overall Rating for Domain 7.0				

Comments (Leader and Evaluator):

Examples of evidence to support rating:

- System for identifying and mentoring potential leaders

- The leader can cite examples in which she coached several emerging leaders to assume greater and greater levels of responsibility within the organization

- Mentor records and emerging leader feedback

- School-wide teacher survey results

- School Improvement Plan

- Leadership responsibility matrix

- The leader can cite examples where she has engaged key stakeholders across the district to develop systems that promote leadership identification and development

- Staff evaluations that document delegation of responsibility and authority to make decisions and take action within defined parameters

Recommended actions for improvement, including needed support:

Domain 8.0: Time/Task/Project Management				
Sub-Domains	Exemplary	Proficient	Progressing	Not Meeting Standards
SD 8.1 Organization of Time and Projects: The leader organizes time and projects for effective leadership.				
SD 8.2 Fiscal Stewardship: The leader provides fiscal stewardship by completing projects on schedule and within budget.				
SD 8.3 Project Objectives and Plans: The leader establishes clear objectives and coherent plans for complex projects.				
Overall Rating for Domain 8.0				

Comments (Leader and Evaluator):	**Examples of evidence to support rating:**
	• Examples of projects that have been adjusted based on the input from a variety of sources
	• Examples of timely project completion
	• Examples of multiple projects and timelines managed by the leader by strategically delegating time, resources, and responsibilities
	• School-wide teacher survey results
	• School Improvement Plan
	• Leadership responsibility matrix
	• School financial information
	• Protocol for accessing school resources, when requested
	• Examples of "systems planning tools" (e.g., tree diagram, matrix diagram, PERT Chart, Gantt Chart) used that display the chronological interdependence of the project events that unfold over time

Recommended actions for improvement, including needed support:

Domain 9.0: Technology				
Sub-Domains	**Exemplary**	**Proficient**	**Progressing**	**Not Meeting Standards**
SD 9.1 Use of Technology to Improve Teaching and Learning: The leader demonstrates use of technology to improve teaching and learning.				
SD 9.2 Personal Proficiency in Electronic Communication: The leader demonstrates personal proficiency in electronic communication.				
Overall Rating for Domain 9.0				

Comments (Leader and Evaluator):	Examples of evidence to support rating:
	• Examples of the leader coaching staff on applications that link technology with school improvement
	• Examples of the leader leveraging technology for greater efficiency and convenience for teachers, parents, and students
	• School-wide teacher survey result
	• Parent survey results
	• School Improvement Plan
	• Examples of opportunities the leader has created for staff and students to experiment with new learning and application of emerging technologies (e.g., WIKI, Skype, camera technologies, software, e-mail, Internet)
	• Examples of the leader's proficient use of e-mail, voicemail, word processing, databases, spreadsheets, presentation software, and district information systems

Recommended actions for improvement, including needed support:

Domain 10.0: Personal Professional Learning

Sub-Domains	Exemplary	Proficient	Progressing	Not Meeting Standards
SD 10.1 Personal Understanding of Research Trends: The leader demonstrates personal understanding of research trends in education and leadership.				
SD 10.2 Personal Professional Focus: The leader creates a personal professional focus.				
SD 10.3 Professional Development Focus: The leader creates a professional development focus.				
SD 10.4 Application of Learning: The leader applies professional development learning.				
Overall Rating for Domain 10.0				

Comments (Leader and Evaluator):	Examples of evidence to support rating:
	• Leader's professional development growth plan, highlighting involvement in professional development topics that are directly linked to the needs of the school, district, or organization
	• Evidence the leader has applied lessons learned from the research to enhance personal leadership practices
	• Case studies of action research shared with subordinates and/or colleagues
	• School-wide teacher survey results
	• Faculty meeting minutes
	• School Improvement Plan
	• Identification of professional readings and reflections that have been used to impact the leader's performance directly
	• Forms, checklists, self-assessments, and other learning tools the leader has created that help the leader apply concepts learned in professional development

Recommended actions for improvement, including needed support:

Multidimensional Leadership Performance Midyear Evaluation Form

Evaluatee's Name:	Position:
School:	School Year:
Evaluator:	District:
Evaluator's Title:	Date Completed:

The evaluator determines whether the principal/assistant principal is making acceptable progress toward goal(s) attainment within each domain. Mark this category as **(P)—progressing** or **(NP)—not progressing**.

Summary of MLP Domains	P	NP	NA
Domain 1: Resilience			
Domain 2: Personal Behavior and Professional Ethics			
Domain 3: Student Achievement			
Domain 4: Decision Making			
Domain 5: Communication			
Domain 6: Faculty Development			
Domain 7: Leadership Development			
Domain 8: Time/Task/Project Management			
Domain 9: Technology			
Domain 10: Personal Professional Learning			

Goal:

Revised Plan/Comment:

Goal:

Revised Plan/Comment:

Principal/Assistant Principal Signature	Date
Superintendent/Designee Signature	Date

Multidimensional Leadership Performance (MLP) System Conference Summary/Proficiency Status Update — Short Form

Leader:

Supervisor:

This form summarizes feedback about proficiency on the sub-domains and domains marked below based on consideration of evidence encountered during this time frame: [enter dates]

Domain 1: Resilience

❑ Exemplary ❑ Proficient ❑ Progressing ❑ Not Meeting Standards

Scale Levels: *(choose one) Where there is sufficient evidence to rate current proficiency on a sub-domain, assign a proficiency level by checking one of the four proficiency levels. If not being rated at this time, leave blank.*

Sub-domain 1.1 – Constructive Reactions: Proficient school leader constructively reacts to disappointment and barriers to success.

❑ Exemplary ❑ Proficient ❑ Progressing ❑ Not Meeting Standards

Sub-domain 1.2 – Willingness to Admit Error: Proficient school leader demonstrates willingness to admit error and learn from it.

❑ Exemplary ❑ Proficient ❑ Progressing ❑ Not Meeting Standards

Sub-domain 1.3 – Disagreement: Proficient school leader constructively handles disagreement with leadership and policy decisions.

❑ Exemplary ❑ Proficient ❑ Progressing ❑ Not Meeting Standards

Sub-domain 1.4 – Dissent: Proficient school leader constructively handles dissent from subordinates.

❑ Exemplary ❑ Proficient ❑ Progressing ❑ Not Meeting Standards

Sub-domain 1.5 – Improvement of Specific Performance Areas: Proficient school leader demonstrates explicit improvement in specific performance areas based on previous evaluations and formative feedback.

❑ Exemplary ❑ Proficient ❑ Progressing ❑ Not Meeting Standards

Domain 2: Personal Behavior and Professional Ethics

❑ Exemplary ❑ Proficient ❑ Progressing ❑ Not Meeting Standards

Scale Levels: *(choose one) Where there is sufficient evidence to rate current proficiency on a sub-domain, assign a proficiency level by checking one of the four proficiency levels. If not being rated at this time, leave blank.*

Sub-domain 2.1 – Integrity: Proficient school leader demonstrates integrity (the quality of possessing and steadfastly adhering to high moral principles or professional standards).

❑ Exemplary ❑ Proficient ❑ Progressing ❑ Not Meeting Standards

Sub-domain 2.2 – Emotional Self-Control: Proficient school leader demonstrates emotional self-control.

❑ Exemplary ❑ Proficient ❑ Progressing ❑ Not Meeting Standards

Sub-domain 2.3 – Ethical and Legal Compliance with Employees: Proficient school leader demonstrates compliance with legal and ethical requirements in relationship to employees.

❑ Exemplary ❑ Proficient ❑ Progressing ❑ Not Meeting Standards

Sub-domain 2.4 – Tolerance: Proficient school leader demonstrates tolerance of different points of view within the boundaries of the values and mission of the organization.

❑ Exemplary ❑ Proficient ❑ Progressing ❑ Not Meeting Standards

Sub-domain 2.5 – Respect: Proficient school leaders honor the time and presence of others.

❑ Exemplary ❑ Proficient ❑ Progressing ❑ Not Meeting Standards

**Multidimensional Leadership Performance (MLP) System
Conference Summary/Proficiency Status Update — Short Form** (continued)

Leader:

Supervisor:

This form summarizes feedback about proficiency on the sub-domains and domains marked below based on consideration of evidence encountered during this time frame: [enter dates]

Domain 3: Student Achievement

❑ Exemplary   ❑ Proficient   ❑ Progressing   ❑ Not Meeting Standards

Scale Levels: *(choose one) Where there is sufficient evidence to rate current proficiency on a sub-domain, assign a proficiency level by checking one of the four proficiency levels. If not being rated at this time, leave blank.*

Sub-domain 3.1 – Planning and Goal Setting: Proficient school leader demonstrates planning and goal setting aligned to the school/district improvement plan to improve student achievement.

❑ Exemplary   ❑ Proficient   ❑ Progressing   ❑ Not Meeting Standards

Sub-domain 3.2 – Student Achievement Results: Proficient school leader demonstrates evidence of student improvement through student achievement results.

❑ Exemplary   ❑ Proficient   ❑ Progressing   ❑ Not Meeting Standards

Sub-domain 3.3 – Instructional Leadership Decisions: Proficient school leader demonstrates the use of student achievement data to make instructional leadership decisions.

❑ Exemplary   ❑ Proficient   ❑ Progressing   ❑ Not Meeting Standards

Sub-domain 3.4 – Student Requirements and Academic Standards: Proficient school leader demonstrates understanding of student requirements and academic standards.

❑ Exemplary   ❑ Proficient   ❑ Progressing   ❑ Not Meeting Standards

Sub-domain 3.5 – Student Performance: Proficient school leader demonstrates understanding of present levels of student performance based on consistent assessments that reflect local and state academic standards.

❑ Exemplary   ❑ Proficient   ❑ Progressing   ❑ Not Meeting Standards

Domain 4: Decision Making

❑ Exemplary   ❑ Proficient   ❑ Progressing   ❑ Not Meeting Standards

Scale Levels: *(choose one) Where there is sufficient evidence to rate current proficiency on a sub-domain, assign a proficiency level by checking one of the four proficiency levels. If not being rated at this time, leave blank.*

Sub-domain 4.1 – Factual Basis for Decisions: Proficient school leader employs factual bases for decisions, including specific reference to internal and external data on student achievement and objective data on curriculum, teaching practices, and leadership practices.

❑ Exemplary   ❑ Proficient   ❑ Progressing   ❑ Not Meeting Standards

Sub-domain 4.2 – Decision-Making Structure: Proficient school leader demonstrates clear identification of decision-making structure, including which decisions are made by consensus or by the staff independently, which decisions are made by the leader after getting input from the staff, and which decisions are made by the leader alone.

❑ Exemplary   ❑ Proficient   ❑ Progressing   ❑ Not Meeting Standards

Sub-domain 4.3 – Decisions Linked to Vision: Proficient school leader links decisions to vision, mission, and strategic priorities reflected in the school/district improvement plans.

❑ Exemplary   ❑ Proficient   ❑ Progressing   ❑ Not Meeting Standards

Sub-domain 4.4 – Decisions Evaluated for Effectiveness: Proficient school leader evaluates decisions for effectiveness and revises, where necessary.

❑ Exemplary   ❑ Proficient   ❑ Progressing   ❑ Not Meeting Standards

Multidimensional Leadership Performance (MLP) System
Conference Summary/Proficiency Status Update — Short Form *(continued)*

Leader:

Supervisor:

This form summarizes feedback about proficiency on the sub-domains and domains marked below based on consideration of evidence encountered during this time frame: [enter dates]

Domain 5: Communication

❏ **Exemplary**　　　❏ **Proficient**　　　❏ **Progressing**　　　❏ **Not Meeting Standards**

Scale Levels: *(choose one) Where there is sufficient evidence to rate current proficiency on a sub-domain, assign a proficiency level by checking one of the four proficiency levels. If not being rated at this time, leave blank.*

Sub-domain 5.1 – Two-Way Communication with Students: Proficient school leader demonstrates two-way communication with students.
　　❏ Exemplary　　　❏ Proficient　　　❏ Progressing　　　❏ Not Meeting Standards

Sub-domain 5.2 – Two-Way Communication with Faculty and Staff: Proficient school leader demonstrates two-way communication with faculty and staff.
　　❏ Exemplary　　　❏ Proficient　　　❏ Progressing　　　❏ Not Meeting Standards

Sub-domain 5.3 – Two-Way Communication with Parents and Community: Proficient school leader demonstrates two-way communication with parents and community.
　　❏ Exemplary　　　❏ Proficient　　　❏ Progressing　　　❏ Not Meeting Standards

Sub-domain 5.4 – Analysis of Input and Feedback: Proficient school leader actively listens and analyzes input and feedback.
　　❏ Exemplary　　　❏ Proficient　　　❏ Progressing　　　❏ Not Meeting Standards

Domain 6: Faculty Development

❏ **Exemplary**　　　❏ **Proficient**　　　❏ **Progressing**　　　❏ **Not Meeting Standards**

Scale Levels: *(choose one) Where there is sufficient evidence to rate current proficiency on a sub-domain, assign a proficiency level by checking one of the four proficiency levels. If not being rated at this time, leave blank.*

Sub-domain 6.1 – Faculty Proficiencies and Needs: Proficient school leader possesses a keen understanding of faculty proficiencies and needs for further development to support and retain proficient and exemplary teachers.
　　❏ Exemplary　　　❏ Proficient　　　❏ Progressing　　　❏ Not Meeting Standards

Sub-domain 6.2 – Leading Professional Development: Proficient school leader personally participates in and leads professional development.
　　❏ Exemplary　　　❏ Proficient　　　❏ Progressing　　　❏ Not Meeting Standards

Sub-domain 6.3 – Formal and Informal Feedback: Proficient school leader demonstrates the use of formal and informal feedback to colleagues with the exclusive purpose of improving individual and organizational performance.
　　❏ Exemplary　　　❏ Proficient　　　❏ Progressing　　　❏ Not Meeting Standards

Sub-domain 6.4 – Modeling, Coaching, and Mentoring: Proficient school leader demonstrates the ability to model coaching and mentoring.
　　❏ Exemplary　　　❏ Proficient　　　❏ Progressing　　　❏ Not Meeting Standards

Sub-domain 6.5 – Recruitment and Hiring of Faculty: Proficient school leader recruits and hires proficient and exemplary teachers.
　　❏ Exemplary　　　❏ Proficient　　　❏ Progressing　　　❏ Not Meeting Standards

Multidimensional Leadership Performance (MLP) System **Conference Summary/Proficiency Status Update — Short Form** (continued)

Leader:

Supervisor:

This form summarizes feedback about proficiency on the sub-domains and domains marked below based on consideration of evidence encountered during this time frame: [enter dates]

Domain 7: Leadership Development

❑ Exemplary ❑ Proficient ❑ Progressing ❑ Not Meeting Standards

Scale Levels: *(choose one) Where there is sufficient evidence to rate current proficiency on a sub-domain, assign a proficiency level by checking one of the four proficiency levels. If not being rated at this time, leave blank.*

Sub-domain 7.1 – Mentoring Emerging Leaders: Proficient school leader mentors emerging leaders to assume key leadership responsibilities.

❑ Exemplary ❑ Proficient ❑ Progressing ❑ Not Meeting Standards

Sub-domain 7.2 – Identification of Potential Future Leaders: Proficient school leader consistently identifies potential future leaders.

❑ Exemplary ❑ Proficient ❑ Progressing ❑ Not Meeting Standards

Sub-domain 7.3 – Delegation and Trust: Proficient school leader provides evidence of delegation and trust in subordinate leaders.

❑ Exemplary ❑ Proficient ❑ Progressing ❑ Not Meeting Standards

Domain 8: Time/Task/Project Management

❑ Exemplary ❑ Proficient ❑ Progressing ❑ Not Meeting Standards

Scale Levels: *(choose one) Where there is sufficient evidence to rate current proficiency on a sub-domain, assign a proficiency level by checking one of the four proficiency levels. If not being rated at this time, leave blank.*

Sub-domain 8.1 – Organization of Time and Projects: Proficient school leader organizes time and projects for effective leadership.

❑ Exemplary ❑ Proficient ❑ Progressing ❑ Not Meeting Standards

Sub-domain 8.2 – Fiscal Stewardship: Proficient school leader provides fiscal stewardship by completing projects on schedule and within budget.

❑ Exemplary ❑ Proficient ❑ Progressing ❑ Not Meeting Standards

Sub-domain 8.3 – Project Objectives and Plans: Proficient school leader establishes clear objectives and coherent plans for complex projects.

❑ Exemplary ❑ Proficient ❑ Progressing ❑ Not Meeting Standards

Domain 9: Technology

❑ Exemplary ❑ Proficient ❑ Progressing ❑ Not Meeting Standards

Scale Levels: *(choose one) Where there is sufficient evidence to rate current proficiency on a sub-domain, assign a proficiency level by checking one of the four proficiency levels. If not being rated at this time, leave blank.*

Sub-domain 9.1 – Use of Technology to Improve Teaching and Learning: Proficient school leades demonstrates use of technology to improve teaching and learning.

❑ Exemplary ❑ Proficient ❑ Progressing ❑ Not Meeting Standards

Sub-domain 9.2 – Personal Proficiency in Electronic Communication: Proficient school leader demonstrates personal proficiency in electronic communication.

❑ Exemplary ❑ Proficient ❑ Progressing ❑ Not Meeting Standards

Multidimensional Leadership Performance (MLP) System
Conference Summary/Proficiency Status Update — Short Form *(continued)*

Leader:

Supervisor:

This form summarizes feedback about proficiency on the sub-domains and domains marked below based on consideration of evidence encountered during this time frame: [enter dates]

Domain 10: Personal Professional Learning

❏ Exemplary ❏ Proficient ❏ Progressing ❏ Not Meeting Standards

Scale Levels: *(choose one) Where there is sufficient evidence to rate current proficiency on a sub-domain, assign a proficiency level by checking one of the four proficiency levels. If not being rated at this time, leave blank.*

Sub-domain 10.1 – Personal Understanding of Research Trends: Proficient school leader demonstrates personal understanding of research trends in education and leadership.

❏ Exemplary ❏ Proficient ❏ Progressing ❏ Not Meeting Standards

Sub-domain 10.2 – Personal Professional Focus: Proficient school leader creates a personal professional focus.

❏ Exemplary ❏ Proficient ❏ Progressing ❏ Not Meeting Standards

Sub-domain 10.3 – Professional Development Focus: Proficient school leader creates a professional development focus.

❏ Exemplary ❏ Proficient ❏ Progressing ❏ Not Meeting Standards

Sub-domain 10.4 – Application of Learning: Proficient school leader applies professional development learning.

❏ Exemplary ❏ Proficient ❏ Progressing ❏ Not Meeting Standards

6 Multidimensional Leadership Performance: Questionnaire

While a questionnaire is an important tool in public opinion research, there are a number of advantages and disadvantages districts must keep in mind prior to using this form of data collection.

Some Advantages of Questionnaires

- Questionnaires are very cost effective when compared to face-to-face interviews. This is especially true for studies involving large sample sizes and large geographic areas. Written questionnaires become even more cost effective as the number of research questions increases.

- Questionnaires are easy to analyze. Data entry and tabulation for nearly all surveys can be done easily with many computer software packages.

- Questionnaires are familiar to most people and they generally do not make people apprehensive.

- Questionnaires reduce bias. Questions are presented uniformly and thus there is no middleman bias. The researcher's own opinions will not influence the respondent to answer questions in a certain manner. There are no verbal or visual clues to influence the respondent.

- Questionnaires are less intrusive than face-to-face surveys. Unlike other research methods, the research instrument does not interrupt the respondent. When a respondent receives a questionnaire in the mailbox, she is free to complete the questionnaire on her own timetable.

Some Disadvantages of Questionnaires

- Questionnaires, like many evaluation methods, occur after the event, so participants may forget important issues.

- Questionnaires are standardized, so it is not possible to explain any points in the questions that participants might misinterpret. This can be solved partially by piloting the questions on a small group of stakeholders. (It is advisable to do this anyway.)

- Respondents may answer superficially, especially if the questionnaire takes a long time to complete. Asking too many questions is a common mistake that should be avoided.

- Stakeholders may not be willing to answer the questions. They might not wish to reveal the information or they might think that they will not benefit from responding. They may even believe they will risk being penalized for giving their real opinions. Respondents should be told why the information is being collected and how the results will be beneficial. They should be asked to reply honestly and told that if their response is negative, this is just as useful as a more positive opinion. If possible, the questionnaire should be anonymous.

If you are going to use a questionnaire, please be sure that it has a nearly 100-percent response rate. The best practice we have seen here at The Center is that it is part of the process for starting or ending the school year. If you only have a 10-percent response rate, you will be inordinately influenced by a few negative responses. Only high response rates put those responses in context. The best result (e.g., "Reframing Teacher Leadership," published by ASCD) shows that there is a big difference between what administrators perceive in teacher actions and what teachers are really doing. You need to make this a "risk-free" exercise; it's just a search for feedback.

In his seminal research on teaching, leadership, and student achievement, John Hattie (2009) found that "feedback was among the most powerful influences on achievement" (p. 173). Clearly, Hattie's comments regarding feedback in his book *Visible Learning: A Synthesis of Over 800 Meta-Analyses Relating to Achievement* referred to student achievement. However, it is not unreasonable to generalize this finding to adult achievement and, in this case, adult achievement in leadership development. Similarly, Michael Fullan and Andy Hargreaves (1996) suggest that a hallmark of professionalism is that individuals "consistently strive for better results, and are always learning to become more effective, from whatever source they can find" (p. 82). This means that you can't just sit back and wait for others to offer you feedback; you must ask for it. Soliciting from other agents (e.g., peers, books and articles, perception data, supervisor, and self) feedback (information) about the leader's practices relative to the identified goal using the MLP Questionnaire is a good use of information.

A key factor to remember about feedback obtained from others: it is one opinion coming from another individual's unique perspective. It is up to you to consider it thoughtfully, compare it to other feedback you have received, and do something constructive with it. It is impossible for us to see ourselves as others see us. However, it is very important that we don't allow these blind spots to jeopardize wonderful opportunities to advance personal growth.

The MLP Questionnaire that follows is organized around "bands" (i.e., groups of shaded and unshaded statements) of leadership statements. These bands of statements correspond with each of the 10 domains. That is, the first band of unshaded statements is related to Domain 1.0, Resilience. The second band of shaded statements is related to Domain 2.0, Personal Behavior and Professional Ethics, and so on. The organization using the bands of statements is purposeful. For example, let's say that you have decided to focus on two domains: Domain 3.0, Student Achievement, and Domain 6.0, Faculty Development. Rather than having to hunt through the document to find the statements that are related to these two domains, you will find them conveniently grouped together. Consequently, you could send out a modified questionnaire that contains only those statements. Or, you could send out the entire questionnaire, so that you get feedback on all aspects of leadership, but use the data from those two bands of statements (e.g., Domains 3.0 and 6.0) for your areas of focus.

Multidimensional Leadership Performance Questionnaire Template

Administrator's Name: Date:

Directions: Read each of the following items carefully. To rate your response to each statement, please check the appropriate box based on the following scale: "5=Strongly Agree," "4=Agree," "3=Disagree," "2=Strongly Disagree," or "1=Not Observed." Your responses are completely confidential and will be an important part of this administrator's self-assessment process for her or his continuous improvement. Thank you for providing your feedback.

Leadership Practice(s)	SA-5	A-4	D-3	SD-2	NO-1
The leader reacts to disappointment and barriers to success constructively.					
The leader demonstrates willingness to admit error and learn from it.					
The leader handles disagreement with leadership and policy decisions constructively.					
The leader handles dissent from subordinates constructively.					
The leader demonstrates explicit improvement in specific performance areas based on previous evaluations and formative feedback.					
The leader demonstrates integrity.					
The leader demonstrates emotional self-control.					
The leader demonstrates compliance with legal and ethical requirements in relationship to employees.					
The leader demonstrates tolerance of different points of view within the boundaries of the value and mission of the organization.					
The leader honors the time and presence of others.					
The leader demonstrates planning and goal setting to upgrade student achievement.					
The leader demonstrates evidence of student improvement through student achievement results.					
The leader demonstrates the use of student achievement data to make instructional leadership decisions.					
The leader demonstrates understanding of student requirements and academic standards.					
The leader demonstrates understanding of present levels of student performance based on consistent assessments that reflect local and state academic standards.					
The leader employs factual bases for decisions, including specific reference to internal and external data on student achievement and objective data on curriculum, teaching practices, and leadership practices.					
The leader demonstrates clear identification of a decision-making structure, including which decisions are made by consensus or by the staff independently, which decisions are made by the leader after getting input from the staff, and which decisions are made by the leader alone with or without staff input.					

Leadership Practice(s)	SA-5	A-4	D-3	SD-2	NO-1
Multidimensional Leadership Performance Questionnaire Template *(continued)*					
The leader links decisions to vision, mission, and strategic priorities.					
The leader evaluates decisions for effectiveness and revises where necessary.					
The leader engages in two-way communication with students.					
The leader engages in two-way communication with faculty and staff.					
The leader engages in two-way communication with parents and community.					
The leader listens actively and analyzes input and feedback.					
The leader understands faculty proficiencies and the needs for further development that will support and retain proficient and exemplary teachers.					
The leader personally leads professional development sessions.					
The leader provides formal and informal feedback to colleagues, with the exclusive purpose of improving individual and organizational performance.					
The leader models coaching and mentoring.					
The leader recruits and hires proficient and exemplary teachers.					
The leader mentors emerging leaders to assume key leadership responsibilities.					
The leader consistently identifies potential future leaders.					
The leader provides evidence of delegation and trust in subordinate leaders.					
The leader organizes time and projects for effective leadership.					
The leader provides fiscal stewardship by completing projects on schedule and within budget.					
The leader establishes clear objectives and coherent plans for complex projects.					
The leader demonstrates use of technology to improve teaching and learning.					
The leader demonstrates personal proficiency in electronic communication.					
The leader demonstrates personal understanding of research trends in education and leadership.					
The leader creates a personal professional focus.					
The leader creates a professional development focus.					
The leader applies professional development learning.					

7 Multidimensional Leadership Performance: Coaching Protocol

Purpose of the Coaching Protocol

This protocol is useful as a coaching tool to support a leader's thinking, problem solving, and goal achievement within the Multidimensional Leadership Performance Assessment Coaching Protocol. The outcomes of a coaching relationship are increased expertise and effectiveness in planning, reflecting, decision making, and continual professional development.

Use of the Coaching Protocol

Skillful coaching by the leader's supervisor supports the leader in accessing internal resources and capacities for self-directed learning. In this sense, the coach "referees" the leader's thinking and supports construction of new understandings. The protocol can be repeated for multiple domains of the MLP System.

Coaching Protocol "Moves"

In our work with clients at The Center, we have found that highly skilled supervisors will simultaneously use three coaching "moves" (refer to the middle column of the MLP Coaching Protocol) to increase leaders' expertise and effectiveness in planning, reflecting, and decision making, and to foster continual professional development. While these three coaching moves are not the only process skills (Smith, 2011) that effective supervisors should have within their repertoire of skills, this trio of process skills, when used artfully, forms the basic conversational lubricant that ensures effective interaction between supervisors and the leaders with whom they are working to improve their performance.

Brief descriptions of these three coaching moves follow:

Delayed Response. This process skill is grounded in the "wait time" research of Rowe (1972, 1987), Tobin (1987), and, more recently, the "think time" research conducted by Robert Stahl (1994). Wait time is the period of silence that follows teacher questions and students' completed responses. What Rowe discovered in her research was that teacher wait ime" rarely lasted more than one and one-half seconds in typical classrooms. More importantly, she discovered that when these periods of teacher silence lasted at least three seconds, many positive things happened to students' and teachers' behaviors and attitudes. For instance, when students are provided with three or more seconds of undisturbed wait time after a question is asked and before they are asked to respond to it, there are certain positive outcomes:

- The length and correctness of student responses increase;

- The number of "I don't know" as well as "no answer" responses decreases;

- The number of volunteered, appropriate answers by larger numbers of students greatly increases; and

- The scores of students on academic achievement tests tend to increase.

Similarly, when teachers wait patiently in silence for three or more seconds after students have responded to a question before asking another question, positive changes in their own teacher behaviors also occur:

- Their questioning strategies tend to be more varied and flexible;

- They decrease the quantity and increase the quality and variety of their questions; and

- They ask additional questions that require more complex information processing and higher-level thinking on the part of students.

Simply put, thinking takes time. Moreover, high-level thinking takes even more time. For example, Pezdek and Miceli (1982) found that it took some third-grade students, on one particular task, 15 seconds to integrate pictorial and verbal information. Learning cannot be rushed. Thinking, like good coffee, requires percolation time. Wait time provides students as well as adult learners with time for a question to percolate down through their brain cells, allowing them to form an appropriate response. Furthermore, if teachers let students' responses percolate before they ask another question, they will end up with a better brew of thinking within their classroom.

You might be asking yourself, "How does this research apply to adult learners and leaders?" The National Research Council (2000) found in their study of human learning that their research design framework assumed "that the learners are children, but the principles apply to adult learning as well" (p. 26). Thus, Rowe's (1972, 1987) and Tobin's (1987) "wait-time" research, followed by Stahl's (1994) "think-time" research findings dealing with adolescent learners can easily be generalized to adult learners and more specifically to the interactions between evaluators and evaluatees within the MLP System process.

In her research, Rowe identified four "species of wait time" (1972, p. 6):

- *Structuring*, which occurs after the teacher gives directions;
- *Soliciting*, which occurs after someone asks a question;
- *Responding*, which occurs when an individual answers a solicitation or responds to a structuring suggestion or builds on the response of others or reports on data; and
- *Reacting*, in which an individual evaluates statements made by others.

The first two types of wait time require each member of the group to monitor and control her own behavior. These are intentional pauses that provide other people with time to think. The person being asked the question controls the third type of wait time, *responding*. This is personal reflection time in which that person waits before answering. Often a person will signal the need for this time by saying, "Let me think about that for a minute." The last type of wait time, *reacting*, takes place throughout a conversation between the leader and the leader's supervisor, who use shared pauses to allow ideas and questions to percolate as well as for personal reflection and/or note-taking.

Use of the processing skill *delaying response* begins a conversational configuration in which *rephrasing* and *exploring* can be practiced. Supervisors greatly enhance the mental functioning of a leader when they routinely practice this configuration: delaying response, or extending to self and others the time to think; rephrasing, or listening with the intent of supporting the leader's thinking; and exploring or asking for details and precision in thinking.

Rephrasing. Rephrasing is perhaps one of the most valuable process skills in a supervisor's conversational toolbox. By definition, rephrasing is simply restating a text, passage, conversation, or work to offer the meaning in another form. This processing skill, when used by the supervisor within a coaching setting, requires two things: listening to understand and attempting to see the other person's point of view (Covey, 1991).

The architecture of a well-designed rephrase includes three structural supports. To begin with, a good rephrase reflects the speaker's content back to the speaker for further consideration. Next, it replicates the speaker's emotion about the content. Last, it constructs containers that hold the speaker's thought processes, as reflected in Figure 7.1. When supervisors consciously use well-designed rephrases, they communicate to the leader a desire to listen, they establish rapport between themselves and the speaker (leader), and they gain permission to explore (the next process skill to be described) for additional details, examples, and greater precision of thinking.

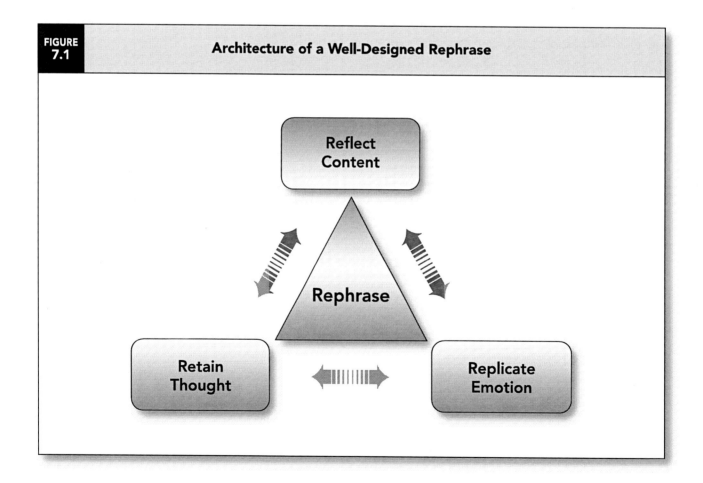

FIGURE 7.1 — Architecture of a Well-Designed Rephrase

What follows are several examples of sentence stems that can be used to begin a rephrase. (Notice that the use of the personal pronouns "I" and "me," as in "*I* hear you saying …" or "Let *me* see if this is what you mean …," is avoided, because the use of these first-person pronouns directs the attention away from the speaker to the one rephrasing. In addition, the use of personal pronouns communicates intent on the part of the listener to interpret, not reflect, the speaker's thoughts.)

- You are concerned about …
- On the one hand, you think we should start now, but on the other hand …
- You value …
- So, your short-term goal is …
- So far, you have identified three qualities …

- In other words, …
- You are noticing that …
- An assumption you are making is …
- You are feeling …
- So, you believe that our objective is to …
- You are suggesting that we …

There are three basic types of rephrases (depicted in Figure 7.2). Supervisors who become skilled in their use of the three types of rephrases will increase the range of possible responses from leaders and, at the same time, will support understanding, relationship, and learning. The three types of rephrases acknowledge and clarify thinking, summarize and organize thinking, and shift another's level of abstraction.

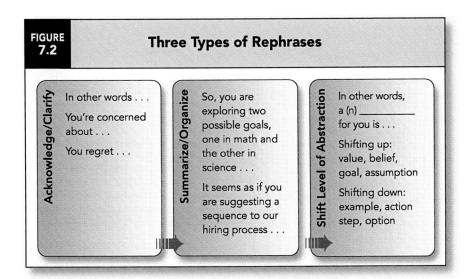

FIGURE 7.2 — **Three Types of Rephrases**

Acknowledge/Clarify
In other words . . .
You're concerned about . . .
You regret . . .

Summarize/Organize
So, you are exploring two possible goals, one in math and the other in science . . .
It seems as if you are suggesting a sequence to our hiring process . . .

Shift Level of Abstraction
In other words, a (n) _____ for you is . . .
Shifting up: value, belief, goal, assumption
Shifting down: example, action step, option

Exploring. The *exploring* through asking questions process skill joins *delaying response* and *rephrasing* within supervisors' toolboxes to enable them to facilitate growth in their evaluatees and to aid in successfully completing the leader's tasks as she explores ideas, analyzes cause-and-effect data, develops goals and strategies for improvement, monitors her collective efforts, and makes adjustments to practice based on the results. Essentially, there are two types of exploring questions supervisors may ask: those that open up thinking and those that focus another's thought processes.

Another way of thinking about these two forms of exploring is to liken them to the effects of a floodlight and a spotlight. For example, questions that open thinking, much like a floodlight, shed light on a wide range of thinking, thereby inviting a diverse number of potential responses. Conversely, probing questions, similar to a spotlight that focuses a precise beam of light on a small area, support precision in the leader's thinking by identifying and clarifying details.

Margaret Wheatley and Debbie Frieze (2010), in their article "Leadership in the Age of Complexity: From Hero to Host," believe that we must abandon our reliance on the antiquated notion that some "visionary, inspiring, brilliant, trustworthy" leader-hero will sweep in and make all of our problems go away (p. 1). Rather, these authors believe we must replace our leader-as-a-hero notion with the idea of a leader-as-a-host who re-engages people in the problem-solving process. As a consequence, these leaders-as-hosts must "extend sincere invitations, ask good questions, and have courage to support risk-taking and experimentation" (p. 4).

So, how would these leaders-as-hosts (supervisors) ask good questions? If supervisors truly want to invite leaders into a coaching conversation, what does a good question look like or sound like? What kind of question encourages open thinking and builds a culture of collaborative inquiry? Laura Lipton and Bruce Wellman (2003), in their book *Mentoring Matters: A Practical Guide to Learning-Focused Relationships,* contend that expert facilitators (supervisors) invite thinking by paying attention to four invitational elements.

The process begins with "sincere invitations" and with the supervisor paying full attention to the leader, which signals a commitment of undivided attention to the conversation. Next, the supervisor asks invitational questions using an "approachable voice … a voice that is well-modulated and tends to rise at the end of the statement, paraphrase or question" (p. 18). Next, invitational questions should use plural forms (e.g., "ideas" instead of "idea," "choices" instead of "choice," "thoughts" instead of "thought," etc.) so that in responding to the question, the leader need not be concerned about having to sort through or rank ideas. Last, invitational questions ought to contain "exploratory phrasing" (p. 18)—words like "might," "some," "possible," "may," and "promising," which serve to expand others' range of thinking. Some examples of questions that contain both plural forms and exploratory language are:

- "In light of these results, *what are some* criteria you *might* use to help you determine which is most important?"

- "What are *some* of your *hunches* as to what *might* need to happen next?"

- "What are *some* of the *instructional trends or patterns* you observed during your learning walk?"

- "If you take this course of action, what are *some things* you anticipate you will see or hear from staff that *might* influence your *actions or outcomes*?"

The second type of *exploring* question introduces specificity to the coaching conversation. These questions cause leaders to make their reasoning explicit, to explore more deeply their point of view, to clarify their assumptions, and to provide greater details in order to clear up vague thinking and language patterns.

One important way that supervisors make a difference for their evaluatees is by supporting precision in their thinking. Robert Garmston and Bruce Wellman, in their book *The Adaptive School: A Sourcebook for Developing Collaborative Groups* (1999, 2009), identify five major categories of vague thinking and language patterns that are prominent within human speech—vague nouns and pronouns, vague verbs, comparator words and phrases, rule words, and universal qualifiers. These are briefly described in Figure 7.3, which follows.

FIGURE 7.3	Vague Thinking and Language Patterns	
Categories of Vague Thinking and Language Patterns	**Description(s)**	**Example(s)**
Vague nouns and pronouns	A part of one's speech that refers to people, places, or things as if each is clearly identified	"Our students" or "the central office" or "the union" or "the parents" or "the administrators"
Vague verbs	A part of one's speech that refers to an action that is taking place as though it is plainly understood	"Implement" or "understand" or "improve" or "be on time and prepared" or "plan"
Comparators	A part of one's speech that references an undefined qualitative or quantitative measure	"This meeting was better than the last" or "It's important that our students show growth in their achievement"
Rule words	A part of one's speech that conveys to others the speaker's undefined beliefs as to how the world works and how people are to operate within it	"We have to ..." or "We must ..." or "We shouldn't ..." or "I can't ..."
Universal qualifiers	A part of one's speech that infers a universal truth understood by all	"All teachers in the school are upset with the new policy" or "Everyone knows that this program is great" or "Our students always do poorly on short constructed responses"

The three process skills (delaying response, rephrasing, and exploring) are foundational skills in a supervisor's coaching toolbox. Moreover, highly effective supervisors have a well-established pattern of routine, proficient use of these essential skills during coaching sessions. Exploring with questions that either "illuminate," or open up a leader's thinking, or "spotlight," or focus a leader's thinking, will, regardless of how well crafted and invitational the questions are, be perceived as an inquisition unless the questions are preceded by appropriate periods of silence (delaying response). The silences will allow the leader time to think, plus well crafted rephrases by the supervisor will communicate that the supervisor cares about the leader's ideas and wants to provide the leader with the opportunity to enhance communication by reflecting on her comments. Consequently, it is important to consider these three skills collectively. The three coaching moves are now combined into the Multidimensioal Leadership Performance Coaching Protocol Conversation Map that follows.

The Multidimensional Leadership Performance Coaching Protocol Conversation Map

Planning Protocol Elements	Coaching Moves	Reflecting Protocol Elements
Planning queries: • As you think about your self-assessment using the MLP Rubric, what are some areas of focus that come to mind? • As you plan for this improvement effort, what are some of the outcomes that are important to you? **5 minutes**	**Active listening:** • Listen fully with the intention to understand the principal and support learning. **Use wait-time research:** • Allow time for thinking, elaboration, and to frame your own responses to the principal. **Rephrasing:** • Use rephrasing to acknowledge and clarify speaker's content, emotions, and logical level. • Use reflective comments that help summarize and organize others' thoughts. • Use reflective comments that move others' thinking to a higher or lower logical level. • Use nonverbal communication to enhance the reflective statement.	**Reflection queries:** • As you reflect on your efforts to implement your professional growth plan, what are some things that come to mind? **5 minutes**
Indicators and evidence of success queries: • What do you anticipate you will see or hear as you achieve your outcomes? • What types of data might you gather to determine your success? • How might you depict or chart the relationship of this data to instructional practices and student achievement? **5 minutes**		**Supporting factors (data) queries:** • What are some specific recollections (data) that come to mind that support your thinking? • What are some factors that influenced what happened? • Given these impressions, what might we talk about today that would be most useful to you and your implementation efforts? **5 minutes**
Approaches, strategies, and resources queries: • Given this opportunity to think through your growth plan, what are some specific leadership strategies-in-action you might take that would help you achieve your desired results? **5 minutes**	**Exploring:** • Search for agreement on the meaning of words. • Ask questions to clarify facts, ideas, and narratives. • Ask questions to clarify explanations, implications, and consequences. • Ask questions to reveal assumptions, points of view, beliefs, or values.	**Comparison queries:** • How would you describe any differences between what you planned and what occurred? • What are some things that happened for which you hadn't planned? • As you reflect on your improvement efforts, what are some things you are noticing about your own reactions to this work? **5 minutes**
Potential factors and concerns queries: • What are some factors that might influence your plan? • What are some variables that might influence your actions and outcomes? **5 minutes**	**Personal learning, applications, and generalizations:** <table><tr><td>Planning</td><td>Reflecting</td></tr></table>• What are some ways this conversation has helped to support your thinking? • What do you want to be most aware of as you begin this improvement effort? • How might this experience connect with previous and future events? • How might I best support your work?	**Cause-effect relationship queries:** • What are some possible relationships between these events? • What sequence of events might have led to that? • What are some factors that may have affected the outcomes? **5 minutes**

In addition to providing a "Conversation Map" to those implementing the MLP System to help structure those brief 15- to 20-minute coaching sessions throughout the school year, we have also provided a series of coaching questions by domain in the tables that follow. The coaching questions help by providing a series of questions that supervisors can pose during coaching sessions that will prompt leaders to think about those leadership practices they should consider in order to move from one performance level to the next higher performance level. More importantly, the coaching questions are helpful to the individual being evaluated as they help the leader monitor her own learning processes by posing "self-regulating" (Hattie, 2012, p. 120) questions. For example, a principal who is operating at the "Progressing" level (i.e., only acknowledging personal and organizational failures when confronted with evidence) within Sub-domain 1.1 of Domain 1.0 might find it helpful to think about ways to communicate to staff her openness to suggestions for improving her professional performance. This could move the leader from "Progressing" to "Proficient" in this sub-domain.

The question or questions that are situated in a particular performance level are designed to stir the evaluatee's thinking about leadership performance that might help them rise from the lower performance level to the higher performance level within that sub-domain. It is also important to note that these questions should not be viewed as an exhaustive list, but rather samples of questions that could be posed to the leader. We encourage you to expand the list as you discover your own versions of questions that awaken the thinking of your evaluatees about how they are monitoring, measuring, and analyzing their leadership practices and the impact they are or are not having on student achievement and where they might begin approaching future leadership practices.

Multidimensional Leadership Performance Coaching Questions by Domain

Domain 1.0: Resilience

Exemplary	Proficient	Progressing	Not Meeting Standards
1.1 Constructive Reactions: The leader constructively reacts to disappointment and barriers to success.			
What are some additional insights you can share with others about what you are learning about personal and organizational resiliency?	To what extent is there a system in place that promotes clear suggestions for improvement when mistakes are made or when current strategies are unsuccessful?	What might be some ways you can communicate your openness to suggestions for improving your professional performance?	How might you demonstrate greater openness to suggestions to improve your professional performance?
1.2 Willingness to Admit Error: The leader demonstrates willingness to admit error and learn from it.			
What additional insights can you share with others about your willingness to admit error and learn from your mistakes?	How can you share personal experiences that could guide, inspire, and teach colleagues and your immediate leadership team to build resilience in their own leadership practices?	What are some of the strategies you are using currently to invite feedback from your staff and faculty?	What might be some steps you can take today to communicate to faculty and staff a willingness to acknowledge errors openly?
1.3 Disagreement: The leader handles disagreement with leadership and policy decisions constructively.			
What additional insights are you gaining about the challenges of reconciling points-of-view disagreements and fully supporting and executing organizational policy and leadership decisions? How are you sharing these insights with others?	How might you reconcile your opinions with final decisions in supporting and implementing organizational policy and leadership decisions?	When or how is it appropriate to challenge policy and leadership decisions, if at all?	What might be the impact when unpopular or difficult policy decisions are undermined, ignored, or executed with public disagreement or lack of enthusiasm from your staff and the organization?
1.4 Dissent: The leader handles dissent from subordinates constructively.			
What additional insights have you gained about the challenges of reconciling points-of-view disagreements with your staff? How are you sharing your learning with others?	What are some strategies you can think of to help your staff grow to acknowledge and implement systems for gaining multiple perspectives in decision making?	Even though dissent is tolerated, what leadership practices, structures, and processes could you put in place that would help staff know that it is also welcomed as part of an informed decision-making process?	What might be some of the steps that need to be taken to establish enough trust that faculty and staff feel free to disagree with you often?

Multidimensional Leadership Performance Coaching Questions by Domain (continued)

Domain 1.0: Resilience (continued)

1.5 Improvement of Specific Performance Areas: The leader demonstrates explicit improvement in specific performance areas based on previous evaluations and formative feedback.

Exemplary	Proficient	Progressing	Not Meeting Standards
What insights have you gained with regard to broader sources of feedback and the impact of these on personal leadership and the professional practice of your staff?	How can you include broader sources of feedback for explicit improvement planning for personal leadership and your staff (e.g., student interviews and surveys, community surveys)?	What strategies do you employ to ensure that personal learning translates into improvement planning and changes in professional practice?	What steps will you take to include previous feedback regarding your performance in your tasks and priorities?

Domain 2.0: Personal Behavior and Professional Ethics

2.1 Integrity: The leader demonstrates integrity (the quality of possessing and steadfastly adhering to high moral principles and professional standards).

Exemplary	Proficient	Progressing	Not Meeting Standards
To what extent do you have a system in place that ensures that you model trustworthiness and inspire confidence in your leadership team?	What might you initiate to help staff and faculty value your verbal commitments as if they were written?	Why do many of your staff want to have your commitments in writing?	What message is communicated when leaders fail to follow through on daily commitments at the school and/or district level?

2.2 Emotional Self-Control: The leader demonstrates emotional self-control.

Exemplary	Proficient	Progressing	Not Meeting Standards
How might you assist colleagues to develop their skills in conflict resolution and to deal with unexpected confrontational situations?	What strategies and approaches do you use to defuse confrontational situations with emotional intelligence, empathy, and respect?	What strategies might you employ to assure your faculty and staff that you will handle tense situations calmly and fairly? How might structures and protocols be used for dealing with perceived crises and situations in which passions are high and confrontation is likely?	How might losing your temper or responding emotionally impact a safe and orderly environment and the resolution of problems?

Multidimensional Leadership Performance Coaching Questions by Domain *(continued)*

Domain 2.0: Personal Behavior and Professional Ethics *(continued)*

Exemplary	Proficient	Progressing	Not Meeting Standards
2.3 Ethical and Legal Compliance with Employees: The leader demonstrates compliance with legal and ethical requirements in relationship to employees.			
To what degree can your staff provide examples in which you modeled ethical behavior in terms of decision making?	What statement best describes your ethical commitment to your staff and faculty in areas where you are able to exercise your own discretion?	How do you communicate and ensure that decisions made in your school or district meet the letter of the law and avoid both the fact and appearance of possible impropriety?	How do you communicate and ensure that decisions made in your school or district meet the letter of the law and avoid both the fact and appearance of possible impropriety?
2.4 Tolerance: The leader demonstrates tolerance of different points of view within the boundaries of the values and mission of the organization.			
To what extent do you systematically seek out different perspectives and celebrate different viewpoints?	How might you elicit divergent thinking while maintaining the focus on the mission?	What strategies might you develop to communicate that you welcome differences in viewpoints, but expect behavior to occur within the school framework and organizational requirements?	What changes in your behavior as leader will be necessary to encourage development of alternative viewpoints among your staff and faculty?
2.5 Respect: The leader honors the time and presence of others.			
To what degree is your staff able to identify specific instances when they were afforded time, attention to their concerns, and respect during interactions with you?	What process do you follow (or might you follow) to ensure that you engage others most effectively during the limited time available in meetings?	What changes are needed to ensure that you are consistently on time or early and prepared?	How can you address sidebar conversations that tend to communicate disrespect and cause distractions for those in attendance?

Multidimensional Leadership Performance Coaching Questions by Domain *(continued)*

Domain 3.0: Student Achievement

3.1 Planning and Goal Setting: The leader demonstrates planning and goal setting to improve student achievement.

Exemplary	Proficient	Progressing	Not Meeting Standards
What specific school-improvement strategies have you employed to measure improvements in teaching and innovations in curriculum that serve as predictors of improved student achievement?	What system is in place to ensure that your best ideas and thinking are shared with colleagues, particularly when there is evidence at your school of improved student achievement?	To what extent do goals and strategies reflect a clear relationship between the actions of teachers and the impact of those actions on student achievement?	What processes have you developed to make sure all goals are both measurable and specific?

3.2 Student Achievement Results: The leader demonstrates evidence of student improvement through student achievement results.

Exemplary	Proficient	Progressing	Not Meeting Standards
What new challenges are emerging in terms of student achievement, and what specific and effective interventions do you see as necessary to continue to improve student achievement results?	What learning have you pursued to help you recognize the critical role professional practices play in improving student achievement for all learners?	To what extent have you taken decisive action in terms of teacher assignments, scheduling of time and opportunity, and adjusting curriculum to improve student achievement? What tools or support do you, personally, need to take such actions more consistently?	How large is the gap between current performance and the established target performance at your school? What leadership actions are being considered to close that gap between current performance and the target performance at your school?

3.3 Instructional Leadership Decisions: The leader demonstrates the use of student achievement data to make instructional leadership decisions.

Exemplary	Proficient	Progressing	Not Meeting Standards
To what degree do you help faculty reflect on best practices or emerging research? How might you, as the instructional leader, encourage decision making on the basis of achievement and teaching data?	What do you need to do to ensure that your faculty receive professional development in data analysis and can make changes in their instruction based on that analysis?	To what degree have you instituted a review of data at informal levels? Why is publicly displaying data so important to promoting a culture of data-driven decision making?	What resources and colleagues are available to you to ensure that connections between student achievement results and professional practices (including schedules, time, staffing) are documented and recognized?

Multidimensional Leadership Performance Coaching Questions by Domain *(continued)*

Domain 3.0: Student Achievement *(continued)*

Exemplary	Proficient	Progressing	Not Meeting Standards
3.4 Student Requirements and Academic Standards: The leader demonstrates understanding of student requirements and academic standards.			
What strategies have you employed or considered employing to examine and discuss student work during faculty meetings or professional development? How do you use anchor papers in PLC, department, or Data Team meetings?	Why is it important that leaders help reduce variance in terms of teacher requirements for academic standards by posting expectations and offering needed professional development?	How frequently do you link standards and student performance by providing examples of proficient work?	To what degree do your your report cards reflect student progress in terms of demonstrating proficiency of standards? How might you communicate student progress toward achieving proficiency of standards to parents, teachers, and students?
3.5 Student Performance: The leader demonstrates understanding of present levels of student performance based on consistent assessments that reflect local and state academic standards.			
To what degree do you use faculty meetings to discuss standards and review student work? To what degree does a system exist in your school to make sure standards are posted and professional development around standards is provided to and supported for all faculty members?	What strategies have you considered to ensure that all teachers understand the importance of adhering to academic standards in their classrooms? How do you promote posting of proficient student work—in prominent locations throughout your school—at all levels?	To what extent do you personally promote kid-friendly standards and student-generated rubrics, done in students' own words?	What is currently done to help students understand standards?

Multidimensional Leadership Performance Coaching Questions by Domain (continued)

Domain 4.0: Decision Making

Exemplary	Proficient	Progressing	Not Meeting Standards
4.1 Factual Basis for Decisions: The leader employs factual bases for decisions, including specific reference to internal and external data on student achievement and objective data on curriculum, teaching practices, and leadership practices.			
To what degree is a system in place that ensures due diligence in decision making that is informed by a variety of student achievement data?	How might you augment your current data collection system to provide added insights to you and your faculty that student achievement data alone cannot provide?	What will be needed to ensure that the vast majority of decisions are informed by a reliance on multiple sources of student achievement data?	Why is it necessary to consult multiple sources of evidence (data) consistently to eliminate the perception that decisions are based on the popularity of an idea or the personal preference of the leader?
4.2 Decision-Making Structure: The leader demonstrates clear identification of decision-making structure, including which decisions are made by consensus or by the staff independently, which decisions are made by the leader after getting input from the staff, and which decisions are made by the leader alone.			
What processes have been effective in distinguishing levels of decision making in your setting?	How will you ensure that your use of consensus and unilateral decision making, when necessary, is predictable and clearly defined for your staff in the future?	To what degree do you use perception data to augment understanding of teaching and learning to better inform decisions?	What are you doing now to establish a clearly defined protocol for making decisions that affect your staff and faculty?
4.3 Decisions Linked to Vision: The leader links decisions to vision, mission, and strategic priorities.			
How do you promote and foster continuous improvement with new staff? What changes might you make to your decision-making process for further improvement?	How might you reinforce and establish your efforts so that direct reports and your entire school community understand the link between decisions and your priorities?	Why is it necessary to explicitly reference your vision and mission, even though they are visibly posted in high-traffic areas of your school?	How might you better align your decisions with the vision and mission of your school?
4.4 Decisions Evaluated for Effectiveness: The leader evaluates decisions for effectiveness and revises where necessary.			
How do you continue to clarify the decision-making process in a dynamic, changing environment?	Why is it necessary for you as a school leader to reevaluate prior decisions and programs in light of emerging research, personal experience, and changing situations?	What will you do from now on to ensure previous decisions and programs are revisited and evaluated on a routine basis?	When do you take time with your leadership team to reflect on decisions that have been made? Do you evaluate decisions on the basis of student achievement?

Multidimensional Leadership Performance Coaching Questions by Domain (continued)

Domain 5.0: Communication

Exemplary	Proficient	Progressing	Not Meeting Standards
5.1 Two-Way Communication with Students: The leader demonstrates two-way communication with students.			
How do you communicate the feedback from students with all of your stakeholders as part of your continuous improvement plan?	How confident are you that you are accessible to all students? Are there times during the school day when you deliberately make yourself available to students?	How do you use data gathered from students to inform decisions about student achievement and school policies?	Specifically, what are you doing as a leader to communicate interest in your students every day?
5.2 Two-Way Communication with Faculty and Staff: The leader demonstrates two-way communication with faculty and staff.			
How might you institutionalize an even deeper level of communication with your staff?	What additional opportunities do you have to listen deeply and actively to the concerns and ideas of your staff?	How might you modify your current meetings to increase your level of communication with your staff, to hear their concerns, and to learn from their experiences?	To what degree do you invite questions and comments to check for understanding, beyond those within faculty meetings?
5.3 Two-Way Communication with Parents and Community: The leader demonstrates two-way communication with parents and community.			
How does feedback from parents and community members inform decision making in the school or district?	What benefits might the school gain if parents and community members understood the rationale for most decisions and believed you were accessible to them?	Knowing that some parents are reluctant to initiate conversations with school leaders, what strategies have you employed or considered in which you, as the leader, would initiate communication with parents and stakeholders?	How are you including parents on committees? To what degree are you currently accessible to parents and community stakeholders? What strategies are you using to make certain there are weekly, protected times when parents know they can meet with you?
5.4 Analysis of Input and Feedback: The leader actively listens and analyzes input and feedback.			
How might you capture ideas provided by staff, parents, students, and your community so that important concerns become priorities and priorities produce effective action plans?	How do you document conversations and meetings sufficiently to ensure that you deepen mutual understanding with your audiences?	What strategies might help you capture key details from your routine communications?	To what extent can you describe situations in which you invited input from others to resolve challenges that arose? What are some of the ways that you gather feedback in your decision-making process?

Multidimensional Leadership Performance Coaching Questions by Domain *(continued)*

Domain 6.0: Faculty Development

Exemplary	Proficient	Progressing	Not Meeting Standards
6.1 Faculty Proficiencies and Needs: The leader understands faculty proficiencies and needs for further development to support and retain proficient and exemplary teachers.			
What procedures have you established to increase professional knowledge opportunities for colleagues across the school system?	What system do you use to prioritize learning needs and empower faculty to create individual learning plans?	What strategies have you employed to meet the learning needs of your faculty, from novice to veteran to expert?	How are professional learning opportunities linked to individual faculty needs?
6.2 Leading Professional Development: The leader personally leads professional development sessions.			
What system do you have in place for sharing insights and learning from professional development activities? How do you help colleagues in other schools benefit from your professional development successes?	What are some of the actions you take to communicate the importance of professional learning for you and your staff?	How do you ensure that you are keeping up with the research and are fluent with best practices that can help develop your faculty and staff?	How often do you devote portions of faculty meetings to professional development, such as sharing personal experiences with colleagues or showcasing successful practices?
6.3 Formal and Informal Feedback: The leader provides formal and informal feedback to colleagues with the exclusive purpose of improving individual and organizational performance.			
How frequently do teachers recognize that your feedback is directly linked to improving both their personal and professional performance and that of the school? What might you do to ensure that they see this important connection?	What are some examples of focused, constructive, and meaningful feedback that you provide to your staff? How does this support their learning?	How do you currently recognize faculty in providing feedback and affirmation to them? To what extent do you acknowledge the efforts of teams, as well as that of individuals?	How can frequent, focused, and constructive feedback support teachers in improving their practice?
6.4 Modeling Coaching and Mentoring: The leader models coaching and mentoring.			
To what extent is faculty aware of the National Staff Development Council (NSDC) Standards for faculty development? What might you do to ensure faculty members are fluent with the NSDC Standards and can delineate or define them to colleagues?	Do you currently have a framework for your informal observations that ensures quality and meaningful feedback as perceived by each teacher?	To what extent does your feedback provide sufficient examples and modeling to guide teachers to improve their instruction?	How might you improve the effectiveness of your classroom observations to ensure that you provide meaningful feedback about specific and proven effective instructional strategies?

Domain 6.0: Faculty Development *(continued)*

Exemplary	Proficient	Progressing	Not Meeting Standards
6.5 The Recruitment and Hiring of Faculty: The leader recruits and hires proficient and exemplary teachers.			
How might you further expand your influence within the district to help others become as skilled in recruitment and hiring as you have become?	How are you tracking the success of your recruitment and hiring strategies, learning from past experience, and revisiting the process annually to improve the process continually? What recruitment strategies are you prioritizing based on where you find your most effective teachers? In what ways are you sharing your recruiting and hiring practices with other administrators and colleagues throughout the system?	In what ways have you described your ideal teacher so that the description aligns with your school's vision, culture, and performance expectations based on the type of teacher who has been successful at your school? What hiring selection tool have you developed that helps interviewers focus on key success criteria aligned with Marzano's *Art and Science of Teaching?* What hiring process is established that specifies the steps, which staff is included, who is responsible, and what the leader is looking for?	In what ways have you worked with the staff in the human resources office to write and post a job description for the vacant teaching position? In what ways are the hiring processes you have put into place systematic and systemic in nature?

Domain 7.0: Leadership Development

Exemplary	Proficient	Progressing	Not Meeting Standards
7.1 Mentoring Emerging Leaders: The leader mentors emerging leaders to assume key leadership responsibilities.			
Do you have a system to ensure that you encourage key assistants to pursue job opportunities when they are available? How might you embed this preparation into their job duties and what changes will you need to make to help build such leadership capacity at your school?	What strategies and lessons might you impart to your direct reports to better prepare them for expanded leadership opportunities?	When do you release responsibility to your assistants to own key decisions? How do you leverage school improvement activities to build leadership capacity for assistants and emerging teacher leaders?	How might you spend time explicitly preparing your assistants to assume your role as principal? What steps would you take to spend more time in preparing your assistants to assume your role as principal?

Multidimensional Leadership Performance Coaching Questions by Domain *(continued)*

Domain 7.0: Leadership Development *(continued)*

Exemplary	Proficient	Progressing	Not Meeting Standards
7.2 Identification of Potential Future Leaders: The leader consistently identifies potential future leaders.			
To what degree do you provide guidance and mentorship to emerging leaders outside of your personal job description and leadership responsibilities?	How have you designed the school improvement process to develop leadership capacity from existing faculty?	What process do you employ to encourage participation in leadership development?	What process is available to you that helps you screen and develop potential leaders?
7.3 Delegation and Trust: The leader provides evidence of delegation and trust in subordinate leaders.			
To what extent do you have a systematic process in place for delegating authority to subordinates?	How might you increase the range and scope of tasks and responsibilities you delegate to key individuals or teams? In what areas do faculty and staff bring expertise that will improve the quality of decisions at your school?	Under what circumstances would you be willing to release increased decision-making authority to your staff and faculty? How might you use the function of delegation to empower staff and faculty at your school?	What factors prevent you from releasing responsibilities to staff?

Domain 8.0: Time/Task/Project Management

Exemplary	Proficient	Progressing	Not Meeting Standards
8.1 Organization of Time and Projects: The leader organizes time and projects for effective leadership.			
How are projects organized to ensure that best practices are considered for innovation within the school and across the district?	What system do you have in place to respond to project challenges or successes with flexibility and agility?	How might you begin to organize your work and communicate responsibilities to your faculty that clarify project goals, milestones, deadlines, and resource needs?	What steps can you take to organize major projects to include timelines, project plans, action steps, resources, and person(s) responsible?
8.2 Fiscal Stewardship: The leader provides fiscal stewardship by completing projects on schedule and within budget.			
How would you describe the systematic method you utilize for pursuing grants, partnerships, and combining community resources to increase student achievement.	To what extent are faculty and staff aware of your budgeting expectations? How are your budgeting expectations delineated, published, and communicated?	Have there been instances in which you failed to meet deadlines or where expenditures resulted in budget overruns? What did you learn from that experience and how did you apply lessons from it?	When resources are limited, what actions do you take as the school leader to allocate them most efficiently?

Multidimensional Leadership Performance Coaching Questions by Domain (continued)

Domain 8.0: Time/Task/Project Management (continued)

Exemplary	Proficient	Progressing	Not Meeting Standards
8.3 Project Objectives and Plans: The leader establishes clear objectives and coherent plans for complex projects.			
How prepared are you to describe the importance of systems thinking as it pertains to project management at your school?	To what extent are tasks and major tasks delineated in your overall project design? What might you do to emphasize the most important components over minor tasks?	How do you ensure unanticipated changes do not derail or prevent completion of key projects at your school?	What changes in your practice are needed to ensure projects are realistically designed, carefully implemented, and supported with sufficient time and resources?

Domain 9.0: Technology

Exemplary	Proficient	Progressing	Not Meeting Standards
9.1 Use of Technology to Improve Teaching and Learning: The leader demonstrates use of technology to improve teaching and learning.			
How do you intend to coach your staff and faculty in the coming year in terms of integrating technology into learning activities and managing data in each classroom?	What resources and training will you need to better advocate for instructional technology or to model improvements in communication, analysis, and presentation to your faculty and staff?	To what degree do you rely on faculty and staff to demonstrate the link between technology applications and teaching and learning?	What have you done as a leader to leverage technology for greater efficiency and convenience for teachers, parents, students, and yourself?
9.2 Personal Proficiency in Electronic Communication: The leader demonstrates personal proficiency in electronic communication.			
To what extent are you currently involved with coaching others to refine and expand their skills in leveraging instructional technology to improve student achievement?	What personal skills with technology would your staff identify as your strengths as a school leader (e.g., spreadsheets, presentation software, district management systems)? Is there a professional development structure to familiarize new staff with technology expectations at your school?	In the coming school year, how might you schedule learning opportunities for yourself to acquire new competencies and sharpen your level of fluency with technology?	What steps can you take to develop your technology skills to minimize your dependency on others for information?

Multidimensional Leadership Performance Coaching Questions by Domain (continued)

Domain 10.0: Personal Professional Learning

Exemplary	Proficient	Progressing	Not Meeting Standards
10.1 Personal Understanding of Research Trends: The leader demonstrates personal understanding of research trends in education and leadership.			
What system have you created to promote action research, disseminate meaningful case studies, and develop learning tools?	How might you ensure that your leadership practice is influenced by applied learning from each professional development session you attend?	To what extent is the professional development you receive directly aligned to the needs identified at your school or within your district?	What is needed to provide you regular access to educational research findings or professional learning opportunities to help you grow as a leader?
10.2 Personal Professional Focus: The leader creates a personal professional focus.			
What has been most effective in creating a focus on professional learning? How might you lead this effort across the district?	To what degree do you explicitly identify the focus areas for professional development in faculty and grade level/department meetings?	How do you prioritize your own learning needs in concert with the needs of the school or district?	What steps can you take to participate in professional learning focused on school and district goals with your staff?
10.3 Professional Development Focus: The leader creates a professional development focus.			
To what degree do you employ a systematic evaluation process to strategically eliminate, modify, or expand professional development to further support organizational goals? How might you lead the creation of such a system?	What is needed to determine the impact of your carefully selected professional development initiatives?	How has your leadership created an effective set of criteria that results in a limited number of initiatives that clearly align with your school's or district's needs assessment?	In what ways do your current actions support focused professional development aligned to your school and district goals for student achievement?
10.4 Application of Learning: The leader applies professional development learning.			
How have you synthesized new professional learning into existing learning for more sophisticated application? How have you applied this learning to support and encourage the growth of other leaders? How will you leverage your professional learning throughout the school, district, and beyond?	How will you determine whether application of your own professional learning is impacting student achievement and the school as a whole? How are you adjusting your practice when clear evidence of success is not apparent?	How are you investing your professional learning and applying it to your school on a daily basis? How do you apply this learning in multiple leadership venues?	What steps can you take to begin to apply professional learning to your daily work?

8 Multidimensional Leadership Performance: Professional Growth Plan

Douglas Reeves, in *Transforming Professional Development into Student Results* (2010), makes a strong argument for the importance of action research as a part of educational practitioners' responsibilities. Another way of saying this is that leaders have a responsibility to influence professional practice through the systematic observation of the impact of specific leadership practices on student achievement. Leaders must support continuous sharing of tools and results among those sustaining a culture of collaborative inquiry. This is the practice of groups (e.g., Data Teams) examining together how well students are performing, relating this to how they are teaching and leading, and then making improvements based on the analysis of this relationship. The process driving this culture of inquiry is the same process, with a minor variation, that you may have been introduced to in several seminars developed by our colleagues at The Leadership and Learning Center (e.g., Data-Driven Decision Making, Advanced Data-Driven Decision Making, and Data Teams), which is depicted in Figure 8.1. You will notice that the process reflected in Figure 8.1 incorporates a seventh step (i.e., assessing the effectiveness of your coaching session). Thus, the title was modified from The Center's earlier publications (e.g., Decision Making for Results and Data Teams) to now read *The Decision-Making for Results 6+1 Process* (Smith, 2011).

Ray Smith (2011), in his training manual entitled *Advanced Decision Making for Results*, building off of the earlier work of his colleagues (Besser, et al., 2010; Besser, et al., 2008) at The Center, added this seventh step in order to address what for many has been a missing ingredient in the goal of conducting highly effective coaching sessions—assessing the degree to which coaching sessions are helpful interactions. While it is critical that supervisors and leaders routinely monitor and evaluate the results of their work, the impact of leadership practices on student achievement, this sixth step is insufficient for the continuous improvement of the coaching session. At the conclusion of each coaching session, supervisors must determine how effectively the coaching session helped the leader to deepen her thinking about or reflection on an improvement process. This step doesn't need to take a great deal of time. Supervisors can simply ask, for example, "How has our time together today helped you expand your thinking?"

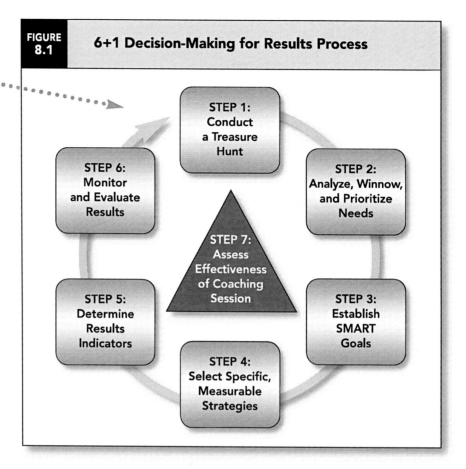

A pursuit into learning begins with a theory, a hunch, or a question

FIGURE 8.1 — **6+1 Decision-Making for Results Process**

STEP 1: Conduct a Treasure Hunt

STEP 2: Analyze, Winnow, and Prioritize Needs

STEP 3: Establish SMART Goals

STEP 4: Select Specific, Measurable Strategies

STEP 5: Determine Results Indicators

STEP 6: Monitor and Evaluate Results

STEP 7: Assess Effectiveness of Coaching Session

Action research of this nature, in addition to using a well-defined process of inquiry as reflected in Figure 8.1, also requires the use of a planning document. Our instincts tell us that high-quality planning should help leaders achieve their goals. But much of the research in this area doesn't support a positive relationship between planning and improved student achievement (Bryson and Roering, 1987; Halachmi, 1986; Mintzberg, 1994; Kannapel, et al., 2005). However, The Leadership and Learning Center's research, which included more than 2,000 schools with more than 1.5 million students from diverse populations (e.g., high- and low-poverty schools, high- and low-second language schools, and schools from urban, suburban, and rural environments), found "correlations between specific elements of building plans and student achievement that can give school leaders insight into how to focus their efforts as they revise and improve their school plans" (Reeves, 2006, p. 69).

Figure 8.2 is a planning template entitled Multidimensional Leadership Performance Professional Growth Plan that contains elements forged from The Center's research on effective planning.

FIGURE 8.2

Multidimensional Leadership Performance Professional Growth Plan Template

School-wide or District-wide or Department-wide Problem-of-Practice:

Theories-of-Action:

SMART Goal #1 Statement:

MLP Matrix Domain: | **Related Sub-domain:**

Leadership Strategies-in-Action	Results Indicators	Desired Benefits	Sources of Data to Monitor
IF I increase the percentage of (insert your 1 to 2 measurable leadership strategies) …	**THEN** I expect to see a measurable (percent) increase in (satisfaction, productivity practices, or student learning results) …	(Create descriptors of successful strategy implementation, as well as changes in staff practices and student work)	(Insert what data you will monitor to determine effectiveness)

What are some things you anticipate you will need to do to ensure success (a list of tasks or steps essential to the strategies-in-action)?

FIGURE 8.3

Instructional Growth Plan

Sample A: Completed Instructional Professional Growth Plan

School-wide or District-wide or Department-wide Problem-of-Practice:

Our NWEA data shows that our students are achieving growth in reading and language arts during the school day. However, our ISTEP+ data, combined with classroom data and teacher feedback, indicate that our students, specifically our special-education, ENL, and Hispanic students, need to make significant growth in reading. This led us to speculate that we don't have a system in place that allows us to systematically discover the instructional practices that we are currently using that most closely relate to increases in reading comprehension. We may not fully understand what the research says about best practice for teaching reading comprehension and English Language Learners. Collectively, we are not doing a good job of helping our students understand and apply the process of analyzing and responding to the content in a piece of text.

Theories-of-Action:

If we focus on reading in the content area on a daily basis and provide frequent feedback to students about the quality of their reading, then we will see improvement in our (Hispanic) language arts (reading comprehension) ISTEP+ scores.

SMART Goal #1 Statement:

Increase the percentage of grade 3 to grade 6 students (Hispanic) scoring at the proficient or higher levels from 65 percent (Hispanic 45 percent) to 75 percent (Hispanic 65 percent) on the language arts (reading comprehension) portion of ISTEP+ by spring of 2011.

MLP Matrix Domain: *Student Achievement 3.0* **Related Sub-domain:** *Student Achievement Results 3.2*

Leadership Strategies-in-Action	Results Indicators	Desired Benefits	Sources of Data to Monitor
IF I increase the percentage of *(insert your 1 to 2 measurable leadership strategies) …*	THEN I expect to see a measurable *(percent) increase in (satisfaction, productivity practices, or student learning results) …*	*(Create descriptors of successful strategy implementation, as well as changes in staff practices and student work)*	*(Insert what data you will monitor to determine effectiveness)*
Increase the percentage of teachers who monitor student achievement gains in reading comprehension by pre/post short-cycle assessments and use the results to inform instructional practice monthly.	Increase the percentage of students scoring at the proficient or higher levels, using a locally developed rubric, on a monthly reading comprehension assessment.	• Greater understanding as to the barriers to proficient student (Hispanic) reading comprehension • Improved awareness of what teachers need and how best to support them • Opportunity to spread instructional best practices	• Classroom observation log • Teacher lesson plans • Reading results

What are some things you anticipate you will need to do to ensure success (a list of tasks or steps essential to the strategies-in-action)?

• Set up a frequent system of classroom observations • Work with staff to create a series of reading comprehension "look fors" to use as a classroom observation guide • Create a common reading comprehension rubric • Provide staff professional development in the use of the rubric • Schedule distributed practice sessions in teacher use of the rubric to achieve a high level of inter-rater reliability • Provide staff professional development in reading comprehension strategies for Hispanic students • Provide follow-up coaching and mentoring of teachers to support the implementation of the professional development.

FIGURE 8.4

Noninstructional Growth Plan

Sample B: Completed Noninstructional Professional Growth Plan

School-wide or District-wide or Department-wide Problem-of-Practice:

Both survey and anecdotal data that we obtain from our customers (school personnel) reveal that repairs to facilities and/or equipment are not made in a timely or quality manner. Our Building Engineers are poorly equipped to "proficiently" resolve minor, nontechnical work orders in at least four areas of need (i.e., small engine [motor] repair and maintenance, drywall repair, furniture repair, and underground sprinkler system repairs). Furthermore, there are a growing number of work orders that become lost within the system and are therefore never acted upon. We lack a cost-effective and efficient set of procedures for processing work orders.

Theories-of-Action:

If I increase the number of Building Engineers who have the capacity to resolve minor work order requests, then our work orders will be processed and resolved in a more expeditious and timely manner.

SMART Goal #1 Statement:

Increase the percentage of work orders completed on time from 70 percent to 95 percent by June 2011 as determined by the summary results from the Information Management System.

MLP Matrix Domain: *Faculty Development 6.0*

Related Sub-domain: *Leading Professional Development 6.2*

Leadership Strategies-in-Action	Results Indicators	Desired Benefits	Sources of Data to Monitor
IF *I increase the percentage of (insert your 1 to 2 measurable leadership strategies) …*	THEN *I expect to see a measurable (percent) increase in (satisfaction, productivity practices, or student learning results) …*	*(Create descriptors of successful strategy implementation, as well as changes in staff practices and student work)*	*(Insert what data you will monitor to determine effectiveness)*
Increase the percentage of Building Engineers (BE) who apply their professional development training at the "proficient" or higher level monthly in each of the four identified areas of need.	*Increase the percentage of minor work orders that are completed on time and at the "proficient" or higher level based on a locally developed rubric.*	• *Greater understanding of the barriers to proficient BE performance in each of the four areas* • *Improved awareness of what BEs need and how best to support them* • *Opportunity to spread repair best practices*	• *Observational data* • *BE self-assessment data* • *Work order rubric data* • *Information Management data*

What are some things you anticipate you will need to do to ensure success (a list of tasks or steps essential to the strategies-in-action)?

• *Secure financial and human resources needed to provide the necessary professional development for BEs* • *Develop an ongoing schedule of professional development* • *Work with professional development trainers to develop a set of training rubrics for each area* • *Develop an implementation plan that addresses the six leadership functions for successful implementation (i.e., developing, articulating, and communicating a shared vision of the intended change; planning and providing resources; investing in professional development; monitoring and checking on progress; providing continuous assistance; and creating a context supportive of the change).*

Two fully completed Professional Growth Plans, one instructional (Figure 8.3) and one noninstructional (Figure 8.4), serve as guides for readers to use in the development of their own professional growth plans.

The Architecture of the MLP Professional Growth Plan

The professional growth plan comprises the essential elements depicted in Figure 8.5 and represented on the MLP Professional Growth Plan template (see Figure 8.2). In his book *Finding Your Leadership Focus: What Matters Most for Student Results,* founder and CEO of The Leadership and Learning Center Douglas Reeves (2011) describes the PIM™ (Planning, Implementation, and Monitoring) studies our colleagues have conducted at The Center based on double-blind reviews of more than 2,000 schools in the United States and Canada, with more than 1.5 million students from diverse populations, including high- and low-poverty schools, high- and low-second language schools, and schools from urban, suburban, and rural environments. While the full details of this study can be found in Appendix A of Reeves' (2011) book, we can say the "data suggest that, after repeated analysis, a focus on some [PIM] variables is more consistently associated with gains in student achievement than on other variables" (p. 109). In short, the elements contained within the suggested format (see Figure 8.2) are strongly associated with improvements in student achievement. Consequently, we are suggesting the following eight elements as key to the development of the MLP Professional Growth Plan.

Problem-of-Practice Statement. The architecture of the professional growth plan begins with the "problem-of-practice statement." The problem-of-practice statement is a critical component of improvement planning for a couple of reasons. It helps focus the attention of the individual—"Of all the demands on my time and the things that I could be paying attention to in the school or department or district, I am going to focus specifically on [specific instructional or leadership or organizational practices, processes, services, etc.]." Such focusing increases the likelihood that the improvement effort will be beneficial to both the individual (helps them understand which leadership practices are most closely associated with organizational improvements and which are not) and the organization (strategic targets are a priority focus of all leaders within the system). The qualities of a "proficient" problem-of-practice statement include:

- *Focuses* on classroom instruction (i.e., the actual interactions between teachers, students, and content in the classroom) or on leadership practices (i.e., how and where leaders use their influence, their learning, and their relationships with staff to impact the core business of teaching and learning and the operation of the organization positively);
- Is *directly observable*;
- Is *actionable* (i.e., is within the school's or department's or district's direct control and influence and can be improved in real time);

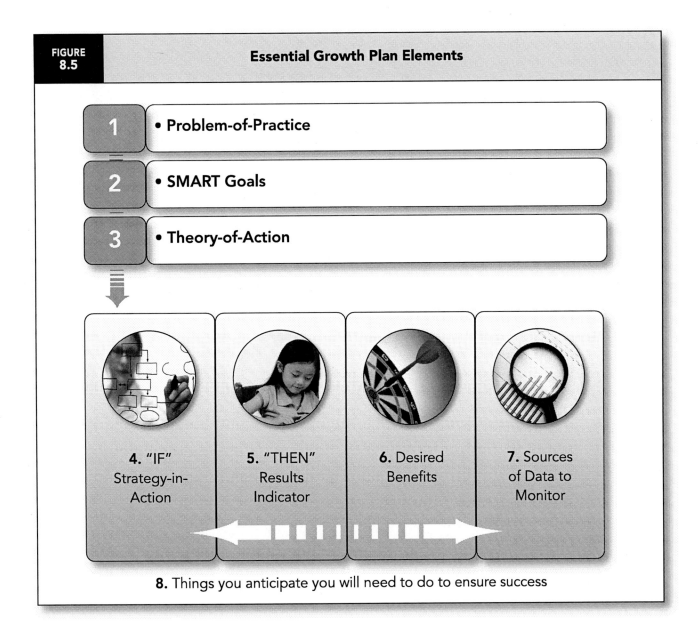

FIGURE 8.5

Essential Growth Plan Elements

1 • **Problem-of-Practice**

2 • **SMART Goals**

3 • **Theory-of-Action**

4. "IF" Strategy-in-Action

5. "THEN" Results Indicator

6. Desired Benefits

7. Sources of Data to Monitor

8. Things you anticipate you will need to do to ensure success

- *Links to a broader strategy* of improvement (i.e., school, department, system); and

- Is *high-leverage* (i.e., if acted upon, it would lead to lasting, significant improvement).

Sample instructional and noninstructional problem-of-practice statements include:

Instructional. Our NWEA data show that our students are achieving growth in reading and language arts during the school day. However, our ISTEP+ data, combined with classroom data and teacher feedback, indicate that our students—specifically our special-education, English Language Learners, and Hispanic students—need significant growth in reading. This led us to speculate that we don't have a system in place that allows us to systematically discover the instructional practices that we are currently using that are most closely related to increases in reading comprehension. We may not fully understand what the research says about best practice for teaching reading comprehension and English Language Learners. Collectively, we are not doing a good job of helping our students understand and apply the process of analyzing and responding to the content in a piece of text.

Noninstructional. Both survey and anecdotal data that we obtained from our customers (school personnel) reveal that repairs to facilities and/or equipment are not made in a timely manner. Furthermore, there are a growing number of work orders that become lost within the system and thus are never acted upon. We lack a cost-effective and efficient set of procedures for processing work orders.

Using the description of a "proficient" problem-of-practice, along with your prioritization of needs (from your school improvement plan), construct your own problem-of-practice statement on the worksheet depicted in Figure 8.6.

Worksheet for the First Three Professional Growth Plan Elements

FIGURE 8.6

Problem-of-Practice Statement:

Theory-of-Action:

IF (I/we) …

THEN we …

SMART Goal Statement:

The percentage of _____ scoring

proficient and higher in _____ will increase

from _____ % to _____ % by _____

measured by the _____

administered _____.

✔ Does your statement **focus** on classroom instruction (i.e., the actual interactions between teachers, students, and content in the classroom) or on leadership practices (i.e., how and where leaders use their influence, their learning, and their relationships with staff to positively impact the core business of teaching and learning and the operation of the organization)?

✔ Is your statement **directly observable**?

✔ Is your statement **actionable** (i.e., is within the school's or department's or district's direct control and influence and can be improved in real time)?

✔ Does your statement **link to a broader strategy** of improvement (i.e., school, department, school district)?

✔ Is your statement **high-leverage** (i.e., if acted upon, it would lead to lasting, significant improvement)?

Theory-of-Action Statement. The next element of your professional growth plan is a theory-of-action statement. When, as leaders, you interact with others, you tend to design or plan your behavior and retain theories for doing so. These theories-of-action comprise the values, strategies, and underlying assumptions that inform our patterns of interpersonal behavior. Theories-of-action operate at two levels: There are espoused theories that we use to explain or justify our behavior. And, there are theories-in-action that are implicit in our patterns of behavior with others. In other words, there are both *intended* theories and *enacted* theories. Leaders must construct explicit theories-of-action and assess those theories against the realities of their work. The architecture of a good theory-of-action has four structural requirements:

- First, it must begin with a statement of *causal relationship* between what you do—in your role as assistant superintendent, director, manager, coordinator, principal, etc.—and what constitutes a good result in your school or department;

- Next, it must be *refutable*; that is, your assertion can be contradicted by an observation or the outcome of a physical experiment;

- After that, it must be *open-ended*. In other words, it must provoke you to make revisions to your actions based upon the consequences of your actions; and

- Last, it must be *aligned* with the other elements of your plan (e.g., your identified problem-of-practice and your SMART goal).

Sample instructional and noninstructional theory-of-action statements include:

Instructional. If we focus on writing in the content area on a daily basis and provide frequent feedback to students about the quality of their writing, then we will see improvement in our language arts (writing) TAKS scores.

Noninstructional. If I increase the percentage of patrons who have a good opinion about the food we prepare in our high school kitchen, then I would expect to see an increase in the number of high school students eating lunch at school.

Based on the criteria of a good theory-of-action statement and the provided examples, return to Figure 8.6 and construct your personal theory-of-action (IF/THEN) statement.

Your Theory-of-Action Statement Checklist

✔ Is it a statement of **causal relationship** between what you do—in your role as assistant superintendent, director, manager, coordinator, principal, etc.—and what constitutes a good result in your school or department?

✔ Is it **refutable**; that is, can your assertion be contradicted by an observation or the outcome of a physical experiment?

✔ Will it **provoke you to make revisions** to your actions based upon the consequences of your actions?

✔ Is it **aligned** with the other elements of your plan (e.g., your identified problem-of-practice and your SMART goal)?

SMART Goal. The next element within a research-based improvement plan is the development of a SMART goal (a goal that is Specific, Measurable, Ambitious, Relevant, and Timely). SMART goals define improvement efforts in ways that are both actionable and attainable. SMART goals offer specificity and measurability to priorities; they provide direction, define desired results, and communicate high but attainable expectations for improvement in ways that can be measured and monitored over time.

Sample SMART goal statements:

- The percentage of Chapel Hill's seventh- and eighth-grade students scoring proficient or higher on the language arts portion of ISTEP+ (literary response and analysis) will increase from 61 percent to 80 percent as measured by the 2011 assessment of ISTEP+ this spring.

- The percentage of patrons who choose food service options rather than vending-machine selections or home lunches will increase from 65 percent to 75 percent by the end of the school year as measured by a locally developed survey administered during the spring of this year.

Based on the definition of a SMART goal and the examples provided, complete the SMART goal template on the worksheet in Figure 8.6.

 Your SMART Goal Statement Checklist

✓ Is it **specific**? Does it have both broad-based and long-term impact because it is focused on the specific content needs of the specific students for whom the goal is intended?

✓ Is it **measurable**? Will you know whether leadership improvement actions result in the kind of result desired (measurable goals simply quantify results to determine the degree of impact or influence)?

✓ Is it **ambitious**? Is it within the realm of your influence or control, sufficiently challenging yet attainable, developed based on current student achievement levels, based on staff belief of their capacity to achieve the goal, and using available resources?

✓ Is it **relevant**? Does it reflect the urgent, critical needs identified through your inquiry process and align well with the school's/district's strategic targets?

✓ Is it **timely**? Does it identify specific dates for assessment and data collection/analysis?

Strategy-in-Action Statement. Based on your theory-of-action statement, you need to translate your theory into one or perhaps two (but no more) strategy-in-action statements as depicted in Figures 8.7 and 8.8. Much like a well-constructed theory-of-action statement, your strategy-in-action statements will consist of several critical attributes. These statements must be:

- *Observable,* subject to frequent public testing, and measurable (i.e., quantifiable; able to be gauged);
- An *obvious* translation (i.e., paraphrase) of the previously identified theory-of-action statement;
- Constructed with *vague language* (e.g., increase the percentage of, reduce the percentage of, increase the amount or number of, etc.), as they are intended to be "dipstick" measures over time, rather than goal statements; and
- *Time-bound:* they should indicate how often the public testing will occur.

Notice in Figure 8.7 that the strategy-in-action statement immediately to the right of the "If/Then" theory-of-action statement is simply a paraphrase of the "If" portion of the theory-of-action statement, which contains each of the critical attributes (e.g., observable, subject to frequent public testing, measurable, etc.). A noninstructional example of a theory-of-action statement translated into a strategy-in-action statement follows in Figure 8.8.

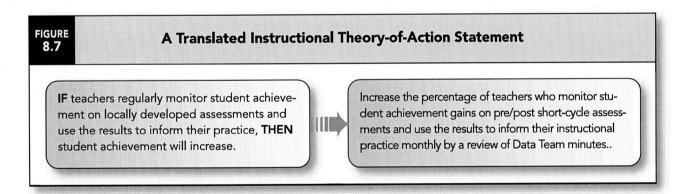

FIGURE 8.7 — **A Translated Instructional Theory-of-Action Statement**

IF teachers regularly monitor student achievement on locally developed assessments and use the results to inform their practice, **THEN** student achievement will increase.

Increase the percentage of teachers who monitor student achievement gains on pre/post short-cycle assessments and use the results to inform their instructional practice monthly by a review of Data Team minutes..

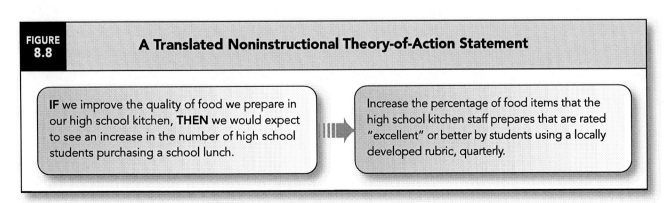

FIGURE 8.8 — **A Translated Noninstructional Theory-of-Action Statement**

IF we improve the quality of food we prepare in our high school kitchen, **THEN** we would expect to see an increase in the number of high school students purchasing a school lunch.

Increase the percentage of food items that the high school kitchen staff prepares that are rated "excellent" or better by students using a locally developed rubric, quarterly.

The two concepts, theories-of-action and strategies-in-action, are adaptations of concepts that derive from the thinking and writing of Donald Schön in his book entitled *Educating the Reflective Practitioner*. Essentially, Schön (1987) believes that each of us, in our interactions with one another, design our behavior and hold theories for doing so. These theories-of-action are made up of the "values, strategies, and underlying assumptions" that inform our patterns of interpersonal behavior. Furthermore, Schön suggests that our theories-of-action operate on two levels. Level one consists of "espoused theories" (p. 255), or theories that we use to rationalize our behavior. Leaders, for example, espouse commitment to continuous improvement and feedback, especially related to their own performance—as in "Just tell it like it is. Be brutally honest." Or, "You are just being nice." Level two, however, consists of theories-in-use, which are naturally embedded within our patterns of unprompted behavior with others. Unlike theories-of-action that we routinely think about and openly discuss, our theories-in-use operate largely at the subconscious level. Many times we are unable to describe these theories and are somewhat surprised to learn, upon reflection, that they may be considerably different from the theories-of-action we espouse. For instance, if we return to our example of the hypothetical leader who espouses the importance of critical feedback as being vital to continuous improvement, she may nonetheless become defensive when receiving performance feedback that is less than complimentary.

Schön (1987) further distinguishes our theories-in-use by dividing them into two "models" (p. 256) of behavior—Model I and Model II. Model I behavior is based on interpersonal interaction that is what he terms "win/lose games." (p. 256). That is, when supervisors interact with their evaluatees using this model of behavior, they design and manage their actions so that they are in control over factors relevant to themselves, irrespective of the needs of the evaluatee. They also tend to keep their dilemmas private and they are not inclined to test their assumptions publicly. For example, a Model I supervisor may understand how to keep her evaluatee focused on a "planning protocol" agenda, but she is unlikely to examine the consequences of her efforts to exercise one-sided control over the evaluatee—especially when the evaluatee may need a different structure of coaching conversation (e.g., reflecting or problem resolving). Model I behavior, according to Schön (1987), represents "single-loop learning" (p. 256), or learning about strategies or tactics for achieving one's own objectives. As a result, there is little to no public testing of one's theories, thus "decreasing" the effectiveness of these types of interactions (p. 257).

Model II behavior, however, aims at creating interpersonal interactions that are controlled jointly, where both supervisor and evaluatee can exchange critical information, even about difficult and sensitive matters, expose personal dilemmas and assumptions to shared inquiry, and make frequent public tests of their theories-of-action. A Model II supervisor, for instance, might publicly test an evluatee's willingness to express how well the supervisor's facilitation of the conversation helped arouse within the evaluatee thoughts about current planned–versus–enacted leadership strategies, resolving dilemmas, and reflecting on performance. Where Model I behavior represented "single-loop" learning, Model II behavior represents "double-loop learning" where you "deliberately challenge your own norms, attitudes, and assumptions" (Senge, et al., 2000). The supervisor and leader mutually consider the tasks they have set for themselves and they try to understand how personal assumptions and perspectives may contribute to the effectiveness of the coaching conversation. Moreover, because Model II behavior demands frequent public testing of theories, the effectiveness of these types of interactions is "increased" (Schön, 1987, p. 258).

We suggest reflective leaders use Model II behavior as they begin to build and test (publicly) a professional learning plan.

Using the examples provided, translate the "IF" portion of your theory-of-action statement into a strategy-in-action statement in the far left-hand column on the worksheet in Figure 8.9. It should contain all of the critical attributes of a well-constructed phrase. Notice that while there is space for two strategy-in-action statements, we highly recommend that you begin the process by focusing on only one strategy-in-action. As evaluation cycles are repeated and leaders gain a comfort level in working these types of improvement efforts, it will then make sense to add more strategies-in-action.

Worksheet for Four Key Planning Elements

FIGURE
8.9

Leadership Strategies-in-Action	Results Indicators	Desired Benefits	Sources of Data to Monitor
IF I increase the percentage of (insert your 1 to 2 measurable leadership strategies) …	THEN I expect to see a measurable (percent) increase in (satisfaction, productivity practices, or student learning results) …	(Create descriptors of successful strategy implementation, as well as changes in staff practices and student work)	(Insert what data you will monitor to determine effectiveness)
1.			
2.			

Your Strategy-in-Action Statement Checklist

✔ Is your statement **observable**, subject to frequent public testing, and measurable (i.e., quantifiable; able to be gauged)?

✔ Is your statement an obvious **translation** (i.e., paraphrase) of the previously identified theory-of-action?

✔ Is your statement constructed with **vague language** (e.g., increase the percentage of, reduce the percentage of, increase the amount or number of, etc.), as it is intended to be a "dipstick" measure over time rather than a goal statement?

✔ Is your statement **time-bound** (it should reflect how often the public testing will occur)?

Results Indicators. To determine results indicators, you will translate your theory-of-action statement into a results indicator statement. Similar in construction to your strategy-in-action statement, your results indicator statement will have several critical attributes. Results indicator statements must be:

- *Observable,* subject to frequent public testing, and measurable (i.e., quantifiable; able to be gauged);

- An *obvious translation* (i.e., paraphrase) of the previously identified "THEN" portion of the theory-of-action;

- A *local assessment* (a measure you control and/or influence) relating to a student or customer (i.e., internal or external) performance measure;

- Constructed with *vague language* (e.g., increase the percentage of, reduce the percentage of, increase the amount or number of, etc.), as they are intended to be "dipstick" measures over time rather than goal statements; and,

- *Time-bound:* they should indicate how often the public testing will occur.

Sample results indicators statements:

- Increase the percentage of students scoring at the proficient level or higher on a monthly writing prompt (using a locally developed rubric).

- Increase the percentage of patrons who rate food "excellent" or better on a locally developed customer satisfaction survey quarterly.

Using the examples and criteria provided, return to Figure 8.9 and write your results indicator statement in the second column of the matrix labeled "Results Indicators."

 Your Results Indicator Statement Checklist

✓ Is your statement **observable**, subject to frequent public testing, and measurable (i.e., quantifiable; able to be gauged)?

✓ Is your statement an **obvious translation** (i.e., paraphrase) of the previously identified "THEN" portion of the theory-of-action?

✓ Is your statement based on a **local assessment** (a measure you control and/or influence) relating to a student or customer (internal or external) performance measure?

✓ Is your statement constructed with **vague language** (e.g., increase the percentage of, reduce the percentage of, increase the amount or number of, etc.), as it is intended to be a "dipstick" measure over time rather than a goal statement?

✓ Is your statement **time-bound** (indicates how often the public testing will occur)?

Desired Benefits. The next step in completing the professional growth plan template is to identify the desired benefits. The desired benefits are simply bulleted descriptors of what successful strategy implementation (primarily related to the leadership strategy) might look like, as well as anticipated improvements in staff practices and student or organizational work. They are derived from the strategy-in-action statement. Here are two examples of what the "desired benefits" might be based on the strategy-in-action statements: Figure 8.10 is from the instructional side of leadership and Figure 8.11 from a noninstructional leadership role.

FIGURE 8.10 | **Instructional Example of Desired Benefits**

Strategy-in-Action: Increase the percentage of teachers who monitor student achievement gains in writing by pre/post short-cycle assessments and use the results to inform instructional practice monthly

Desired Benefits: • Better understanding of teacher needs relative to student writing • Just-in-time support of teachers' writing knowledge and skills • Better awareness of the obstacles to proficient student writing

FIGURE 8.11 | **Noninstructional Example of Desired Benefits**

Strategy-in-Action: Increase the percentage of food items that the high school prepares that are "excellent" or better, using a locally developed rubric, quarterly

Desired Benefits: • Improved understanding of staff needs relative to food preparation • Just-in-time support of staff regarding food preparation knowledge and skills • Better awareness of the obstacles to excellent food preparation

Using your strategy-in-action statement, along with the examples provided, write your desired benefits in the third column of Figure 8.9.

Your Desired Benefits Checklist

✓ Are your desired benefits bulleted statements that reflect those unmeasured qualities you would expect to result from a successfully implemented strategy-in-action and results indicator?

✓ Have you made certain that these bulleted statements are not simply a paraphrase of the strategy-in-action or the results indicator?

✓ Do these bulleted statements talk about the insights (relative to your problem-of-practice) that you and your staff might gain from successful implementation of your plan?

Sources of Data to Monitor. The next to the last step in developing a professional growth plan template is to identify the sources of data to monitor. The goal here is to identify the data from your leadership strategy as well as from your results indicators that you intend to monitor. For example, if your leadership strategy-in-action says you intend to "Increase the percentage of time spent during faculty meeting discussions related to targeted student achievement monthly," then you will most likely want to monitor faculty meeting agendas and time spent during these gatherings talking about your most pressing areas of student achievement needs. Similarly, if your results indicator is "Increasing the percentage of students who produce a 'Proficient' or higher piece of nonfiction writing monthly based on a common writing rubric," then you would probably be collecting student writing scores from your Data Teams (e.g., professional learning communities). Remember, you are testing a hypothesis—"If I …, then I would expect to see …"—so identify the data that you must monitor and measure from these two variables to determine whether your hypothesis is accurate or not. A sample of data sources to monitor is shown in Figure 8.12.

Your Sources of Data to Monitor Checklist

✓ Have you identified the data from your leadership strategy as well as from your results indicators that you intend to monitor?

✓ Have you made certain that these bulleted statements reflect the various measures you are tracking?

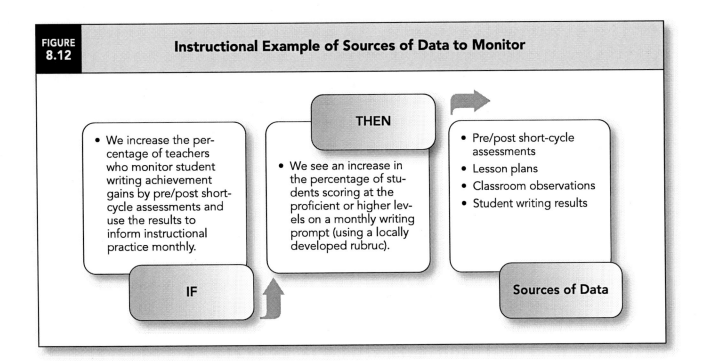

| FIGURE 8.12 | Instructional Example of Sources of Data to Monitor |

THEN

• We increase the percentage of teachers who monitor student writing achievement gains by pre/post short-cycle assessments and use the results to inform instructional practice monthly.

IF

• We see an increase in the percentage of students scoring at the proficient or higher levels on a monthly writing prompt (using a locally developed rubruc).

• Pre/post short-cycle assessments
• Lesson plans
• Classroom observations
• Student writing results

Sources of Data

Using your strategy-in-action statement, along with your results indicators, identify the sources of data to monitor in the far right-hand column of Figure 8.9.

Things You Anticipate You Will Need to Do to Ensure Success. The aim of this last step in the development of your professional growth plan is to do a task analysis of your plan. That is, you will be identifying all of those things you must do in order to implement the strategy. The critical function of this step is to answer the following question: "What are all of those important tasks I/we must complete in order to implement the strategy-in-action and achieve the desired results?" These are the items that typically occupy most improvement plans; they are typically not measurable strategies, beyond a binary measure (did we do them or not), as they represent actions that must happen, but once they are completed they are finished. Sample task analyses may be found in Figure 8.3 (instructional example) and Figure 8.4 (noninstructional example).

Use the worksheet in Figure 8.13 to conduct your task analysis for your professional growth plan.

FIGURE 8.13	Task Analysis Worksheet

Task Analysis
(Brainstorm all tasks or steps essential to accomplishing your strategies-in-action and results indicators)

✔ Things You Anticipate You Will Need to Do to Ensure Success Checklist

✓ Have you identified all of those things you must do in order to implement the strategy?

✓ Do these items generally represent actions that must happen, but once they are completed they are finished?

✔ Quick Check Your Sources of Data to Monitor

✓ Have you identified the data from your leadership strategy as well as from your results indicators that you intend to monitor?

✓ Have you made certain that these bulleted statements reflect the various measures you are tracking?

9 Multidimensional Leadership Performance: Summative Evaluation

"Summative leadership evaluation" is a phrase commonly used to refer to assessment of leaders by their respective supervisors. It is a culminating step in the evaluation process. It is also a condition of employment and therefore imposed onto the leader, and uniformly applied, with the object of measuring all leaders' knowledge, skills, and attitudes on the same criteria to determine the level of their performance. Moreover, it is meant to meet the schools', districts', or state's needs for leader accountability and is intended to provide support for leaders wherever they are on the performance continuum (e.g., coaching and mentoring of performance from one performance level to the next higher performance level).

Highly effective teachers design and expose their students to a sufficient number of formative assessments, accompanied by providing to and/or securing from students immediate feedback, so that they can make inferences about their students' knowledge, skills, and attitudes to help them make sound instructional decisions. Effective supervisors of leaders engage in similar work. In this sense, summative assessment (evaluation) is characterized as assessment of a particular leader's knowledge, skills, and attitudes only after the supervisor has engaged in "an inference-making enterprise" (Popham, 2003, p. 4) in which she collects information along with artifacts from the leader being evaluated in order to arrive at accurate inferences about the leader's overall performance.

It formally communicates to the leader "how they did." But more importantly, by looking at how the leader did, it helps the organization know what specific needs the leader has and how best to support the continued growth of the leader. While summative evaluation is typically quantitative, using numeric scores to assess the leader's performance, the MLP System also relies on qualitative descriptions or narratives, which tell the story behind the numbers.

The MLP Summative Evaluation Process (as described in Chapter 2) includes two steps, starting with Step 6 of the process where the leader prepares a Consolidated Performance Assessment. In other words, the leader will synthesize the information obtained under Steps 4 and 5 (monthly monitoring and the Midyear Evaluation) in order to prepare a consolidated assessment, or comprehensive view, of performance throughout the year. This brief summary of the data and artifacts is used to judge performance and should be provided to the leader's evaluator well in advance (at least two weeks) of the performance discussion at which final performance levels will be discussed.

Next, Step 7, the leader will meet with her evaluator at the end of the year to discuss progress in completing the evaluation process. They will discuss the self-assessment, the results of monthly monitoring, the Midyear Evaluation, Consolidated Assessment, and summary evaluation of the leader, which the evaluator prepares in advance of the meeting. If additional data or artifacts need to be brought into the discussion, the leader should have them readily available to share at this time. At this meeting, the leader and the leader's supervisor will agree upon performance levels, degree of goal attainment, and recommendations for next year's professional growth plan.

A blank template follows as well as a template that depicts a summative evaluation for a fictional leader.

Multidimensional Leadership Performance Summative Evaluation Form

Evaluatee's Name:	Position:
School:	School Year:
Evaluator:	District:
Evaluator's Title:	Date Completed:

This form serves as a permanent record of a leader's performance, based on the specific criteria delineated in the Multidimensional Leadership Performance (MLP) Matrix.

Directions for Supervisors: Examine all sources of evidence for each of the ten domains, using the results from the MLP Self-Reflection Matrix Guide, as it applies to the leader's performance. Refer to the scale requirements and indicate sources of evidence used to determine the evaluation results in each domain. Assign an overall evaluation of the leader's performance, sign the form, and obtain the signature of the leader.

Use the format and tables in Chapter 5 to help calculate sub-domain and domain scores into an MLP System Score.

Inasmuch as all of the MLP domains collectively contribute to the leader's overall success, four of the ten domains carry greater weight to signify their importance in the evaluation process. Consequently, the MLP domains have been weighted using the following percentages as depicted in Figure 9.1.

FIGURE 9.1	Multidimensional Leadership Performance Domain Weighting	
Multidimensional Leadership Performance Domains		**Weighting**
Domain 1: Resilience		5%
Domain 2: Personal Behavior and Professional Ethics		5%
Domain 3: Student Achievement		**10%**
Domain 4: Decision Making		5%
Domain 5: Communication		5%
Domain 6: Faculty Development		**30%**
Domain 7: Leadership Development		**15%**
Domain 8: Time/Task/Project Management		5%
Domain 9: Technology		5%
Domain 10: Personal Professional Learning		15%
	Total	**100%**

Multidimensional Leadership Performance Summative Evaluation Form *(continued)*

Summary of MLP Domains	EX	P	PR	NMS
Domain 1: Resilience				
Domain 2: Personal Behavior and Professional Ethics				
Domain 3: Student Achievement				
Domain 4: Decision Making				
Domain 5: Communication				
Domain 6: Faculty Development				
Domain 7: Leadership Development				
Domain 8: Time/Task/Project Management				
Domain 9: Technology				
Domain 10: Personal Professional Learning				
MLP System Rating Score (Table 9, p. 52)				

		Sources of Evidence *(Check all that apply)*				
1						
2						
3						
4						
5						
6						
7						
8						
9						
10						

Multidimensional Leadership Performance Summative Evaluation Form *(continued)*

Evaluatee's Signature:	Date:
Superintendent/Designee Signature:	Date:
Comments Attached: ○ Yes ○ No	
Superintendent/Designee Signature:	Date:

Note: The leader's signature on this form represents neither acceptance nor approval of the Multidimensional Leadership Performance (MLP) System Evaluation. It does, however, indicate that the leader has reviewed the MLP evaluation with the evaluator and may reply in writing. The signature of the superintendent/designee verifies that the MLP evaluation has been reviewed and that the proper process has been followed according to state statues.

Multidimensional Leadership Performance Summative Evaluation Form

Evaluatee's Name: **Jim Hendstrom**	Position: **Principal**
School: **Whispering Winds High School**	School Year: **2010–2011**
Evaluator: **Cheryl Osage**	District: **Independence SD**
Evaluator's Title: **Area Superintendent**	Date Completed: **June 30, 2011**

This form serves as a permanent record of a leader's performance, based on the specific criteria delineated in the Multidimensional Leadership Performance (MLP) Matrix.

Directions for Supervisors: Examine all sources of evidence for each of the ten domains, using the results from the MLP Self-Reflection Matrix Guide, as it applies to the leader's performance. Refer to the scale requirements and indicate sources of evidence used to determine the evaluation results in each domain. Assign an overall evaluation of the leader's performance, sign the form, and obtain the signature of the leader.

Use the format and tables in Chapter 5 to help calculate sub-domain and domain scores into a MLP System Score.

Inasmuch as all of the MLP domains collectively contribute to the leader's overall success, four of the ten domains carry greater weight to signify their importance in the evaluation process. Consequently, the MLP domains have been weighted using the following percentages as depicted in Figure 9.1.

FIGURE 9.1 — **Multidimensional Leadership Performance Domain Weighting**

Multidimensional Leadership Performance Domains	Weighting
Domain 1: Resilience	5%
Domain 2: Personal Behavior and Professional Ethics	5%
Domain 3: Student Achievement	**10%**
Domain 4: Decision Making	5%
Domain 5: Communication	5%
Domain 6: Faculty Development	**30%**
Domain 7: Leadership Development	**15%**
Domain 8: Time/Task/Project Management	5%
Domain 9: Technology	5%
Domain 10: Personal Professional Learning	**15%**
Total	**100%**

Multidimensional Leadership Performance Summative Evaluation Form *(continued)*					
Summary of MLP Domains	EX	P	PR	NMS	
Domain 1: Resilience			2		
Domain 2: Personal Behavior and Professional Ethics			2		
Domain 3: Student Achievement			2		
Domain 4: Decision Making		3			
Domain 5: Communication		3			
Domain 6: Faculty Development		3			
Domain 7: Leadership Development	4				
Domain 8: Time/Task/Project Management		3			
Domain 9: Technology		3			
Domain 10: Personal Professional Learning		3			
MLP System Rating Score (Table 9, p. 52)		295			

Evaluator Comments:	Sources of Evidence *(Check all that apply)*						
	Formal Observation	Informal Observation	Self-Assessment	Growth Plan	Artifacts	Site Visit	Other *(Explain)*
1	✓	✓					
2				✓			
3				✓			
4			✓				
5					✓		
6					✓		
7	✓	✓				✓	
8				✓	✓		
9		✓					
10				✓	✓		

Evaluator Comments:

- At times, Jim exhibits aggressive or dismissive behaviors, leading to a climate in which people are reluctant to raise sensitive issues. One such issue that typifies this type of behavior was his interaction with the publisher of the Gazette and his disagreement with the way Whispering Winds HS was depicted in her article on "push outs." Jim, you should consider what strategies you might employ to assure your faculty and staff that you will handle tense situations calmly and fairly in the future. How might structures and protocols be used for dealing with perceived crises and situations in which passions are high and confrontation is likely?

- Jim is keenly aware of state and district results and has discussed those results with his staff, but they have not linked specific decisions to the data. Jim, you should think about the degree to which you have instituted a review of data at informal levels. Why is publicly displaying data so important to promoting a culture of data-driven decision making?

Multidimensional Leadership Performance Summative Evaluation Form *(continued)*

Evaluatee's Signature: *Jim Hendstrom*   Date: *6/30/11*

Superintendent/Designee Signature: *Cynthia Osage*   Date: *6/30/11*

Comments Attached: ○ Yes   ☑ No

Superintendent/Designee Signature: Date:

Note: The leader's signature on this form represents neither acceptance nor approval of the Multidimensional Leadership Performance (MLP) System Evaluation. It does, however, indicate that the leader has reviewed the MLP evaluation with the evaluator and may reply in writing. The signature of the superintendent/designee verifies that the MLP evaluation has been reviewed and that the proper process has been followed according to state statues.

10 Case Study Materials and Learning Experiences

In his book *Assessing Educational Leaders* (2nd ed.), Douglas Reeves (2009) encourages organizations to create scenarios, case studies, "realistic stories with rich descriptions of human behavior and decision-making processes—that portray exemplary performance" (p. 81) in each of the 10 domains. These case studies create a hypothetical perspective of leadership practices. In addition, case studies of exemplary leadership performance also help organizations "socialize" its members into the organization (i.e., help them learn the knowledge, skills, behaviors, social values, and beliefs necessary to function effectively as members of the organization). For example, Leadership Domain 5.0 is *"Communication— Leaders in education understand communication as a two-way street. They seek to listen and learn from students, staff, and community. They recognize individuals for good work and maintain high visibility at school and in the community. Regular communications to staff and community keep all stakeholders engaged in the work of the school."* Based on the description of exemplary performance in this leadership domain and its sub-domains (consult the Multidimensional Leadership Matrix in Chapter 3 for details), we might create a case study such as this:

Kim Wong believes that public education needs to be conducted in public, and his school is characterized by transparency in terms of communication with students and their parents. Pikes Peak Middle School was the first district middle school to embrace a technological solution for student records, assessment data, and parent reporting and communication. When Kim became principal, he facilitated a staff effort to know every student by name within the first month of school and required his six administrators and counselors to contact ten parents every week just to encourage them to support their child's education.

In addition to this personal contact with parents and students, learning assessment has also changed. In the past, tests at Pikes Peak were so secret that even the best students were at a loss in predicting content that would be on the tests. Both parents and students were extremely frustrated by the lack of clearly stated expectations. Today, every class in every department utilizes scoring guides that describe proficiency and post essential questions students need to answer by the end of every term. Students know the standards they are working on and help to generate the criteria by which their work will be assessed. These outcomes for learning are also posted on teacher WebPages that students and parents can access with ease. These changes have not come about easily. But student achievement on state-, district-, and teacher-generated measures have improved steadily, and Kim keeps the community up to date with these academic improvements.

Kim proudly points to a robust communication system at his school. His open-door policy features daily time when he has no meetings. He also expects every staff member to return e-mails and phone calls within 24 hours. Every department Data Team meeting publishes minutes with action taken that are distributed school-wide. In addition, information on school attendance, behavior referrals, lunch counts, end-of-course assessments, and proportion of students on track for graduation is available to the general public online and disaggregated by sub-groups. Individual student performance across the same variables is available to every teacher for every student in their classes, and all of the above is available to counselors and administrators in real time.

Three years ago, Kim created a listening system for all stakeholders that collected data systematically across the following areas: satisfaction surveys, perception interviews and focus groups, and Web site and onsite complaints. These three forms of stakeholder feedback are collected and analyzed on explicit dates throughout the year for students, parents, patrons, faculty, and staff. A few schools have adopted this process, and several district-level departments borrowed ideas from Kim. Success at Pikes Peak resulted in several national conference presentations and a growing number of requested speaking engagements.

In most cases, the characters depicted are either creating problems through their own actions or are being confronted with problems resulting from the behavior of others. It is the problem dimension of human behavior in school administration, however, rather than the routine duties that should be studied. Organizations committed to "growing your own leaders" (Byham, Smith, and Paese, 2002) and developing preparation and professional development training programs need to direct most of their attention to the area of human behavior if prospective and experienced administrators and supervisors are to be equipped with the knowledge and skills required for the 21st century and beyond. The value of case study examinations is in the discussions and interaction they generate. When people see and discuss similarities between the case study and your own organization, learning is taking place.

The examination of these cases will reveal that most of them are limited in their contextual information. For example, the nature of the case study community and school district and other details that the reader might desire in order to resolve a problem may be missing from the study. This approach of limiting the available information has been taken for two reasons: a) It allows for a much larger number of cases to be presented in the book; and b) It provides the instructor or group leader with an excellent opportunity to tailor a case to specific local circumstances by supplementing the case with pertinent details: for example, urban versus suburban or rural setting, elementary student body versus secondary, large versus small school, and so on.

It should also be noted that the cases in the book are open-ended. While the studies sometimes describe the attempted resolution of subsidiary problems, the administrator in each case is generally left with the need to resolve a major conflict or dilemma. Some individuals have mixed feelings about this type of case study. There is little doubt that an unresolved problem or conflict will demand more thought and effort from the student and the instructor. But the construction of the cases was based on the premise that organizations would derive greater benefit from cases that require a resolution to the problems identified than from cases presenting a ready-made solution. Each leadership case study is meant to simulate real life. In real leadership situations, we have to use all the known facts to make the best decision possible. There is never a guarantee of the outcome. Leaders have to become comfortable with uncertainty.

Such open discussion helps supervisors to better understand leadership best practices and helps them all to align their own styles with the culture and values of their organization. There are no "right answers" for these case studies. But some possible good answers following each are suggested for you to consider.

The Nature of Case Studies

Case studies have been used for training programs for a long time, with a wide variety of content and formats (Connelly, Allen, and Waples, 2007). Although we hope the case studies in this book will provide interesting reading, their primary purpose is to stimulate individual and group involvement in situations requiring the application of the concepts presented in the Multidimensional Leadership Performance (MLP) Matrix and the MLP Coaching Protocol. Each leadership case study emphasizes critical problems in educational administration and supervision and is organized around the 10 domains of leadership presented in the MLP Matrix. Furthermore, we have constructed 40 Instructional Leadership Scenarios (case studies) in which we depict 24 problems of principalship and 16 problems of assistant principalship. In addition, we have created 39 Noninstructional Leadership Scenarios, cases devoted to problems associated with other administrative and supervisory non-instructional positions, such as superintendent and the central office supervisor (e.g., assistant superintendent; directors of elementary, middle, and high school; human resources; grounds and maintenance; food services; and transportation).

Many readers, if not most, will have difficulty in using rubrics reliably at first without some practice. No assessment tool is effective if it is not used on a regular basis. Rubrics are most effective when we practice using them with our staffs over and over again. For example, Reeves (2006) found that effective teacher collaboration that focuses on a collective examination of real student work using a common rubric not only improved (e.g., percent agreement achieved) over time, with repeated practice, it took teacher groups less time to achieve an effective level of agreement. Developing effective rubrics requires revision based on feedback from staff. The best rubrics are products of an iterative effort. Therefore, the remainder of this book presents a large number of representative case studies and suggested learning activities designed to help the reader become more skilled in applying the research on effective leadership practices to improve the work of leaders at all levels of the organization.

Developing and Using Rubrics Reliably

What is a rubric? Rubrics (or "*scoring tools*") are a way of describing evaluation criteria (or "*grading standards*") based on the expected outcomes and performances of students and adults. Typically, rubrics are used in scoring or grading written assignments or oral presentations. However, they may also be used to score any form of student or adult performance. Similarly, the Multidimensional Leadership Performance Matrix, consisting of domains and related sub-domains, is a series of leadership competency rubrics. Each rubric consists of a set of scoring criteria (word picture descriptions of leadership behavior) and point values associated with these criteria. In most rubrics, the criteria are grouped into categories so the instructor, or supervisor in our case, and the leader being evaluated can discriminate among the categories by level of performance. In organizational use, the rubric provides an "objective" *external standard* against which leadership performance may be compared.

Even the best leadership evaluation model cannot succeed without equally effective implementation. It is critical to the overall accuracy and reliability of the evaluation system that evaluators share a common understanding of performance expectations and rating levels. To achieve overall accuracy and reliability of the evaluation system, we recommend that organizations conduct "norming sessions," where all leaders review leadership performance in the form of case studies, assign a score, and then discuss their scores and specify why they gave them. Using a rubric and holding "norming sessions" help organizations achieve "inter-rater reliability" (Jonsson and Svingby, 2007).

The "norming sessions" are a critical part of an organization's work toward common understanding of performance expectations and consistency in use. Consequently, we suggest that you meet once or twice a semester and invite all supervisors of leaders. During a session, you would review key leadership domains (e.g., student achievement, faculty development, leadership development, and personal, professional learning) and their related rubrics, silently evaluate a few sample case studies, and then discuss your scores with each other. Based on our work with clients across the nation, we have found, as you will find, these discussions to be quite lively and important because you are talking about your leadership standards, your expectations for performance, and your schools and/or departments in a productive, focused way. Following such a meeting, leaders leave the "norming session" reflecting on their own leadership practices.

Another variation of this supervisor of leaders "norming session" is to use the rubrics and "norming sessions" during your monthly district-wide meetings with all administrators. That is, each administrator is given the same amount of time and the same case studies to review (again, you might want to select key leadership domains on which to focus your organizational thinking) ahead of the actual meeting. On the day of your district-wide meeting, you have your own "norming session" in small, six- to seven-member teams of administrators. First, give the administrators copies of the specific rubrics (the leadership domains and their related sub-domains) and explain how to use them. Next, have them silently score each of the case studies or scenarios. Last, spend the rest of the allotted time discussing each of the scenarios in great depth. Why did you give the scores you gave? It is important that you keep referring to the rubrics, which, of course, are a clear statement of your leadership standards and a reflection of expected leadership practices you are trying to replicate across the district. There is great value in this process. The administrators quickly see some of the errors or weaknesses in their own leadership practices. More importantly, by frequently engaging your administrators in the process of assessment, you can:

• Develop a clearly articulated and widely held and understood point of view on what high-quality leadership looks like.

• Build a collaborative learning culture that replaces the compliance orientation typical of most districts with one of engagement, collaboration, and continuous learning. To facilitate student learning and the higher-order skills of analysis, inquiry, and creative problem solving successfully, districts must develop and encourage these same skills in adults.

• Develop and implement coherent system-wide leadership strategies that support the kinds of teaching and learning that districts want in all of their schools. This means building a theory of action that articulates the leader's belief about how to improve instruction and student learning most effectively, focusing deeply on a few key strategies that bring their theory of action to life, and then aligning the allocation of human and financial resources and support and accountability systems to these strategies.

In the following sections, a large number of case studies (scenarios) are presented, along with their respective scoring guides (i.e., how and why the authors scored the leadership performance the way they did). That is, each of the 79 instructional and noninstructional scenarios is immediately followed by a scoring guide for each scenario to aid with your "norming sessions." The variety of case studies represented should provide sufficient opportunity to gain experience in applying the Multidimensional Leadership Performance Matrix rubrics and to gain additional insights into the reality of school/district administration and supervision. Figure 10.1, which follows, shows how each of the case studies relates to other aspects of school/district administration and supervision.

FIGURE 10.1	Analysis of Cases, According to Level, Type of Position, and Area of Administration													
	Level			Position				Areas of Administration						
Case #	Elementary	Middle School	High School	Principal	Asst. Principal	Superintendent or Asst. Supt.	Director	Dir. Elementary	Dir. Middle School	Dir. High School	Transportation	Food Service	Human Resources	Grounds & Maintenance
Domain 1.0: Resilience														
1	x			x										
2		x			x									
3			x	x										
4	x						x	x						
5		x					x		x					
6			x				x			x				
7						x								
Domain 2.0: Personal Behavior and Professional Ethics														
8	x			x										
9	x				x									
10		x		x										
11			x	x										
12							x					x		
13							x						x	
14						x								
Domain 3.0: Student Achievement														
15	x			x										
16	x				x									
17		x			x									
18		x		x										
19			x	x										
20			x	x										
21							x					x		
22	x						x	x						
23							x							x
24		x					x			x				
25						x								
Domain 4.0: Decision Making														
26	x			x										
27		x			x									
28			x	x										
29							x					x		
30							x						x	
31						x								

| FIGURE 10.1 | Analysis of Cases, According to Level, Type of Position, and Area of Administration (continued) |

Case #	Elementary	Middle School	High School	Principal	Asst. Principal	Superintendent or Asst. Supt.	Director	Dir. Elementary	Dir. Middle School	Dir. High School	Transportation	Food Service	Human Resources	Grounds & Maintenance
	Level			Position				Areas of Administration						
Domain 5.0: Communication														
32	x				x									
33		x		x										
34			x	x										
35							x					x		
36							x							x
37			x				x			x				
Domain 6.0: Faculty Development														
38	x			x										
39		x		x										
40			x		x									
41	x						x	x						
42		x					x		x					
43						x								
Domain 7.0: Leadership Development														
44	x			x										
45	x				x									
46		x		x										
47		x			x									
48			x	x										
49			x	x										
50							x				x			
51							x					x		
52							x						x	
53							x							x
54					x									
55			x				x			x				
Domain 8.0: Time/Task/Project Management														
56	x			x										
57		x			x									
58			x	x										
59	x						x	x						
60		x					x		x					
61						x								

FIGURE
10.1

Analysis of Cases, According to Level, Type of Position, and Area of Administration *(continued)*

Case #	Level			Position				Areas of Administration						
	Elementary	Middle School	High School	Principal	Asst. Principal	Superintendent or Asst. Supt.	Director	Dir. Elementary	Dir. Middle School	Dir. High School	Transportation	Food Service	Human Resources	Grounds & Maintenance
Domain 9.0: Technology														
62	x			x										
63		x		x										
64			x		x									
65							x				x			
66							x						x	
67						x								
Domain 10.0: Personal Professional Learning														
68	x			x										
69	x			x										
70		x		x										
71		x			x									
72			x		x									
73			x	x										
74							x					x		
75	x						x	x						
76							x							x
77		x					x		x					
78			x				x			x				
79						x								

Domain 1.0: Resilience

Resilience is defined as the ability of the leader to overcome setbacks and absorb any learning offered by those setbacks quickly and at the minimum cost. Resilience includes coping well with high levels of ongoing disruptive change, sustaining energy when under constant pressure, bouncing back from disappointment and setbacks easily, overcoming adversity, changing ways of working to incorporate learning when old ways are no longer feasible, and doing all of this without acting in dysfunctional or harmful ways to others within the organization. More importantly, when leaders practice resilient behaviors, their actions are contagious because they model the way for others to act in similar ways.

Scenario #1—Darbie
1.0: Resilience

Over the past three years, the staff at Madison Elementary School in Denver, Colorado, had strategically and collectively worked hard to increase student achievement for all kindergarten through sixth-grade students. Each year they had seen significant improvement at all grade levels and made adjustments based on student growth data. This year, the third- through sixth-grade teachers were positive that their students would perform exceptionally well on the writing, math, and language arts sections on the Colorado Student Assessments Performance (CSAP). On Monday, August 22, when the final CSAP results data were shared by Darbie, their principal, the entire community cheered. For the first time in the school's history, Madison Elementary was rated as an exemplary school, which was the highest rating they could achieve in the state. Student attendance and teacher morale was up and the teachers were excited to celebrate their success.

On Wednesday of that week, Darbie and her school leadership team, which consisted of grade-level and non-core academic teachers, and parents met to decide on their celebration plan. After much discussion, they agreed on a school-wide "pride" assembly and a special field trip to the Denver Mint, followed by lunch on the Capital lawn for all the Madison students in third grade through fifth grade who were proficient or above on the CSAP and who had 96 percent attendance for the year. The celebration events were to be sponsored and supported by the school activity fund and the Parent Teacher Organization. Darbie was to announce the plan to the rest of the staff, students, and community on Monday of the following week during morning announcements.

However, at school on Thursday, it was evident that teachers throughout the school had heard about the leadership team plans and there were serious concerns that not all students would be included in the field trip. Primary and special education teachers approached Darbie, wondering why their students who had not taken the CSAP or students who had shown growth but did not meet the target were not allowed to attend the celebration. By noon, Darbie had also heard similar concerns from several parents and had a message on her desk to call her district elementary director, who had also received a couple of calls from concerned parents. Darbie was both frustrated and thankful to receive this feedback, as she knew in her heart that the celebration plan did not reflect the mission of the school and her own values. She was also relieved that it came prior to making the celebration plan announcement to the entire community. She quickly thought about her previous coaching sessions with her elementary director, and she knew exactly what she needed to do.

Immediately, Darbie called her elementary director and was very open to hearing the parent concerns and suggestions by her supervisor and shared that she also questioned the decision that she had supported. After the conversation, she canceled the school-wide Monday announcement and called a stand-up meeting for all staff on Friday and a leadership meeting on Tuesday morning to listen to all concerns and to brainstorm alternative school-wide celebrations. After the meetings and when a new celebration plan had been developed, Darbie called her elementary director back and was able to assure her that she had taken action to reevaluate and change the celebration plans and that she was in total agreement with the feedback. Darbie also shared that this had been a personal learning experience for her and that she would only approve plans that were inclusive of all students and that upheld the core values of the district and aligned with all district policies.

Peruse the MLP Matrix and assess Darbie's performance in Domain 1.0: Resilience. Make mental notes and be prepared to respond as to the reason for your score on that dimension. Please be prepared to report out in 15 minutes.

Scenario #1—Darbie
1.0: Resilience

PROFICIENT

Over the past three years, the staff at Madison Elementary School in Denver, Colorado, had strategically and collectively worked hard to increase student achievement for all kindergarten through sixth-grade students. Each year they had seen significant improvement at all grade levels and made adjustments based on student growth data. This year, the third- through sixth-grade teachers were positive that their students would perform exceptionally well on the writing, math, and language arts sections on the Colorado Student Assessments Performance (CSAP). On Monday, August 22, when the final CSAP results data were shared by Darbie, their principal, the entire community cheered. For the first time in the school's history, Madison Elementary was rated as an exemplary school, which was the highest rating they could achieve in the state. Student attendance and teacher morale was up and the teachers were excited to celebrate their success.

On Wednesday of that week, Darbie and her school leadership team, which consisted of grade-level and non-core academic teachers, and parents met to decide on their celebration plan. After much discussion, they agreed on a school-wide "pride" assembly and a special field trip to the Denver Mint, followed by lunch on the Capital lawn for all the Madison students in third grade through fifth grade who were proficient or above on the CSAP and who had 96 percent attendance for the year. The celebration events were to be sponsored and supported by the school activity fund and the Parent Teacher Organization. Darbie was to announce the plan to the rest of the staff, students, and community on Monday of the following week during morning announcements.

However, at school on Thursday, it was evident that teachers throughout the school had heard about the leadership team plans and there were serious concerns that not all students would be included in the field trip. Primary and special education teachers approached Darbie, wondering why their students who had not taken the CSAP or students who had shown growth but did not meet the target were not allowed to attend the celebration. By noon, Darbie had also heard similar concerns from several parents and had a message on her desk to call her district elementary director, who had also received a couple of calls from concerned parents. **(1.4)** Darbie was both frustrated and thankful to receive this feedback, as she knew in her heart that the celebration plan did not reflect the mission of the school and her own values. She was also relieved that it came prior to making the celebration plan announcement to the entire community. **(1.5)** She quickly thought about her previous coaching sessions with her elementary director, and she knew exactly what she needed to do.

(1.3, 1.2) Immediately, Darbie called her elementary director and was very open to hearing the parent concerns and suggestions by her supervisor and shared that she also questioned the decision that she had supported. After the conversation, she canceled the school-wide Monday announcement and called a stand-up meeting for all staff on Friday and a leadership meeting on Tuesday morning to listen to all concerns and to brainstorm alternative school-wide celebrations. After the meetings and when a new celebration plan had been developed,

1.4: When dissent surfaced from staff and parents regarding the decision, Darbie used the information to reevaluate her decision. SCORE 1.4 AT PROFICIENT.

1.5: Darbie reflected upon her previous evaluations with her director and used the feedback to help her prioritize what needed to be done. SCORE 1.5 AT PROFICIENT.

1.3 and 1.2: Darbie immediately brought concerns to her immediate supervisor. SCORE 1.3 AT PROFICIENT.

Darbie openly and with a nondefensive attitude admitted to her supervisor that she was wrong in supporting the decision. SCORE 1.2 AT PROFICIENT.

CASE STUDY MATERIALS AND LEARNING EXPERIENCES

1.1 and 1.3: Darbie admitted that she had not thought through the school-wide ramifications of the celebration decision and talked about her own personal learning. SCORE 1.1 AT PROFICIENT.

Darbie proactively talked with her supervisor about how she handled the differing points of view regarding student celebrations in her school and reevaluated the decision based on district core values and policies. SCORE 1.3 AT PROFICIENT.

(1.1, 1.3) Darbie called her elementary director back and was able to assure her that she had taken action to reevaluate and change the celebration plans and that she was in total agreement with the feedback. Darbie also shared that this had been a personal learning experience for her and that she would only approve plans that were inclusive of all students and that upheld the core values of the district and aligned with all district policies.

Scenario #2—Susan
1.0: Resilience

Susan is an assistant principal at Grander City Middle School. This is the spring of her fifth year in this role. Some of Susan's duties include handling student discipline, creating the master schedule, supervising assessments, and the data collection process. The school district just finished the second round of state testing. Susan was responsible for the administration, supervision, and collection of the testing for the entire middle school. She was pleased with the testing procedures and practices that she put in place this school year. It was the end of the day and Susan had just finished the testing check-in process at the district office. The district testing coordinator gave the following suggestions to Susan for the testing window for next year:

- Ensure all testing booklets are accounted for and in alphabetical and numerical order.

- Guarantee all students have completed all sections of the test or the proper invalidations will be in place for each incomplete student booklet.

- Verify that all teachers have followed proper testing procedures.

When Susan returned to the school, she met with Mrs. Duncan, the principal, to give a report of the check-in process. Susan shared with Mrs. Duncan the criticisms from the district testing coordinator. It was apparent that Susan was a little upset about the feedback given. She acknowledged that some of the test booklets were out of order due to the number of enrollments prior to the testing window. Mrs. Duncan suggested that she should create a system for students who enroll and withdraw during the testing window.

Susan admitted that this was an issue from the previous year as well.

She continued to say that the district should create a system for this issue to ensure consistency and that it should not be the assistant principal's responsibility.

Mrs. Duncan responded quickly by saying it was the responsibility of the assistant principal to put procedures in place for their testing site because of the individual school dynamics. Susan concluded the debriefing by stating that she was aware that this issue was a concern before and that she would look into procedures for addressing this issue. Mrs. Duncan stated that she expects that this issue will not be a concern again for the fall testing window.

Peruse the MLP Matrix and assess Susan's performance in Domain 1.0: Resilience. Make mental notes and be prepared to respond as to the reason for your score on that dimension. Please be prepared to report out in 15 minutes.

Scenario #2—Susan
1.0: Resilience

PROGRESSING

Susan is an assistant principal at Grander City Middle School. This is the spring of her fifth year in this role. Some of Susan's duties include handling student discipline, creating the master schedule, supervising assessments, and the data collection process. The school district just finished the second round of state testing. Susan was responsible for the administration, supervision, and collection of the testing for the entire middle school. She was pleased with the testing procedures and practices that she put in place this school year. It was the end of the day and Susan had just finished the testing check-in process at the district office. The district testing coordinator gave the following suggestions to Susan for the testing window for next year:

- Ensure all testing booklets are accounted for and in alphabetical and numerical order.

- Guarantee all students have completed all sections of the test or the proper invalidations will be in place for each incomplete student booklet.

- Verify that all teachers have followed proper testing procedures.

When Susan returned to the school, she met with Mrs. Duncan, the principal, to give a report of the check-in process. Susan shared with Mrs. Duncan the criticisms from the district testing coordinator. It was apparent that Susan was a little upset about the feedback given. **(1.1) She acknowledged that some of the test booklets were out of order due to the number of enrollments prior to the testing window. Mrs. Duncan suggested that she should create a system for students who enroll and withdraw during the testing window.**

(1.2) Susan admitted that this was an issue from the previous year as well.

(1.3) She continued to say that the district should create a system for this issue to ensure consistency and that it should not be the assistant principal's responsibility.

Mrs. Duncan responded quickly by saying it was the responsibility of the assistant principal to put procedures in place for their testing site because of the individual school dynamics. **(1.5) Susan concluded the debriefing by stating that she was aware that this issue was a concern before and that she would look into procedures for addressing this issue.** Mrs. Duncan stated that she expects that this issue will not be a concern again for the fall testing window.

1.1: Susan acknowledges the organizational failure to have the testing booklets in alphabetical and numerical order.
SCORE 1.1 AT PROGRESSING.

1.2: Susan admitted that it was an issue from the previous year as well, but said she really believed that the district rather than individual schools should create a system for this issue to ensure consistency and that it should not be the assistant principal's responsibility.
SCORE 1.2 AT PROGRESSING.

1.3: Susan suggested that it was the district's responsibility to create a system for this issue.
SCORE 1.3 AT PROGRESSING.

1.5: Susan stated that she was aware of this issue and that she would explore ways to address the concern for the future.
SCORE 1.5 AT PROGRESSING.

Scenario #3—Rebecca
1.0: Resilience

Rebecca was nearing the end of her fifth year as principal at Running Rock High School. For the first time this year, Rebecca was finally feeling that she clearly knew who she was as leader. She also recognized that her learning continued each day, and that much of that came from her work with others in multiple venues. It was not uncommon for Rebecca to experience great joy in her work as well as challenges on the same day. She now understood both to be an integral part of leadership, knowing that her greatest growth as a leader always seemed to be the result of facing some of her greatest challenges.

This school year started out much like the past four. However, within the first month of school, a series of events occurred that tested her leadership, decision making, and, on occasion, her desire to continue this work. Her staff and community never knew about her doubts. Rather, she sought coaching from those whom she trusted to coach her and to help her access her own reserves for problem-solving and coping.

Running Rock High School experienced both a tragedy and a scandal. A senior who was beloved by the students, staff, and community lost his life in a car accident and created a crisis situation in the building. Through the well-designed crisis response plan, Rebecca was able to mobilize her own staff and seek support from other schools to assist with the significant counseling needs in her school. Throughout the crisis and beyond, she offered praise for risk-taking and both individual and collective efforts. Additionally, she offered feedback that was both positive and that encouraged continuous learning. However, as Rebecca shared with her staff later in the year, she pushed back her own need for support in the interest of leading others through this crisis. In hindsight, Rebecca told her staff that she might have gone through the process better by "taking her own oxygen first." Running Rock and Rebecca weathered the tragedy together and modified their crisis plan based on their reflections after things settled down.

Just two weeks later, Rebecca's athletic director was suspected of violating the state student athletic code of ethics by encouraging coaches to recruit students for three major sports. Rebecca initially pushed back at both the association investigators and human resources because of her difficulty believing such behavior from the athletic director was likely. The investigation revealed that he had been blatantly violating recruiting rules over the course of the past two years. Rebecca, along with the human resources department, put the athletic director on administrative leave and ultimately dismissed him. From that point forward, Rebecca was fully supportive of the decision and backed it with evidence whenever she was challenged.

Since her former athletic director was well liked by the staff, students, and community, there was a political backlash that Rebecca expected but found extremely disconcerting as a leader. Staff members, students, and parents confronted her publicly and some even expressed their discontent with the decision at a school board meeting. Although it was emotionally taxing, Rebecca listened carefully to each dissenting viewpoint, validating the emotions behind the anger and offering what she could legally in terms of her confidence in the final decision to dismiss the athletic director. Rebecca was glad that she had had extensive cognitive coaching experience, as this allowed her to use skills such as paraphrasing, empathetic listening, and inquiry to maintain relationships during this difficult period. It became clear to her during this process that a broad spectrum of voices needed to be involved when the school hired to fill the position. Rebecca made sure that all groups were represented to give feedback about the right person for the position and had the opportunity to participate in the process fully.

It was now the end of the year. Rebecca had worked through her earlier feelings of uncertainty and felt strongly that all of her decisions were the right ones for students. She also recognized what an incredible learning experience the year had provided her. It was just another reminder that every year brings new learning, regardless of how many years one has served as a principal. When Rebecca received feedback from staff, students, and community via her 360 surveys, she reflected on those trends that gave her an opportunity for further learning. Rebecca used the lessons from these trends to build her professional growth plan for the following year. Rebecca was pleasantly surprised that, given the unique circumstances of the year, the manner in which she handled both major issues during the year was perceived in a generally positive manner. Rebecca had an even greater commitment to her role as a building leader than before because of the challenges she had overcome.

Peruse the MLP Matrix and assess Rebecca's performance in Domain 1.0: Resilience. Make mental notes and be prepared to respond as to the reason for your score on that dimension. Please be prepared to report out in 15 minutes.

Scenario #3—Rebecca
1.0: Resilience

Exemplary

Rebecca was nearing the end of her fifth year as principal at Running Rock High School. For the first time this year, Rebecca was finally feeling that she clearly knew who she was as leader. She also recognized that her learning continued each day, and that much of that came from her work with others in multiple venues. It was not uncommon for Rebecca to experience great joy in her work as well as challenges on the same day. She now understood both to be an integral part of leadership, knowing that her greatest growth as a leader always seemed to be the result of facing some of her greatest challenges.

This school year started out much like the past four. However, within the first month of school, a series of events occurred that tested her leadership, decision making, and, on occasion, her desire to continue this work. Her staff and community never knew about her doubts. Rather, she sought coaching from those whom she trusted to coach her and to help her access her own reserves for problem-solving and coping.

Running Rock High School experienced both a tragedy and a scandal. A senior who was beloved by the students, staff, and community lost his life in a car accident and created a crisis situation in the building. Through the well-designed crisis response plan, Rebecca was able to mobilize her own staff and seek support from other schools to assist with the significant counseling needs in her school. **(1.2) Throughout the crisis and beyond, she offered praise for risk-taking and both individual and collective efforts. Additionally, she offered feedback that was both positive and that encouraged continuous learning.** However, as **(1.1, 1.2) Rebecca shared with her staff later in the year, she pushed back her own need for support in the interest of leading others through this crisis. In hindsight, Rebecca told her staff that she might have gone through the process better by "taking her own oxygen first." Running Rock and Rebecca weathered the tragedy together and modified their crisis plan based on their reflections after things settled down.**

Just two weeks later, Rebecca's athletic director was suspected of violating the state student athletic code of ethics by encouraging coaches to recruit students for three major sports. **(1.3) Rebecca initially pushed back at both the association investigators and human resources because of her difficulty believing such behavior from the athletic director was likely.** The investigation revealed that he had been blatantly violating recruiting rules over the course of the past two years. Rebecca, along with the human resources department, put the athletic director on administrative leave and ultimately dismissed him. **(1.3) From that point forward, Rebecca was fully supportive of the decision and backed it with evidence whenever she was challenged.**

Since her former athletic director was well liked by the staff, students, and community, there was a political backlash that Rebecca expected but found extremely disconcerting as a leader. Staff members, students, and parents confronted her publicly and some even expressed their discontent with the decision

> **1.2:** Rebecca has offered feedback and supports continuous learning by individuals and the organization through encouraging risk-taking through positive support. Score 1.2 at Exemplary.

> **1.1 and 1.2:** Rebecca is willing to acknowledge errors and make suggestions, which results in system-wide learning. Score 1.1 and 1.2 at Exemplary.

> **1.3:** Rebecca was not afraid to challenge authority until the evidence became clear that the athletic director was, in fact, violating ethics. Score 1.3 at Exemplary.

> **1.3:** Once the decision was final and backed with evidence, Rebecca supported it, even in the face of dissent from others. Score 1.3 at Exemplary.

1.4: Rebecca listened to dissenting voices and used multiple perspectives.
SCORE 1.4 AT EXEMPLARY.

1.4: Rebecca deliberately generated multiple perspectives so that the final decision could be more broadly supported.
SCORE 1.4 AT EXEMPLARY.

1.5: Rebecca used 360 survey data to reflect on her performance and create an action plan for the following year.
SCORE 1.5 AT EXEMPLARY.

at a school board meeting. Although it was emotionally taxing, **(1.4)** Rebecca listened carefully to each dissenting viewpoint, validating the emotions behind the anger and offering what she could legally in terms of her confidence in the final decision to dismiss the athletic director. Rebecca was glad that she had had extensive cognitive coaching experience, as this allowed her to use skills such as paraphrasing, empathetic listening, and inquiry to maintain relationships during this difficult period. It became clear to her during this process that a broad spectrum of voices needed to be involved when the school hired to fill the position. **(1.4)** Rebecca made sure that all groups were represented to give feedback about the right person for the position and had the opportunity to participate in the process fully.

It was now the end of the year. Rebecca had worked through her earlier feelings of uncertainty and felt strongly that all of her decisions were the right ones for students. **(1.5)** She also recognized what an incredible learning experience the year had provided her. It was just another reminder that every year brings new learning, regardless of how many years one has served as a principal. When Rebecca received feedback from staff, students, and community via her 360 surveys, she reflected on those trends that gave her an opportunity for further learning. Rebecca used the lessons from these trends to build her professional growth plan for the following year. Rebecca was pleasantly surprised that, given the unique circumstances of the year, the manner in which she handled both major issues during the year was perceived in a generally positive manner. Rebecca had an even greater commitment to her role as a building leader than before because of the challenges she had overcome.

Scenario #4—Linda
1.0: Resilience

As the executive director of elementary education in a large suburban school district, Linda had been charged with the development of the new elementary standards-based report card. Prior to starting the process, she met with the superintendent and leadership cabinet for support in outlining a strategic plan and timeline to accomplish this task. Up front, the superintendent and Linda knew this was not going to be an easy task, as many teachers as well as parents were reluctant to give up grades and to move to a standards-based rubric. Having recalled previous district-wide initiatives she had led and the organizational as well as personal mistakes made, Linda has learned from the past and understands she needs to integrate the group feedback and use the mission and values of the district to guide her work.

Linda took time to reflect upon this advice from the superintendent and upon her previous experiences before setting out to pull together a working committee that truly represented all district as well as community stakeholders. Additionally, she formed an internal and external communication loop, set a rigorous time-line, and developed a decision-making framework that was clearly articulated and orchestrated.

Having laid this groundwork, Linda began her biweekly meetings with the committee and quickly learned that the middle school principals and parents in the group were struggling to support this district initiative. They felt that it would be too difficult for students and parents to transition back to grades in middle school. After several meetings and many lengthy discussions, Linda was feeling a little overwhelmed, as she knew her charge was to develop a K–5 standards-based report card. The middle school objections would be a setback to her charge from the superintendent. Even though Linda supported this feedback, she had to share these concerns with the superintendent proactively and outline the committee recommendations. Students in grades K–4 would use the standards-based report card in all content areas, while students in grade 5 would use the same report card for all nonacademic core content and would be given grades in reading and math. Linda felt that this reflected the "groupthink" and was prepared to advocate for district alignment between levels since the middle school was not moving to a standards-based report card.

Upon contacting the superintendent, she was told that this information would be shared with the superintendent's cabinet and that they would support the decision or give further guidance to her and the committee. During the presentation, the group praised Linda for providing great leadership to the standards-based report card committee through her willingness to listen to all the concerns, remaining calm when the initiative was challenged, being open to suggestions, and being an advocate for district grade-level alignment and consistency. The superintendent's cabinet supported the decision, and Linda and her committee moved from the planning stage to first-year implementation.

Peruse the MLP Matrix and assess Linda's performance in Domain 1.0: Resilience. Make mental notes and be prepared to respond as to the reason for your score on that dimension. Please be prepared to report out in 15 minutes.

CASE STUDY MATERIALS AND LEARNING EXPERIENCES

Scenario #4—Linda
1.0 Resilience

PROFICIENT

As the executive director of elementary education in a large suburban school district, Linda had been charged with the development of the new elementary standards-based report card. Prior to starting the process, she met with the superintendent and leadership cabinet for support in outlining a strategic plan and timeline to accomplish this task. Up front, the superintendent and Linda knew this was not going to be an easy task, as many teachers as well as parents were reluctant to give up grades and to move to a standards-based rubric. **(1.1, 1.2) Having recalled previous district-wide initiatives she had led and the organizational as well as personal mistakes made, Linda has learned from the past and understands she needs to integrate the group feedback and use the mission and values of the district to guide her work.**

(1.5) Linda took time to reflect upon this advice from the superintendent and upon her previous experiences before setting out to pull together a working committee that truly represented all district as well as community stakeholders. Additionally, she formed an internal and external communication loop, set a rigorous timeline, and developed a decision-making framework that was clearly articulated and orchestrated.

Having laid this groundwork, Linda began her biweekly meetings with the committee and quickly learned that **(1.4) the middle school principals and parents in the group were struggling to support this district initiative.** They felt that it would be too difficult for students and parents to transition back to grades in middle school. After several meetings and many lengthy discussions, **(1.4) Linda was feeling a little overwhelmed, as she knew her charge was to develop a K–5 standards-based report card. The middle school objections would be a setback to her charge from the superintendent. (1.3) Even though Linda supported this feedback, she had to share these concerns with the superintendent proactively and outline the committee recommendations.** Students in grades K–4 would use the standards-based report card in all content areas, while students in grade 5 would use the same report card for all nonacademic core content and would be given grades in reading and math. Linda felt that this reflected the "groupthink" and was prepared to advocate for district alignment between levels since the middle school was not moving to a standards-based report card.

Upon contacting the superintendent, she was told that this information would be shared with the superintendent's cabinet and that they would support the decision or give further guidance to her and the committee. During the presentation, the group praised Linda for providing great leadership to the standards-based report card committee through her willingness to listen to all the concerns, remaining calm when the initiative was challenged, being open to suggestions, and being an advocate for district grade-level alignment and consistency. The superintendent's cabinet supported the decision, and Linda and her committee moved from the planning stage to first-year implementation.

Scenario #5—Jeffrey
1.0: Resilience

Jeffrey has been in his position as director of middle schools for the school district of Fort Warren for the last three years. Jeffrey was a middle school principal in the district for eight years. He was known for being an instructional leader and having an energy that others envied. In analyzing the middle school academic and discipline data, his main goals for this year are to align the grades 7 and 8 curriculum to the curriculum of the elementary schools and the high school and to decrease expulsion rates at the two middle schools.

On Monday morning, Jeffrey enters the boardroom for a cabinet meeting with the superintendent, Jonathon Outlaw, the assistant superintendent, Kristen McCann, the business manager, Tony Monroe, and the human resource director, Nick Jones. Nick Jones is an outspoken messenger for the teachers about the newly implemented discipline policy. The policy states that students will only be expelled in instances involving drugs and weapons. The teachers are upset because they feel that the policy does not support them as classroom teachers. They believe, as in the past, that if a student has 10 or more suspensions, he should be expelled from school. Jeffrey firmly believes in the new policy in order to decrease the expulsion rate at the middle schools. Superintendent Outlaw begins the meeting by having the cabinet share highlights from the previous week. Several highlights are shared. Then he has the cabinet share the concerns. At this time, Nick Jones speaks up by stating that there is an eighth-grade student who has already accumulated 12 two-day suspensions for defiance and fighting. He then continues by saying the newly implemented expulsion policy does not foster a safe environment for teachers and students. Nick looks boldly at Jeffrey and shares that the two principals of both middle schools feel the same way as the teachers. Jeffrey looks at Superintendent Outlaw and acknowledges this student example and some of the teachers' concerns. He asks the superintendent if it would be wise for him to assemble a team of teachers, counselors, and the two principals to discuss their concerns and possible remedies for the problem. Superintendent Outlaw tells Jeffrey that he should have formed a team prior to the implementation of the policy and that it would not be smart to have them brainstorm remedies to the problem. Jeffrey interrupts by saying that he knows he should have brought representatives together before implementing the policy, but he believes that it is not too late to bring them together to share suggestions on making the policy more acceptable. Jeffrey concludes his comments by stating that he will meet with the two middle school principals tomorrow to learn their thoughts regarding the policy and he would meet with teacher representatives about improvements that can be made to support the teachers.

The next day at the meeting with the middle school principals, Jeffrey shares what was said in the cabinet meeting yesterday. One of the principals, Robert Flack, shouts that his teachers are upset at him because of the constant misbehavior of the students and their loss of control of their classrooms. Jeffrey listens and nods, but does not say anything. Then principal Dorothy Anderson agrees with Robert by saying the policy is causing students to be more disruptive and that Jeffrey should have consulted with them prior to implementing the policy. She then states that he handled the new attendance policy in the same way last year, and that the policy is still causing problems with teachers and parents because of the leniency of the truancy consequences.

Later that afternoon, the superintendent calls Jeffrey to his office to debrief the meeting with principals. Jeffrey shares the concerns of the principals and states that they are mad at him because he did not elicit their input prior to the implementation of the policy. Superintendent Outlaw tells Jeffrey that he concurs with the principals because this has happened before and Jeffrey did not make changes to ensure that he would not lead like this in the future. Jeffrey apologizes and states that he will improve his leadership style by being more collaborative in the future.

Peruse the MLP Matrix and assess Jeffrey's performance in Domain 1.0: Resilience. Make mental notes and be prepared to respond as to the reason for your score on that dimension. Please be prepared to report out in 15 minutes.

Scenario #5—Jeffrey
1.0: Resilience

PROGRESSING

Jeffrey has been in his position as director of middle schools for the school district of Fort Warren for the last three years. Jeffrey was a middle school principal in the district for eight years. He was known for being an instructional leader and having an energy that others envied. In analyzing the middle school academic and discipline data, his main goals for this year are to align the grades 7 and 8 curriculum to the curriculum of the elementary schools and the high school and to decrease expulsion rates at the two middle schools.

On Monday morning, Jeffrey enters the boardroom for a cabinet meeting with the superintendent, Jonathon Outlaw, the assistant superintendent, Kristen McCann, the business manager, Tony Monroe, and the human resource director, Nick Jones. Nick Jones is an outspoken messenger for the teachers about the newly implemented discipline policy. The policy states that students will only be expelled in instances involving drugs and weapons. The teachers are upset because they feel that the policy does not support them as classroom teachers. They believe, as in the past, that if a student has 10 or more suspensions, he should be expelled from school. Jeffrey firmly believes in the new policy in order to decrease the expulsion rate at the middle schools. Superintendent Outlaw begins the meeting by having the cabinet share highlights from the previous week. Several highlights are shared. Then he has the cabinet share the concerns. At this time, Nick Jones speaks up by stating that there is an eighth-grade student who has already accumulated 12 two-day suspensions for defiance and fighting. He then continues by saying the newly implemented expulsion policy does not foster a safe environment for teachers and students. Nick looks boldly at Jeffrey and shares that the two principals of both middle schools feel the same way as the teachers. **(1.1) Jeffrey looks at Superintendent Outlaw and acknowledges this student example and some of the teachers' concerns. He asks the superintendent if it would be wise for him to assemble a team of teachers, counselors, and the two principals to discuss their concerns and possible remedies for the problem.** Superintendent Outlaw tells Jeffrey that he should have formed a team prior to the implementation of the policy and that it would not be smart to have them brainstorm remedies to the problem. **(1.2) Jeffrey interrupts by saying that he knows he should have brought representatives together before implementing the policy, (1.3) but he believes that it is not too late to bring them together to share suggestions on making the policy more acceptable.** Jeffrey concludes his comments by stating that he will meet with the two middle school principals tomorrow to learn their thoughts regarding the policy and he would meet with teacher representatives about improvements that can be made to support the teachers.

The next day at the meeting with the middle school principals, Jeffrey shares what was said in the cabinet meeting yesterday. **(1.4) One of the principals, Robert Flack, shouts that his teachers are upset at him because of the constant misbehavior of the students and their loss of control of their classrooms. Jeffrey listens and nods, but does not say anything. Then principal Dorothy Anderson agrees with Robert by saying the policy is causing**

1.1: Jeffrey acknowledges the concerns with the policy when Nick shares the example of the student.
SCORE 1.1 AT PROGRESSING.

1.2: Jeffrey is able to accept the evidence of mistakes when offered by others.
SCORE 1.2 AT PROGRESSING.

1.3: Jeffrey challenges Superintendent Outlaw and decides to assemble the teachers regardless of whether Dr. Outlaw agrees or not.
SCORE 1.3 AT PROGRESSING.

1.4: Jeffrey tolerates the dissent of the principals by nodding and listening.
SCORE 1.4 AT PROGRESSING.

1.5: Jeffrey has not created an action plan to ensure that this behavior will not happen again. SCORE 1.5 AT PROGRESSING.

students to be more disruptive and that Jeffrey should have consulted with them prior to implementing the policy. She then states that he handled the new attendance policy in the same way last year, and that the policy is still causing problems with teachers and parents because of the leniency of the truancy consequences.

Later that afternoon, the superintendent calls Jeffrey to his office to debrief the meeting with principals. Jeffrey shares the concerns of the principals and states that they are mad at him because he did not elicit their input prior to the implementation of the policy. **(1.5) Superintendent Outlaw tells Jeffrey that he concurs with the principals because this has happened before and Jeffrey did not make changes to ensure that he would not lead like this in the future. Jeffrey apologizes and states that he will improve his leadership style by being more collaborative in the future.**

Scenario #6—Adrienne
1.0: Resilience

This was now Adrienne's fifth year working for West Metro School District as a director of high schools. Adrienne joined the district leadership team after being recruited by the superintendent from another district. With more than 18 years of experience in education, Adrienne had multiple educational experiences from which to draw when responding to the daily demands of her job. Most recently, Adrienne's former position as principal of a large urban high school reminded her that the district should never lose sight of the needs of principals and the unique challenges they face at the building level.

For the past three years, Adrienne had built a system of support for high school principals, which was constantly evolving. In addition to monthly meetings and professional development with all district and building leadership, the high school principals met monthly to engage in common professional development time. Principals now cited this time together as something they wouldn't miss and around which they planned their calendars. This wasn't always the case. Adrienne learned from her mistakes during her first year as a director of high schools. In an effort to develop rapport with the group, Adrienne had tried to connect with the group more as a fellow principal who understood their trials and tribulations.

The meetings that first year started as professional book studies, but then seemed always to devolve into complaint sessions. When Herb, a high school principal, confronted Adrienne about how annoying the sessions had become, Adrienne listened carefully to what he had to say. At first she felt misunderstood. After some reflection, she began to come to terms with the idea that this colleague was right. As she was completing her end-of-year evaluation conference with the assistant superintendent, she noticed similar trends in her 360 survey data. Others in the district felt that her efforts to be seen as empathetic to the needs of principals caused her to sacrifice some of her leadership talent for moving the district forward. When writing her goals for the following year, Adrienne made sure this area for growth was highlighted.

When Adrienne began her second year as a director, she admitted to the group that her leadership the previous year had not been all she had hoped for. She asked the group to work collaboratively to achieve their goals regarding ongoing professional development. She reminded them that she was able to understand their world, but was also there to support them as they engaged in continuous improvement. Without this continuous improvement, they would not reach their full potential as a learning organization.

With his permission, Adrienne publicly thanked Herb for holding her accountable and encouraged others to do the same. Several principals spoke up and requested that in order for them to truly grow professionally, they should engage in their own cross-school Data Team (small teams that strategically improve practice through the use of data). Adrienne accepted this idea and worked with the group of principals to assign roles and determine the best way to approach this professional development endeavor.

CASE STUDY MATERIALS AND LEARNING EXPERIENCES

The first year they implemented the Data Team, there were significant bumps in the road. At one point, the group wanted to abandon the plan because of pressure Adrienne was receiving from the superintendent to spend more time developing a plan for a new high school sports initiative. The group expressed multiple opinions and not all agreed on the next steps. The group agreed to two additional sessions one month to work through a plan that would justify continuing the work the Data Team group had started, rather than take on this new initiative. The plan included a timeline for taking on the high school sports initiative the following year with the group's full support. Adrienne facilitated a protocol with the group that allowed them to create a compelling argument to the superintendent, who ultimately agreed to drop the initiative until the following year when Adrienne presented him with their plan. He was pleased with his decision, as Adrienne's group of high school principals gained incredible momentum in their Data Team over the next two years and served as a model for similar cross-district professional development throughout West Fork.

Peruse the MLP Matrix and assess Adrienne's performance in Domain 1.0: Resilience. Make mental notes and be prepared to respond as to the reason for your score on that dimension. Please be prepared to report out in 15 minutes.

Scenario #6—Adrienne
1.0: Resilience

EXEMPLARY

This was now Adrienne's fifth year working for West Metro School District as a director of high schools. Adrienne joined the district leadership team after being recruited by the superintendent from another district. With more than 18 years of experience in education, Adrienne had multiple educational experiences from which to draw when responding to the daily demands of her job. Most recently, Adrienne's former position as principal of a large urban high school reminded her that the district should never lose sight of the needs of principals and the unique challenges they face at the building level.

For the past three years, Adrienne had built a system of support for high school principals, which was constantly evolving. In addition to monthly meetings and professional development with all district and building leadership, the high school principals met monthly to engage in common professional development time. Principals now cited this time together as something they wouldn't miss and around which they planned their calendars. This wasn't always the case. Adrienne learned from her mistakes during her first year as a director of high schools. In an effort to develop rapport with the group, Adrienne had tried to connect with the group more as a fellow principal who understood their trials and tribulations.

The meetings that first year started as professional book studies, but then seemed always to devolve into complaint sessions. **(1.4) When Herb, a high school principal, confronted Adrienne about how annoying the sessions had become, Adrienne listened carefully to what he had to say. At first she felt misunderstood. After some reflection, she began to come to terms with the idea that this colleague was right.** As she was completing her **(1.5) end-of-year evaluation conference with the assistant superintendent, she noticed similar trends in her 360 survey data.** Others in the district felt that her efforts to be seen as empathetic to the needs of principals caused her to sacrifice some of her leadership talent for moving the district forward. **(1.5) When writing her goals for the following year, Adrienne made sure this area for growth was highlighted.**

When **(1.1, 1.2) Adrienne began her second year as a director, she admitted to the group that her leadership the previous year had not been all she had hoped for. She asked the group to work collaboratively to achieve their goals regarding ongoing professional development. She reminded them that she was able to understand their world, but was also there to support them as they engaged in continuous improvement. Without this continuous improvement, they would not reach their full potential as a learning organization.**

(1.4) With his permission, Adrienne publicly thanked Herb for holding her accountable and encouraged others to do the same. Several principals (1.4) spoke up and requested that in order for them to truly grow professionally, they should engage in their own cross-school Data Team (small teams that strategically improve practice through the use of data). Adrienne accepted this idea and worked with the group of principals to assign roles and determine the best way to approach this professional development endeavor.

1.4: Adrienne uses Herb's comment as an opportunity to reflect on her leadership and ultimately acknowledges her error.
SCORE 1.4 AT EXEMPLARY.

1.5: Adrienne uses data from the 360 survey and the evaluation process to reflect and change her priorities to impact her own growth and that of the organization positively.
SCORE 1.5 AT EXEMPLARY.

1.5: Adrienne integrates the learning from her reflection to create goals for the following year and ultimately change her priorities to impact the district as a whole positively.
SCORE 1.5 AT EXEMPLARY.

1.1 and **1.2:** Adrienne admits her error and begins a plan to make positive change. Although her intention was good, mistakes were made; new learning has occurred that can inform future plans.
SCORE 1.1 AND 1.2 AT EXEMPLARY.

1.4: Adrienne recognizes Herb's thoughtful dissent and encourages others to do the same if needed.
SCORE 1.4 AT EXEMPLARY.

1.4: Adrienne utilizes principals in multiple roles and encourages this thoughtful dissent. These behaviors, combined with her encouragement of multiple viewpoints when the group was faced with the superintendent initiative, demonstrate her willingness to create constructive contention for the good of the organization. SCORE 1.4 AT EXEMPLARY.

1.3: Adrienne works collaboratively on a plan that will challenge the need to implement the new initiative immediately. She uses appropriate tools to justify continuing their work, but also shows a willingness to take on the new initiative and support it the following year. SCORE 1.3 AT EXEMPLARY.

(1.3) The first year they implemented the Data Team, there were significant bumps in the road. At one point, the group wanted to abandon the plan because of pressure Adrienne was receiving from the superintendent to spend more time developing a plan for a new high school sports initiative. **(1.4, cont.)** The group expressed multiple opinions and not all agreed on the next steps. The group agreed to two additional sessions one month to work through a plan that would justify continuing the work the Data Team group had started, rather than take on this new initiative. **(1.3)** The plan included a timeline for taking on the high school sports initiative the following year with the group's full support. **(1.4, cont.)** Adrienne facilitated a protocol with the group that allowed them to create a compelling argument to the superintendent, who ultimately agreed to drop the initiative until the following year when Adrienne presented him with their plan. He was pleased with his decision, as Adrienne's group of high school principals gained incredible momentum in their Data Team over the next two years and served as a model for similar cross-district professional development throughout West Fork.

Scenario #7—Carlos
1.0: Resilience

This year, Carlos was definitely feeling the pressure from what he believed to be an unreasonable board of education. When Carlos first became the superintendent of Idlewood School District two years ago, the board seemed excited about the work he was doing. Now, with two new members of the board, things felt significantly different. Carlos had heard of situations like his own, but couldn't believe that he would have to endure these unreasonable expectations.

There was much to do in Idlewood when Carlos arrived. Although the previous superintendent had left on good terms with the staff and board, Carlos could see clearly that things could be better. Under the prior leadership, practices and policies in the district had become much too safe and it didn't appear to Carlos that people were taking the risk of innovating. In the interest of being seen as the leader who was on the cutting edge, Carlos considered himself someone who needed to create a bit of chaos.

One of the first initiatives Carlos took on was to push out a new reading program system-wide. His personal passion and belief system drove this project forward and he was excited about the possibilities. In an effort to get the project moving, Carlos did not engage his district leadership team in the perfunctory representative team from schools, as he determined this would be a burden on the system. Instead, he met with his director of curriculum and instruction, Sheila, and gave her the task of getting the reading program in place district-wide within three months. She initially pushed back, citing that ownership and feedback from the system needed to be included in the project rollout or it was likely to fail. Carlos told her it was fine for her to express her disagreement, but she needed to do it behind closed doors so that it wouldn't jeopardize the initiative.

By early winter, the system was on fire. Principals refused to move forward with the reading program. Board members found themselves constantly fielding concerns from principals and the teacher's union and raised these concerns with Carlos at several board work sessions. In one particular session, the board president reminded Carlos of the board policy that required a representative team to be utilized whenever large-scale curricular issues were to be decided. The board directed Carlos to follow the policy. Carlos was angered by their interference and felt they did not understand fully what was best for the district.

When Carlos convened his cabinet the next week, he told his district leaders that they were moving forward with the reading program as planned. Each cabinet member was charged with a group of principals or union members to convince to "settle down" and get on board with the initiative. For a while, things did settle down, as promises were made to survey staff about their apprehensions about the new program. When the survey results came back negative, Carlos reiterated his passion for the project to his cabinet and directed them to continue work as planned. He knew that when they started to see results, everyone would get on board eventually.

Close to the end of the school year, the board met with Carlos to review his performance and complete his evaluation. They addressed the issue of Carlos ignoring board directives and policies. Carlos defended his decisions and reminded the board that he was the educator, not they. He also felt it important to remind the board that he had an advanced degree in literacy and he was best able to make these kinds of decisions for the board. The board was not convinced and created goals for his improvement the following year.

The pace of the program implementation remained much the same the following year. Amidst all the pushback, Carlos remained true to his ideals and continued an aggressive implementation timeline. Two new members were elected to the board in November, and it seemed to Carlos that the interference from the board grew exponentially. Sometime in February, the director of curriculum announced that she had accepted a position as a consultant and would be leaving in early March. Within a couple of months, eight principals also submitted their resignations for various reasons. When the board confronted Carlos about his lack of progress on his goals from the previous year, Carlos became agitated and annoyed, once again citing that he knew what was best for this district. Now it was May and it had become clear that Carlos was going to be removed by the Idlewood Board of Education. He found it disappointing that they didn't even wait to see what kinds of results he was able to get.

Peruse the MLP Matrix and assess Carlos's performance in Domain 1.0: Resilience. Make mental notes and be prepared to respond as to the reason for your score on that dimension. Please be prepared to report out in 15 minutes.

Scenario #7—Carlos
1.0: Resilience

NOT MEETING STANDARDS

This year, Carlos was definitely feeling the pressure from what he believed to be an unreasonable board of education. When Carlos first became the superintendent of Idlewood School District two years ago, the board seemed excited about the work he was doing. Now, with two new members of the board, things felt significantly different. Carlos had heard of situations like his own, but couldn't believe that he would have to endure these unreasonable expectations.

There was much to do in Idlewood when Carlos arrived. Although the previous superintendent had left on good terms with the staff and board, Carlos could see clearly that things could be better. Under the prior leadership, practices and policies in the district had become much too safe and it didn't appear to Carlos that people were taking the risk of innovating. In the interest of being seen as the leader who was on the cutting edge, Carlos considered himself someone who needed to create a bit of chaos.

One of the first initiatives Carlos took on was to push out a new reading program system-wide. His personal passion and belief system drove this project forward and he was excited about the possibilities. In an effort to get the project moving, Carlos did not engage his district leadership team in the perfunctory representative team from schools, as he determined this would be a burden on the system. Instead, he met with his director of curriculum and instruction, Sheila, and gave her the task of getting the reading program in place district-wide within three months. She initially pushed back, citing that ownership and feedback from the system needed to be included in the project rollout or it was likely to fail. **(1.4) Carlos told her it was fine for her to express her disagreement, but she needed to do it behind closed doors so that it wouldn't jeopardize the initiative.**

> **1.4: Carlos tolerates private dissent from the curriculum and instruction director.**
> SCORE 1.4 AT PROGRESSING.

By early winter, the system was on fire. Principals refused to move forward with the reading program. Board members found themselves constantly fielding concerns from principals and the teacher's union and raised these concerns with Carlos at several board work sessions. In one particular session, the board president reminded Carlos of the board policy that required a representative team to be utilized whenever large-scale curricular issues were to be decided. **(1.2) The board directed Carlos to follow the policy. Carlos was angered by their interference and felt they did not understand fully what was best for the district.**

> **1.2: Carlos is defensive and unwilling to acknowledge or learn from the mistake.**
> SCORE 1.2 AT NOT MEETING STANDARDS.

(1.3) When Carlos convened his cabinet the next week, he told his district leaders that they were moving forward with the reading program as planned. Each cabinet member was charged with a group of principals or union members to convince to "settle down" and get on board with the initiative. For a while, things did settle down, as promises were made to survey staff about their apprehensions about the new program. When the survey results came back negative, Carlos reiterated his passion for the project to his cabinet and directed them to continue work as planned. He knew that when they started to see results, everyone would get on board eventually.

> **1.3: Carlos ignores directives from the board and moves forward with his own plan.**
> SCORE 1.3 AT NOT MEETING STANDARDS.

1.1: Carlos becomes defensive and does not acknowledge his error. SCORE 1.1 AT NOT MEETING STANDARDS.

1.5: Carlos ignores the goals developed as a result of his evaluation and pushes forward in the same manner as before. SCORE 1.5 AT NOT MEETING STANDARDS.

1.2: Carlos continues to be defensive, believing he is right, and refuses to see where change may need to happen. SCORE 1.2 AT NOT MEETING STANDARDS.

Close to the end of the school year, the board met with Carlos to review his performance and complete his evaluation. They addressed the issue of Carlos ignoring board directives and policies. **(1.1) Carlos defended his decisions and reminded the board that he was the educator, not they. He also felt it important to remind the board that he had an advanced degree in literacy and he was best able to make these kinds of decisions for the board. (1.5) The board was not convinced and created goals for his improvement the following year.**

The pace of the program implementation remained much the same the following year. Amidst all the pushback, Carlos remained true to his ideals and continued an aggressive implementation timeline. Two new members were elected to the board in November, and it seemed to Carlos that the interference from the board grew exponentially. Sometime in February, the director of curriculum announced that she had accepted a position as a consultant and would be leaving in early March. Within a couple of months, eight principals also submitted their resignations for various reasons. **(1.2) When the board confronted Carlos about his lack of progress on his goals from the previous year, Carlos became agitated and annoyed, once again citing that he knew what was best for this district.** Now it was May and it had become clear that Carlos was going to be removed by the Idlewood Board of Education. He found it disappointing that they didn't even wait to see what kinds of results he was able to get.

Domain 2.0:
Personal Behavior and Professional Ethics

Leaders in education demonstrate personal behaviors consistent with community values and ethics. They keep commitments, work with students, and act in service of the best interests of the students, staff, and community.

Scenario #8—Mike
2.0: Personal Behavior and Professional Ethics

Mike, a fourth-year principal at Thunder Ridge Elementary School, had just finished his final observation of the day. He was rather pleased. All of his observations had proved productive. The students in these classes were well behaved and on task and the lessons in all but one class were obviously well organized. He returned to his office and finalized his written notes and placed them in the four teacher's mailboxes, with a note requesting a meeting with him the next day before attending to other duties.

The following day, he met with all four teachers. The last two teacher conferences were like night and day. Mrs. Black, the former, was a veteran teacher of 15 years. She had established a routine that varied only slightly to adjust to student needs in each class. In Mike's mind, Mrs. Black was the ideal teacher. She had perfect control and inspired her students to learn. She rarely, if ever, had any discipline problems that she herself could not deal with in her classroom. As Mike completed his meeting with Mrs. Black, he did note that he failed to see her lesson plans for the week, or day for that matter. When Mike asked Mrs. Black about them, she proceeded to inform him that she kept daily lesson plans in an old logbook and very rarely consulted the book since she had her plans securely ingrained in her mind. Mike noted this and gave Mrs. Black an excellent review and a letter of commendation. Mike's last meeting was with Ms. White, a second-year teacher. For the most part, her students were well behaved and stayed on task. As Mike reviewed his notes, however, he expressed concern that Ms. White's class was not quite as organized as he would like to see. Furthermore, he had noticed that she had produced a sketchy set of lesson plans that did not follow the prescribed method set forth in the Thunder Ridge Teacher Handbook. Mike concluded the conference with Ms. White by suggesting she write up next week's lesson plans in the correct method and submit them to him in advance for his review. He noted this on the evaluation and gave her an average review.

Later that day, Ms. White returned to Mike's office. She was visibly upset. Mike had noticed that she was somewhat of a perfectionist and sensed that she was less than happy with her evaluation. Ms. White, however, confronted him with copies of both her and Mrs. Black's evaluations. Her argument was that Mike had obviously not been totally objective or consistent in his two reviews. Besides, Ms. White knew for a fact that Mrs. Black did not keep lesson plans, nor did she consult them for that matter and hadn't done so for several years. Furthermore, Mrs. Black, who was Ms. White's mentor, had actually told her that the lesson plans were only necessary for first-year teachers. Mrs. Black had also said that Mike rarely, if ever, considered them to be important. Mike was furious! First, he demanded to know how she had obtained a copy of Mrs. Black's evaluation. Second, he dismissed Mrs. Black's contention that lesson plans were not important as being an inaccurate interpretation. After all, they had a well-established policy in the school's handbook that addressed this issue. Last, he was openly critical of Ms. White's confrontation of him and questioning of his integrity. Mike wondered whether a letter in Ms. White's file documenting this affront was needed.

Peruse the MLP Matrix and assess Mike's performance in Domain 2.0: Personal Behavior and Professional Ethics. Make mental notes and be prepared to respond as to the reason for your score on that dimension. Please be prepared to report out in 15 minutes.

Scenario #8—Mike
2.0: Personal Behavior and Professional Ethics
NOT MEETING STANDARDS

Mike, a fourth-year principal at Thunder Ridge Elementary School, had just finished his final observation of the day. He was rather pleased. All of his observations had proved productive. The students in these classes were well behaved and on task and the lessons in all but one class were obviously well organized. He returned to his office and finalized his written notes and placed them in the four teacher's mailboxes, with a note requesting a meeting with him the next day before attending to other duties.

The following day, he met with all four teachers. The last two teacher conferences were like night and day. Mrs. Black, the former, was a veteran teacher of 15 years. She had established a routine that varied only slightly to adjust to student needs in each class. In Mike's mind, Mrs. Black was the ideal teacher. She had perfect control and inspired her students to learn. She rarely, if ever, had any discipline problems that she herself could not deal with in her classroom. As Mike completed his meeting with Mrs. Black, he did note that he failed to see her lesson plans for the week, or day for that matter. When Mike asked Mrs. Black about them, she proceeded to inform him that she kept daily lesson plans in an old logbook and very rarely consulted the book since she had her plans securely ingrained in her mind. Mike noted this and gave Mrs. Black an excellent review and a letter of commendation. Mike's last meeting was with Ms. White, a second-year teacher. For the most part, her students were well behaved and stayed on task. As Mike reviewed his notes, however, he expressed concern that Ms. White's class was not quite as organized as he would like to see. Furthermore, he had noticed that she had produced a sketchy set of lesson plans that did not follow the prescribed method set forth in the Thunder Ridge Teacher Handbook. Mike concluded the conference with Ms. White by suggesting she write up next week's lesson plans in the correct method and submit them to him in advance for his review. He noted this on the evaluation and gave her an average review.

Later that day, Ms. White returned to Mike's office. She was visibly upset. Mike had noticed that she was somewhat of a perfectionist and sensed that she was less than happy with her evaluation. Ms. White, however, confronted him with copies of both her and Mrs. Black's evaluations. **(2.1) Her argument was that Mike had obviously not been totally objective or consistent in his two reviews.** Besides, Ms. White knew for a fact that Mrs. Black did not keep lesson plans, nor did she consult them for that matter and hadn't done so for several years. Furthermore, Mrs. Black, who was Ms. White's mentor, had actually told her that the lesson plans were only necessary for first-year teachers. **(2.3) Mrs. Black had also said that Mike rarely, if ever, considered them to be important. (2.2) Mike was furious! First, he demanded to know how she had obtained a copy of Mrs. Black's evaluation. Second, he dismissed Mrs. Black's contention that lesson plans were not important as being an inaccurate interpretation. After all, they had a well-established policy in the school's handbook that addressed this issue. Last, he was openly critical of Ms. White's confrontation of him and questioning of his integrity. (2.4) Mike wondered whether a letter in Ms. White's file documenting this affront was needed.**

2.1: The fact that Mike violated his own values by not holding all teachers to the same set of standard practices greatly impacts his integrity. SCORE 2.1 AT NOT MEETING STANDARDS.

2.3: Mike's inconsistent treatment of these two teachers constitutes a violation of policy, even if unintentional. SCORE 2.3 AT NOT MEETING STANDARDS.

2.2: The leader loses his temper and is emotionally unstable. SCORE 2.2 AT NOT MEETING STANDARDS.

2.4: Mike's considering a letter of reprimand suggests that his desire is to suppress other points of view rather than inviting differences of opinion. SCORE 2.4 AT NOT MEETING STANDARDS.

Scenario #9—Luis
2.0: Personal Behavior and Professional Ethics

After school on Friday, Mack O'Brien, sixth-grade teacher at Rolling Hills, demanded a meeting with his assistant principal, Luis. Overhearing Mack's angry comments to his secretary, Luis came out to see what was so upsetting. When Mack tried to share his frustrations regarding his struggles with meeting the needs of his special education students, Luis, who was eager to head out for the weekend himself, told Mack to pack up his bag and head home for the weekend and that they would talk on Monday. As Mack walked out, Luis suggested that they meet early Monday morning at 7:30 a.m. and they could discuss his concerns.

At exactly 7:30 a.m., Mack was in the office and Luis had not arrived at school yet. Mack waited patiently and finally saw Luis enter the school at 7:45 a.m. carrying a fresh cup of coffee from a local shop. Luis smiled at Mack, never acknowledged that he was late, and invited Mack to come in his office. Mack stormed in, threw his books angrily onto his desk, and slumped into his seat. "I hope you had a great weekend, as mine was awful," he exclaimed. Luis looked up and saw his anger and frustration. "Now, Mack, what can be so wrong that a few days away from your students and teaching wouldn't cure?"

This comment infuriated Mack because he was genuinely seeking support and guidance from the assistant principal. Mack, no longer able to control his anger, began to attack Luis verbally, making comments about his lack of faculty support. Similarly, with each comment Mack made, Luis could feel his anger rising and could no longer contain his thoughts. In a very loud and sharp tone of voice, Luis challenged all of Mack's comments and told Mack that if he did not leave immediately, his evaluation would reflect this altercation. Just then, the bell rang signaling the start of class, so Mack picked up his bag and stomped out the door.

Following Mack's departure, Luis left his office and shared the entire conversation he had with Mack with his secretary, just as parents and staff were passing by the front office. He ended the conversation by saying, "Mack needs to retire, and he can no longer handle this job." Just then, the principal, having heard the comments, walked up and asked him to come into his office. Luis remained calm and shared how insubordinate Mack had been to him, taking no ownership in the altercation.

Peruse the MLP Matrix and assess Luis's performance in Domain 2.0: Personal Behavior and Professional Ethics. Make mental notes and be prepared to respond as to the reason for your score on that dimension. Please be prepared to report out in 15 minutes.

Scenario #9—Luis
2.0: Personal Behavior and Professional Ethics
NOT MEETING STANDARDS

2.1: Luis is not willing to take the time to listen to Mack's frustrations because he wants to go home. He puts off meeting with Mack until Monday, at which time he arrives late and thus has not honored his commitment. SCORE 2.1 AT NOT MEETING STANDARDS.

After school on Friday, Mack O'Brien, sixth-grade teacher at Rolling Hills, demanded a meeting with his assistant principal, Luis. Overhearing Mack's angry comments to his secretary, Luis came out to see what was so upsetting. When Mack tried to share his frustrations regarding his struggles with meeting the needs of his special education students, **(2.1) Luis, who was eager to head out for the weekend himself, told Mack to pack up his bag and head home for the weekend and that they would talk on Monday.** As Mack walked out, Luis suggested that they meet early Monday morning at 7:30 a.m. and they could discuss his concerns.

2.5: By arriving 15 minutes late for the meeting, Luis does not honor Mack's time. SCORE 2.5 AT NOT MEETING STANDARDS.

(2.5) At exactly 7:30 a.m., Mack was in the office and Luis had not arrived at school yet. Mack waited patiently and finally saw Luis enter the school at 7:45 a.m. carrying a fresh cup of coffee from a local shop. Luis smiled at Mack, never acknowledged that he was late, and invited Mack to come in his office. Mack stormed in, threw his books angrily onto his desk, and slumped into his seat. "I hope you had a great weekend, as mine was awful," he exclaimed. Luis looked up and saw his anger and frustration. **(2.4) "Now, Mack, what can be so wrong that a few days away from your students and teaching wouldn't cure?"**

2.4: Luis is not respectful in his comment back to Mack and discourages an open conversation. SCORE 2.4 AT NOT MEETING STANDARDS.

This comment infuriated Mack because he was genuinely seeking support and guidance from the assistant principal. Mack, no longer able to control his anger, began to attack Luis verbally, making comments about his lack of faculty support. **(2.2, 2.3) Similarly, with each comment Mack made, Luis could feel his anger rising and could no longer contain his thoughts. In a very loud and sharp tone of voice, Luis challenged all of Mack's comments and told Mack that if he did not leave immediately, his evaluation would reflect this altercation.** Just then, the bell rang signaling the start of class, so Mack picked up his bag and stomped out the door.

2.2: Luis loses his self-control and engages in an argument with Mack. SCORE 2.2 AT NOT MEETING STANDARDS.

Following Mack's departure, Luis left his office and shared the entire conversation he had with Mack with his secretary, just as parents and staff were passing by the front office. He ended the conversation by saying, "Mack needs to retire, and he can no longer handle this job." Just then, the principal, having heard the comments, walked up and asked him to come into his office. Luis remained calm and shared how insubordinate Mack had been to him, taking no ownership in the altercation.

2.3: In his anger, Luis threatens Mack and implies that his evaluation could be compromised, thus creating an even greater distance between them. SCORE 2.3 AT NOT MEETING STANDARDS.

Scenario # 10—Leslie
2.0: Personal Behavior and Professional Ethics

Leslie had just finished meeting with the parents at Broadway Middle School Back-to-School Night. This was her very first Back-to-School night as a principal at Broadway Middle School. As she was walking to her office to leave for the evening, a parent stopped her to thank her for her clear focus, always being visible, her well-articulated expectations, and her sense of urgency to improve behavior and academic achievement at this school. Broadway Middle School had not met Annual Yearly Progress standards for the last two years. The district hired Leslie to decrease the disciplinary referrals and to increase student achievement in the areas of reading and writing. Leslie, a veteran principal with 15 years of experience and success at another middle school in the district, was best known for closing the achievement gap for Latino and African-American males in the areas of literacy and mathematics. Leslie was not excited about leaving her previous school to come to Broadway Middle School. She felt as though she was punished for being successful.

The next day, Leslie had to deal with a discipline issue regarding two students who were involved in horseplay in the restroom. One of the students who was misbehaving in the restroom was the son of the parent who stopped to thank her the previous night at Back-to-School Night. Leslie immediately called the parents to discuss the incident and consequences with them. She shared with the parents at Back-to-School Night that she would always call parents whenever an issue arose, and that she believed communication and follow-through were imperative to improve the behavior of students. When Leslie called the parent to tell her that her son would have to serve a detention for his horseplay, the parent was furious, stating that the detention was not fair and the consequence was too severe. Leslie told the mother that she understood why she would be upset. Then she referred the parent to the school handbook where it stated the consequences for various infractions. The mother responded that she never received the school handbook. Leslie reminded the mother that she should have received one at Back-to-School night. She then told the mother that she would send one home with Michael, her son. Leslie restated that the detention was the proper consequence based on the school and district policy.

Leslie further explained to the mother that, as principal, it was her responsibility to ensure that the students were safe and that the mission of Broadway Middle School was achieved. She also invited the mother to schedule a meeting to discuss further her concerns about the severity of the consequence and the policies in the handbook. Leslie assured the mother that they would work as a team to ensure that Michael was successful. She also asked the mother if she had any suggestions about what could be done to improve the communication between parents and the school so that parents could know the expectations as well as the consequences when those expectations were not met.

Peruse the MLP Matrix and assess Leslie's performance in Domain 2.0: Personal Behavior and Professional Ethics. Make mental notes and be prepared to respond as to the reason for your score on that dimension. Please be prepared to report out in 15 minutes.

Scenario # 10—Leslie
2.0: Personal Behavior and Professional Ethics

PROFICIENT

Leslie had just finished meeting with the parents at Broadway Middle School Back-to-School Night. This was her very first Back-to-School night as a principal at Broadway Middle School. As she was walking to her office to leave for the evening, a parent stopped her to thank her for her clear focus, always being visible, her well-articulated expectations, and her sense of urgency to improve behavior and academic achievement at this school. Broadway Middle School had not met Annual Yearly Progress standards for the last two years. The district hired Leslie to decrease the disciplinary referrals and to increase student achievement in the areas of reading and writing. Leslie, a veteran principal with 15 years of experience and success at another middle school in the district, was best known for closing the achievement gap for Latino and African-American males in the areas of literacy and mathematics. Leslie was not excited about leaving her previous school to come to Broadway Middle School. She felt as though she was punished for being successful.

The next day, Leslie had to deal with a discipline issue regarding two students who were involved in horseplay in the restroom. One of the students who was misbehaving in the restroom was the son of the parent who stopped to thank her the previous night at Back-to-School Night. Leslie immediately called the parents to discuss the incident and consequences with them. **(2.1) She shared with the parents at Back-to-School Night that she would always call parents whenever an issue arose, and that she believed communication and follow-through were imperative to improve the behavior of students. When Leslie called the parent to tell her that her son would have to serve a detention for his horseplay, the parent was furious, stating that the detention was not fair and the consequence was too severe. (2.2) Leslie told the mother that she understood why she would be upset. Then she referred the parent to the school handbook where it stated the consequences for various infractions.** The mother responded that she never received the school handbook. Leslie reminded the mother that she should have received one at Back-to-School night. She then told the mother that she would send one home with Michael, her son. **(2.3) Leslie restated that the detention was the proper consequence based on the school and district policy.**

(2.4) Leslie further explained to the mother that, as principal, it was her responsibility to ensure that the students were safe and that the mission of Broadway Middle School was achieved. She also invited the mother to schedule a meeting to discuss further her concerns about the severity of the consequence and the policies in the handbook. Leslie assured the mother that they would work as a team to ensure that Michael was successful. **(2.5) She also asked the mother if she had any suggestions about what could be done to improve the communication between parents and the school so that parents could know the expectations as well as the consequences when those expectations were not met.**

2.1: Leslie meets commitments. Verbal commitments have the same weight as written commitments. She immediately called Michael's mother. SCORE 2.1 AT PROFICIENT.

2.2: Leslie dealt with the furious mother with dignity and self-control. Leslie defuses the confrontational situation with emotional intelligence by referring the mother to the school handbook. SCORE 2.2 AT PROFICIENT.

2.3: The consequence does not cross the line in terms of the handbook's policy. SCORE 2.3 AT PROFICIENT.

2.4: Leslie focuses on achieving the school's mission. She invites the mother to discuss her concerns. Leslie values differences in points of views. SCORE 2.4 AT PROFICIENT.

2.5: Leslie is willing to listen and respect others in planned and unplanned meetings. She believes in engaging others in meaningful dialogue. SCORE 2.5 AT PROFICIENT.

Scenario #11—Jason
2.0: Personal Behavior and Professional Ethics

Running a large rural high school was a dream job for Jason. When he was first named as the new principal of Sunset Ridge High School two years ago, Jason felt that he finally had the opportunity to steer the ship in the direction he wanted. Prior to serving as principal, Jason spent nearly five years as the assistant principal of Sunset Ridge. The first two years Jason spent adjusting the sails, since he didn't always agree with the previous principal's decisions. He regularly received positive feedback from the community and staff about his commitment to the school and felt strongly that the school was now positioned well in terms of its reputation among rural high schools.

This year, Jason was taking things to a new level with the school improvement plan. In the past, Jason had maintained the same school leadership structure that was put into place by the previous principal, mostly because he didn't want to rock the boat too much in his new role. He was now ready to engage the staff and community more fully in a more authentic input process. His intent was to use a new representative leadership team to brainstorm strategies for the school improvement plan. Jason was incredibly excited about the potential of this new structure, having selected just the right leaders for the team.

The first two leadership team meetings went smoothly. Jason arrived early, fully prepared with agenda and materials. The team members were excited about the opportunity to have input into the school improvement plan for the first time. Jason invited diverse opinions during the brainstorming process, and everyone was feeling positive about the meetings. He was prepared for each meeting with background knowledge that the team members would need to understand current student achievement and analyze potential causes. Team members freely shared ideas back and forth between their representative groups and the leadership team and reported that they were honored that Jason was so open to listening to their concerns and ideas.

During the third meeting of the year, a situation erupted that seemed to derail the process. The group had worked through the data analysis and had successfully set a few specific goals for the plan. When the conversations shifted to strategies, a philosophical battle between Jason and several of the department leaders escalated into an aggressive shouting match between Jason and the others. Given the fact that a parent representative was in the room, Jason felt it was necessary to demonstrate his command over the situation publicly, so that the parent would not feel he had lost control of his own staff. Given previous experiences in similar situations, Jason was careful not to reprimand the teachers publicly, but did make it clear that he disagreed with their opinions based on his knowledge of research-based practices.

When the teachers spoke privately with Jason later, they felt compelled to remind him that he had asked for diverse opinions during their first meeting. Jason redirected the teachers to the school's decision-making matrix to remind them that he would make final decisions about instructional programs ultimately, and the action plan discussion fell into the instructional program arena. Jason stood his ground on principle, explaining that unless the group could come to some consensus on research-based practices, he would be making the final decision about the particular action step they were stuck on as a group.

From that point forward, the leadership team meetings remained much more controlled. Opinions and ideas continued to be freely offered. However, the staff began to view these meetings as simply an opportunity to speak, not a real opportunity to participate in the decision-making process. Jason felt better about the level of control in the meetings, but continued to feel that the leadership meetings were not getting at the kind of ownership for the school improvement plan that he wanted. In the interest of getting through the year with less chaos, Jason took over more of the actual writing of the school improvement plan and just used the group to provide feedback until the plan was finalized.

Peruse the MLP Matrix and assess Jason's performance in Domain 2.0: Personal Behavior and Professional Ethics. Make mental notes and be prepared to respond as to the reason for your score on that dimension. Please be prepared to report out in 15 minutes.

Scenario #11—Jason
2.0: Personal Behavior and Professional Ethics

PROGRESSING

Running a large rural high school was a dream job for Jason. When he was first named as the new principal of Sunset Ridge High School two years ago, Jason felt that he finally had the opportunity to steer the ship in the direction he wanted. Prior to serving as principal, Jason spent nearly five years as the assistant principal of Sunset Ridge. The first two years Jason spent adjusting the sails, since he didn't always agree with the previous principal's decisions. He regularly received positive feedback from the community and staff about his commitment to the school and felt strongly that the school was now positioned well in terms of its reputation among rural high schools.

This year, Jason was taking things to a new level with the school improvement plan. In the past, Jason had maintained the same school leadership structure that was put into place by the previous principal, mostly because he didn't want to rock the boat too much in his new role. He was now ready to engage the staff and community more fully in a more authentic input process. His intent was to use a new representative leadership team to brainstorm strategies for the school improvement plan. Jason was incredibly excited about the potential of this new structure, having selected just the right leaders for the team.

(2.5) The first two leadership team meetings went smoothly. Jason arrived early, fully prepared with agenda and materials. The team members were excited about the opportunity to have input into the school improvement plan for the first time. **(2.5)** Jason invited diverse opinions during the brainstorming process, and everyone was feeling positive about the meetings. He was prepared for each meeting with background knowledge that the team members would need to understand current student achievement and analyze potential causes. Team members freely shared ideas back and forth between their representative groups and the leadership team and reported that they were honored that Jason was so open to listening to their concerns and ideas.

During the third meeting of the year, a situation erupted that seemed to derail the process. The group had worked through the data analysis and had successfully set a few specific goals for the plan. **(2.2, 2.3)** When the conversations shifted to strategies, a philosophical battle between Jason and several of the department leaders escalated into an aggressive shouting match between Jason and the others. Given the fact that a parent representative was in the room, Jason felt it was necessary to demonstrate his command over the situation publicly, so that the parent would not feel he had lost control of his own staff. Given previous experiences in similar situations, Jason was careful not to reprimand the teachers publicly, but did make it clear that he disagreed with their opinions based on his knowledge of research-based practices.

(2.1) When the teachers spoke privately with Jason later, they felt compelled to remind him that he had asked for diverse opinions during their first meeting. Jason redirected the teachers to the school's decision-making matrix to remind them that he would make final decisions about instructional programs

2.5: Jason arrives early and is fully prepared for the meetings. SCORE 2.5 AT PROFICIENT.

2.5: Jason encourages diverse opinions, brings knowledge, and offers resources to support team's decisions. Team members feel encouraged to share opinions. SCORE 2.5 AT PROFICIENT.

2.2: Jason demonstrates aggressive behavior when a philosophical disagreement erupts. SCORE 2.2 AT PROGRESSING.

2.3: Although Jason is aggressive, he does not cross the line into illegal or unethical behavior when he makes the decision not to reprimand the teachers publicly. SCORE 2.3 AT PROFICIENT.

2.1: Jason refers to written commitments as the reference for such actions over the verbal commitment that teachers felt he expressed during the meeting. SCORE 2.1 AT PROGRESSING.

CASE STUDY MATERIALS AND LEARNING EXPERIENCES

2.4: Jason does not punish alternative points of view, but he does not encourage developing the ideas that are shared, and ultimately he alone makes the final decisions. SCORE 2.4 AT PROGRESSING.

ultimately, and the action plan discussion fell into the instructional program arena. Jason stood his ground on principle, explaining that unless the group could come to some consensus on research-based practices, he would be making the final decision about the particular action step they were stuck on as a group.

From that point forward, the leadership team meetings remained much more controlled. **(2.4)** Opinions and ideas continued to be freely offered. However, the staff began to view these meetings as simply an opportunity to speak, not a real opportunity to participate in the decision-making process. Jason felt better about the level of control in the meetings, but continued to feel that the leadership meetings were not getting at the kind of ownership for the school improvement plan that he wanted. In the interest of getting through the year with less chaos, Jason took over more of the actual writing of the school improvement plan and just used the group to provide feedback until the plan was finalized.

Scenario #12—Jerry
2.0: Personal Behavior and Professional Ethics

Jerry was recently hired to join a large suburban school district as the director of transportation. Prior to this position, Jerry had been the assistant director of transportation in a neighboring school district that was half the size of his new district. While Jerry was very excited about his position, he was under a lot of pressure to perform well and the stress was causing him many restless nights.

Just into his third month, late in the day on Friday, a middle school principal contacted him about a persistent student and parent concern regarding one of their bus drivers. Jerry listened, took a few notes, and told the principal that he would work on the issue and get back with her the following week. Jerry put the notes on his desk and left for the weekend. Feeling frustrated after not hearing from Jerry in more than two weeks, the principal once again contacted the transportation office and this time was put on hold and then told to call Jerry back the following Monday, at which time he should have time to talk to her. Jerry once again looked at the note with every intent to get back to it later in the day, but other issues kept him from attending to this issue.

When Monday came around, Jerry once again did not make himself available to talk with the principal, as he knew that he had not had time to investigate the issue with the bus driver. This time the principal had had enough and decided to call Jerry's supervisor to complain about his lack of follow-through and ability to solve an issue in a timely manner. Jerry was immediately called into his supervisor's office, whereby he shared that he had been working on the issue and promised that he would get back to the principal immediately. Jerry left the office livid at the principal for calling his supervisor and drove directly to the school and demanded to see the principal.

The principal was glad to see Jerry and hopeful that the situation would soon be resolved. She invited Jerry into her office, where Jerry refused to sit down and began to holler at the principal for contacting his supervisor. Seeing that Jerry was visibly upset and exhausted, the principal tried to calmly explain her concerns in hopes they could work together to resolve the issue. Jerry proceeded to raise his voice again and give excuses for not getting back with her the previous week. When it was obvious that the conversation was not going to be resolved and that Jerry was in no state of mind to listen, the principal asked him to leave, noting that it was obvious that they were not going to resolve anything that day and that they both needed time away to reflect upon what to do next. Jerry left with no further comment.

The following week, the principal was contacted by one of her principal colleagues who asked her what had happened between her and the new director of transportation. She had heard from her bus driver that the two of them had had an argument. The principal, understandably upset, called her director.

Peruse the MLP Matrix and assess Jerry's performance in Domain 2.0: Personal Behavior and Professional Ethics. Make mental notes and be prepared to respond as to the reason for your score on that dimension. Please be prepared to report out in 15 minutes.

Scenario #12—Jerry
2.0: Personal Behavior and Professional Ethics
NOT MEETING STANDARDS

Jerry was recently hired to join a large suburban school district as the director of transportation. Prior to this position, Jerry had been the assistant director of transportation in a neighboring school district that was half the size of his new district. While Jerry was very excited about his position, he was under a lot of pressure to perform well and the stress was causing him many restless nights.

Just into his third month, late in the day on Friday, a middle school principal contacted him about a persistent student and parent concern regarding one of their bus drivers. **(2.1) Jerry listened, took a few notes, and told the principal that he would work on the issue and get back with her the following week. Jerry put the notes on his desk and left for the weekend. Feeling frustrated after not hearing from Jerry in more than two weeks,** the principal once again contacted the transportation office and this time was put on hold and then told to call Jerry back the following Monday, at which time he should have time to talk to her. **(2.5) Jerry once again looked at the note with every intent to get back to it later in the day, but other issues kept him from attending to this issue.**

When Monday came around, **(2.1) Jerry once again did not make himself available to talk with the principal, as he knew that he had not had time to investigate the issue with the bus driver.** This time the principal had had enough and decided to call Jerry's supervisor to complain about his lack of follow-through and ability to solve an issue in a timely manner. **(2.4) Jerry was immediately called into his supervisor's office, whereby he shared that he had been working on the issue and promised that he would get back to the principal immediately. Jerry left the office livid at the principal for calling his supervisor and drove directly to the school and demanded to see the principal.**

The principal was glad to see Jerry and hopeful that the situation would soon be resolved. She invited Jerry into her office, where **(2.2) Jerry refused to sit down and began to holler at the principal for contacting his supervisor.** Seeing that Jerry was visibly upset and exhausted, the principal tried to calmly explain her concerns in hopes they could work together to resolve the issue. **(2.1) Jerry proceeded to raise his voice again and give excuses for not getting back with her the previous week. (2.4) When it was obvious that the conversation was not going to be resolved and that Jerry was in no state of mind to listen,** the principal asked him to leave, noting that it was obvious that they were not going to resolve anything that day and that they both needed time away to reflect upon what to do next. Jerry left with no further comment.

(2.3) The following week, the principal was contacted by one of her principal colleagues who asked her what had happened between her and the new director of transportation. She had heard from her bus driver that the two of them had had an argument. The principal, understandably upset, called her director.

2.1: Jerry does not follow through with the request and, after two weeks, the principal has to take the initiative to check back with Jerry. SCORE 2.1 AT NOT MEETING STANDARDS.

2.5: By not following up with the principal, Jerry is not honoring the time-sensitive issue and concerns. SCORE 2.5 AT NOT MEETING STANDARDS.

2.1: Jerry continues not to follow through with the principal's request to investigate the issue. SCORE 2.1 AT NOT MEETING STANDARDS.

2.4: In his anger, Jerry cannot see or hear the principal's concerns about Jerry's reluctance to get back with her in a timely manner regarding the issue. SCORE 2.4 AT NOT MEETING STANDARDS.

2.2: Jerry loses his temper with the principal and is emotionally upset. SCORE 2.2 AT NOT MEETING STANDARDS.

2.1: Jerry continues to raise his voice and gives excuses that are unacceptable. SCORE 2.1 AT NOT MEETING STANDARDS.

2.4: Jerry is not open to listening to the principal. SCORE 2.4 AT NOT MEETING STANDARDS.

2.3: Jerry violated the relationship between himself and the principal by sharing privileged information with another colleague. SCORE 2.3 AT NOT MEETING STANDARDS.

Scenario #13—Sharon
2.0: Personal Behavior and Professional Ethics

Human resource administrator Sharon has been in her position for five years in the Indian Creek School District. As human resource administrator, one of her responsibilities is to lead the district advisory council. The Indian Creek School District human relations department has a monthly forum for staff members to voice their concerns regarding nonacademic policies, practices, and procedures in order to improve communication between teachers and administrators for furthering quality education. The forum also allows teachers and administrators to identify concerns and attempt to resolve conflict within the workplace. Sharon fosters healthy relationships by honoring her word and following through on her commitments. She is always present at the monthly DAC meetings and believes in starting and ending meetings on time.

Oftentimes at these meetings, staff members can share their concerns anonymously, which sometimes leads to cynicism and negative comments directed toward district personnel.

The meeting began with Sharon greeting the staff members and thanking them for attending. Sharon then reviewed the professional meeting norms. Then Sharon collected the staff concerns and praises, and began reading the praises. After the praises were read, she then read the main concern—the newly adopted evaluation system for teachers and administrators that includes a point system for merit pay. The staff members were upset because they believe that the system is too subjective and that the merit pay philosophy is punitive. As others gave input, the concern got personal and heated. Sharon remained calm and centered as she stated the facts with respect and dignity. She defused the angry comments by sharing the rationale behind the decision to adopt the merit pay evaluation point system. She also shared the district data to support the decision of implementing the new evaluation system. Sharon referred to the Indiana State policy on merit pay and explained to the DAC attendees that the district had adopted the policy in its true form and, by so doing, it did not cross the line of the state policy.

As the meeting concluded, Sharon thanked the attendees for voicing their concerns about the new evaluation system and assured the teachers and administrators that the evaluation system would support the mission and vision of Indian Creek School District. Sharon continued her closing remarks to the staff by offering her support to any teacher or administrator as they prepared for the implementation of the evaluation system. She stated her willingness to meet with schools, departments, or individual teachers. Sharon knows the importance of immediate feedback, so prior to leaving for the evening she wrote a summary of the meeting to disseminate to all staff first thing the next morning.

Peruse the MLP Matrix and assess Sharon's performance in Domain 2.0: Personal Behavior and Professional Ethics. Make mental notes and be prepared to respond as to the reason for your score on that dimension. Please be prepared to report out in 15 minutes.

Scenario #13—Sharon
2.0: Personal Behavior and Professional Ethics

PROFICIENT

2.1: Sharon attends every meeting and believes in starting and ending on time. Her verbal commitments have the same weight as written commitments. SCORE 2.1 AT PROFICIENT.

2.2: Sharon deals with the attacks regarding this sensitive subject with dignity and self-control.

The leader never meets anger with anger: instead, she remains calm and centered. SCORE 2.2 AT PROFICIENT.

2.3: Sharon does not cross the line of state policy. There are no instances of illegal or unethical conduct with employees or the policy. SCORE 2.3 AT PROFICIENT.

2.4: Sharon focuses on achieving the mission and vision of the school district. SCORE 2.4 AT PROFICIENT.

2.5: Sharon offered support to the teachers and administrators. She acknowledged their concerns and showed them respect during the meeting. SCORE 2.5 AT PROFICIENT.

Human resource administrator Sharon has been in her position for five years in the Indian Creek School District. As human resource administrator, one of her responsibilities is to lead the district advisory council. The Indian Creek School District human relations department has a monthly forum for staff members to voice their concerns regarding nonacademic policies, practices, and procedures in order to improve communication between teachers and administrators for furthering quality education. The forum also allows teachers and administrators to identify concerns and attempt to resolve conflict within the workplace. **(2.1) Sharon fosters healthy relationships by honoring her word and following through on her commitments. She is always present at the monthly DAC meetings and believes in starting and ending meetings on time.**

Oftentimes at these meetings, staff members can share their concerns anonymously, which sometimes leads to cynicism and negative comments directed toward district personnel.

The meeting began with Sharon greeting the staff members and thanking them for attending. Sharon then reviewed the professional meeting norms. Then Sharon collected the staff concerns and praises, and began reading the praises. After the praises were read, she then read the main concern—the newly adopted evaluation system for teachers and administrators that includes a point system for merit pay. The staff members were upset because they believe that the system is too subjective and that the merit pay philosophy is punitive. As others gave input, the concern got personal and heated. **(2.2) Sharon remained calm and centered as she stated the facts with respect and dignity. She defused the angry comments by sharing the rationale behind the decision to adopt the merit pay evaluation point system. She also shared the district data to support the decision of implementing the new evaluation system. (2.3) Sharon referred to the Indiana State policy on merit pay and explained to the DAC attendees that the district had adopted the policy in its true form and, by so doing, it did not cross the line of the state policy.**

As the meeting concluded, **(2.4) Sharon thanked the attendees for voicing their concerns about the new evaluation system and assured the teachers and administrators that the evaluation system would support the mission and vision of Indian Creek School District. (2.5) Sharon continued her closing remarks to the staff by offering her support to any teacher or administrator as they prepared for the implementation of the evaluation system. She stated her willingness to meet with schools, departments, or individual teachers.** Sharon knows the importance of immediate feedback, so prior to leaving for the evening she wrote a summary of the meeting to disseminate to all staff first thing the next morning.

Scenario #14—Juliana
2.0: Personal Behavior and Professional Ethics

Juliana dreamed of becoming a superintendent from the time she first entered the administrative ranks 10 years ago. She had certainly earned the title after demonstrating successful leadership as an assistant principal, principal, district director, and chief academic officer. Now her time had arrived and she was excited to make a difference in the Waterfront School District. Juliana was well aware that board relationships could be tricky, so she intentionally set out to ensure she built a strong relationship with board members as a group and individually. Regardless of the warnings she received during her superintendent licensure program, she knew that meeting one on one with board members was the right thing to do if she wanted to build trust.

The board had given Juliana a clear directive when they hired her. They realized that progress had been stalled for the past five years at Waterfront and valuable time had been wasted. On that point, the entire board could agree. However, how to get things moving became a matter of personal opinion, and Juliana found herself juggling seven different personal agendas all at once. On several occasions, Juliana found herself feeling unsure of what she had agreed to after private sessions with board members. In the interest of keeping the peace and the board members happy, Juliana often told board members what good ideas they had, but then "massaged" the ideas so that they seemed more acceptable by all when written plans were developed.

When the board's ideas moved into an arena that seemed "below the line" to the assistant superintendent, he approached Juliana with the concern. Juliana reminded him that the position of superintendent was highly political and that she was managing the situation carefully. Since his concern was with regard to some individual board members' push for a completely new approach to mathematics, he felt compelled to remind Juliana of the results they were getting with the current program and the strain it would put on the system to implement something new just because it was part of a personal agenda for a few board members.

Juliana became argumentative with the assistant superintendent, sarcastically stating, "It is easy for you to criticize when you aren't the one sitting in the superintendent's chair." She also reminded him that she had more experience as an administrator than he and could navigate the political waters more deftly. Juliana left the conversation, annoyed that he would bring this up with her at a time when she was working so hard to manage the various personalities on the board.

Given the assistant superintendent's comment, Juliana decided it would be a good idea to bring together district leaders to review mathematics data and give some feedback about whether a new math program was in order. At the meeting, she told the group that she welcomed their ideas and wanted to weigh the push from the board members against the need for the change. She included one board member in the meeting so that he could hear what they had to say. After the meeting, she met privately with the board member to ask his opinion of the day's feedback session. He acknowledged that there was data to support that the current math program was working, but it didn't fit the philosophical framework that parents in the community were advancing. When Juliana agreed that perhaps a new math program would make the community happier with the district, he felt confident that she was ready to move forward with the new initiative.

At the next board meeting, Juliana presented the board with a plan for implementing a new approach to mathematics. She decided she would deal with the pushback from principals and other district leaders by telling everyone that the board was demanding this change. Most board members lacked the detailed knowledge about either the previous math program or the proposed new program, and the resulting vote was 6–1, in favor of the new math program.

Peruse the MLP Matrix and assess Juliana's performance in Domain 2.0: Personal Behavior and Professional Ethics. Make mental notes and be prepared to respond as to the reason for your score on that dimension. Please be prepared to report out in 15 minutes.

Scenario #14—Juliana
2.0: Personal Behavior and Professional Ethics

PROGRESSING

Juliana dreamed of becoming a superintendent from the time she first entered the administrative ranks 10 years ago. She had certainly earned the title after demonstrating successful leadership as an assistant principal, principal, district director, and chief academic officer. Now her time had arrived and she was excited to make a difference in the Waterfront School District. Juliana was well aware that board relationships could be tricky, so she intentionally set out to ensure she built a strong relationship with board members as a group and individually. Regardless of the warnings she received during her superintendent licensure program, she knew that meeting one on one with board members was the right thing to do if she wanted to build trust.

The board had given Juliana a clear directive when they hired her. They realized that progress had been stalled for the past five years at Waterfront and valuable time had been wasted. On that point, the entire board could agree. However, how to get things moving became a matter of personal opinion, and Juliana found herself juggling seven different personal agendas all at once. **(2.1)** On several occasions, Juliana found herself feeling unsure of what she had agreed to after private sessions with board members. In the interest of keeping the peace and the board members happy, Juliana often told board members what good ideas they had, but then "massaged" the ideas so that they seemed more acceptable by all when written plans were developed.

When the board's ideas moved into an arena that seemed "below the line" to the assistant superintendent, he approached Juliana with the concern. Juliana reminded him that the position of superintendent was highly political and that she was managing the situation carefully. Since his concern was with regard to some individual board members' push for a completely new approach to mathematics, he felt compelled to remind Juliana of the results they were getting with the current program and the strain it would put on the system to implement something new just because it was part of a personal agenda for a few board members.

(2.2) Juliana became argumentative with the assistant superintendent, sarcastically stating, "It is easy for you to criticize when you aren't the one sitting in the superintendent's chair." **(2.3)** She also reminded him that she had more experience as an administrator than he and could navigate the political waters more deftly. Juliana left the conversation, annoyed that he would bring this up with her at a time when she was working so hard to manage the various personalities on the board.

Given the assistant superintendent's comment, **(2.4)** Juliana decided it would be a good idea to bring together district leaders to review mathematics data and give some feedback about whether a new math program was in order. At the meeting, she told the group that she welcomed their ideas and wanted to weigh the push from the board members against the need for the change. She included one board member in the meeting so that he could hear what they had to say. After the meeting, she met privately with the board member

---

2.1: Juliana does not demonstrate that verbal agreements hold the same weight as written agreements and ultimately manipulates agreements in written form in an attempt to please all.
SCORE 2.1 AT PROGRESSING.

2.2: Juliana speaks to the assistant superintendent in a demeaning manner, which may cause reluctance to raise issues on future occasions.
SCORE 2.2 AT PROGRESSING.

2.3: Although Juliana's comment is demeaning, it does not cross the line in terms of policy or law.
SCORE 2.3 AT PROFICIENT.

2.4: Juliana encourages alternative points of view. However, she does not really consider them in her final decision.
SCORE 2.4 AT PROGRESSING.

2.5: Juliana is on time and fully prepared for meetings. She encourages diverse opinions in the context of this meeting as well as the meeting with district leaders, but does not engage these diverse opinions in a meaningful or consistent manner. SCORE 2.5 AT PROGRESSING.

to ask his opinion of the day's feedback session. He acknowledged that there was data to support that the current math program was working, but it didn't fit the philosophical framework that parents in the community were advancing. When Juliana agreed that perhaps a new math program would make the community happier with the district, he felt confident that she was ready to move forward with the new initiative.

At the next board meeting, Juliana presented the board with a plan for implementing a new approach to mathematics. **(2.5)** She decided she would deal with the pushback from principals and other district leaders by telling everyone that the board was demanding this change. Most board members lacked the detailed knowledge about either the previous math program or the proposed new program, and the resulting vote was 6–1, in favor of the new math program.

Domain 3.0:
Student Achievment

Leaders in education make student learning their top priority. They direct energy and resources toward data analysis for instructional improvement and the development and implementation of quality standards-based curricula, and they evaluate, monitor, and provide feedback to staff on instructional delivery.

Scenario #15—Marek
3.0: Student Achievement

Marek is a principal at Range View Elementary and is held in high esteem by his colleagues throughout the district and, specifically, in his Mark Twain feeder area. As a result of the successes his school has experienced over the past five years, his peers seek him out for advice. Marek is known for his ability to research best practices that align with his students' needs and is not enamored by the latest instructional fad or program. Marek views his staff as leaders and decision makers in his school and knows the power of their influence on student learning, behavior, and motivation.

As a tenured principal in his feeder area, Marek is keenly aware of the significant high school dropout rates. He is concerned that if his Title I school fails to engage and excite students in taking ownership of their learning, the majority will become part of the district dropout statistics. Eighty-five percent of his students are on free and reduced lunch and 58 percent are minority students from families with limited English speaking.

When accepting the principalship, Marek knew it was going to be one of the most challenging opportunities in his career and he was committed to doing whatever it took to turn the school around. Knowing the federal and state demands placed on his learning community and leadership, he set out to improve student achievement for all students and specifically to close the gap between his highest- and lowest-performing students. With his staff and community, a five-year plan was developed that included a strong focus on professional development targeting the "unwrapping" of Power Standards (a process to identify the concepts and skills found in both the standards and the indicators to determine what students need to know and be able to do). His staff prioritized their goals and participated in Data Teams (PLCs) to ensure that instructional leadership decisions were made based on relevant and timely achievement data from multiple sources. Additionally, they documented the relationship between the actions of the teachers (cause data) and the achievement of students (effect data). Teachers worked in teams to score student work as a means to refine their skills of inter-rater reliability and posted examples of student work based on each standard proficiency level. While Marek knew the impact of his decisions on his learning community, he led with his heart as well as his head and used collaborative decision-making processes to ensure his staff had a voice in establishing goals based on student needs.

For the past five years, Range View Elementary has seen student performance gains in all content areas. In their fourth year, they outperformed their demographics so dramatically that state assessments showed improvement in all second through fifth grades in math, writing, and reading. Students showed an average gain of 45 percent in proficient or advanced scorings from previous years. As Marek and his staff disaggregated the data, it was clear that their performance gap was closing and their transient and ESL populations were also improving dramatically. The local newspaper published an article that acknowledged Marek and his staff for commitment to student achievement in their feeder area.

In the privacy of his office, when his supervisor asked him what he needed to do to sustain this effort, he shared that his staff needed to refine their Data Teams process to ensure that 100 percent of their time remained focused on student achievement. Additionally, they needed to move from monthly reporting of student achievement data to biweekly reporting. His supervisor also asked Marek if he would be willing to share his five-year plan and success data with his peers at their next principal meeting, and he respectfully declined, stating, "My time needs to be focused on the work of my building."

Peruse the MLP Matrix and assess Marek's performance in Domain 3.0: Student Achievement. Make mental notes and be prepared to respond as to the reason for your score on that dimension. Please be prepared to report out in 15 minutes.

Scenario #15—Marek
3.0: Student Achievement

PROFICIENT

Marek is a principal at Range View Elementary and is held in high esteem by his colleagues throughout the district and, specifically, in his Mark Twain feeder area. As a result of the successes his school has experienced over the past five years, his peers seek him out for advice. Marek is known for his ability to research best practices that align with his students' needs and is not enamored by the latest instructional fad or program. Marek views his staff as leaders and decision makers in his school and knows the power of their influence on student learning, behavior, and motivation.

As a tenured principal in his feeder area, Marek is keenly aware of the significant high school dropout rates. He is concerned that if his Title I school fails to engage and excite students in taking ownership of their learning, the majority will become part of the district dropout statistics. Eighty-five percent of his students are on free and reduced lunch and 58 percent are minority students from families with limited English speaking.

When accepting the principalship, Marek knew it was going to be one of the most challenging opportunities in his career and he was committed to doing whatever it took to turn the school around. Knowing the federal and state demands placed on his learning community and leadership, he set out to improve student achievement for all students and specifically to close the gap between his highest- and lowest-performing students. **(3.5) With his staff and community, a five-year plan was developed that included a strong focus on professional development targeting the "unwrapping" of Power Standards (a process to identify the concepts and skills found in both the standards and the indicators to determine what students need to know and be able to do). (3.3) His staff prioritized their goals and participated in Data Teams (PLCs) to ensure that instructional leadership decisions were made based on relevant and timely achievement data from multiple sources. (3.1) Additionally, they documented the relationship between the actions of the teachers (cause data) and the achievement of students (effect data). (3.4) Teachers worked in teams to score student work as a means to refine their skills of inter-rater reliability and posted examples of student work based on each standard proficiency level.** While Marek knew the impact of his decisions on his learning community, he led with his heart as well as his head and used collaborative decision-making processes to ensure his staff had a voice in establishing goals based on student needs.

(3.2) For the past five years, Range View Elementary has seen student performance gains in all content areas. In their fourth year, they outperformed their demographics so dramatically that state assessments showed improvement in all second through fifth grades in math, writing, and reading. Students showed an average gain of 45 percent in proficient or advanced scorings from previous years. As Marek and his staff disaggregated the data, it was clear that their performance gap was closing and their transient and ESL populations were also improving dramatically.

3.5: Standards have been analyzed and translated into what students need to know and be able to do. They are widely shared by all staff.
SCORE 3.5 AT PROFICIENT.

3.3: Marek empowered his staff to set goals and make decisions based on student achievement data from multiple sources.
SCORE 3.3 AT PROFICIENT.

3.1: At Range View, Marek and his staff look at the relationship between actions and student achievement.
SCORE 3.1 AT PROFICIENT.

3.4: Teachers worked in teams to score student work and to review based on proficiency levels on standards.
SCORE 3.4 AT PROFICIENT.

3.2: There is evidence of consistent improvement across multiple indicators. Data shows Range View is closing the achievement gap, and the use of previous and current data is used to continually challenge his staff and students.
SCORE 3.2 AT EXEMPLARY.

CASE STUDY MATERIALS AND LEARNING EXPERIENCES

The local newspaper published an article that acknowledged Marek and his staff for commitment to student achievement in their feeder area.

In the privacy of his office, when his supervisor asked him what he needed to do to sustain this effort, he shared that his staff needed to refine their Data Teams process to ensure that 100 percent of their time remained focused on student achievement. Additionally, they needed to move from monthly reporting of student achievement data to biweekly reporting. His supervisor also asked Marek if he would be willing to share his five-year plan and success data with his peers at their next principal meeting, and he respectfully declined, stating, "My time needs to be focused on the work of my building."

Scenario #16—Silas
3.0: Student Achievement

Silas was recently appointed assistant principal at Marten Elementary School when the school moved to a four-track calendar. The superintendent made the decision as a result of rapid growth in the area and the overcrowding of classrooms and common areas when all students were in school. Prior to taking this position, Silas had no year-round school experience. He was hired due to his exemplary teaching practices, which had led to significant achievement gains for his students over the past five years. His new principal was so busy dealing with unhappy parents and four-track logistics, that she asked Silas to take charge of the school improvement planning for the year.

Eager to begin, Silas reviewed the school and state achievement data for his new building and was beginning to see trends in student achievement at each grade level. Having previously only used disaggregated data in his own classroom, he was uncertain of how to link school-wide data to their decision-making framework. Knowing the standards for each grade level, Silas decided to start out by making sure that his staff had the required trainings they needed to implement the standards across the curriculum successfully. He discussed the school and district results, but did not link the data to their standards work and professional development efforts. The school data showed a three-year decline in writing performance. He went on to ask his staff to share professional development topics they wanted to see addressed throughout the year and was surprised when writing was not a topic of focus.

The week following, Silas used a faculty meeting to review the student achievement data and to communicate the goals he had developed. Staff shared that they felt they had too many goals and standards to teach and did not know how to go about prioritizing their standards and working as grade-level teams to plan instruction. With this information, Silas knew he would focus professional development time around prioritizing standards and using assessment to guide instructional decisions. He would begin by bringing in outside consultants to teach structures and practices that would be used during Data Team (PLC) meetings to help his staff focus on their new writing goals.

Teachers felt that Silas had heard their concerns and were excited about the implementation of Data Teams. Additionally, they were very open to using monthly planning time to implement the structure within their grade levels. Silas monitored the efforts by conducting monthly walk-throughs and giving teachers feedback on their instructional practices and use of the standards. While he saw that teachers made changes slowly, there was evidence of a greater focus on the standards. For the first time, teachers and students were working together to align standards and grade-level course objectives.

Over the course of the year, while teachers could see only minor improvement in test results on writing, they could see improvement in student attitudes toward school and daily work. Silas made sure to celebrate even the small gains and to acknowledge staff publicly for their commitment to their improvement efforts. At the end of the year, he invited input and suggestions from staff and from parents on his building accountability committee and used the data to help revise their school improvement plan and to inform their goals for the following year. In his final review with his principal, Silas acknowledged he had grown significantly this year and that he would use the data he received from her and the staff to set his goals for the next year.

Peruse the MLP Matrix and assess Silas's performance in Domain 3.0: Student Achievement. Make mental notes and be prepared to respond as to the reason for your score on that dimension. Please be prepared to report out in 15 minutes.

Scenario #16—Silas
3.0: Student Achievement

PROGRESSING

Silas was recently appointed assistant principal at Marten Elementary School when the school moved to a four-track calendar. The superintendent made the decision as a result of rapid growth in the area and the overcrowding of classrooms and common areas when all students were in school. Prior to taking this position, Silas had no year-round school experience. He was hired due to his exemplary teaching practices, which had led to significant achievement gains for his students over the past five years. His new principal was so busy dealing with unhappy parents and four-track logistics, that she asked Silas to take charge of the school improvement planning for the year.

Eager to begin, Silas reviewed the school and state achievement data for his new building and was beginning to see trends in student achievement at each grade level. Having previously only used disaggregated data in his own classroom, he was uncertain of how to link school-wide data to their decision-making framework. Knowing the standards for each grade level, Silas decided to start out by making sure that his staff had the required trainings they needed to implement the standards across the curriculum successfully. **(3.3) He discussed the school and district results, but did not link the data to their standards work and professional development efforts.** The school data showed a three-year decline in writing performance. He went on to ask his staff to share professional development topics they wanted to see addressed throughout the year and was surprised when writing was not a topic of focus.

The week following, Silas used a faculty meeting to review the student achievement data and to communicate the goals he had developed. **(3.5) Staff shared that they felt they had too many goals and standards to teach and did not know how to go about prioritizing their standards and working as grade-level teams to plan instruction.** With this information, **(3.4) Silas knew he would focus professional development time around prioritizing standards and using assessment to guide instructional decisions. He would begin by bringing in outside consultants to teach structures and practices that would be used during Data Team (PLC) meetings to help his staff focus on their new writing goals.**

Teachers felt that Silas had heard their concerns and were excited about the implementation of Data Teams. Additionally, they were very open to using monthly planning time to implement the structure within their grade levels. **(3.1) Silas monitored the efforts by conducting monthly walk-throughs and giving teachers feedback on their instructional practices and use of the standards. While he saw that teachers made changes slowly, there was evidence of a greater focus on the standards. (3.4) For the first time, teachers and students were working together to align standards and grade-level course objectives.**

3.3: Silas shared the school and district data with his staff, but did not help them understand the link between the data and their school goals. SCORE 3.3 AT PROGRESSING.

3.5: While staff are aware of the standards, they do not use them widely. SCORE 3.5 AT PROGRESSING.

3.4: Silas understands the student requirements and academic standards and knows what his staff needs. His staff is struggling to understand the link between the standards and student performance and he is hopeful that Data Teams will help his staff focus more on student achievement. SCORE 3.4 AT PROGRESSING.

3.1: Silas developed goals related to student needs in writing and is working with staff to improve student achievement. To date, the practices have not resulted in significant improvement. SCORE 3.1 AT PROGRESSING.

3.4: Teachers are beginning to work together, focused on standards and aligning their grade-level course objectives. They have yet to make the strong connection between standards and student performANCE. SCORE 3.4 AT PROGRESSING.

3.2: Test scores did not show improvement in writing the first year, but teachers were confident that more subjective, formative data existed that showed evidence of improvements in their classrooms. SCORE 3.2 AT PROGRESSING.

(3.2) Over the course of the year, while teachers could see only minor improvement in test results on writing, they could see improvement in student attitudes toward school and daily work. Silas made sure to celebrate even the small gains and to acknowledge staff publicly for their commitment to their improvement efforts. At the end of the year, he invited input and suggestions from staff and from parents on his building accountability committee and used the data to help revise their school improvement plan and to inform their goals for the following year. In his final review with his principal, Silas acknowledged he had grown significantly this year and that he would use the data he received from her and the staff to set his goals for the next year.

Scenario #17—Shannon
3.0: Student Achievement

Shannon is a third-year assistant principal at Sandy Middle School. Sandy hosts students in seventh and eighth grade, and the district's gifted-and-talented program is housed in the building. Shannon's role is to support the building principal in all capacities, but he has recognized data and curriculum as two of his strengths. Shannon is honored to be the lead when it comes to carrying out the responsibilities for assuring student achievement and academic growth within the building.

Shannon worked closely with the principal and the school improvement planning team to develop a focused plan to help the school increase language arts and math scores on the state assessment. The plan has not changed much over the previous two years. It defines two main goals for implementation and monitoring. Shannon and the building principal know that, after so little growth the previous year, they need to increase the amount of time they spend in classrooms observing the effectiveness of the strategies in the school improvement plan to determine if they are being implemented with fidelity. The previous year, the school worked on learning the strategies. The administration observed many of the teachers implementing the strategies, but did not use a checklist or measurement tool to document their observations. There is evidence around the building that teachers are focused on these strategies and are waiting for a large increase in student achievement to accompany their hard work in trying to implement the new strategies.

Shannon continuously stays up to date on school-wide and district data, but has had difficulty in making time to share it and its implications with the whole staff. The focus has been more on implementing and teaching the strategies that are in the plan. School-wide data has been shared only once or twice a year. The data reviewed during the meeting only related to the state's summative assessment tool. Shannon is working on creating a plan to evaluate the school's formative data on a monthly basis, but has not been able to meet with the staff to take them through the process. Shannon has studied and is working on how to empower teacher leaders to assume facilitator roles when analyzing data, but he is experiencing some pushback. Teachers are not on board with the positive effects that data analysis and formative assessments can have on student achievement because the students' scores the previous year did not increase.

Shannon has also been presented with the challenge of communicating the new state standards to his staff. They have been available for two years. The teachers are used to having writing standards in their lesson plans, but they are now anxious to get started on implementing the new standards on which they were recently trained. Some teachers in Shannon's building are on the district standards committee, but they have not had time to meet as a staff to identify the Power Standards. The staff is having difficulty seeing the connection between student achievement and the new standards. They feel they need to see the correlation between their common formative assessments and the new standards.

Shannon is so focused on the state assessment data that other curricular areas are not being addressed. He and many of his teachers understand how the new

CASE STUDY MATERIALS AND LEARNING EXPERIENCES

standards and achievement results fit together, but he has not yet developed a plan to help teachers connect instruction, standards, and data-driven decision making systematically in a single ongoing process they understand and can facilitate independently.

Peruse the MLP Matrix and assess Shannon's performance in Domain 3.0: Student Achievement. Make mental notes and be prepared to respond as to the reason for your score on that dimension. Please be prepared to report out in 15 minutes.

Scenario #17—Shannon
3.0: Student Achievement

Proficient

Shannon is a third-year assistant principal at Sandy Middle School. Sandy hosts students in seventh and eighth grade, and the district's gifted-and-talented program is housed in the building. Shannon's role is to support the building principal in all capacities, but he has recognized data and curriculum as two of his strengths. Shannon is honored to be the lead when it comes to carrying out the responsibilities for assuring student achievement and academic growth within the building.

(3.1) Shannon worked closely with the principal and the school improvement planning team to develop a focused plan to help the school increase language arts and math scores on the state assessment. The plan has not changed much over the previous two years. It defines two main goals for implementation and monitoring. Shannon and the building principal know that, after so little growth the previous year, they need to increase the amount of time they spend in classrooms observing the effectiveness of the strategies in the school improvement plan to determine if they are being implemented with fidelity. The previous year, the school worked on learning the strategies. The administration observed many of the teachers implementing the strategies, but did not use a checklist or measurement tool to document their observations. **(3.2) There is evidence around the building that teachers are focused on these strategies and are waiting for a large increase in student achievement to accompany their hard work in trying to implement the new strategies.**

(3.3) Shannon continuously stays up to date on school-wide and district data, but has had difficulty in making time to share it and its implications with the whole staff. The focus has been more on implementing and teaching the strategies that are in the plan. School-wide data has been shared only once or twice a year. The data reviewed during the meeting only related to the state's summative assessment tool. Shannon is working on creating a plan to evaluate the school's formative data on a monthly basis, but has not been able to meet with the staff to take them through the process. Shannon has studied and is working on how to empower teacher leaders to assume facilitator roles when analyzing data, but he is experiencing some pushback. Teachers are not on board with the positive effects that data analysis and formative assessments can have on student achievement because the students' scores the previous year did not increase.

(3.5) Shannon has also been presented with the challenge of communicating the new state standards to his staff. They have been available for two years. The teachers are used to having writing standards in their lesson plans, but they are now anxious to get started on implementing the new standards on which they were recently trained. Some teachers in Shannon's building are on the district standards committee, but they have not had time to

3.1: Shannon has implemented a plan that has specific and measurable goals related to student achievement, but these efforts have yet to result in improved student achievement.
Score 3.1 at Proficient.

3.2: Shannon has implemented leadership practices that will influence teaching practices. However there is insufficient evidence of changes in teaching and curricula that will create the improvements necessary to achieve student performance goals.
Score 3.2 at Proficient.

3.3: Shannon is aware of state and district results and has discussed those results with staff, but has not linked specific decisions to the data.
Score 3.3 at Proficient.

3.5: Shannon has presented the new standards to the staff. The Power Standards are developed, but not widely known or used by faculty.
Score 3.5 at Proficient.

meet as a staff to identify the Power Standards. **(3.4)** The staff is having difficulty seeing the connection between student achievement and the new standards. They feel they need to see the correlation between their common formative assessments and the new standards.

Shannon is so focused on the state assessment data that other curricular areas are not being addressed. He and many of his teachers understand how the new standards and achievement results fit together, but he has not yet developed a plan to help teachers connect instruction, standards, and data-driven decision making systematically in a single ongoing process they understand and can facilitate independently.

Scenario #18—Edward
3.0: Student Achievement

Edward, a middle school principal in his fifth year at Arlington Middle School Academy, met with the English department on the first day of school. In an effort to improve the benchmark assessment scores this school year, Edward introduced a pre- and post-year survey to students. These surveys were used to identify the common errors on the English benchmark. Determined to ensure student achievement, Edward collaborated with the Data Team to create specific curriculum and instructional strategies that addressed the challenges in the benchmark assessment. He utilized the assistant principals and lead teachers to coach other team members on curriculum mapping and measuring students' improvements. He worked with the team members in setting professional and personal SMART goals to improve student achievement.

In addition to addressing the students' challenges, Edward led the team in identifying students' strengths to facilitate improvements in student achievement. Based on multiple indicators, such as student writing samples, bell ringers, teacher observations, and benchmark assessments, Edward and the team concluded the need to differentiate literacy instruction. He challenged the team to implement a peer-mentoring model for students below and above literacy proficiency. He also indicated the need for the staff to exhibit cultural "responsiveness" due to the performance of various sub-groups on the benchmark assess. He insisted that the mentoring program involve students of various ethnic and socioeconomic groups, as well as exceptional learners.

Edward concluded the meeting by instructing the English department to display their data results from the benchmark assessment, student surveys, and the participation data from the mentoring program by posting in both the data room and electronically. He modeled the need to have a data binder for documentation and reflections with teachers, colleagues, and his supervisors.

The next day in the entire staff meeting, Edward shared successes from the previous school year, along with the English department's SMART goal to continue and increase student achievement in literacy. To create staff buy-in, he led the staff members through the data analysis process. The staff then identified the Power Standards that focused on literacy skills in their content areas in order to support the goal of increased student achievement. Edward encouraged them to identify practices to improve literacy across the content.

That evening, Edward created a student achievement section on the Web, sharing data, effective teaching practices, and spotlighting individual students with significant achievements in the literacy area.

Peruse the MLP Matrix and assess Edward's performance in Domain 3.0: Student Achievement. Make mental notes and be prepared to respond as to the reason for your score on that dimension. Please be prepared to report out in 15 minutes.

3.1: Edward shares examples of specific teaching and curriculum strategies that are associated with improved student achievement by discussing the benchmark assessment with staff.
SCORE 3.1 AT EXEMPLARY.

3.2: Edward used a variety of measuring tools to identify student weaknesses and successes. Edward also identified groups of disadvantaged students who were not successful on the assessments.
SCORE 3.2 AT EXEMPLARY.

3.3: Edward used the data from the assessment surveys and mentoring program, along with reflections.
SCORE 3.3 AT EXEMPLARY.

3.4: Edward begins every faculty meeting sharing successes and goals.
SCORE 3.4 AT EXEMPLARY.

3.5: Edward led the staff in the creation of Power Standards in order to improve literacy achievement.
SCORE 3.5 AT EXEMPLARY.

Scenario #18—Edward
3.0: Student Achievement

EXEMPLARY

Edward, a middle school principal in his fifth year at Arlington Middle School Academy, met with the English department on the first day of school. **(3.1) In an effort to improve the benchmark assessment scores this school year, Edward introduced a pre- and post-year survey to students. These surveys were used to identify the common errors on the English benchmark. Determined to ensure student achievement, Edward collaborated with the Data Team to create specific curriculum and instructional strategies that addressed the challenges in the benchmark assessment. He utilized the assistant principals and lead teachers to coach other team members on curriculum mapping and measuring students' improvements. He worked with the team members in setting professional and personal SMART goals to improve student achievement.**

In addition to addressing the students' challenges, Edward led the team in identifying students' strengths to facilitate improvements in student achievement. **(3.2) Based on multiple indicators, such as student writing samples, bell ringers, teacher observations, and benchmark assessments, Edward and the team concluded the need to differentiate literacy instruction. He challenged the team to implement a peer-mentoring model for students below and above literacy proficiency. He also indicated the need for the staff to exhibit cultural "responsiveness" due to the performance of various sub-groups on the benchmark assess. He insisted that the mentoring program involve students of various ethnic and socioeconomic groups, as well as exceptional learners.**

(3.3) Edward concluded the meeting by instructing the English department to display their data results from the benchmark assessment, student surveys, and the participation data from the mentoring program by posting in both the data room and electronically. He modeled the need to have a data binder for documentation and reflections with teachers, colleagues, and his supervisors.

(3.4) The next day in the entire staff meeting, Edward shared successes from the previous school year, along with the English department's SMART goal to continue and increase student achievement in literacy. To create staff buy-in, he led the staff members through the data analysis process. **(3.5) The staff then identified the Power Standards that focused on literacy skills in their content areas in order to support the goal of increased student achievement.** Edward encouraged them to identify practices to improve literacy across the content.

That evening, Edward created a student achievement section on the Web, sharing data, effective teaching practices, and spotlighting individual students with significant achievements in the literacy area.

Scenario #19—Maurice
3.0: Student Achievement

Maurice was thrilled to be in charge of monitoring school improvement efforts at Longraven High School. After having served four years as the assistant principal, he had proved he had a good knowledge of research-based practices to improve student achievement. Over the last two years, Maurice carefully guided the staff through a process where all academic standards were analyzed and prioritized and for which common formative assessments were developed. Maurice felt fortunate that his principal understood Maurice's knowledge and ability to focus the staff on the right work most likely exceeded his own ability in this area. Regardless, Maurice's principal did not let this difference interfere with Maurice's leading the staff forward in this process.

The building leadership team was able to work together to define specific goals for the current year. Given their analysis of student growth in reading for the past three years, it was clear that the work they did to monitor the results of short-cycle common formative assessments the previous year was beginning to pay off in terms of predicting how students might then perform on the state reading assessments. A fairly good correlation between these formative and summative measures now existed, and both indicated that students were making some gains in reading achievement. Additionally, the students who were struggling the most seemed to be achieving more than a year's growth on both their internal bench-mark and the state assessments. Through the targeted reading intervention that had been put in place for all students reading below grade level, the staff was also able to see "short-term wins" on a regular basis. Although overall reading achievement was still not where it needed to be, triangulated data showed clearly that students were making progress.

This year, they would continue to monitor the same school improvement goals with regard to instructional strategies. The goals would focus on increasing deployment of these strategies, as well as continuously monitoring the results of the common assessments. Although the student demographics were challenging, Maurice worked with the staff on disaggregating data so that these differences could be analyzed more easily. He also brought articles and other resources to the staff to develop background knowledge about schools that had been successful in the face of these challenges. Through the work in department Data Teams (small teams that strategically improve practice through the use of data), specific strategies were implemented and the correlation between these strategies and student achievement were regularly monitored. Because of the results they were beginning to see, the entire staff and community were beginning to embrace fully their own efficacy at making a difference.

On a recent classroom walk-through visit, Maurice was pleased to see that indi-vidual departments had remained committed to posting priority standards in accessible student language. In many classrooms, students were able to articulate how their work fit into essential questions tied to these priority standards.

Maurice was still a bit frustrated with a few teachers who seemed to be offering mere lip service to the goals and who hadn't really engaged in the process fully. He continued to talk with colleagues about the best manner in which to move

CASE STUDY MATERIALS AND LEARNING EXPERIENCES

these teachers along, but was still learning the hard lesson that sometimes the group's momentum needs to carry initiatives forward, even if a few lag behind. Maurice wondered if this would be sufficient and what else he could do to engage these few teachers in the process. He had hoped that the data displays throughout the school that demonstrated how students were growing, as well as the writing exemplars that demonstrated how students were applying reading strategies in other content areas, would convince them that this was the right work. But they remained unconvinced.

Maurice still had challenges ahead and Longraven had much work to do. But each day seemed to bring him closer to understanding how best to change the course of student achievement through the work of the staff in the building. He had confidence that they were headed in the right direction.

Peruse the MLP Matrix and assess Maurice's performance in Domain 3.0: Student Achievement. Make mental notes and be prepared to respond as to the reason for your score on that dimension. Please be prepared to report out in 15 minutes.

Scenario #19—Maurice
3.0: Student Achievement

PROFICIENT

Maurice was thrilled to be in charge of monitoring school improvement efforts at Longraven High School. After having served four years as the assistant principal, he had proved he had a good knowledge of research-based practices to improve student achievement. **(3.5) Over the last two years, Maurice carefully guided the staff through a process where all academic standards were analyzed and prioritized and for which common formative assessments were developed.** Maurice felt fortunate that his principal understood Maurice's knowledge and ability to focus the staff on the right work most likely exceeded his own ability in this area. Regardless, Maurice's principal did not let this difference interfere with Maurice's leading the staff forward in this process.

The building leadership team was able to work together **(3.1) to define specific goals for the current year. Given their analysis of student growth in reading for the past three years, it was clear that the work they did to monitor the results of short-cycle common formative assessments the previous year was beginning to pay off** in terms of predicting how students might then perform on the state reading assessments. A fairly good correlation between these formative and summative measures now existed, **(3.2) and both indicated that students were making some gains in reading achievement. Additionally, the students who were struggling the most seemed to be achieving more than a year's growth on both their internal benchmark and the state assessments. Through the targeted reading intervention that had been put in place for all students reading below grade level, (3.1, cont.) the staff was also able to see "short-term wins" on a regular basis.** Although overall reading achievement was still not where it needed to be, **(3.3) triangulated data showed clearly that students were making progress.**

This year, they would continue to monitor the same school improvement goals with regard to instructional strategies. The goals would focus on increasing deployment of these **(3.3, cont.) strategies, as well as continuously monitoring the results of the common assessments. Although the student demographics were challenging, Maurice worked with the staff on disaggregating data so that these differences could be analyzed more easily.** He also brought articles and other resources to the staff to develop background knowledge about schools that had been successful in the face of these challenges. **(3.3) Through the work in department Data Teams (small teams that strategically improve practice through the use of data), specific strategies were implemented and the correlation between these strategies and student achievement were regularly monitored.** Because of the results they were beginning to see, the entire staff and community were beginning to embrace fully their own efficacy at making a difference.

On a recent classroom walk-through visit, Maurice was pleased to see that **(3.5) individual departments had remained committed to posting priority standards in accessible student language.** In many classrooms, students were able to articulate how their work fit into essential questions tied to these priority standards.

3.5: Maurice has ensured that standards have been prioritized and common formative assessments have been created tied to these prioritized standards.
SCORE 3.5 AT PROFICIENT.

3.1: Maurice has guided the staff to define specific goals and analyze data. Results show improvement based on the work.
SCORE 3.1 AT PROFICIENT

3.2: Students, both overall and in targeted groups, are demonstrating improvement, and interventions for struggling students have been put into play.
SCORE 3.2 AT PROFICIENT.

3.3: Maurice uses multiple data sources to analyze student achievement.
SCORE 3.3 AT PROFICIENT.

3.3: Data Teams are used as a consistent professional development structure to analyze data and improve practice.
SCORE 3.3 AT PROFICIENT.

3.5: Student-friendly prioritized standards are posted throughout the school.
SCORE 3.5 AT PROFICIENT.

Maurice was still a bit frustrated with a few teachers who seemed to be offering mere lip service to the goals and who hadn't really engaged in the process fully. He continued to talk with colleagues about the best manner in which to move these teachers along, but was still learning the hard lesson that sometimes the group's momentum needs to carry initiatives forward, even if a few lag behind. Maurice wondered if this would be sufficient and what else he could do to engage these few teachers in the process. He had hoped that the **(3.4, 3.5) data displays throughout the school that demonstrated how students were growing, as well as the writing exemplars** that demonstrated how students were applying reading strategies in other content areas, would convince them that this was the right work. But they remained unconvinced.

Maurice still had challenges ahead and Longraven had much work to do. But each day seemed to bring him closer to understanding how best to change the course of student achievement through the work of the staff in the building. He had confidence that they were headed in the right direction.

Scenario #20—Trevor
3.0: Student Achievement

As a former assistant principal in charge of building positive school culture, Trevor was the man to return the fun to life at West Milborn High School. As the new principal of a large urban high school where morale was low and the former principal ruled as a dictator, Trevor gave the staff a new sense of excitement about what he could do to bring back a positive culture. The previous principal had made some gains in terms of student academic growth, but made the decision to leave West Milborn when he was offered a position as a director in another school district.

In an effort to win over the staff and set himself apart from the previous principal, Trevor decided to revamp the school improvement plan to better reflect a culture where individuality was honored in his teaching staff. He realized that this was a bold move, given the school was only two years into a five-year plan. However, he felt he needed to reinstate the staff's feelings of empowerment. In early staff meetings, Trevor expressed agreement with teachers' complaints that the socioeconomic backgrounds of the students who attended West Milborn would always be an obstacle to real growth in student achievement. Trevor suggested, "Let's make these kids feel positive about the relationships they have with us since they probably aren't getting this at home." He felt strongly that the students would reach their natural potential if they were given a sense of security and knew that the staff liked them. Given the challenges of lack of parental involvement at West Milborn, this plan had the advantage of not relying on parents to help with the goals that Trevor set forth. Additionally, Trevor's experience had shown him that gathering specific data from teachers only intimidated the staff and made them feel less creative about the best way to get results. He would know when things were improving by simply walking down the halls and observing the tone of the building. This would encourage students to spend more time at school, participating in athletics and other activities, something Trevor knew was tied to higher student achievement.

Things seemed to be going well by October. Incidents with student discipline were down, as staff focused on talking through issues with students rather than engaging in consequences that would take students away from the one stable environment they had—school. Trevor often heard from teachers how much more relaxed the staff meetings were and that they finally felt they had permission to teach and monitor student progress in their own way. This new surge of individualism throughout the building created a wealth of ideas for how to engage students in more after-school activities. To allow teachers time to focus on the after-school activities, Trevor made the decision to remove a few things from teachers' plates. He was confident that he would get enough of a bump in achievement just by changing the culture, so preparing for and administering the previously required benchmark assessments seemed like it would detract from teacher creativity. When Trevor announced the elimination of the assessments at a staff meeting, the teachers gave him a standing ovation. At that moment, Trevor realized that he had truly changed the culture and empowered his staff to make the best possible environment for teachers.

When the school year closed, Trevor felt good about what he had accomplished.

The staff welcomed him into classrooms, team meetings, and lounges and he felt completely comfortable joining in on conversations, as he understood fully how hard their jobs were and simply wanted to make it easier for them to focus on their craft. When the state testing results arrived over the summer, Trevor was surprised at the slight dip in student test scores, but decided not to waste too much brainpower on speculating why. He was busy planning a phenomenal kickoff for the new school year and couldn't allow something he had little control of to get him down.

Peruse the MLP Matrix and assess Trevor's performance in Domain 3.0: Student Achievement. Make mental notes and be prepared to respond individually as to the reason for your score on that dimension. Please be prepared to report out in 15 minutes.

Scenario #20—Trevor
3.0: Student Achievement

NOT MEETING STANDARDS

As a former assistant principal in charge of building positive school culture, Trevor was the man to return the fun to life at West Milborn High School. As the new principal of a large urban high school where morale was low and the former principal ruled as a dictator, Trevor gave the staff a new sense of excitement about what he could do to bring back a positive culture. The previous principal had made some gains in terms of student academic growth, but made the decision to leave West Milborn when he was offered a position as a director in another school district.

In an effort to win over the staff and set himself apart from the previous principal, Trevor decided to revamp the school improvement plan to better reflect a culture where individuality was honored in his teaching staff. He realized that this was **(3.1) a bold move, given the school was only two years into a five-year plan. However, he felt he needed to reinstate the staff's feelings of empowerment. (3.2) In early staff meetings, Trevor expressed agreement with teachers' complaints that the socioeconomic backgrounds of the students who attended West Milborn would always be an obstacle to real growth in student achievement.** Trevor suggested, "Let's make these kids feel positive about the relationships they have with us since they probably aren't getting this at home." He felt strongly that the students would reach their natural potential if they were given a sense of security and knew that the staff liked them. Given the challenges of lack of parental involvement at West Milborn, this plan had the advantage of not relying on parents to help with the goals that Trevor set forth. Additionally, **(3.2, cont.) Trevor's experience had shown him that gathering specific data from teachers only intimidated the staff and made them feel less creative about the best way to get results. (3.2) He would know when things were improving by simply walking down the halls and observing the tone of the building.** This would encourage students to spend more time at school, participating in athletics and other activities, something Trevor knew was tied to higher student achievement.

Things seemed to be going well by October. Incidents with student discipline were down, as staff focused on talking through issues with students rather than engaging in consequences that would take students away from the one stable environment they had—school. **(3.4) Trevor often heard from teachers how much more relaxed the staff meetings were and that they finally felt they had permission to teach and monitor student progress in their own way.** This new surge of individualism throughout the building created a wealth of ideas for how to engage students in more after-school activities. To allow teachers time to focus on the after-school activities, Trevor made the decision to remove a few things from teachers' plates. He was confident that he would get enough of a bump in achievement just by changing the culture, so preparing for and

3.1: Trevor makes a decision to abandon the current achievement-based school improvement plan and move to a plan based on something difficult to measure in terms of impact on student achievement. SCORE 3.1 AT NOT MEETING STANDARDS.

3.2: Trevor agrees with staff that students will never achieve at high levels due to their socio-economic background. SCORE 3.2 AT NOT MEETING STANDARDS.

3.2: Trevor has not taken decisive steps to use data or change practices in the building to impact student achievement. SCORE 3.2 AT NOT MEETING STANDARDS.

3.4: Trevor does not intrude on individual teacher's classroom practice or curriculum and does not see individual practice as something important to monitor or be involved in. SCORE 3.4 AT NOT MEETING STANDARDS.

3.5: Trevor eliminates the standards-based benchmark assessments; thus he removes any tie to monitoring standards in a universal manner in the building. SCORE 3.5 AT NOT MEETING STANDARDS.

3.3: Trevor is indifferent to the data. SCORE 3.3 AT NOT MEETING STANDARDS.

(3.5) administering the previously required benchmark assessments seemed like it would detract from teacher creativity. When Trevor announced the elimination of the assessments at a staff meeting, the teachers gave him a standing ovation. At that moment, Trevor realized that he had truly changed the culture and empowered his staff to make the best possible environment for teachers.

When the school year closed, Trevor felt good about what he had accomplished. The staff welcomed him into classrooms, team meetings, and lounges and he felt completely comfortable joining in on conversations, as he understood fully how hard their jobs were and simply wanted to make it easier for them to focus on their craft. When the state testing results arrived over the summer, Trevor was surprised at the slight dip in student test scores, **(3.3) but decided not to waste too much brainpower on speculating why.** He was busy planning a phenomenal kickoff for the new school year and couldn't allow something he had little control of to get him down.

Scenario #21—Samuel
3.0: Student Achievement

Samuel had worked in the food industry for six years before joining Golden School District as their director of food service. As a chef at a local restaurant, he had worked long hours and was rarely home before midnight. With a new baby on the way, he wanted to secure a position in which he could still contribute to his community but have a more stable family schedule. During his interview, the superintendent had made it clear that the district had a comprehensive accountability system, which gave central office support departments visibility, responsibility, and accountability. The accountability plan sent a clear message to building leaders, teachers, and community members that all administrators in the district were held accountable in the same way that teachers and principals were held accountable.

Samuel was just beginning his second year in this position, having spent his first year getting to know each of his 41 school leaders and learning what was working and what his customers would like to see his department focus on for this next year. Given Samuel's transition from a business to a public position, he also made himself very familiar with state and district expectations, which he shared with his department leaders. Samuel reviewed the central office goals, making sure that his department goals were rigorous, relevant, and aligned. In addition, Samuel also reviewed the past three years of survey data from parents, staff, and students. Based on feedback from each of the school leaders and the previous years' data, Samuel was able to identify contributions his department could make to district common goals that served students.

As a result of this comprehensive review, it was clear to Samuel and his department leaders that they needed to increase the percentage of patrons who chose food service options over vending-machine selections or home lunches. When averaging the data from all of his schools, Samuel could see they were feeding about 52 percent of the students on any given day. Furthermore, the self-reported survey data from principals and teachers indicated that they were concerned that their students were not eating nutritional lunches—many were just eating candy and pop from the vending machines. Or, they had packed their own lunches from home, which often did not contain a proper nutritional food balance. More importantly, staff could see a significant decline in student motivation and performance directly following lunch. Samuel and his team set a goal of an 18 percent increase in food service patrons, which in a year's time would translate to 60 percent of students eating school lunches.

Shortly thereafter, Samuel sent an e-mail that identified his department goals for the year to all schools, as well as the plans for collecting and assessing the data to make needed changes. Samuel started by evaluating menu choices, soliciting food option ideas from students and parents, and making the changes immediately. Goals and expectations were posted in each cafeteria so that everyone in the organization could support the goals. By the end of his first year, Samuel's department did not meet their goal, but did see small improvements. Yet, Samuel remained optimistic and used the survey data to reevaluate his department improvement efforts. The feedback was clear. Samuel needed to be more inclusive when making decisions that affected each of his schools. Samuel created a food service committee, consisting of students, staff, and parents, whose main objective was to problem-solve ways to ensure that food service became the option of choice for students. Samuel is certain that his team will meet and exceed their new goal of 65 percent this year.

Peruse the MLP Matrix and assess Samuel's performance in Domain 3.0: Student Achievement. Make mental notes and be prepared to respond as to the reason for your score on that dimension. Please be prepared to report out in 15 minutes.

Scenario #21—Samuel
3.0: Student Achievement

PROGRESSING

Samuel had worked in the food industry for six years before joining Golden School District as their director of food service. As a chef at a local restaurant, he had worked long hours and was rarely home before midnight. With a new baby on the way, he wanted to secure a position in which he could still contribute to his community but have a more stable family schedule. During his interview, the superintendent had made it clear that the district had a comprehensive accountability system, which gave central office support departments visibility, responsibility, and accountability. The accountability plan sent a clear message to building leaders, teachers, and community members that all administrators in the district were held accountable in the same way that teachers and principals were held accountable.

Samuel was just beginning his second year in this position, having spent his first year getting to know each of his 41 school leaders and learning what was working and what his customers would like to see his department focus on for this next year. Given Samuel's transition from a business to a public position, he also made himself very familiar with state and district expectations, which he shared with his department leaders. **(3.3) Samuel reviewed the central office goals, making sure that his department goals were rigorous, relevant, and aligned. In addition, Samuel also reviewed the past three years of survey data from parents, staff, and students. Based on feedback from each of the school leaders and the previous years' data, Samuel was able to identify contributions his department could make to district common goals that served students.**

(3.3) As a result of this comprehensive review, it was clear to Samuel and his department leaders that they needed to increase the percentage of patrons who chose food service options over vending-machine selections or home lunches. When averaging the data from all of his schools, Samuel could see they were feeding about 52 percent of the students on any given day. Furthermore, the self-reported survey data from principals and teachers indicated that they were concerned that their students were not eating nutritional lunches—many were just eating candy and pop from the vending machines. Or, they had packed their own lunches from home, which often did not contain a proper nutritional food balance. More importantly, staff could see a significant decline in student motivation and performance directly following lunch. Samuel and his team set a goal of an 18 percent increase in food service patrons, which in a year's time would translate to 60 percent of students eating school lunches.

Shortly thereafter, **(3.5) Samuel sent an e-mail that identified his department goals for the year to all schools, as well as the plans for collecting and assessing the data to make needed changes.** Samuel started by evaluating menu choices, soliciting food option ideas from students and parents, and making the changes immediately. **(3.4) Goals and expectations were posted in each cafeteria so that everyone in the organization could support the goals.**

3.3: Samuel and his team review multiple data sources from the past three years and use the information to determine priorities for the department. SCORE 3.3 AT PROFICIENT.

3.3: Samuel and his department systematically examined the data to determine strengths and challenges. Goals were set based on this analysis. SCORE 3.3 AT PROFICIENT.

3.5: After analyzing all of the survey data, Samuel e-mailed all principals, translating the data into goals and strategies for his department. SCORE 3.5 AT PROFICIENT.

3.4: Samuel and his leadership team posted their expectations and goals in each school. SCORE 3.4 AT PROGRESSING.

3.1: Measurable goals were established, but these efforts did not result in meeting department goals in the first year. SCORE 3.1 AT PROGRESSING.

3.2: While some evidence of improvement exists, Samuel and his team receive feedback regarding improvements necessary to achieve their department goals. SCORE 3.2 AT PROGRESSING.

(3.1) By the end of his first year, Samuel's department did not meet their goal, but did see small improvements. Yet, Samuel remained optimistic and used the survey data to reevaluate his department improvement efforts. **(3.2)** The feedback was clear. Samuel needed to be more inclusive when making decisions that affected each of his schools. Samuel created a food service committee, consisting of students, staff, and parents, whose main objective was to problem-solve ways to ensure that food service became the option of choice for students. Samuel is certain that his team will meet and exceed their new goal of 65 percent this year.

Scenario #22—Sonje
3.0: Student Achievement

Over the past eight years as director of elementary schools for East Lake District, Sonje viewed herself as a lifelong learner and looked upon each new school year as an opportunity to learn and grow as a leader. With the recent introduction of the Common Core State Standards in her district, she knew that this year would once again provide her with the excitement and mental stimulation of taking on another new challenge. Student achievement would remain the top priority, and she would direct her energy and focus to ensure that her principals were well trained and could lead their building through the successful implementation of the new standards, while increasing student achievement.

As one of two elementary directors, Sonje was known for her expertise in the area of data-driven decision making. District leaders sought out her guidance, and she was always available to provide support at all levels of the organization. Sonje had previously attended and was certified in the development of district Data Teams (small district-level teams that strategically improve practice through the use of data) and was in charge of monitoring the teams and providing guidance and training to elementary principals in the implementation of their school Data Teams. Using this structure and the data-driven decision-making process, Sonje trained district and school leaders to implement the Common Core State Standards. During her tenure in this position, student achievement grew slightly over the years and Sonje felt that if the core standards were implemented with fidelity district-wide, the achievement of all students across the district would increase.

In previous years under Sonje's leadership, during monthly principals' meetings and her biweekly meetings with each of her principals, they developed a keen understanding of how to "unwrap" standards (the process of making standards manageable to help educators extract from the wording of the standards the concepts and skills students need to know and be able to do) and how to identify the Power Standards that, when taught using researched-based instructional practices, would yield high levels of student achievement. Sonje also put together feeder area principal Data Teams who met to analyze their feeder data patterns and to set a school improvement feeder alignment SMART goal. While Sonje provided three-year summative district-level data, disaggregated by school, principals also brought classroom assessment data and proficient writing exemplars to share and review with colleagues. As a result of this process, principals were able to provide greater focus and support to their staff during their Data Team meetings and biweekly walk-throughs.

During the year-long implementation of the Common Core State Standards, Sonje led her principals in analyzing data focused on cause/effect data and their relationship to student data. Past analysis had focused mainly on student achievement data, and Sonje really wanted her principals to understand the power and relationship of the adult actions within their learning system vis-à-vis their impact on student achievement. Sonje encouraged her school to focus on two to three school improvement goals and measure their SMART goals by using both cause and effect data for adult practices on student achievement.

At the end of the year, Sonje convened the district Data Team, which consisted of the superintendents' leadership group reviewing the student achievement data. While 50 percent of the schools saw slight gains in performance, all schools at least maintained their previous averages. Sonje was pleased that, at a time when a new initiative of this magnitude was implemented, student achievement stayed constant. Principals were excited about the new school year, feeling that with the guidance they received from Sonje and the implementation of the Common Core State Standards, all sub-populations of students would show significant growth results.

Peruse the MLP Matrix and assess Sonje's performance in Domain 3.0: Student Achievement. Make mental notes and be prepared to respond as to the reason for your score on that dimension. Please be prepared to report out in 15 minutes.

Scenario #22—Sonje
3.0: Student Achievement

PROFICIENT

Over the past eight years as director of elementary schools for East Lake District, Sonje viewed herself as a lifelong learner and looked upon each new school year as an opportunity to learn and grow as a leader. With the recent introduction of the Common Core State Standards in her district, she knew that this year would once again provide her with the excitement and mental stimulation of taking on another new challenge. Student achievement would remain the top priority, and she would direct her energy and focus to ensure that her principals were well trained and could lead their building through the successful implementation of the new standards, while increasing student achievement.

As one of two elementary directors, Sonje was known for her expertise in the area of data-driven decision making. District leaders sought out her guidance, and she was always available to provide support at all levels of the organization. Sonje had previously attended and was certified in the development of district Data Teams (small district-level teams that strategically improve practice through the use of data) and was in charge of monitoring the teams and providing guidance and training to elementary principals in the implementation of their school Data Teams. Using this structure and the data-driven decision-making process, Sonje trained district and school leaders to implement the Common Core State Standards. During her tenure in this position, student achievement grew slightly over the years and Sonje felt that if the core standards were implemented with fidelity district-wide, the achievement of all students across the district would increase.

In previous years under Sonje's leadership, **(3.1) during monthly principals' meetings and her biweekly meetings with each of her principals, they developed a keen understanding of how to "unwrap" standards (the process of making standards manageable to help educators extract from the wording of the standards the concepts and skills students need to know and be able to do) and how to identify the Power Standards that, when taught using researched-based instructional practices, would yield high levels of student achievement. (3.3) Sonje also put together feeder area principal Data Teams who met to analyze their feeder data patterns and to set a school improvement feeder alignment SMART goal. (3.5) While Sonje provided three-year summative district-level data, disaggregated by school, principals also brought classroom assessment data and proficient writing exemplars to share and review with colleagues.** As a result of this process, principals were able to provide greater focus and support to their staff during their Data Team meetings and biweekly walk-throughs.

(3.4) During the year-long implementation of the Common Core State Standards, Sonje led her principals in analyzing data focused on cause/effect data and their relationship to student data. Past analysis had focused mainly on student achievement data, and Sonje really wanted her principals to understand the power and relationship of the adult actions within their learning system vis-à-vis their impact on student achievement. Sonje

3.1: Goals and strategies used reflect a clear relationship between the actions of principals/teachers, school improvement goals, and student achievement. Sonje routinely shares specific teaching and curriculum strategies with principals. SCORE 3.1 AT EXEMPLARY.

3.3: Data insights are regularly the topic of meetings and professional development sessions. SCORE 3.3 AT PROFICIENT.

3.5: Feeder area principals are sharing and reviewing achievement data and student writing exemplars to determine the link between their standards work and student achievement. SCORE 3.5 AT PROFICIENT.

3.4: Every principal and staff development meeting is focused on student achievement. SCORE 3.4 AT EXEMPLARY.

encouraged her school to focus on two to three school improvement goals and measure their SMART goals by using both cause and effect data for adult practices on student achievement.

At the end of the year, Sonje convened the district Data Team, which consisted of the superintendents' leadership group reviewing the student achievement data. **(3.2) While 50 percent of the schools saw slight gains in performance, all schools at least maintained their previous averages.** Sonje was pleased that, at a time when a new initiative of this magnitude was implemented, student achievement stayed constant. Principals were excited about the new school year, feeling that with the guidance they received from Sonje and the implementation of the Common Core State Standards, all sub-populations of students would show significant growth results.

Scenario #23—Mitchell
3.0: Student Achievement

Mitchell is the buildings and grounds supervisor for the Metropolitan Kingston Public School System. He has been employed in facility management for 17 years. Mitchell was assigned to coordinate and manage a team consisting of head custodians, administrators, and teachers to discuss the immediate needs and plans for renovation of one of their schools. He has been recognized for his commitment to the profession, his outstanding leadership, and his ability to work with other administrators/employees for the betterment of their school district.

Newberry Middle School, the school to be renovated, was established in 1968 and is one of the oldest schools in the district. Since then, the school has undergone a facelift of the main entrance and the addition of a larger gym. Due to the proposal for integrating technology in classrooms, creating more energy-efficient schools, and designing a multifaceted resource/student services center, Mitchell informs his team that they will have to develop a plan that aligns with the school district improvement plan to improve student achievement. During their initial meeting, Mitchell clearly states that facility maintenance planning involves setting operational and performance goals that are long-term. He shares his ideas and his past experiences of leading a team of custodians who were committed to maintaining excellent building repairs, cleanliness, and sanitization. Their knowledge of the standards they were to uphold contributed to the academic and operational success in other schools within the district. A survey was distributed to students, teachers, and parents rating the school's appearance and its impact on learning. The survey results acknowledged the link between the two. Consistent high scores from students' academic achievement tests were another proof.

During the planning process, Mitchell reiterated to his team that the appearance, upkeep, and available resources of a school have been shown to be linked with student achievement. He wants to ensure that his team understands that their focus is centered on student achievement. He explains that the challenges ahead, such as creating a smooth flow of student traffic in the building, providing functional classrooms and workspaces for administrators, creating a student service office accessible to all students, and implementing security measures, will require the efforts of all involved in order to create a more conducive environment for learning and success. His team is very receptive to his observations and all agree to make decisions that are effective in promoting student learning.

During staff meetings and staff development forums, Mitchell makes it clear that good housekeeping requires the full cooperation of students and faculty members, and knowledge by custodians to uphold the standards of the district. Everyone understands the importance of maintaining attractive and clean schools and the effect it can have on student learning and achievement.

Peruse the MLP Matrix and assess Mitchell's performance in Domain 3.0: Student Achievement. Make mental notes and be prepared to respond as to the reason for your score on that dimension. Please be prepared to report out in 15 minutes.

Scenario #23—Mitchell
3.0: Student Achievement

EXEMPLARY

3.1: Mitchell demonstrates that his focus on planning and goal setting aligns with the school district improvement plan. SCORE 3.1 AT EXEMPLARY.

3.2: Mitchell demonstrates evidence of student achievement on a consistent basis. He creates reports to communicate results to all stakeholders. SCORE 3.2 AT EXEMPLARY.

3.3: Mitchell demonstrates gauging student achievement to make leadership decisions. SCORE 3.3 AT EXEMPLARY.

Mitchell is the buildings and grounds supervisor for the Metropolitan Kingston Public School System. He has been employed in facility management for 17 years. Mitchell was assigned to coordinate and manage a team consisting of head custodians, administrators, and teachers to discuss the immediate needs and plans for renovation of one of their schools. He has been recognized for his commitment to the profession, his outstanding leadership, and his ability to work with other administrators/employees for the betterment of their school district.

Newberry Middle School, the school to be renovated, was established in 1968 and is one of the oldest schools in the district. Since then, the school has undergone a facelift of the main entrance and the addition of a larger gym. Due to the proposal for integrating technology in classrooms, creating more energy-efficient schools, and designing a multifaceted resource/student services center, **(3.1) Mitchell informs his team that they will have to develop a plan that aligns with the school district improvement plan to improve student achievement. During their initial meeting, Mitchell clearly states that facility maintenance planning involves setting operational and performance goals that are long-term. He shares his ideas and his past experiences of leading a team of custodians who were committed to maintaining excellent building repairs, cleanliness, and sanitization. Their knowledge of the standards they were to uphold contributed to the academic and operational success in other schools within the district. (3.2) A survey was distributed to students, teachers, and parents rating the school's appearance and its impact on learning. The survey results acknowledged the link between the two. Consistent high scores from students' academic achievement tests were another proof.**

During the planning process, **(3.3) Mitchell reiterated to his team that the appearance, upkeep, and available resources of a school have been shown to be linked with student achievement. He wants to ensure that his team understands that their focus is centered on student achievement. He explains that the challenges ahead, such as creating a smooth flow of student traffic in the building, providing functional classrooms and workspaces for administrators, creating a student service office accessible to all students, and implementing security measures, will require the efforts of all involved in order to create a more conducive environment for learning and success.** His team is very receptive to his observations and all agree to make decisions that are effective in promoting student learning.

During staff meetings and staff development forums, Mitchell makes it clear that good housekeeping requires the full cooperation of students and faculty members, and knowledge by custodians to uphold the standards of the district. Everyone understands the importance of maintaining attractive and clean schools and the effect it can have on student learning and achievement.

Scenario #24—Marsha
3.0: Student Achievement

Marsha is beginning her second year in the role of director of middle schools in the Valley Mills School District. Valley Mills services grades K–12 and has an enrollment of more than 14,000 students. Marsha serves as an overseer of the middle school curriculum, acts as an instructional leader for the three middle schools, and ensures the district/middle school educational objectives are aligned to state frameworks. She prides herself on knowing what instructional practices yield the highest standards in student achievement and knows instructional excellence when observed.

Marsha is responsible for the development of annual goals and action planning for the teaching and learning program. She meets with the three middle school principals every week to discuss the district improvement goals that have remained constant for the last two years. The district plan identifies specific and measurable goals related to student achievement in all core areas. The plan includes the administration of common formative assessments in reading, writing, science, and math; the formation of monthly Data Teams in the English, math, and science departments; and professional development on strategies for engagement. The annual goals are based on the needs of the middle schools; however, their efforts have not resulted in any improvements in student achievement at the present. The middle school principals support the need for district goals for improvement, but they are more vested in their individual school goals and strategies for improvement.

It is Friday afternoon and Marsha is meeting with the three principals to discuss strategy implementation based on the district plan. In the meeting, the principals share with Marsha that they all have their own professional development plans that focus on strategies that their teachers are implementing with fidelity. Marsha shares with the principals that if their teachers do not implement the strategies from the district plan, then improvements will not be made. The principals respond that their plans are based on the state and district data and that the district plan does not include any evidence that state and district data were used to create the instructional strategies defined in the plan. Marsha reminds the principals that in August they reviewed data and "unwrapped" standards at the July training, so she is confused about why they think the plan did not include the state and district data. One of the principals then states, "We did review the data and standards are unwrapped and posted, but there is not a link between the district plan and student achievement." She adds, "There is not even a link between our data and the strategies listed in the plan."

Marsha becomes very confused and concludes the meeting by reiterating that standards had been analyzed and "unwrapped" during the summer and standards posted in every school. As the principals walk to their cars, one says very angrily to the others, "Yeah, they're posted. But they do not reflect proficiency in achievement on the common formative assessments that we administer four times a year, so why post them?"

Peruse the MLP Matrix and assess Marsha's performance in Domain 3.0: Student Achievement. Make mental notes and be prepared to respond as to the reason for your score on that dimension. Please be prepared to report out in 15 minutes.

Scenario #24—Marsha
3.0: Student Achievement

PROGRESSING

Marsha is beginning her second year in the role of director of middle schools in the Valley Mills School District. Valley Mills services grades K–12 and has an enrollment of more than 14,000 students. Marsha serves as an overseer of the middle school curriculum, acts as an instructional leader for the three middle schools, and ensures the district/middle school educational objectives are aligned to state frameworks. She prides herself on knowing what instructional practices yield the highest standards in student achievement and knows instructional excellence when observed.

(3.1) Marsha is responsible for the development of annual goals and action planning for the teaching and learning program. She meets with the three middle school principals every week to discuss the district improvement goals that have remained constant for the last two years. The district plan identifies specific and measurable goals related to student achievement in all core areas. The plan includes the administration of common formative assessments in reading, writing, science, and math; the formation of monthly Data Teams in the English, math, and science departments; and professional development on strategies for engagement. The annual goals are based on the needs of the middle schools; however, their efforts have not resulted in any improvements in student achievement at the present. **(3.2)** The middle school principals support the need for district goals for improvement, but they are more vested in their individual school goals and strategies for improvement.

It is Friday afternoon and Marsha is meeting with the three principals to discuss strategy implementation based on the district plan. In the meeting, the principals share with Marsha that they all have their own professional development plans that focus on strategies that their teachers are implementing with fidelity. Marsha shares with the principals that if their teachers do not implement the strategies from the district plan, then improvements will not be made. **(3.3)** The principals respond that their plans are based on the state and district data and that the district plan does not include any evidence that state and district data were used to create the instructional strategies defined in the plan. **(3.4)** Marsha reminds the principals that in August they reviewed data and "unwrapped" standards at the July training, so she is confused about why they think the plan did not include the state and district data. One of the principals then states, "We did review the data and standards are unwrapped and posted, but there is not a link between the district plan and student achievement." She adds, "There is not even a link between our data and the strategies listed in the plan."

(3.5) Marsha becomes very confused and concludes the meeting by reiterating that standards had been analyzed and "unwrapped" during the summer and standards posted in every school. As the principals walk to their cars, one says very angrily to the others, "Yeah, they're posted. But they do not reflect proficiency in achievement on the common formative assessments that we administer four times a year, so why post them?"

3.1: Marsha has developed specific and measurable goals related to student achievement, but these efforts have yet to result in improved student achievement. SCORE 3.1 AT PROFICIENT.

3.2: Some evidence of improvement exists, but there is insufficient evidence of changes in the teaching strategies that will create the improvements necessary to achieve student performance goals. SCORE 3.2 AT PROGRESSING.

3.3: Marsha is aware of state and district results and has discussed those results with staff, but has not linked specific decisions to the data. SCORE 3.3 AT PROGRESSING.

3.4: Standards are posted and required training has been conducted, but the link between standards and student performance is not readily evident to faculty or students. SCORE 3.4 AT PROGRESSING.

3.5: Standards have been analyzed and Power Standards are developed. Student work is posted, but does not reflect proficient work throughout the building. SCORE 3.5 AT PROGRESSING.

Scenario #25—Larry
3.0: Student Achievement

Panorama Point was a pretty good school district as far as Larry was concerned. In his previous district, Larry always felt that learning was stifled and unevenly skewed toward a focus on state assessment results. Larry was willing to recognize the importance of these results as a dipstick measure of student performance, but always felt that state achievement results were unrealistic and unfair to districts with challenging demographics.

When Larry first began his teaching career, things were different. Teachers were honored for their expertise and were considered the best judges of student progress. The current state of education hardly seemed to be sending this message, so Larry considered it his place to make sure that all instructional staff knew that he knew the students they worked with had significant challenges that most likely would keep their achievement quite low. What was important was all that was being done to keep student behavior under control and make sure kids stayed in school as long as possible. As long as students left high school with a diploma, they could consider their work successful.

Various leaders had come and gone, but Larry stuck with Panorama because he felt he had fallen into a nicely paced system, where tradition could continue and change was kept to a reasonable level to avoid creating too much angst. The resources provided to teachers had been updated a few times, but generally Panorama stuck with programs that teachers were comfortable teaching and that wouldn't require a lot of new professional development. As far as Larry was concerned, teachers had enough on their plates and they didn't need to be learning a new program every few years on top of everything else.

As the assistant superintendent, Larry led the curriculum adoption process in the district. He always had the opportunity to keep this potential disruption under control. Textbooks were updated to new editions when budget allowed, but programs didn't really change. In Larry's experience, teachers always tailored the resources and curriculum to their own style anyway, so it really wasn't necessary for the district to provide a lot of guidance with regard to using the resources.

When a superintendent arrived at Panorama last spring, Larry was initially excited about connecting with this new leader. Larry found him to be very approachable and laid-back in the interview and thought he would be a perfect fit for the district. Now that the year was underway, Larry was discovering that they had hired someone completely different than he expected. The superintendent was constantly asking questions about data and monitoring the progress of curriculum, teaching, and a variety of other things that seemed irrelevant given the district's demographics. Monitoring data was not going to tell them anything they didn't already know about their students. Larry told him that the students' backgrounds kept most of the students in the unsatisfactory range on state and classroom assessments.

Larry limped along with the new superintendent and tried to listen to his ideas and even found many of them to be great ideas—for another district. It was clear to Larry when the new superintendent started talking about posting standards and student work that he completely misunderstood this student population. Making public displays of each student's lack of understanding would only embarrass the students and would do nothing to improve their achievement. Larry decided to give the new superintendent a year and see if he settled down a bit once he became familiar with the district.

Peruse the MLP Matrix and assess Larry's performance in Domain 3.0: Student Achievement. Make mental notes and be prepared to respond as to the reason for your score on that dimension. Please be prepared to report out in 15 minutes.

Scenario #25—Larry
3.0: Student Achievement

NOT MEETING STANDARDS

Panorama Point was a pretty good school district as far as Larry was concerned. In his previous district, Larry always felt that learning was stifled and unevenly skewed toward a focus on state assessment results. **(3.2, 3.3) Larry was willing to recognize the importance of these results as a dipstick measure of student performance, but always felt that state achievement results were unrealistic and unfair to districts with challenging demographics.**

When Larry first began his teaching career, things were different. Teachers were honored for their expertise and were considered the best judges of student progress. The current state of education hardly seemed to be sending this message, so **(3.2) Larry considered it his place to make sure that all instructional staff knew that he knew the students they worked with had significant challenges that most likely would keep their achievement quite low. (3.1) What was important was all that was being done to keep student behavior under control and make sure kids stayed in school as long as possible. As long as students left high school with a diploma, they could consider their work successful.**

Various leaders had come and gone, but Larry stuck with Panorama because he felt he had fallen into a nicely paced system, where tradition could continue and change was kept to a reasonable level to avoid creating too much angst. **(3.2) The resources provided to teachers had been updated a few times, but generally Panorama stuck with programs that teachers were comfortable teaching and that wouldn't require a lot of new professional development. As far as Larry was concerned, teachers had enough on their plates and they didn't need to be learning a new program every few years on top of everything else.**

As the assistant superintendent, Larry led the curriculum adoption process in the district. He always had the opportunity to keep this potential disruption under control. Textbooks were updated to new editions when budget allowed, but programs didn't really change. **(3.4) In Larry's experience, teachers always tailored the resources and curriculum to their own style anyway, so it really wasn't necessary for the district to provide a lot of guidance with regard to using the resources.**

When a superintendent arrived at Panorama last spring, Larry was initially excited about connecting with this new leader. Larry found him to be very approachable and laid-back in the interview and thought he would be a perfect fit for the district. Now that the year was underway, Larry was discovering that they had hired someone completely different than he expected. The superintendent was constantly asking questions about data and monitoring the progress of curriculum, teaching, and a variety of other things that seemed irrelevant given the district's demographics.

3.2 and 3.3: Larry does not believe the data is valuable, especially in light of challenging demographics. SCORE 3.2 AND 3.3 AT NOT MEETING STANDARDS.

3.2: Larry blames the student demographics for results and does not believe that student achievement can improve. SCORE 3.2 AT NOT MEETING STANDARDS.

3.1: Larry does not have specific goals in mind. Rather, a general outcome is noted and focus is on the student characteristics controlling achievement outcomes. SCORE 3.1 AT NOT MEETING STANDARDS.

3.2: Larry does not take any action to match curriculum or instructional decisions to student achievement. SCORE 3.2 AT NOT MEETING STANDARDS.

3.4: Outside of supplying resources, he leaves the implementation of these up to individual teacher discretion. SCORE 3.4 AT NOT MEETING STANDARDS.

3.2: Larry blames the student demographics for results and does not believe that student achievement can improve. SCORE 3.2 AT NOT MEETING STANDARDS.

3.5: Larry has not influenced standards-based assessment or understanding and believes the superintendent's recommendation to do so is misguided. SCORE 3.5 AT NOT MEETING STANDARDS.

(3.2) Monitoring data was not going to tell them anything they didn't already know about their students. Larry told him that the students' backgrounds kept most of the students in the unsatisfactory range on state and classroom assessments.

Larry limped along with the new superintendent and tried to listen to his ideas and even found many of them to be great ideas—for another district. **(3.5)** It was clear to Larry when the new superintendent started talking about posting standards and student work that he completely misunderstood this student population. Making public displays of each student's lack of understanding would only embarrass the students and would do nothing to improve their achievement. Larry decided to give the new superintendent a year and see if he settled down a bit once he became familiar with the district.

Domain 4.0:
Decision Making

Leaders in education make decisions based on vision and mission and using facts and data. They use a transparent process for making decisions and articulate clearly who makes which decisions. The leader uses the process to empower others and distribute leadership when appropriate.

Scenario #26—Jillian
4.0: Decision Making

Jillian is the principal at Lincoln Elementary, which is an inner-city school with more than 75 percent of its enrollment students of color. She is just beginning her sixth year at the school. Jillian is well respected in the community by all stakeholders and known for her ability to inspire a shared vision and to work collaboratively with her staff in making decisions based on data. Under her leadership, the staff has worked diligently in their Data Teams (a professional learning community) and during professional development to change their culture from one that was measured by student attendance, students completing each year, and retaining students from year to year, to one that translates high expectations into high student achievement. Over her tenure, the school has seen a significant closing of the achievement gap between her highest- and lowest-performing students, with the greatest gains coming from her students of color. Lincoln Elementary was recently recognized in its district for being the school that made the greatest growth gains between all sub-populations.

Lincoln Elementary School's gap-closing success was the direct result of the entire community taking responsibility for the learning of all students. Jillian developed and articulated a decision-making model to ensure that decisions were made based on the vision and mission of the school, together with facts and data. Student achievement, objective data on curriculum, and research-based teaching practices were used during weekly staff meetings to build consensus on the focus of school improvement goals and objectives. Teachers were looked upon as leaders in their school and consistently participated in professional development sessions and job-embedded training in Decision Making for Results (a continuous improvement process) and Data Teams to ensure a standards-based approach with assessments and practices aligned with individual student needs. During their weekly Data Team meetings that focused on the school improvement goal of reading, grade-level teachers made decisions collaboratively on the effectiveness of teaching and learning.

Yearly, when the staff reviews the state summative data for the school, Jillian makes sure that they take the time to celebrate their successes and to recognize individual accomplishments. This is also a time when Jillian and the staff can discuss openly in a trusting environment what is not working and what needs to be changed. After analyzing and charting the data, the teachers head back to their respective Data Teams to reset their SMART (Strategic, Measurable, Achievable, Relevant, and Timely) goals and to select and determine instructional strategies and results indicators.

While Jillian and her staff have formed a tight web of interdependence around improving student achievement, the school also sees parents as important partners in the achievement of their school improvement goals. Jillian has articulated and used the school decision-making model during large- and small-group community meetings and makes sure that parents know and appreciate that their voices are heard.

Prior to starting the new school year, Jillian reviewed the data collected from the staff and parent survey and knows that her learning community is headed in the right direction. Student achievement is rising, gaps are closing, and all stakeholders feel empowered and take personal responsibility for the success of all students and of their learning community.

Peruse the MLP Matrix and assess Jillian's performance in Domain 4.0: Decision Making. Make mental notes and be prepared to respond as to the reason for your score on that dimension. Please be prepared to report out in 15 minutes.

Scenario #26—Jillian
4.0: Decision Making

EXEMPLARY

Jillian is the principal at Lincoln Elementary, which is an inner-city school with more than 75 percent of its enrollment students of color. She is just beginning her sixth year at the school. Jillian is well respected in the community by all stakeholders and known for her ability to inspire a shared vision and to work collaboratively with her staff in making decisions based on data. Under her leadership, the staff has worked diligently in their Data Teams (a professional learning community) and during professional development to change their culture from one that was measured by student attendance, students completing each year, and retaining students from year to year, to one that translates high expectations into high student achievement. Over her tenure, the school has seen a significant closing of the achievement gap between her highest- and lowest-performing students, with the greatest gains coming from her students of color. Lincoln Elementary was recently recognized in its district for being the school that made the greatest growth gains between all sub-populations.

Lincoln Elementary School's gap-closing success was the direct result of the entire community taking responsibility for the learning of all students. **(4.2) Jillian developed and articulated a decision-making model** to ensure that **(4.1) decisions were made based on the vision and mission of the school, together with facts and data. Student achievement, objective data on curriculum, and research-based teaching practices were used** during weekly staff meetings **(4.3) to build consensus on the focus of school improvement goals and objectives.** Teachers were looked upon as leaders in their school and consistently participated in professional development sessions and job-embedded training in Decision Making for Results (a continuous improvement process) and Data Teams to ensure a standards-based approach with assessments and practices aligned with individual student needs. During their weekly Data Team meetings that focused on the school improvement goal of reading, **(4.2) grade-level teachers made decisions collaboratively on the effectiveness of teaching and learning.**

Yearly, when the staff reviews the state summative data for the school, Jillian makes sure that they take the time to celebrate their successes and to recognize individual accomplishments. This is also a time when **(4.4) Jillian and the staff can discuss openly in a trusting environment what is not working and what needs to be changed.** After analyzing and charting the data, the teachers head back to their respective Data Teams to reset their SMART (Strategic, Measurable, Achievable, Relevant, and Timely) goals and to select and determine instructional strategies and results indicators.

While Jillian and her staff have formed a tight web of interdependence around improving student achievement, the school also sees parents as important partners in the achievement of their school improvement goals. **(4.2) Jillian has articulated and used the school decision-making model during large- and small-group community meetings** and makes sure that parents know and appreciate that their voices are heard.

4.2: Jillian articulated the decision-making model to staff.
SCORE **4.2** AT EXEMPLARY.

4.1: Jillian and staff make fact- and data-driven decisions. They use a variety of data sources.
SCORE **4.1** AT EXEMPLARY.

4.3: Decisions are made based on the vision/mission of the school and on strategic school improvement goals.
SCORE **4.3** AT EXEMPLARY.

4.2: The leader clarifies the decision-making method for major decisions and shares decisions with the staff, using data to the greatest extent possible to support those decisions.
SCORE **4.2** AT EXEMPLARY.

4.4: Jillian has created a trusting culture whereby staff can openly discuss areas of need and growth and make changes based on the data.
SCORE **4.4** AT EXEMPLARY.

4.2: Jillian has made sure that all stakeholders understand the decision-making model.
SCORE **4.2** AT EXEMPLARY.

4.2: Jillian surveyed and asked for feedback from staff and parents. All stakeholders are taking responsibility for organizational success. SCORE 4.2 AT EXEMPLARY.

Prior to starting the new school year, Jillian reviewed the **(4.2) data collected from the staff and parent survey** and knows that her learning community is headed in the right direction. Student achievement is rising, gaps are closing, and **(4.2, cont.) all stakeholders feel empowered and take personal responsibility for the success of all students and of their learning community.**

Scenario #27—Ian
4.0: Decision Making

Ian is a second-year assistant principal at Boswell Middle School. Boswell services students in grades 6–8. Ian's role is to support the principal in communicating the vision of the school as well as manage the building responsibilities. Most of his time should be dedicated to supporting the sixth grade with academics and behavior.

Ian is responsible for leading department meetings, in which he is supposed to communicate important information from the principal, as well as lead the group in analyzing common assessment data. Ian typically covers all the topics quickly and tries to dismiss the teachers from the meeting early. He does not create a written agenda for team leaders to follow and does not assign anyone to take notes. Ian quickly shares with them his interpretation of what the principal has discussed in their last administrative meeting. He rushes through the information and tells teachers that if they have questions about the information, they should e-mail the principal. During meetings, team leaders often bring to his attention their concerns about how low their students' scores were in relation to the school's common assessment benchmark. Ian has commented that the assessment was not really a good assessment and that they should not worry about the scores. Instead, he tells them they should worry about how the students are doing in class and that the students' grades are the best reflection of their academic progress.

Ian does not seem organized and is not communicating well. He has canceled multiple department chair meetings and has given no reason as to why they were canceled. The principal has noticed that the sixth-grade teachers are not following the specific guidelines that were discussed in the previous administrative meetings. This leads her to believe that Ian is not communicating important information to the sixth-grade team. It also seems that the sixth-grade students are not meeting the school's expectations for behavior or academics.

Peruse the MLP Matrix and assess Ian's performance in Domain 4.0: Decision Making. Make mental notes and be prepared to respond as to the reason for your score on that dimension. Please be prepared to report out in 15 minutes.

Scenario #27—Ian
4.0: Decision Making

NOT MEETING STANDARDS

4.3: Ian is unaware of or disconnected from the organization's vision, mission, and strategic priorities. There is little or no evidence of the relationship of leadership decisions to these organizational guideposts. He is not able to communicate the school's focus or vision in meetings. SCORE 4.3 AT NOT MEETING STANDARDS.

4.1: Ian rarely uses data for decisions. For example, he communicates to teachers not to be concerned about common assessment data. He also tries to end meetings too quickly because he thinks it will make him more popular with his staff. SCORE 4.1 AT NOT MEETING STANDARDS.

4.2: Ian's approach to decision making has no clear method and bewilders the staff. SCORE 4.2 AT NOT MEETING STANDARDS.

4.4: Ian shows little or no evidence of reflection and reevaluation in previous decisions. SCORE 4.4 AT NOT MEETING STANDARDS.

Ian is a second-year assistant principal at Boswell Middle School. Boswell services students in grades 6–8. Ian's role is to support the principal in communicating the vision of the school as well as manage the building responsibilities. Most of his time should be dedicated to supporting the sixth grade with academics and behavior.

Ian is responsible for leading department meetings, in which he is supposed to communicate important information from the principal, as well as lead the group in analyzing common assessment data. Ian typically covers all the topics quickly and tries to dismiss the teachers from the meeting early. He does not create a written agenda for team leaders to follow and does not assign anyone to take notes. **(4.3) Ian quickly shares with them his interpretation of what the principal has discussed in their last administrative meeting. He rushes through the information and tells teachers that if they have questions about the information, they should e-mail the principal. (4.1) During meetings, team leaders often bring to his attention their concerns about how low their students' scores were in relation to the school's common assessment benchmark. Ian has commented that the assessment was not really a good assessment and that they should not worry about the scores. Instead, he tells them they should worry about how the students are doing in class and that the students' grades are the best reflection of their academic progress.**

(4.2) Ian does not seem organized and is not communicating well. He has canceled multiple department chair meetings and has given no reason as to why they were canceled. The principal has noticed that the sixth-grade teachers are not following the specific guidelines that were discussed in the previous administrative meetings. This leads her to believe that Ian is not communicating important information to the sixth-grade team. **(4.4) It also seems that the sixth-grade students are not meeting the school's expectations for behavior or academics.**

THE REFLECTIVE LEADER: IMPLEMENTING A MULTIDIMENSIONAL LEADERSHIP PERFORMANCE SYSTEM

Scenario #28—Ethan
4.0: Decision Making

Ethan had been serving as principal of Rolling River High School for eight years. During his tenure, Ethan had the opportunity to lead his high school through both triumph and adversity. As a seasoned principal, he felt capable of handling either, obviously preferring the former. As Ethan considered the state of student achievement at Rolling River, he judged that this year had the potential to be either.

Last year's state assessment results were in hand and Ethan was disappointed in how flat the results were given the incredible gains the school had made over the past few years. His staff embraced significant reform measures enthusiastically over the course of the past five years and were buoyed by the impact they were having on student achievement. Ethan worried that they were now becoming somewhat complacent and needed a new boost. Recently, his physical education department chair shared that people were feeling that they had gotten through the emergency of improving student achievement and now felt that the school was remaining tied to cross-content writing strategies that worked well in the past but didn't appear to be pushing students any further. The physical education teacher confessed that teachers were feeling they couldn't change the instructional approach because Ethan seemed quite tied to the past success of these results.

Ethan took this information to heart and decided to use an upcoming staff meeting to remind staff about the decision-making matrix that had not been revisited by the full staff in a couple of years. Ethan had developed the matrix to clearly outline what types of decisions were made by whom and for what purpose. In this instance, Ethan brought the staff back to the original reason for the decision to move forward with the writing framework they had developed as a staff. He also took the opportunity to let the staff know that it was okay to revisit this decision, as this should ultimately be a shared decision given its immediate impact on teaching and students. Ethan reminded the staff of several other initiatives that had been revised based on emerging data trends, even admitting the failure of his own idea for improving parent involvement, which had been dropped completely after two years of data suggested it was discouraging instead of encouraging parent involvement.

Ethan encouraged anyone with a strong interest in reworking the framework to become involved. Ethan then worked with the school leadership team to analyze trends in state and district writing assessments to pinpoint where students were stalled. The team also examined the types of instructional strategies that Data Teams (small teams that strategically improve practice through the use of data) used throughout the course of the last year. When the English department approached Ethan about a potential change in curriculum that would better support the revised framework, Ethan suggested that the teachers bring this curriculum to the team. During their next few meetings, the ad hoc group used several tools to explore this curriculum as well as several others that had been recommended in current research reviews. Ethan had suggested that they use these tools to vet other curricula as well.

Ethan worked with the team to ensure that any changes made to the framework or curriculum still fit within the mission and vision of the school. Additionally, the team met with the building leadership team to ensure that appropriate revisions were made to the school improvement plan to reflect the new framework and curriculum. The team was pleased to see the staff embrace the changes when they worked through a professional development protocol designed to help build understanding of the thinking behind the changes. Feedback from the meeting indicated that the staff felt the team had represented their thinking well throughout the process.

Peruse the MLP Matrix and assess Ethan's performance in Domain 4.0: Decision Making. Make mental notes and be prepared to respond as to the reason for your score on that dimension. Please be prepared to report out in 15 minutes.

Scenario #28—Ethan
4.0: Decision Making

PROFICIENT

Ethan had been serving as principal of Rolling River High School for eight years. During his tenure, Ethan had the opportunity to lead his high school through both triumph and adversity. As a seasoned principal, he felt capable of handling either, obviously preferring the former. As Ethan considered the state of student achievement at Rolling River, he judged that this year had the potential to be either.

Last year's state assessment results were in hand and Ethan was disappointed in how flat the results were given the incredible gains the school had made over the past few years. His staff embraced significant reform measures enthusiastically over the course of the past five years and were buoyed by the impact they were having on student achievement. Ethan worried that they were now becoming somewhat complacent and needed a new boost. Recently, his physical education department chair shared that people were feeling that they had gotten through the emergency of improving student achievement and now felt that the school was remaining tied to cross-content writing strategies that worked well in the past but didn't appear to be pushing students any further. The physical education teacher confessed that teachers were feeling they couldn't change the instructional approach because Ethan seemed quite tied to the past success of these results.

Ethan took this information to heart and **(4.2) decided to use an upcoming staff meeting to remind staff about the decision-making matrix that had not been revisited by the full staff in a couple of years. Ethan had developed the matrix to clearly outline what types of decisions were made by whom and for what purpose.** In this instance, Ethan brought the staff back to the original reason for the decision to move forward with the writing framework they had developed as a staff. He also **(4.4) took the opportunity to let the staff know that it was okay to revisit this decision,** as this should ultimately be a shared decision given its immediate impact on teaching and students. **(4.4) Ethan reminded the staff of several other initiatives that had been revised based on emerging data trends, even admitting the failure of his own idea for improving parent involvement, which had been dropped completely after two years of data suggested it was discouraging instead of encouraging parent involvement.**

Ethan encouraged anyone with a strong interest in reworking the framework to become involved. **(4.1, 4.2) Ethan then worked with the school leadership team to analyze trends in state and district writing assessments to pinpoint where students were stalled.** The team also examined the types of instructional strategies that Data Teams (small teams that strategically improve practice through the use of data) used throughout the course of the last year. When the English department approached Ethan about a potential change in curriculum that would better support the revised framework, Ethan suggested that the teachers bring this curriculum to the team. During their next few meetings, the ad hoc group used several tools to explore this curriculum as well as several others that had been recommended in current research reviews. Ethan had suggested that they use these tools to vet other curricula as well.

> **4.2:** Ethan revisits the decision-making matrix to clarify how decisions are made.
> SCORE 4.2 AT PROFICIENT.

> **4.4:** Ethan revisits a previous decision and shares with staff that this decision can be reevaluated in the current light.
> SCORE 4.4 AT EXEMPLARY.
>
> **4.4:** Ethan reminds staff of multiple initiatives that have been revised and even admits to a failure of his own initiative that had to be "sunsetted" due to ineffectiveness in improving parent involvement.
> SCORE 4.4 AT EXEMPLARY.

> **4.1** and **4.2:** Ethan uses data to guide the decisions regarding any revisions to the plan. Trends are analyzed from multiple sources.
> SCORE 4.1 AND 4.2 AT PROFICIENT.

CASE STUDY MATERIALS AND LEARNING EXPERIENCES

4.3: Ethan guides the team to ensure that changes reflected vision, mission, curriculum, and the school improvement plan. SCORE 4.3 AT PROFICIENT.

(4.3) Ethan worked with the team to ensure that any changes made to the framework or curriculum still fit within the mission and vision of the school. Additionally, the team met with the building leadership team to ensure that appropriate revisions were made to the school improvement plan to reflect the new framework and curriculum. The team was pleased to see the staff embrace the changes when they worked through a professional development protocol designed to help build understanding of the thinking behind the changes. Feedback from the meeting indicated that the staff felt the team had represented their thinking well throughout the process.

Scenario #29—John
4.0: Decision Making

John has been the director of transportation for the past eight years in a large suburban school district outside of Chicago, Illinois. Upon first taking his new position, the district provided training for him in the Baldridge Continuous Quality Improvement Model (a national customer-focused service model to improve organizational performance) and a leadership institute that had as one of its main focuses how to make decisions for results. Two years ago, the district saw a significant decline in enrollment resulting in cuts to John's transportation department. This was not the first time in his tenure as director of transportation that John had had to make similar cuts. John prided himself on knowing the transportation budget well and had been recognized for his strategic work in keeping costs low, while still maintaining a high degree of stakeholder (parents, students, and bus drivers) satisfaction.

When John first heard of these cuts, he immediately reflected on the last time his department had to make similar cuts and reviewed the processes he used and the results of his actions. With this data and feedback in mind, he set out to bring together all members of his team—bus drivers, schedulers, and his leadership team—to articulate the plan they would use to make these difficult decisions. While John knew that this was his decision to make ultimately, he also knew that a district value and part of the vision and mission of the district focused on collaboration and a partnership with all stakeholders. Consequently, John and his leadership team worked to develop a survey to be distributed to principals, parents, and students, which not only communicated the nature and magnitude of cuts needed but also asked for specific feedback and suggestions that would ensure everyone had a chance to have their voices heard in the process.

After a very thorough review of the feedback from his meetings with his internal transportation team and the survey data, it was clear to John and his team that the only way to reduce costs and to balance the budget was to maximize ridership by reorganizing bus routes. With this decision made, John and his team began to work on the plan they had previously developed. They began by reviewing all of the school boundaries, current routes, and school start and end times. Additionally, they referred to the survey, noting a significant and consistent piece of data from parents regarding a concern for discipline issues that arose when students of different grade levels, elementary and secondary, were at the same bus stop or rode the same bus together. After countless hours of reviewing the data, the team was able to make significant changes to the bus schedules, which resulted in fewer and shorter routes. In addition, the team was able to enlist parents who volunteered to be at each of the individual bus stops to monitor student behavior. All bus drivers attended professional development sessions focused on proactive strategies to support positive student behavior while riding the bus. The plan was communicated to all schools and parents and met with great support. The schools also agreed to be proactive by talking with their older students about taking responsibility to support positive behavior on the bus. John was pleased that parents and schools were satisfied with the decisions made and that his goal of balancing the budget was achieved.

CASE STUDY MATERIALS AND LEARNING EXPERIENCES

After the first couple of weeks, John and his team once again reached out for feedback by hosting a series of focus group meetings with parents and heard concerns from a variety of sources. Upon reviewing this data, plus personally riding buses and visiting bus stops, John and his team worked to make the changes needed to remedy the viable concerns.

Peruse the MLP Matrix and assess John's performance in Domain 4.0: Decision Making. Make mental notes and be prepared to respond as to the reason for your score on that dimension. Please be prepared to report out in 15 minutes.

Scenario #29—John
4.0: Decision Making

EXEMPLARY

John has been the director of transportation for the past eight years in a large suburban school district outside of Chicago, Illinois. Upon first taking his new position, the district provided training for him in the Baldridge Continuous Quality Improvement Model (a national customer-focused service model to improve organizational performance) and a leadership institute that had as one of its main focuses how to make decisions for results. Two years ago, the district saw a significant decline in enrollment resulting in cuts to John's transportation department. This was not the first time in his tenure as director of transportation that John had had to make similar cuts. John prided himself on knowing the transportation budget well and had been recognized for his strategic work in keeping costs low, while still maintaining a high degree of stakeholder (parents, students, and bus drivers) satisfaction.

When John first heard of these cuts, **(4.1) he immediately reflected on the last time his department had to make similar cuts and reviewed the processes he used and the results of his actions.** With this data and feedback in mind, **(4.2) he set out to bring together all members of his team—bus drivers, schedulers, and his leadership team—to articulate the plan they would use to make these difficult decisions. (4.2) While John knew that this was his decision to make ultimately, (4.3) he also knew that a district value and part of the vision and mission of the district focused on collaboration and a partnership with all stakeholders.** Consequently, John and his leadership team **(4.2) worked to develop a survey to be distributed to principals, parents, and students, which not only communicated the nature and magnitude of cuts needed but also asked for specific feedback and suggestions** that would ensure everyone had a chance to have their voices heard in the process.

After a very **(4.2) thorough review of the feedback from his meetings with his internal transportation team and the survey data, it was clear to John and his team that the only way to reduce costs and to balance the budget was to maximize ridership by reorganizing bus routes.** With this decision made, John and his team began to work on the plan they had previously developed. They began by **(4.1) reviewing all of the school boundaries, current routes, and school start and end times. Additionally, they referred to the survey, noting a significant and consistent piece of data from parents regarding a concern for discipline issues that arose when students of different grade levels, elementary and secondary, were at the same bus stop or rode the same bus together.** After countless hours of reviewing the data, the team was able to make significant changes to the bus schedules, which resulted in fewer and shorter routes. In addition, the team was able to enlist parents who volunteered to be at each of the individual bus stops to monitor student behavior. All bus drivers attended professional development sessions focused on proactive strategies to support positive student behavior while riding the bus. The plan was communicated to all schools and parents and met with great support. The schools also agreed to be proactive by talking with their older students about taking responsibility to support positive behavior on the bus. John was pleased

4.1: John reflected upon previous data and results. SCORE **4.1** AT EXEMPLARY.

4.2: John made sure that all stakeholders involved knew how decisions would be made. SCORE **4.2** AT EXEMPLARY.

4.2: John identified that this was his decision to make and that he was ultimately responsible for balancing the budget, while keeping customer satisfaction high. SCORE **4.2** AT EXEMPLARY.

4.3: John used the vision and mission of the district to guide his actions. SCORE **4.3** AT EXEMPLARY.

4.2: The plan was articulated and stakeholders surveyed. SCORE **4.2** AT EXEMPLARY.

4.2: While the decision was ultimately made by John, the data collected was compelling and supported by all involved. SCORE **4.2** AT EXEMPLARY.

4.1: Data is reflected in all the decisions made to support the transportation decision. SCORE **4.1** AT EXEMPLARY.

4.1: After the decision was made and implemented, John and his team following up by collecting data on how the plan was working. SCORE 4.1 AT EXEMPLARY.

4.4: John and his team evaluated the decision for effectiveness and revised as needed. SCORE 4.4 AT EXEMPLARY.

that parents and schools were satisfied with the decisions made and that his goal of balancing the budget was achieved.

After the first couple of weeks, John and his **(4.1) team once again reached out for feedback by hosting a series of focus group meetings with parents and heard concerns from a variety of sources.** Upon reviewing this data, plus personally riding buses and visiting bus stops, **(4.4) John and his team worked to make the changes needed to remedy the viable concerns.**

Scenario #30—Ronald
4.0: Decision Making

Ronald is a manager for recruitment and staffing in the Hartman County School District, Human Resources Office. He has been in this position with this district for three years. He has established a good working relationship with his colleagues and other administrators in the district. The district is in the process of accepting applications for administrative and teaching positions for a new school that will be opening at the start of the next academic year.

During the staff planning meetings, Ronald did not note the number and kinds of students to be served, the number of teachers needed, the types of educational programs and support services that would be needed, nor the availability of funding to operate this new school. When staff members questioned him about the failure to provide this information, he stated that his plan was to look at the organizational structure at another similar school and base his decisions on that information. This reply bewildered the staff. Without this critical information, he was not aware of the qualities that the candidates should possess that would be helpful in this school, nor the criteria needed to select the staff. This type of approach for selecting qualified candidates was disconnected from the district's vision, mission, and strategic priorities.

As he began screening applications for possible candidates who would qualify for positions in the new school, Ronald paid little attention to the lack of diversity and experience the pool of applicants represented. After reviewing the applications and hand selecting the ones he thought would be good candidates, he began contacting them for interviews. Some of the candidates were friends or family members of Ronald's, who were previous applicants or who were already in the school system and wanted to transfer to the new school. Because he was aware prior to receiving the applications that these people would apply for a position, he made sure that they got a good interview that would lead to their being hired. When the candidates were hired, it made him feel important and popular with his friends and family, and he didn't want to risk losing that status. His failure to review the evaluations of applicants who were currently employed with the district, as well as complete a verification check on each applicant, demonstrated his lack of leadership and his neglecting to use data to assist him with his decision making that would impact student learning and achievement.

Peruse the MLP Matrix and assess Ronald's performance in Domain 4.0: Decision Making. Make mental notes and be prepared to respond as to the reason for your score on that dimension. Please be prepared to report out in 15 minutes.

Scenario #30—Ronald
4.0: Decision Making

Not Meeting Standards

Ronald is a manager for recruitment and staffing in the Hartman County School District, Human Resources Office. He has been in this position with this district for three years. He has established a good working relationship with his colleagues and other administrators in the district. The district is in the process of accepting applications for administrative and teaching positions for a new school that will be opening at the start of the next academic year.

During the staff planning meetings, **(4.2) Ronald did not note the number and kinds of students to be served, the number of teachers needed, the types of educational programs and support services that would be needed, nor the availability of funding to operate this new school. When staff members questioned him about the failure to provide this information, he stated that his plan was to look at the organizational structure at another similar school and base his decisions on that information. This reply bewildered the staff. (4.3) Without this critical information, he was not aware of the qualities that the candidates should possess that would be helpful in this school, nor the criteria needed to select the staff. This type of approach for selecting qualified candidates was disconnected from the district's vision, mission, and strategic priorities.**

As he began screening applications for possible candidates who would qualify for positions in the new school, Ronald paid little attention to the lack of diversity and experience the pool of applicants represented. After reviewing the applications and hand selecting the ones he thought would be good candidates, he began contacting them for interviews. Some of the candidates were friends or family members of Ronald's, who were previous applicants or who were already in the school system and wanted to transfer to the new school. **(4.1) Because he was aware prior to receiving the applications that these people would apply for a position, he made sure that they got a good interview that would lead to their being hired. When the candidates were hired, it made him feel important and popular with his friends and family, and he didn't want to risk losing that status. His failure to review the evaluations of applicants who were currently employed with the district, as well as complete a verification check on each applicant, demonstrated his lack of leadership and his neglecting to use data to assist him with his decision making that would impact student learning and achievement.**

4.2: Ronald's approach to decision making has no clear method and bewilders the staff. SCORE 4.2 AT NOT MEETING STANDARDS.

4.3: Ronald's lack of critical information on which to base his decision shows a disconnection from the organization's vision, mission, and strategic planning. SCORE 4.3 AT NOT MEETING STANDARDS.

4.1: Ronald fails to use data when making hiring decisions. He makes decisions to be popular with his friends and family. SCORE 4.1 AT NOT MEETING STANDARDS.

Scenario #31—Isabel
4.0: Decision Making

Isabel was well into her seventh year as superintendent of Clear Crest School District. She had come into the role as an assistant superintendent with years of administrative and teaching experience in the district. If there was one thing Isabel knew, it was Clear Crest. She knew the expectations, the achievement, the history, and the people well, and this familiarity guided her decisions on a daily basis. There were both advantages and disadvantages to such a high level of background knowledge, and Isabel was discovering both sides of the coin on a regular basis. Feeling too entrenched in the history of Clear Crest caused Isabel to hire a new assistant superintendent two years ago from outside the district and the state. She thought some fresh new ideas might provide a good shot in the arm for Clear Crest.

The new assistant superintendent proved to complement Isabel's strengths well. He brought a deep understanding of how to reach high levels of performance with students, regardless of demographics. Given the rapidly changing face of Clear Crest, this understanding was essential. Together they were able to set Clear Crest on a course that took into consideration past successes as well as initiatives that had less than desirable results.

Isabel was quick to share such "learning opportunities" with the entire administrative and teaching staff on a yearly basis. This year was no different. During the initial kickoff with all staff, Isabel spoke at great length about the intentional decision to end the reading initiative that was producing lackluster results for the sixth year in a row. Based on the results of the state assessment and district benchmarks, it was clear that this program was not worth continuing. Clear Crest had also been gathering implementation data for the past five years that indicated no correlation between extensive professional development, full implementation of teaching strategies, and increased student achievement. Quite the contrary, it seemed the more they relied on the fidelity of the program, the less they were likely to see any change in summative assessment results.

Last year, a new three-year improvement plan had been crafted with the assistance of a team of consultants, who provided professional development and guidance in the application of the Decision Making for Results process (improvement planning and monitoring process). Isabel and the new assistant superintendent led a team through a process that specifically addressed the cause-and-effect data that had been gathered regarding student reading achievement. They developed a plan that not only addressed the needs and the potential causes, but also considered the culture of the district and did not compromise the current vision or mission.

Although district leaders were familiar with the Decision Making for Results process and how the district team came to the goals, actions, results indicators, and monitoring related to the District Improvement Plan, other staff members in the district had less exposure. In an effort to help staff and community members better understand the process that led to the plan, Isabel provided an overview of how decisions were made throughout the district and included detailed information about the Decision Making for Results process. This overview was provided to staff and community in multiple venues throughout the spring of the previous year with a focus on how data was used in the decision process.

Peruse the MLP Matrix and assess Isabel's performance in Domain 4.0: Decision Making. Make mental notes and be prepared to respond as to the reason for your score on that dimension. Please be prepared to report out in 15 minutes.

Scenario #31—Isabel
4.0: Decision Making

PROFICIENT

Isabel was well into her seventh year as superintendent of Clear Crest School District. She had come into the role as an assistant superintendent with years of administrative and teaching experience in the district. If there was one thing Isabel knew, it was Clear Crest. She knew the expectations, the achievement, the history, and the people well, and this familiarity guided her decisions on a daily basis. There were both advantages and disadvantages to such a high level of background knowledge, and Isabel was discovering both sides of the coin on a regular basis. Feeling too entrenched in the history of Clear Crest caused Isabel to hire a new assistant superintendent two years ago from outside the district and the state. She thought some fresh new ideas might provide a good shot in the arm for Clear Crest.

The new assistant superintendent proved to complement Isabel's strengths well. He brought a deep understanding of how to reach high levels of performance with students, regardless of demographics. Given the rapidly changing face of Clear Crest, this understanding was essential. Together they were able to set Clear Crest on a course that took into consideration past successes as well as initiatives that had less than desirable results.

(4.4) Isabel was quick to share such "learning opportunities" with the entire administrative and teaching staff on a yearly basis. This year was no different. During the initial kickoff with all staff, Isabel spoke at great length about the intentional decision to end the reading initiative that was producing lackluster results for the sixth year in a row. **(4.1)** Based on the results of the state assessment and district benchmarks, it was clear that this program was not worth continuing. Clear Crest had also been gathering implementation data for the past five years that indicated no correlation between extensive professional development, full implementation of teaching strategies, and increased student achievement. Quite the contrary, it seemed the more they relied on the fidelity of the program, the less they were likely to see any change in summative assessment results.

Last year, **(4.3)** a new three-year improvement plan had been crafted with the assistance of a team of consultants, who provided professional development and guidance in the application of the Decision Making for Results process (improvement planning and monitoring process). **(4.3, cont.)** Isabel and the new assistant superintendent led a team through a process that specifically addressed the cause-and-effect data that had been gathered regarding student reading achievement. They developed a plan that not only addressed the needs and the potential causes, but also considered the culture of the district and did not compromise the current vision or mission.

Although district leaders were familiar with the Decision Making for Results process and how the district team came to the goals, actions, results indicators, and monitoring related to the District Improvement Plan, other staff members in the district had less exposure. In an effort to help staff and community members

> **4.4:** Isabel provides an honest view of the multiple data points that guided the decision to sunset a program. Also refers to this as a regular practice, at least annually. SCORE 4.4 AT EXEMPLARY.

> **4.1:** Isabel has cited state and district data sources, as well as curriculum implementation data. SCORE 4.1 AT PROFICIENT.

> **4.3:** Isabel leads the team through a process that ensures alignment with vision and mission and the district improvement plan. SCORE 4.3 AT PROFICIENT.

CASE STUDY MATERIALS AND LEARNING EXPERIENCES

4.2: Isabel provides information on how decisions are made in the district and includes a focus on data analysis. SCORE 4.2 AT PROFICIENT.

better understand the process that led to the plan, **(4.2) Isabel provided an overview of how decisions were made throughout the district and included detailed information about the Decision Making for Results process. This overview was provided to staff and community in multiple venues throughout the spring of the previous year with a focus on how data was used in the decision process.**

Scenarios 32–37

Domain 5.0:
Communication

Leaders in education understand communication as a two-way street. They seek to listen and learn from students, staff, and community. They recognize individuals for good work and maintain high visibility at school and in the community. Regular communications with staff and community keep all stakeholders engaged in the work of the school.

CASE STUDY MATERIALS AND LEARNING EXPERIENCES

Scenario #32—Alexandra
5.0: Communication

Alexandra, after 12 very successful years as a primary teacher, was in her first year as an assistant principal at a brand-new suburban elementary school with just over 500 students. Having just finished her administrative certification program, she was excited about her new administrative role. She was enjoying the new challenges, the freedom of being out of the classroom, and her time to interact with students more freely. She found great joy in visiting with students on the playground and took on lunch duty so she could get to know the names of her students personally and to give her teachers a break. Alexandra was also highly visible within the school. She met the children as they arrived on the buses, frequently visited classrooms, and made certain that dismissal at the end of the day was uneventful. In just over three months' time, Alexandra prided herself on knowing the names of the majority of the students—and not just the students she saw frequently in her office for discipline concerns, but other students as well.

Alexandra's principal, Mary, saw great strength in Alexandra's ability to communicate with staff, parents, and students and was excited for her to become involved in all aspects of the school. As a result, their working relationship was mutually positive and collaborative. Her principal could see that Alexandra was compassionate with staff. She knew the long hours they put in and the hard work they did to ensure that all student needs were being met. The principal also observed that Alexandra was a great reflective listener and coach. Staff openly gave feedback and remarked about the close bond that their school leaders had formed with them; they trusted their leadership and sought out their guidance and support. Alexandra felt empowered and eager to take on a leadership challenge.

Having such confidence in Alexandra's leadership skills, Mary appointed Alexandra to be the school's representative on the District Crisis Team and scheduled her to attend a crisis prevention conference in mid-October. Alexandra would take on the main responsibility for any crisis that would occur during Mary's absence.

At the beginning of December, Mary was out of the building attending her monthly principal meeting when Alexandra was paged to the front office. Knowing that pages during academic schooltime were off-limits, Alexandra knew this must be an emergency and that she needed to get to the office quickly. As she entered the office, the principal's secretary shared that they just received a call from the district office that there had been a bank robbery three blocks from the school. The gunman had been seen last headed in the school's direction on foot. Alexandra remained calm and knew exactly what she needed to do.

Immediately, Alexandra got on the PA system and announced that all teachers were to check their attendance. This was the code that Mary and Alexandra had communicated early to their staff that would be used in case of an emergency lockdown. Teachers calmly closed their doors and asked all students to move to the front of the class and sit on the floor closer to the teachers, away from the windows, and shared that they had decided to read a story to the class at this time. This was also part of the lockdown crisis plan that Alexandra put together with her staff based on what she learned at the crisis prevention conference. Alexandra had trained the staff and, as a result, they knew exactly what to do in the case of a school lockdown. Alexandra made a quick sweep throughout the entire building and returned to the office, at which time she received a call from the central office that it was all clear and that they could resume normal school procedures. Alexandra made an announcement on the PA system that reflected the lockdown had been lifted and it was all clear. At the end of the day, Alexandra held a quick stand-up meeting and shared what had happened near the school, applauded her staff for responding so quickly and calmly, and asked for feedback on her leadership during this crisis. After the meeting, Alexandra also crafted a memo to send home to parents the next day that shared the situation and acknowledged how proud she was of her staff for the way they responded during the crisis. When Mary returned from her principals' meeting shortly after, she applauded Alexandra for her quick and strategic responses and direct communication during a crisis situation. Alexandra smiled and said, "Wow! I might have looked calm on the outside, but my insides were shaking."

Peruse the MLP Matrix and assess Alexandra's performance in Domain 5.0: Communication. Make mental notes and be prepared to respond as to the reason for your score on that dimension. Please be prepared to report out in 15 minutes.

Scenario #32—Alexandra
5.0: Communication

PROFICIENT

Alexandra, after 12 very successful years as a primary teacher, was in her first year as an assistant principal at a brand-new suburban elementary school with just over 500 students. Having just finished her administrative certification program, she was excited about her new administrative role. She was enjoying the new challenges, the freedom of being out of the classroom, and her time to interact with students more freely. **(5.1) She found great joy in visiting with students on the playground and took on lunch duty so she could get to know the names of her students personally and to give her teachers a break. Alexandra was also highly visible within the school. She met the children as they arrived on the buses, frequently visited classrooms, and made certain that dismissal at the end of the day was uneventful. In just over three months' time, Alexandra prided herself on knowing the names of the majority of the students—and not just the students she saw frequently in her office for discipline concerns, but other students as well.**

Alexandra's principal, **(5.3) Mary, saw great strength in Alexandra's ability to communicate with staff, parents, and students and was excited for her to become involved in all aspects of the school.** As a result, their working relationship was mutually positive and collaborative. Her principal could see that **(5.4) Alexandra was compassionate with staff. She knew the long hours they put in and the hard work they did to ensure that all student needs were being met. The principal also observed that Alexandra was a great reflective listener and coach. Staff openly gave feedback and remarked about the close bond that their school leaders had formed with them; they trusted their leadership and sought out their guidance and support. Alexandra felt empowered and eager to take on a leadership challenge.**

Having such confidence in Alexandra's leadership skills, Mary appointed Alexandra to be the school's representative on the District Crisis Team and scheduled her to attend a crisis prevention conference in mid-October. Alexandra would take on the main responsibility for any crisis that would occur during Mary's absence.

At the beginning of December, Mary was out of the building attending her monthly principal meeting when Alexandra was paged to the front office. Knowing that pages during academic schooltime were off-limits, Alexandra knew this must be an emergency and that she needed to get to the office quickly. As she entered the office, the principal's secretary shared that they just received a call from the district office that there had been a bank robbery three blocks from the school. The gunman had been seen last headed in the school's direction on foot. Alexandra remained calm and knew exactly what she needed to do.

(5.4) Immediately, Alexandra got on the PA system and announced that all teachers were to check their attendance. This was the code that Mary and Alexandra had communicated early to their staff that would be used in case of an emergency lockdown. Teachers calmly closed their doors and asked all students to move to the front of the class and sit on the floor closer to the teachers,

---

5.1: Alexandra is highly visible at her school during critical student transition times and regularly visits classrooms. She greets students by name and spends time getting to know her students personally.
SCORE **5.1** AT PROFICIENT.

5.3: Alexandra has developed strong communication skills when interacting with parents, staff, and students.
SCORE **5.3** AT PROFICIENT.

5.4: Alexandra's staff see her as a caring and compassionate listener. They trust her feedback and seek her guidance.
SCORE **5.4** AT PROFICIENT.

5.4: Alexandra listened carefully to her secretary regarding the news of the gunman. With this information, she was able to communicate clearly with her staff regarding what needed to happen. Following school crisis plan procedures, the school went into lockdown.
SCORE **5.4** AT PROFICIENT.

5.2: Staff were part of the decision-making team regarding the systems they would put in place during a lockdown.
SCORE 5.2 AT PROFICIENT.

5.2: Alexandra knows her staff well and takes it upon herself to recognize them for their work and contributions to the school publicly.
SCORE 5.2 AT PROFICIENT.

5.3: Alexandra routinely communicates with parents regarding events during the day.
SCORE 5.3 AT PROFICIENT.

away from the windows, and shared that they had decided to read a story to the class at this time. **(5.2) This was also part of the lockdown crisis plan that Alexandra put together with her staff based on what she learned at the crisis prevention conference. Alexandra had trained the staff and, as a result, they knew exactly what to do in the case of a school lockdown.** Alexandra made a quick sweep throughout the entire building and returned to the office, at which time she received a call from the central office that it was all clear and that they could resume normal school procedures. Alexandra made an announcement on the PA system that reflected the lockdown had been lifted and it was all clear. At the end of the day, Alexandra held a quick stand-up meeting and shared what had happened near the school, applauded her staff for responding so quickly and calmly, and asked for feedback on her leadership during this crisis. **(5.2) After the meeting, Alexandra also crafted a memo to send home to parents the next day that shared the situation and acknowledged how proud she was of her staff (5.3) for the way they responded during the crisis. When Mary returned from her principals' meeting shortly after, she applauded Alexandra for her quick and strategic responses and direct communication during a crisis situation.** Alexandra smiled and said, "Wow! I might have looked calm on the outside, but my insides were shaking."

Scenario #33—Alicia
5.0: Communication

Alicia, principal at Thunder Ridge Middle School, has been in this position for the last 13 years. She prides herself on being a veteran educator with more than 25 years of experience. As principal, she supervises more than 95 certified staff and 43 classified staff. She has led her school in curriculum mapping of the Common Core State Standards and is considered to be a curriculum and instruction guru among her peers.

It is Thursday morning. Alicia begins each school day at the buses greeting the students as they arrive. She greets all the eighth graders by name. She is still learning the names of the seventh-grade students; greeting them by name is difficult. Alicia's morning message is always to tell the students to do their personal best and to have a great day. The teachers highly respect Alicia for her instructional leadership style and appreciate her visibility during the noninstructional times of the day, such as lunch and in the hallways between classes.

After the morning bell rings, Alicia conducts walkabouts in all the team hallways. One teacher stops her to share a concern in the lunchroom. However, Alicia interrupts her and tells her to bring up all concerns during this afternoon's weekly faculty meeting. The teacher is highly upset and shares with another teacher that Alicia will have informal conversations with the teachers about personal matters, like family or other nonschool-related issues. "Things that don't matter," she states, rolling her eyes. Alicia believes that if something is a concern for one teacher, it is a concern for others.

Later, after school, Alicia begins the weekly staff meeting with praises. After a few of the teachers share their praises, she then asks if there are any concerns. The teacher who stopped her in the hallway raises her hand and shares that students are arriving late to the third-period lunch and they do not have enough time to eat. She also states that many parents have called and want this issue resolved. Alicia just stares at the teacher and says that she has not noticed students not having enough time to eat all of their lunch, and she believes that they are talking and socializing way too much. She continues to say that the teachers need to be more proactive by walking around during their lunch duty. The teacher puts her head down and shakes her head in disgust. She whispers to her teammate, "This is not the issue."

Another teacher raises her hand. Once called on, she states the same concern. Alicia listens and asks who the parents are who want explanations. After being given the names of the parents who are complaining, Alicia calls all of these parents to hear their concerns. Alicia tells each parent that she will look into the lunch situation.

Peruse the MLP Matrix and assess Alicia's performance in Domain 5.0: Communication. Make mental notes and be prepared to respond as to the reason for your score on that dimension. Please be prepared to report out in 15 minutes.

Scenario #33—Alicia
5.0: Communication

PROGRESSING

Alicia, principal at Thunder Ridge Middle School, has been in this position for the last 13 years. She prides herself on being a veteran educator with more than 25 years of experience. As principal, she supervises more than 95 certified staff and 43 classified staff. She has led her school in curriculum mapping of the Common Core State Standards and is considered to be a curriculum and instruction guru among her peers.

(5.1) It is Thursday morning. Alicia begins each school day at the buses greeting the students as they arrive. She greets all the eighth graders by name. She is still learning the names of the seventh-grade students; greeting them by name is difficult. Alicia's morning message is always to tell the students to do their personal best and to have a great day. The teachers highly respect Alicia for her instructional leadership style and appreciate her visibility during the noninstructional times of the day, such as lunch and in the hallways between classes.

(5.2) After the morning bell rings, Alicia conducts walkabouts in all the team hallways. One teacher stops her to share a concern in the lunchroom. However, Alicia interrupts her and tells her to bring up all concerns during this afternoon's weekly faculty meeting. The teacher is highly upset and shares with another teacher that Alicia will have informal conversations with the teachers about personal matters, like family or other nonschool-related issues. "Things that don't matter," she states, rolling her eyes. Alicia believes that if something is a concern for one teacher, it is a concern for others.

Later, after school, Alicia begins the weekly staff meeting with praises. After a few of the teachers share their praises, she then asks if there are any concerns. **(5.4)** The teacher who stopped her in the hallway raises her hand and shares that students are arriving late to the third-period lunch and they do not have enough time to eat. She also states that many parents have called and want this issue resolved. Alicia just stares at the teacher and says that she has not noticed students not having enough time to eat all of their lunch, and she believes that they are talking and socializing way too much. She continues to say that the teachers need to be more proactive by walking around during their lunch duty. The teacher puts her head down and shakes her head in disgust. She whispers to her teammate, "This is not the issue."

Another teacher raises her hand. Once called on, she states the same concern. **(5.3)** Alicia listens and asks who the parents are who want explanations. After being given the names of the parents who are complaining, Alicia calls all of these parents to hear their concerns. Alicia tells each parent that she will look into the lunch situation.

5.1: Alicia knows most students' names, is visible, often greets students by name, and talks with students frequently. SCORE 5.1 AT PROGRESSING.

5.2: Alicia typically limits her listening to time during faculty meetings. SCORE 5.2 AT PROGRESSING.

5.4: Alicia appears to listen to the teachers, but she relies on her own interpretation of the problem with the students. SCORE 5.4 AT PROGRESSING.

5.3: Alicia calls each parent, but only after they initiate the concern. The parents receive a respectful hearing from Alicia. SCORE 5.3 AT PROGRESSING.

Scenario #34—Aaron
5.0: Communication

Aaron loved all aspects of his work as the principal of Northridge High School, but he especially loved his job this time of year. The beginning of the school year in a large comprehensive high school was always a time of intense energy and renewal. During the first three months of school, Aaron sought every opportunity to set the tone for the year. Once the tone was positive with all stakeholders, the garden simply needed to be watered and tended. Aaron knew that sowing and tending the garden required positive interactions and acknowledgment of each individual's contribution to the greater good.

Aaron began each year with an all-day professional development kickoff. During this year's kickoff, the building leadership team shared the game plan for the year in terms of school improvement strategies and the tie to the school's mission and vision. He always invited district leaders, classified staff, his building engineer, and all staff who supported students in his school to these meetings each year and made sure he followed up with these individuals throughout the year. Staff had the opportunity to break into small cross-content groups to share their greatest hopes and fears about the year and how they planned to support the vision and mission of the school through the school improvement work. Aaron made sure he visited with each of these groups throughout the day to ensure that he understood their various perspectives.

Aaron's staff was already very familiar with the school improvement plan because of the involvement they had in creating the plan. Aaron used a representative leadership team to do the detail work of the plan and serve as a conduit of information and feedback between their own representative teams and the leadership team. Additionally, Aaron made sure that several parents from the school advisory committee, a classified staff member, and student government representatives were also included in the building leadership team.

In addition to creating this representative framework for input and feedback, Aaron made sure that he had multiple opportunities for feedback from all of his representative stakeholders. One of his favorite avenues for student feedback was a monthly lunch with 10 students who were recruited to share their concerns or ideas about Northridge High School. Students were selected from various groups intentionally to provide for a cross section of backgrounds. Not only was this a great way to hear what students had to say, it also encouraged students to understand the perspectives of others in a smaller, more personal group setting. The students often mentioned Aaron's openness to ideas whenever specific student concerns were raised in both informal and formal settings. Aaron also attended more formal meetings with student government, parent advisory groups, and community forums; however, the more informal settings proved to be the most informative for Aaron.

Northridge stakeholders weren't always able to attend meetings, so Aaron and his leadership team developed various other systems of communication to meet the community's needs. But Aaron felt that still more could be done in this area. The Web site and e-mail provided great tools for pushing out information, but Aaron knew that getting access to the Web was a challenge for some of his families. When the leadership team developed a comprehensive survey with a target response rate of 80 percent, Aaron knew they would need to solve the technology problem for many of his families who lacked Internet access. This prompted Aaron to set up stations for access on community night, in the libraries, and in several local fast-food restaurants. The targeted 80 percent response rate was achieved. The opportunities for enhanced communication were so well received by families that the arrangement continued beyond the survey period, and regular free access to computers and the Internet was provided throughout the community. Suddenly, Aaron had parents, students, community members, and staff commenting on the information they had accessed on the Web site.

This new electronic traffic prompted Aaron to set up a regular two-way communication loop via the Web site so that he could constantly remain in touch with ideas and needs of the community and school. What started as a way to gain feedback about the school improvement plan blossomed into a new way of life at Northridge High School. Aaron was especially pleased about how important the input of staff, students, and community members had been in making this happen. Aaron could cite how he had used the data from multiple forms of interaction with large groups, small groups, electronic communication, and surveys to guide the mission and work of the school. The stakeholders' pleas for more opportunities to share information was what really set the project in motion. Aaron ended the year with a sense that he had a strong pulse on what his community was thinking, and the opportunities for expanding this new connection seemed wide open.

Peruse the MLP Matrix and assess Aaron's performance in Domain 5.0: Communication. Make mental notes and be prepared to respond as to the reason for your score on that dimension. Please be prepared to report out in 15 minutes.

Scenario #34—Aaron
5.0: Communication

EXEMPLARY

Aaron loved all aspects of his work as the principal of Northridge High School, but he especially loved his job this time of year. The beginning of the school year in a large comprehensive high school was always a time of intense energy and renewal. During the first three months of school, Aaron sought every opportunity to set the tone for the year. Once the tone was positive with all stakeholders, the garden simply needed to be watered and tended. Aaron knew that sowing and tending the garden required positive interactions and acknowledgment of each individual's contribution to the greater good.

Aaron began each year with an all-day professional development kickoff. During this year's kickoff, the building leadership team shared the game plan for the year in terms of school improvement strategies and the tie to the school's mission and vision. **(5.2) He always invited district leaders, classified staff, his building engineer, and all staff who supported students in his school to these meetings each year and made sure he followed up with these individuals throughout the year.** Staff had the opportunity to break into small cross-content groups to share their greatest hopes and fears about the year and how they planned to support the vision and mission of the school through the school improvement work. **(5.2) Aaron made sure he visited with each of these groups throughout the day to ensure that he understood their various perspectives.**

(5.2) Aaron's staff was already very familiar with the school improvement plan because of the involvement they had in creating the plan. Aaron used a representative leadership team to do the detail work of the plan and serve as a conduit of information and feedback between their own representative teams and the leadership team. **(5.3) Additionally, Aaron made sure that several parents from the school advisory committee, a classified staff member, and student government representatives were also included in the building leadership team.**

In addition to creating this representative framework for input and feedback, Aaron made sure that he had multiple opportunities for feedback from all of his representative stakeholders. One of his favorite avenues for student feedback was a **(5.1) monthly lunch with 10 students who were recruited to share their concerns or ideas about Northridge High School. Students were selected from various groups intentionally to provide for a cross section of backgrounds. (5.1) Not only was this a great way to hear what students had to say, it also encouraged students to understand the perspectives of others in a smaller, more personal group setting. (5.1) The students often mentioned Aaron's openness to ideas whenever specific student concerns were raised in both informal and formal settings. (5.1, 5.3) Aaron also attended more formal meetings with student government, parent advisory groups, and community forums;** however, the more informal settings proved to be the most informative for Aaron.

5.2: Aaron made sure that all groups were included in opportunities for discussion and feedback.
SCORE 5.2 AT EXEMPLARY.

5.2: Aaron made sure he listened to small groups and understood perspectives.
SCORE 5.2 AT EXEMPLARY.

5.2: Aaron made sure that all were very involved in the creation and implementation of the plan.
SCORE 5.2 AT EXEMPLARY.

5.3: Aaron makes sure the parent voice is heard and includes parent representation in the school leadership team.
SCORE 5.3 AT EXEMPLARY.

5.1: Aaron ensures student representation on the leadership team.
SCORE 5.1 AT EXEMPLARY.

5.1: Aaron also makes sure that he has regular opportunities to hear the diverse voices of students in small-group settings.
SCORE 5.1 AT EXEMPLARY.

5.1: Students refer to Aaron's ability to listen and take in student ideas.
SCORE 5.1 AT EXEMPLARY.

5.1 and 5.3: Aaron has regular formal meetings with both students and parents.
SCORE 5.1 AND 5.3 AT EXEMPLARY.

5.3: Aaron ensures that communication is adapted to fit the needs of the community. SCORE 5.3 AT EXEMPLARY.

5.4: Aaron reads the situation and creatively solves for the lack of Internet access. SCORE 5.4 AT EXEMPLARY.

5.3: Aaron uses technology to increase lines of communication with community. SCORE 5.3 AT EXEMPLARY.

5.3: A regular communication loop is established to ensure ongoing feedback between school and community. SCORE 5.3 AT EXEMPLARY.

5.4: Aaron used multiple listening strategies and used this data to make meaningful changes in the school's direction. SCORE 5.4 AT EXEMPLARY.

Northridge stakeholders weren't always able to attend meetings, so **(5.3) Aaron and his leadership team developed various other systems of communication to meet the community's needs.** But Aaron felt that still more could be done in this area. **(5.3, cont.) The Web site and e-mail provided great tools** for pushing out information, but **(5.4) Aaron knew that getting access to the Web was a challenge for some of his families.** When the leadership team **(5.3, cont.) developed a comprehensive survey with a target response rate of 80 percent, Aaron knew they would need to solve the technology problem for many of his families who lacked Internet access. (5.3) This prompted Aaron to set up stations for access on community night, in the libraries, and in several local fast-food restaurants. The targeted 80 percent response rate was achieved.** The opportunities for enhanced communication were so well received by families that the arrangement continued beyond the survey period, and regular free access to computers and the Internet was provided throughout the community. Suddenly, Aaron had parents, students, community members, and staff commenting on the information they had accessed on the Web site.

This new electronic traffic **(5.3) prompted Aaron to set up a regular two-way communication loop via the Web site so that he could constantly remain in touch with ideas and needs of the community and school. (5.4) What started as a way to gain feedback about the school improvement plan blossomed into a new way of life at Northridge High School. Aaron was especially pleased about how important the input of staff, students, and community members had been in making this happen. Aaron could cite how he had used the data from multiple forms of interaction with large groups, small groups, electronic communication, and surveys to guide the mission and work of the school.** The stakeholders' pleas for more opportunities to share information was what really set the project in motion. Aaron ended the year with a sense that he had a strong pulse on what his community was thinking, and the opportunities for expanding this new connection seemed wide open.

Scenario #35—Myra
5.0: Communication

Myra had been director of food services for the past 10 years in a large urban school district with more than 65 schools district-wide. During this time, Myra had experienced many personnel changes at the central office within each department, and this year was no different. While staff changes in other departments were irregular, Myra's food service department had remained fairly stable over the years, a phenomenon she attributed to the strong and trusting relationships she had developed with her department chairs, cafeteria leads, and her school principals. Myra made it a point to visit her schools on a regular basis and knew all of the principals and most of her cafeteria team members by name. Another quality that limited turnover in her department was Myra's leadership team, which helped to focus and align their department goals with central office goals.

Myra's drive to create and nurture strong relationships with her staff and principals (internal customers) also extended to the way she worked with her external customers, the parents of the students her staff served. Consequently, when Myra created her accountability committee, she made certain it consisted of representatives reflecting both her internal and external customers. This comprehensive group came together quarterly to monitor food service goals and to serve as a proactive problem-solving team when issues arose or new initiatives were to be implemented. Agendas were sent out well ahead of time and meetings were facilitated in a manner that encouraged open discussion and two-way conversations.

This year, with the changing of central office leadership, the decision was made to move to a district-wide integrated management system that would include student achievement and personnel data. The impact on the food services department and on schools would be a change in the manner in which teachers took the lunch count and the way that cafeteria leads kept count of full and à la carte lunches served daily in each school.

Myra knew this would challenge her leadership skills. She understood the key to success would be to make sure that there was a communication system put in place that was transparent, one that could push information out to but also pull information in from stakeholders. In preparation for this change, Myra called upon her accountability committee to develop a comprehensive strategic plan that would ensure a smooth implementation of the new system when school started in the fall. Once the plan was in place, it was important to communicate with all stakeholders. Myra was able to meet with all principals during their beginning-of-the-year meetings to outline the plan clearly and ask for feedback and support in working with teachers. Principals were very excited with the change, as they saw this system as a way to move their lunch lines along much more quickly so students were not waiting so long for their lunches. It would also allow students time to eat in a leisurely way and time to take a recess break. Principals trusted Myra and supported the plan by giving 30 minutes of their beginning-of-the-year workweek meetings to the cafeteria leads (who had previously been trained over the summer by Myra) to train teachers on the new system.

CASE STUDY MATERIALS AND LEARNING EXPERIENCES

While there would be little impact on parents and students (besides getting through the line much more quickly), Myra knew it was important to communicate with parents about a change in process. Myra used the system to send out a carefully crafted e-mail to parents registered in the system and a letter in the mail to those parents not registered, so that all would receive the information at about the same time.

During the first week of school, Myra and her food service leadership team divided up the schools and visited all 65 schools. Their goal was to observe the new process, ask for feedback, and immediately address any on-site concerns. While there were a few bumps over the first several months, the schools quickly settled into using the new management system. All in all, Myra was pleased with the implementation process.

Peruse the MLP Matrix and assess Myra's performance in Domain 5.0: Communication. Make mental notes and be prepared to respond as to the reason for your score on that dimension. Please be prepared to report out in 15 minutes.

Scenario #35—Myra
5.0: Communication

PROFICIENT

Myra had been director of food services for the past 10 years in a large urban school district with more than 65 schools district-wide. During this time, Myra had experienced many personnel changes at the central office within each department, and this year was no different. While staff changes in other departments were irregular, Myra's food service department had remained fairly stable over the years, a phenomenon she attributed to the strong and trusting relationships she had developed with her department chairs, cafeteria leads, and her school principals. **(5.2) Myra made it a point to visit her schools on a regular basis and knew all of the principals and most of her cafeteria team members by name.** Another quality that limited turnover in her department was Myra's leadership team, which helped to focus and align their department goals with central office goals.

(5.3, 5.2) Myra's drive to create and nurture strong relationships with her staff and principals (internal customers) also extended to the way she worked with her external customers, the parents of the students her staff served. Consequently, when Myra created her accountability committee, she made certain it consisted of representatives reflecting both her internal and external customers. This comprehensive group came together quarterly to monitor food service goals and to serve as a proactive problem-solving team when issues arose or new initiatives were to be implemented. Agendas were sent out well ahead of time and meetings were facilitated in a manner that encouraged open discussion and two-way conversations.

This year, with the changing of central office leadership, the decision was made to move to a district-wide integrated management system that would include student achievement and personnel data. The impact on the food services department and on schools would be a change in the manner in which teachers took the lunch count and the way that cafeteria leads kept count of full and à la carte lunches served daily in each school.

Myra knew this would challenge her leadership skills. She understood **(5.4) the key to success would be to make sure that there was a communication system put in place that was transparent, one that could push information out to but also pull information in from stakeholders. In preparation for this change, Myra called upon her accountability committee to develop a comprehensive strategic plan that would ensure a smooth implementation of the new system when school started in the fall.** Once the plan was in place, it was important to communicate with all stakeholders. **(5.4) Myra was able to meet with all principals during their beginning-of-the-year meetings to outline the plan clearly and ask for feedback and support in working with teachers.** Principals were very excited with the change, as they saw this system as a way to move their lunch lines along much more quickly so students were not waiting so long for their lunches. It would also allow students time to eat in a leisurely way and time to take a recess break. Principals trusted Myra and supported the plan by giving 30 minutes of their beginning-of-the-year workweek meetings to the cafeteria leads (who had previously been trained over the summer by Myra) to train teachers on the new system.

5.2: Myra visits her schools regularly and has worked to get to know principals and her staff by name. SCORE 5.2 AT PROFICIENT.

5.3 and **5.2:** Decisions in the food service department are made by an accountability committee, which consists of parents and staff. SCORE 5.3 AT EXEMPLARY.

Accountability meetings are set up to include open two-way discussions. SCORE 5.2 AT PROFICIENT.

5.4: Myra, together with her accountability committee, created a comprehensive communication plan to keep all stakeholders informed. SCORE 5.4 AT PROFICIENT.

5.4: There was evidence of the creation of a communication plan that consisted of openly sharing information, and principals were receptive to new ideas and suggestions. SCORE 5.4 AT PROFICIENT.

CASE STUDY MATERIALS AND LEARNING EXPERIENCES

5.3: Once the plan has been implemented, Myra continues to communicate any changes with parents. SCORE 5.3 AT PROFICIENT.

5.4: Myra is highly visible in her schools and uses this time to evaluate the strengths and needs at each of her sites. She continually asks for feedback on the implementation of the new systems and uses the information to make adjustments. SCORE 5.4 AT PROFICIENT.

While there would be little impact on parents and students (besides getting through the line much more quickly), **(5.3)** Myra knew it was important to communicate with parents about a change in process. Myra used the system to send out a carefully crafted e-mail to parents registered in the system and a letter in the mail to those parents not registered, so that all would receive the information at about the same time.

(5.4) During the first week of school, Myra and her food service leadership team divided up the schools and visited all 65 schools. Their goal was to observe the new process, ask for feedback, and immediately address any on-site concerns. While there were a few bumps over the first several months, the schools quickly settled into using the new management system. All in all, Myra was pleased with the implementation process.

Scenario #36—David
5.0: Communication

David has been the grounds and maintenance administrator for five years at Ridgetop School District. In the city of Ridgetop, recent severe rains have caused leaks and flooding in many of the schools. David is reviewing the work orders from all the buildings concerning the leaks and flood damage. After reading that most of the buildings are still experiencing moisture and leaks, he contacts all the principals and head custodians to notify them of his plans to address the damage.

David has assembled a meeting involving the co-op students, the day-shift custodians, and all the head custodians. In the meeting, he greets all the custodial staff and some of the co-op students by name. He engages in informal conversations with some of the co-op students before the start of the meeting. He shares with them that their high school has really been affected by the storm. He asks them if they have seen a lot of damage in the hallways, classrooms, and in other locations. He listens to their observations. David then begins the meeting by thanking everyone for attending on such short notice. Next he describes the effects of moisture and leaks, stating that moisture and leaks will contribute to mold growth, which can trigger asthma episodes and allergic reactions, cause severe odors, and lead to a variety of other problems.

At this time, two of the custodians raise their hands to share their current needs at their schools, but David tells them to wait until he is done talking. He then begins sharing with the staff how to inspect the buildings for signs of moisture and leaks. He tells them to look for signs of water damage by checking for moldy odors, looking for stains on the walls and ceiling, and checking cold surfaces. He then looks at one of the custodians and nods as a gesture to indicate that he can speak. The custodian shares that his team has already located the moisture and leaks and that they have responded by cleaning and drying damp materials and furnishings. David listens but does not respond. He then looks at the other custodian to listen to him. The second custodian reiterates that his team did the same thing to prevent mold. David does not make eye contact with the custodian who is speaking, nor does he encourage him to elaborate on what was done in his building. Instead, David nods to acknowledge what was said, then restates what needs to be done when responding to moisture and leaks.

Another custodian raises his hand and states that several parents are unhappy with the moldy smell of the building and are demanding some answers. David listens with his hand on his chin and then states that he will invite parents to a community forum to discuss the conditions of the building.

The next day, David calls an emergency meeting with the Parent Human Relations Council to discuss the storm damage.

Peruse the MLP Matrix and assess David's performance in Domain 5.0: Communication. Make mental notes and be prepared to respond individually as to the reason for your score on that dimension. Please be prepared to report out in 15 minutes.

Scenario #36—David
5.0: Communication

PROGRESSING

David has been the grounds and maintenance administrator for five years at Ridgetop School District. In the city of Ridgetop, recent severe rains have caused leaks and flooding in many of the schools. David is reviewing the work orders from all the buildings concerning the leaks and flood damage. After reading that most of the buildings are still experiencing moisture and leaks, he contacts all the principals and head custodians to notify them of his plans to address the damage.

(5.1) David has assembled a meeting involving the co-op students, the day-shift custodians, and all the head custodians. In the meeting, he greets all the custodial staff and some of the co-op students by name. He engages in informal conversations with some of the co-op students before the start of the meeting. He shares with them that their high school has really been affected by the storm. He asks them if they have seen a lot of damage in the hallways, classrooms, and in other locations. (5.2) He listens to their observations. David then begins the meeting by thanking everyone for attending on such short notice. Next he describes the effects of moisture and leaks, stating that moisture and leaks will contribute to mold growth, which can trigger asthma episodes and allergic reactions, cause severe odors, and lead to a variety of other problems.

At this time, two of the custodians raise their hands to share their current needs at their schools, but David tells them to wait until he is done talking. He then begins sharing with the staff how to inspect the buildings for signs of moisture and leaks. He tells them to look for signs of water damage by checking for moldy odors, looking for stains on the walls and ceiling, and checking cold surfaces. He then looks at one of the custodians and nods as a gesture to indicate that he can speak. **(5.4) The custodian shares that his team has already located the moisture and leaks and that they have responded by cleaning and drying damp materials and furnishings. David listens but does not respond. He then looks at the other custodian to listen to him. The second custodian reiterates that his team did the same thing to prevent mold. David does not make eye contact with the custodian who is speaking, nor does he encourage him to elaborate on what was done in his building. Instead, David nods to acknowledge what was said, then restates what needs to be done when responding to moisture and leaks.**

Another custodian raises his hand and states that several **(5.3) parents are unhappy with the moldy smell of the building and are demanding some answers. David listens with his hand on his chin and then states that he will invite parents to a community forum to discuss the conditions of the building.**

The next day, David calls an emergency meeting with the Parent Human Relations Council to discuss the storm damage.

5.1: David knows most student names, is visible, often greets students by name, and talks with students frequently. SCORE 5.1 AT PROGRESSING.

5.2: David typically limits his listening to time during faculty meetings. SCORE 5.2 AT PROGRESSING.

5.4: David appears to listen to others, but he relies on his interpretation of what needs to be done. SCORE 5.4 AT PROGRESSING.

5.3: David calls a parent meeting only after they initiate the concern. The parents receive a respectful hearing with him. SCORE 5.3 AT PROGRESSING

Scenario #37—Raul
5.0: Communication

When Raul looked back on his time as a director of high schools in the Rapid Falls School District, he realized that many events had shaped his understanding of the best way to navigate change. Early in his career, he learned the difficult lesson of assuming too much during turbulent times. Having served as a district leader for more than seven years, Raul had firsthand knowledge of how teachers, administrators, parents, students, and board members would react when change became uncomfortable. During his early years, he pushed forward through these events, believing that all would accept the change in the end if they just forged ahead. He couldn't have been more wrong.

Over the past couple of years, Raul had led one of his high schools through a significant change, and it was a vast improvement upon earlier transition processes. Two years ago, it had become evident that the high school needed major remodeling and, in some cases, reconstruction. The board of education was initially hesitant about moving forward with requests to taxpayers to support a bond initiative. When Raul and the superintendent first presented the results of a long-range plan to the board, four of the seven board members made it clear they would never support this measure in such difficult economic times.

In an effort to earn their support, Raul and the superintendent's cabinet members organized a two-day planning and brainstorming session that included representation from the board of education, district and building administration, certified and classified staff from both the building and district levels, and students and community members. In these sessions, Raul organized teams to work through a protocol to examine current and desired states with regard to the high school facility. The sessions were exhausting, but incredibly fruitful as Raul listened carefully to ideas and made sure he acknowledged and responded to group participants. Everyone involved left with a strong commitment to the project, and their excitement was evident. In addition to examining the facility needs and dreams, the protocol gave teams the opportunity to examine current curriculum and instructional objectives in the light of a new 21st-century facility.

This was only the beginning. After the success of the two-day work session, it was clear that input was the key to making this project successful. Once the pre-bond construction and design firm was selected, more intentional dialogue sessions began to develop. The superintendent was cautious about getting too many people involved initially, but Raul and the now fully supportive board members successfully convinced him that this level of input was needed to fully engage the community and ensure a positive vote for the bond on election day.

Over the next year, Raul worked closely with various groups to hear their ideas, to gain input regarding draft designs, and to make sure that instruction and facilities would successfully complement each other. In addition to meeting with student groups, building and district advisory committees, and employee groups, Raul and the high school principal arranged for small focus group meetings with bus drivers, nutrition services staff, secretaries, budget office staff, students, parents, seniors, and community service organizations. The year it took to complete this feedback loop was intense and often exhausting, but an amazing thing happened along the way. The electronic feedback tool that had been set up on the district and school Web sites became alive with unique ideas for design and funding. Eventually, it also led to grassroots efforts to engage every neighbor in the community fully in a campaign drive once the board of education officially put the bond question on the ballot.

Raul was not surprised when the parent, staff, and survey data came back regarding the potential bond. It fully supported what he had been hearing throughout the year. Students felt very involved and even co-created a student publication with Raul and the principal that gave regular updates on the design process. The parents and families reported similar feelings. This survey data, combined with the anecdotal data Raul received from the various focus groups and meetings, became the blueprint for a new direction, not just for the high school, but for future district projects. Raul collaborated with various district leaders to develop a project management process modeled after the approach the district took with the reconstruction initiative. Not everything had gone well, so the process included "lessons learned" and suggested changes for future initiatives. This new process proved useful not only in large-scale projects, but was also simplified to guide smaller-scale change initiatives. Raul was pleased to know that his own learning had contributed to this organizational learning.

Peruse the MLP Matrix and assess Raul's performance in Domain 5.0: Communication. Make mental notes and be prepared to respond as to the reason for your score on that dimension. Please be prepared to report out in 15 minutes.

Scenario #37—Raul
5.0: Communication

EXEMPLARY

When Raul looked back on his time as a director of high schools in the Rapid Falls School District, he realized that many events had shaped his understanding of the best way to navigate change. Early in his career, he learned the difficult lesson of assuming too much during turbulent times. Having served as a district leader for more than seven years, Raul had firsthand knowledge of how teachers, administrators, parents, students, and board members would react when change became uncomfortable. During his early years, he pushed forward through these events, believing that all would accept the change in the end if they just forged ahead. He couldn't have been more wrong.

Over the past couple of years, Raul had led one of his high schools through a significant change, and it was a vast improvement upon earlier transition processes. Two years ago, it had become evident that the high school needed major remodeling and, in some cases, reconstruction. The board of education was initially hesitant about moving forward with requests to taxpayers to support a bond initiative. When Raul and the superintendent first presented the results of a long-range plan to the board, four of the seven board members made it clear they would never support this measure in such difficult economic times.

In an effort to earn their support, (5.2, 5.4) Raul and the superintendent's cabinet members organized a two-day planning and brainstorming session that included representation from the board of education, district and building administration, certified and classified staff from both the building and district levels, and students and community members. In these sessions, Raul organized teams to work through a protocol to examine current and desired states with regard to the high school facility. The sessions were exhausting, but incredibly fruitful as Raul listened carefully to ideas and made sure he acknowledged and responded to group participants. Everyone involved left with a strong commitment to the project, and their excitement was evident. (5.3) In addition to examining the facility needs and dreams, the protocol gave teams the opportunity to examine current curriculum and instructional objectives in the light of a new 21st-century facility.

This was only the beginning. After the success of the two-day work session, it was clear that input was the key to making this project successful. Once the pre-bond construction and design firm was selected, more intentional dialogue sessions began to develop. The superintendent was cautious about getting too many people involved initially, but Raul and the now fully supportive board members successfully convinced him that this level of input was needed to fully engage the community and ensure a positive vote for the bond on election day.

(5.2) Over the next year, Raul worked closely with various groups to hear their ideas, to gain input regarding draft designs, and to make sure that instruction and facilities would successfully complement each other. (5.1, 5.3) In addition to meeting with student groups, building and district advisory committees, and employee groups, Raul and the high school principal

---

5.2 and **5.4:** Raul reads the situation and responds accordingly to schedule an intensive feedback session that will include board members. Raul engages in active involvement and listening as teams work through his protocol.
SCORE 5.2 AND 5.4 AT EXEMPLARY.

5.3: Raul also uses this venue to engage stakeholders in input and conversations regarding curriculum and instruction.
SCORE 5.3 AT EXEMPLARY.

5.2: Raul's calendar reflects time to engage in high levels of input and communication.
SCORE 5.2 AT EXEMPLARY.

5.1 and **5.3:** Raul engages with various groups in various venues and models a high level of listening by ensuring that all are involved and that settings are small enough to encourage feedback.
SCORE 5.1 AND 5.3 AT EXEMPLARY.

CASE STUDY MATERIALS AND LEARNING EXPERIENCES

arranged for small focus group meetings with bus drivers, nutrition services staff, secretaries, budget office staff, students, parents, seniors, and community service organizations. The year it took to complete this feedback loop was intense and often exhausting, but an amazing thing happened along the way. **(5.3)** The electronic feedback tool that had been set up on the district and school Web sites became alive with unique ideas for design and funding. Eventually, it also led to grassroots efforts to engage every neighbor in the community fully in a campaign drive once the board of education officially put the bond question on the ballot.

Raul was not surprised when the parent, staff, and survey data came back regarding the potential bond. It fully supported what he had been hearing throughout the year. **(5.1)** Students felt very involved and even co-created a student publication with Raul and the principal that gave regular updates on the design process. **(5.3)** The parents and families reported similar feelings. This survey data, combined with the anecdotal data Raul received from the various focus groups and meetings, **(5.4)** became the blueprint for a new direction, not just for the high school, but for future district projects. Raul collaborated with various district leaders to develop a project management process modeled after the approach the district took with the reconstruction initiative. Not everything had gone well, so the process included "lessons learned" and suggested changes for future initiatives. This new process proved useful not only in large-scale projects, but was also simplified to guide smaller-scale change initiatives. Raul was pleased to know that his own learning had contributed to this organizational learning.

Domain 6.0:
Faculty Development

Leaders recruit, hire, and retain proficient and exemplary teachers. In their efforts to retain proficient and exemplary teachers, leaders focus on evidence, research, and classroom realities faced by teachers. They link professional practice with student achievement to demonstrate the cause-and-effect relationship. Leaders also facilitate effective professional development, monitor implementation of critical initiatives, and provide timely feedback to teachers so that feedback can be used to enhance teacher professional practice.

Scenario #38—Bernadette
6.0: Faculty Development

Bernadette has been an elementary principal in a small rural district in Bridgeport County for the past 19 years. Having previously taught at the middle school level and having attended kindergarten through high school in Bridgeport, Bernadette is seen as an icon in the district. While her student achievement data shows that approximately 70 percent of her students are not proficient, she has an attendance rate of 97 percent. Parents, staff, and students all support Bernadette's decisions and, during her tenure at Taylor Elementary, there have been very few community or staff concerns about the operation of the building and/or the school's student achievement results. As a result, Bernadette neither asks for nor receives district-level coaching or feedback on her leadership.

Even though there seems to be a high turnover of staff each year at Taylor Elementary, teachers are experienced and eager to learn. During her tenure, Bernadette has been fortunate to continue to hire highly qualified teachers each year, even as this turnover occurs. Bernadette attributes her ability to hire well-honed teachers to her interviewing processes, which include a close working relationship with human resources to post vacant positions. More importantly, Bernadette takes it upon herself to interview candidates and to be solely responsible for making the hiring decisions.

Bernadette provides support for her staff by engaging in a process each summer before the start of the new school year, during which she makes a list of possible staff development topics for her staff. During teacher workweek, the staff development topics are posted and teachers are asked to prioritize their top three professional development choices for the year. Once the top areas of interest are decided, Bernadette creates a professional development calendar and blocks out two staff meetings a month for workshops in the designated areas of focus. Bernadette sees her role at Taylor Elementary more as that of an efficient manager than as an instructional leader and therefore asks for volunteers from teachers to lead these biweekly staff development sessions.

Given Bernadette's focus on effective management, she is highly visible in the school and uses classroom observations as a time to ensure that students and teachers are on task and working hard. Rather than seeing this as an opportunity to provide teachers with feedback on their instructional practices or to ensure that the objectives taught align with district and school improvement plans, she chooses to provide feedback that is mainly focused on the organization of the classroom, student behavioral management, and engagement.

Peruse the MLP Matrix and assess Bernadette's performance in Domain 6.0: Faculty Development. Make mental notes and be prepared to respond as to the reason for your score on that dimension. Please be prepared to report out in 15 minutes.

Scenario #38—Bernadette
6.0: Faculty Development

NOT MEETING STANDARDS

Bernadette has been an elementary principal in a small rural district in Bridgeport County for the past 19 years. Having previously taught at the middle school level and having attended kindergarten through high school in Bridgeport, Bernadette is seen as an icon in the district. While her student achievement data shows that approximately 70 percent of her students are not proficient, she has an attendance rate of 97 percent. Parents, staff, and students all support Bernadette's decisions and, during her tenure at Taylor Elementary, there have been very few community or staff concerns about the operation of the building and/or the school's student achievement results. As a result, Bernadette neither asks for nor receives district-level coaching or feedback on her leadership.

Even though there seems to be a high turnover of staff each year at Taylor Elementary, teachers are experienced and eager to learn. During her tenure, Bernadette has been fortunate to continue to hire highly qualified teachers each year, even as this turnover occurs. **(6.5) Bernadette attributes her ability to hire well-honed teachers to her interviewing processes, which include a close working relationship with human resources to post vacant positions. More importantly, Bernadette takes it upon herself to interview candidates and to be solely responsible for making the hiring decisions.**

(6.1) Bernadette provides support for her staff by engaging in a process each summer before the start of the new school year, during which she makes a list of possible staff development topics for her staff. During teacher workweek, the staff development topics are posted and teachers are asked to prioritize their top three professional development choices for the year. Once the top areas of interest are decided, Bernadette creates a professional development calendar and blocks out two staff meetings a month for workshops in the designated areas of focus. (6.2) Bernadette sees her role at Taylor Elementary more as that of an efficient manager than as an instructional leader and therefore asks for volunteers from teachers to lead these biweekly staff development sessions.

(6.4) Given Bernadette's focus on effective management, she is highly visible in the school and uses classroom observations as a time to ensure that students and teachers are on task and working hard. (6.3) Rather than seeing this as an opportunity to provide teachers with feedback on their instructional practices or to ensure that the objectives taught align with district and school improvement plans, she chooses to provide feedback that is mainly focused on the organization of the classroom, student behavioral management, and engagement.

6.5: Bernadette works with the human resources department to write and post job descriptions. Beyond hiring teachers independently, she has no system/process in place to acquire feedback from staff. SCORE 6.5 AT PROGRESSING.

6.1: Professional development in the school is not based on specific faculty needs nor student achievement needs. This could be one indication as to why there is so much turnover in Bernadette's school. SCORE 6.1 AT NOT MEETING STANDARDS.

6.2: Bernadette devotes faculty meetings to professional development and relies on her staff to lead each professional development opportunity. SCORE 6.2 AT PROGRESSING.

6.4: Bernadette views classroom observations as a time to ensure that all teachers are teaching and students are on task, versus collecting feedback regarding student learning. SCORE 6.4 AT NOT MEETING STANDARDS.

6.3: Bernadette provides limited, nonspecific, and nonconstructive feedback to her staff. SCORE 6.3 AT NOT MEETING STANDARDS.

Scenario #39—Kyle
6.0: Faculty Development

Kyle, a fourth-year principal at Riddle Middle School, is reviewing the needs of the School Improvement Plan. He is developing what professional development is needed from the needs assessments of each teacher that he and the instructional coach developed based on the Decision Making for Results seminar they attended last month. Kyle shared with Stacey, the instructional coach, that it is imperative that the professional development for second semester is differentiated based on student data and teacher needs.

Kyle also told Stacey they needed to create choice boards for each teacher with a list of various professional development initiatives from the School Improvement Plan. The choices include Cooperative Learning, Writing across the Curriculum, Five Easy Steps to a Balanced Math Program, and Multiple Intelligences. Kyle and Stacey used walk-through data to create the choices on the choice boards. Each teacher will have the opportunity to choose two professional development initiatives to focus on for the second semester and summer learning modules.

That evening when Kyle was working at home, he revised his monthly meeting calendar in order to devote the hour that he had with teachers to focusing on professional development. Each meeting would start with a cooperative learning strategy of the month. He planned to facilitate explaining how to use the strategy and the philosophy for incorporating the strategy.

The following week, Kyle met with the staff after school to share the format of professional development for the second semester. He communicated to the staff that the professional development initiatives would be on the walk-through checklist to ensure that all teachers implemented the strategies with fidelity. After each walk-through, feedback forms would be given to the teachers whose classes were observed. Kyle also stated that Stacey would start to generate data charts on teacher implementation. The two of them would then create a plan for individual teacher support.

At the end of the day, Kyle felt the need to call Mr. Mavis, the human resource director, to notify him of his professional development plan and the teacher-coaching model. He also shared that future teacher candidates should be able to provide evidence of implementing best practices either in previous teaching experience or during their student teaching.

Peruse the MLP Matrix and assess Kyle's performance in Domain 6.0: Faculty Development. Make mental notes and be prepared to respond as to the reason for your score on that dimension. Please be prepared to report out in 15 minutes.

Scenario #39—Kyle
6.0: Faculty Development

PROFICIENT

Kyle, a fourth-year principal at Riddle Middle School, is reviewing the needs of the School Improvement Plan. **(6.1) He is developing what professional development is needed from the needs assessments of each teacher that he and the instructional coach developed based on the Decision Making for Results seminar they attended last month. Kyle shared with Stacey, the instructional coach, that it is imperative that the professional development for second semester is differentiated based on student data and teacher needs.**

Kyle also told Stacey they needed to create choice boards for each teacher with a list of various professional development initiatives from the School Improvement Plan. The choices include Cooperative Learning, Writing across the Curriculum, Five Easy Steps to a Balanced Math Program, and Multiple Intelligences. Kyle and Stacey used walk-through data to create the choices on the choice boards. Each teacher will have the opportunity to choose two professional development initiatives to focus on for the second semester and summer learning modules.

That evening when Kyle was working at home, **(6.2) he revised his monthly meeting calendar in order to devote the hour that he had with teachers to focusing on professional development. Each meeting would start with a co-operative learning strategy of the month. He planned to facilitate explaining how to use the strategy and the philosophy for incorporating the strategy.**

The following week, Kyle met with the staff after school to share the format of professional development for the second semester. **(6.3) He communicated to the staff that the professional development initiatives would be on the walk-through checklist to ensure that all teachers implemented the strategies with fidelity. After each walk-through, feedback forms would be given to the teachers whose classes were observed. (6.4) Kyle also stated that Stacey would start to generate data charts on teacher implementation. The two of them would then create a plan for individual teacher support.**

(6.5) At the end of the day, Kyle felt the need to call Mr. Mavis, the human resource director, to notify him of his professional development plan and the teacher-coaching model. He also shared that future teacher candidates should be able to provide evidence of implementing best practices either in previous teaching experience or during their student teaching.

6.1: Kyle implements faculty development based on the needs of the School Improvement Plan, and some effort has been made to differentiate and embed professional development. SCORE 6.1 AT PROFICIENT.

6.2: Kyle personally leads professional development at various times throughout the school year. Kyle devotes faculty meetings to professional development, not announcements. SCORE 6.2 AT PROFICIENT.

6.3: Kyle provides formal feedback consistent with the school initiatives to reinforce effective/highly effective performance and highlight the strengths of colleagues. SCORE 6.3 AT PROFICIENT.

6.4: Kyle engages in coaching to improve teaching and learning. SCORE 6.4 AT PROFICIENT.

6.5: Kyle works collaboratively with Mr. Mavis in the human resources office to define the ideal teacher, based upon the school's vision, culture, and performance expectations. SCORE 6.5 AT PROFICIENT.

Scenario #40—Margo
6.0: Faculty Development

Margo loved working as an assistant principal at Twin Peaks High School. She had been a leader at Twin Peaks for the past five years and felt very good about her relationships with the staff. The principal was a strong instructional leader, which sometimes proved intimidating for Margo. But she found her niche in leadership and stuck with it. Her niche was being in charge of the school's professional development team.

During meetings with the team, Margo often had the chance to share some ideas of things she had seen done in her previous district. The staff seemed to like her ideas, with the exception of one who seemed to continue to ask for the results of these ideas. Margo felt it was difficult to quantify the impact on student achievement precisely; therefore, she relied heavily on positive comments from teachers after the professional development days. She just knew they were successful because of the positive response that staff members had.

Recently, a teacher on the team brought some research to the group that talked about the importance of embedding professional development experiences in staff meetings. Margo loved this idea and encouraged the teacher to approach the principal about using the regularly scheduled faculty meetings for this purpose. The team created a plan that outlined how each faculty meeting would be used for a different topic that they felt staff was interested in. In order to determine this interest, Margo volunteered to send out a survey to the staff that would allow the team to gather interests and tailor each meeting to these interests.

When the results of the survey came in, Margo was pleased that the most popular requests from teachers were clearly tied in to individual strengths of the professional development team. Given the unique nature of high schools, the team had to discard the ideas that were content specific, and instead focused on those topics that could apply to all content areas. Although Margo was quite uncomfortable speaking in front of large groups, she agreed to lead her own session on a topic she was very familiar with: character education.

The team also agreed that classroom observations and evaluations should be closely tied to the topics they covered in the faculty meeting professional development sessions. Margo eagerly created a new observation tool that would capture the elements of the new faculty learning. Margo decided to use this herself during her observations and was able to provide feedback to teachers during their post-observation conferences that specifically tied to these areas of focus.

This work with staff during pre- and post-conferences proved to be Margo's favorite part of the professional development initiatives. Given her training in counseling, Margo felt she was well equipped to provide expert coaching. Margo was able to visit classrooms frequently, conducting both informal and formal observations tied directly to the common understandings of practice that had been shared during the professional development sessions. Many teachers were so excited about the feedback they received from Margo that they agreed to work on an action research project that tied their implementation of professional development learning to student achievement. Margo's excitement about the observation/feedback project prompted her to create a very systematic approach to classroom observations that included both a schedule and a system for regular visits. During a recent visit with her principal, Margo shared some of the tools she had created. The principal was impressed with Margo's initiative in this area and agreed to try out these tools during his own classroom observations. He encouraged Margo to include the proficiency elements of her evaluation tool in the job posting she was sending to the human resources department. Margo agreed that this was a great idea and would certainly attract higher-quality candidates.

Margo was pleased with the staff development efforts at her school this year. She felt that she had created a new system of evaluation and feedback that was directly tied to the work of the professional development team. Given the interest that teachers expressed in this new learning, Margo considered the year a success.

Peruse the MLP Matrix and assess Margo's performance in Domain 6.0: Faculty Development. Make mental notes and be prepared to respond as to the reason for your score on that dimension. Please be prepared to report out in 15 minutes.

Scenario #40—Margo
6.0: Faculty Development

PROGRESSING

Margo loved working as an assistant principal at Twin Peaks High School. She had been a leader at Twin Peaks for the past five years and felt very good about her relationships with the staff. The principal was a strong instructional leader, which sometimes proved intimidating for Margo. But she found her niche in leadership and stuck with it. Her niche was being in charge of the school's professional development team.

During meetings with the team, Margo often had the chance to share some ideas of things she had seen done in her previous district. The staff seemed to like her ideas, with the exception of one who seemed to continue to ask for the results of these ideas. **(6.1) Margo felt it was difficult to quantify the impact on student achievement precisely; therefore, she relied heavily on positive comments from teachers after the professional development days. She just knew they were successful because of the positive response that staff members had.**

Recently, a teacher on the team brought some research to the group that talked about the **(6.2) importance of embedding professional development experiences in staff meetings. Margo loved this idea and encouraged the teacher to approach the principal about using the regularly scheduled faculty meetings for this purpose. The team created a plan that outlined how each faculty meeting would be used for a different topic that they felt staff was interested in.** In order to determine this interest, **(6.1) Margo volunteered to send out a survey to the staff that would allow the team to gather interests and tailor each meeting to these interests.**

When the results of the survey came in, Margo was pleased that the most popular requests from teachers were clearly tied in to individual strengths of the professional development team. Given the unique nature of high schools, the team had to discard the ideas that were content specific, and instead focused on those topics that could apply to all content areas. Although Margo was quite uncomfortable speaking in front of large groups, **(6.2) she agreed to lead her own session on a topic she was very familiar with: character education.**

6.1: Margo did not use the school improvement plan or results of evaluations to determine specific goals for professional development. However, she does acknowledge differentiated needs (paragraph 3).
SCORE 6.1 AT PROGRESSING.

6.2: Margo did help develop a plan for using faculty meetings for professional development, but only led professional development on one occasion in an area she felt comfortable.
SCORE 6.2 AT PROFICIENT/PROGRESSING.

6.1: Margo was aware of differentiated needs of staff, but professional development is only embedded in faculty meetings.
SCORE 6.1 AT PROGRESSING.

6.2: Margo did agree to lead one professional development session herself.
SCORE 6.2 AT PROFICIENT/PROGRESSING.

CASE STUDY MATERIALS AND LEARNING EXPERIENCES

The team also agreed that **(6.3)** classroom observations and evaluations should be closely tied to the topics they covered in the faculty meeting professional development sessions. Margo eagerly created a new observation tool that would capture the elements of the new faculty learning. Margo decided to use this herself during her observations and was able to provide feedback to teachers during their post-observation conferences that specifically tied to these areas of focus.

This work with staff during pre- and post-conferences proved to be Margo's favorite part of the professional development initiatives. Given her training in counseling, **(6.4)** Margo felt she was well equipped to provide expert coaching. Margo was able to visit classrooms frequently, conducting both informal and formal observations tied directly to the common understandings of practice that had been shared during the professional development sessions. Many teachers were so excited about the feedback they received from Margo that they agreed to work on an action research project that tied their implementation of professional development learning to student achievement. Margo's excitement about the observation/feedback project prompted her to create a very systematic approach to classroom observations that included both a schedule and a system for regular visits. During a recent visit with her principal, Margo shared some of the tools she had created. The principal was impressed with Margo's initiative in this area and agreed to try out these tools during his own classroom observations. **(6.5)** He encouraged Margo to include the proficiency elements of her evaluation tool in the job posting she was sending to the human resources department. Margo agreed that this was a great idea and would certainly attract higher-quality candidates.

Margo was pleased with the staff development efforts at her school this year. She felt that she had created a new system of evaluation and feedback that was directly tied to the work of the professional development team. Given the interest that teachers expressed in this new learning, Margo considered the year a success.

Scenario #41—Juan
6.0: Faculty Development

After 15 years as a middle school principal in a neighboring school, Juan became one of three directors of elementary education in a suburban school district with an approximate enrollment of 50,000 students. At the same time Juan was hired as director of elementary education, the district had just lost a budget election and was facing a salary freeze, reduction in staff, and significant cuts to the professional development budget. As a result, many elementary principals who were close to retirement decided to go ahead and retire, which left the district with 10 principal vacancies. Additionally, in an effort to help deal with budgetary shortfalls, the district decided to cut the number of professional development days and eliminate the weekly early-release days designated for Data Team meetings.

Juan viewed each of these situations as an opportunity to demonstrate to the district his leadership strengths and volunteered to be the director in charge of the principal hiring and the reorganization of professional development for the district.

Knowing the leadership that Juan had exhibited at the middle school, he was given support from the superintendent to move forward with responsibility in these two areas. With the start of school only five weeks away, Juan was excited to prove himself and knew that the first priority needed to be the hiring of elementary principals. Juan began by contacting the director of human resources, and together they proceeded to write and post the positions. With little time to plan the process and knowing that current principals were on summer break in July, Juan utilized hiring practices he had used in his previous role as middle school principal when hiring teachers in his school, rather than researching past district hiring practices. Soon into the process, he very quickly realized that there were key differences between hiring classroom teachers and hiring principal leaders and needed to seek support of the other two directors to help him standardize the process and align to district recruitment and hiring criteria.

Simultaneously, Juan was developing a staff development restructuring plan he would present to principals at their first meeting at the end of August. Knowing that the professional development budget had been cut in half, he developed a plan that relied solely on principals in the group to lead all professional development opportunities during the year. Additionally, he developed a calendar that utilized one hour of each bimonthly principal meeting as the designated time for these professional development sessions and determined the six topics of focus for the year.

With the professional development early-release days cut, Juan devised a plan in which principals would be put into feeder teams and three times a year would visit on another's schools to see how their colleagues were working with staff around the identified professional development topics. Specifically, they would do walk-through observations in hopes of acquiring new learning from their colleagues that they could then take back to their schools and staff.

In Juan's mind, having principals, rather than himself, take charge of the professional development would free up his time to visit principals in his designated schools, which was one of his job responsibilities. Furthermore, he would use this time to get to know his new principals and to make sure they knew that he saw his role as one of supporting when needed, but normally standing back and letting the principal lead his learning community. Toward that end, he communicated to his principals that in addition to his scheduled visits, he was always available by phone and that he would only contact them if he had a concern for student safety or community issues that parents had brought to his attention As this was the leadership he received and valued from his middle-level directorship, he felt it would also serve him well with his elementary principals.

Peruse the MLP Matrix and assess Juan's performance in Domain 6.0: Faculty Development. Make mental notes and be prepared to respond as to the reason for your score on that dimension. Please be prepared to report out in 15 minutes.

Scenario #41—Juan
6.0: Faculty Development

Not Meeting Standards

After 15 years as a middle school principal in a neighboring school, Juan became one of three directors of elementary education in a suburban school district with an approximate enrollment of 50,000 students. At the same time Juan was hired as director of elementary education, the district had just lost a budget election and was facing a salary freeze, reduction in staff, and significant cuts to the professional development budget. As a result, many elementary principals who were close to retirement decided to go ahead and retire, which left the district with 10 principal vacancies. Additionally, in an effort to help deal with budgetary shortfalls, the district decided to cut the number of professional development days and eliminate the weekly early-release days designated for Data Team meetings.

Juan viewed each of these situations as an opportunity to demonstrate to the district his leadership strengths and volunteered to be the director in charge of the principal hiring and the reorganization of professional development for the district.

Knowing the leadership that Juan had exhibited at the middle school, he was given support from the superintendent to move forward with responsibility in these two areas. With the start of school only five weeks away, Juan was excited to prove himself and knew that the first priority needed to be the hiring of elementary principals. **(6.5)** Juan began by contacting the director of human resources, and together they proceeded to write and post the positions. With little time to plan the process and knowing that current principals were on summer break in July, Juan utilized hiring practices he had used in his previous role as middle school principal when hiring teachers in his school, rather than researching past district hiring practices. Soon into the process, he very quickly realized that there were key differences between hiring classroom teachers and hiring principal leaders and needed to seek support of the other two directors to help him standardize the process and align to district recruitment and hiring criteria.

Simultaneously, Juan was developing a staff development restructuring plan he would present to principals at their first meeting at the end of August. **(6.2)** Knowing that the professional development budget had been cut in half, he developed a plan that relied solely on principals in the group to lead all professional development opportunities during the year. **(6.1)** Additionally, he developed a calendar that utilized one hour of each bimonthly principal meeting as the designated time for these professional development sessions and determined the six topics of focus for the year.

With the professional development early-release days cut, **(6.2)** Juan devised a plan in which principals would be put into feeder teams and three times a year would visit one another's schools to see how their colleagues were working with staff around the identified professional development topics. Specifically, they would do walk-through observations in hopes of acquiring new learning from their colleagues that they could then take back to their schools and staff.

6.5: Juan works with the human resource department to write his job descriptions for principals. He utilized a process he had used before as a principal in hiring teachers and did not think about the differences needed in a system for hiring principals.
SCORE **6.5** AT PROGRESSING.

6.2: Juan devotes time during bimonthly principal meetings for professional development and relies solely on principals in the group to lead the professional development.
SCORE **6.2** AT PROGRESSING.

6.1: Juan planned the professional development topics for the year without feedback from principals and without looking at district student achievement data.
SCORE **6.1** AT NOT MEETING STANDARDS.

6.2: Juan set up time for his principals to meet in feeder teams to discuss their professional development topics. Principals independently observed each other's schools and learned from each other.
SCORE **6.2** AT PROGRESSING.

6.4: Juan views principal observations as part of his job responsibilities/ obligations to manage compliance issues. He does not see this as an opportunity to give constructive and proactive feedback regarding the improvement efforts. SCORE 6.4 AT NOT MEETING STANDARDS.

6.3: Juan believes that feedback is only given regarding parent issues or student safety concerns. Therefore, his feedback to principals is limited and not specific to effective performance toward meeting specific goals. SCORE 6.3 AT NOT MEETING STANDARDS.

In Juan's mind, having principals, rather than himself, take charge of the professional development would free up his time to visit principals in his designated schools, which was one of his job responsibilities. **(6.4)** Furthermore, he would use this time to get to know his new principals and to make sure they knew that he saw his role as one of supporting when needed, but normally standing back and letting the principal lead his learning community. **(6.3)** Toward that end, he communicated to his principals that in addition to his scheduled visits, he was always available by phone and that he would only contact them if he had a concern for student safety or community issues that parents had brought to his attention As this was the leadership he received and valued from his middle-level directorship, he felt it would also serve him well with his elementary principals.

Scenario #42—Eric
6.0: Faculty Development

Eric is ecstatic about the prospects for the new school year. This is his third year as director of middle schools for the Newburg School District. Prior to assuming this district-level position, Eric was a very successful middle school principal for 10 years in the neighboring district of Portage. He is known for increasing student achievement in the areas of reading and math during his years at Portage Middle School. Last year, his state assessments were 90 percent passing for ELA and 93 percent passing for math for both grades 7 and 8. Eric attributes his successes as a leader to the development of others. He believes, like Ernest Boyer in his book *The Basic School*, that "school improvement means people improvement." In this new position of director of middle schools, Eric oversees the functions of the district's four middle schools, including supervising the principals, facilitating the curriculum writing meetings, analyzing middle school academic and discipline data, supporting the development of school improvement plans, and handling community and parent concerns at the district level.

One of the middle school principals was recently appointed as principal of one of the high schools. Therefore, Eric has to hire a new middle school principal. He firmly believes in getting the right people on the bus and also making sure that they are in the right seat. All summer, Eric has worked with Derek Bradshaw, the human resource administrator, to find the best candidate for the position of middle school principal. He worked collaboratively with Mr. Bradshaw to establish an interview process aligned with the district's performance expectations of the principals, the vision of the school and district, and the culture of the building.

Once the new middle school principal is hired, Eric will begin his monthly meetings with the middle school principals, focusing on professional development. He believes in job-embedded professional development that is focused, consistent, and based on the needs of the schools and district. He limits covering the "nuts and bolts" orientation information during these meetings, because they reflect the prioritized needs of the district and school improvement plans. Eric utilizes the data from each school to meet the individual needs of the four principals. The middle school principals and Eric use the Data Teams process and Decision Making for Results as they identify cause-and-effect data (e.g., adult practice and student achievement data). After his meetings with principals, Eric provides each principal with a written summary of what was discussed, learned, and agreed upon as the next step. This summary is in the format of an action plan, which provides the principals with a road map that leads to accountability. The principals appreciate Eric's focus, support, and organization.

After the principals receive their action plans, Eric visits each principal to support her in implementing initiatives. During his one-hour visit, he meets with the principal for 30 minutes, allowing her to create agenda topics based on her current needs. In the last half-hour of the visit, the principal conducts classroom visits accompanied by Eric to observe what instructional strategies need further emphasis during the school's professional development time. The principals really value this time with Eric because they not only feel empowered to share their focuses in teaching and learning, but they also receive coaching from him on what new approaches they can implement based on research and data.

Peruse the MLP Matrix and assess Eric's performance in Domain 6.0: Faculty Development. Make mental notes and be prepared to respond as to the reason for your score on that dimension. Please be prepared to report out in 15 minutes.

Scenario #42—Eric
6.0: Faculty Development

PROFICIENT

Eric is ecstatic about the prospects for the new school year. This is his third year as director of middle schools for the Newburg School District. Prior to assuming this district-level position, Eric was a very successful middle school principal for 10 years in the neighboring district of Portage. He is known for increasing student achievement in the areas of reading and math during his years at Portage Middle School. Last year, his state assessments were 90 percent passing for ELA and 93 percent passing for math for both grades 7 and 8. Eric attributes his successes as a leader to the development of others. He believes, like Ernest Boyer in his book *The Basic School*, that "school improvement means people improvement." In this new position of director of middle schools, Eric oversees the functions of the district's four middle schools, including supervising the principals, facilitating the curriculum writing meetings, analyzing middle school academic and discipline data, supporting the development of school improvement plans, and handling community and parent concerns at the district level.

One of the middle school principals was recently appointed as principal of one of the high schools. Therefore, Eric has to hire a new middle school principal. **(6.5)** He firmly believes in getting the right people on the bus and also making sure that they are in the right seat. All summer, Eric has worked with Derek Bradshaw, the human resource administrator, to find the best candidate for the position of middle school principal. He worked collaboratively with Mr. Bradshaw to establish an interview process aligned with the district's performance expectations of the principals, the vision of the school and district, and the culture of the building.

Once the new middle school principal is hired, **(6.2)** Eric will begin his monthly meetings with the middle school principals, focusing on professional development. He believes in job-embedded professional development that is focused, consistent, and based on the needs of the schools and district. He limits covering the "nuts and bolts" orientation information during these meetings, because **(6.1)** they reflect the prioritized needs of the district and school improvement plans. Eric utilizes the data from each school to meet the individual needs of the four principals. The middle school principals and Eric use the Data Teams process and Decision Making for Results as they identify cause-and-effect data (e.g., adult practice and student achievement data). **(6.3)** After his meetings with principals, Eric provides each principal with a written summary of what was discussed, learned, and agreed upon as the next step. This summary is in the format of an action plan, which provides the principals with a road map that leads to accountability. The principals appreciate Eric's focus, support, and organization.

6.5: Eric works collaboratively with the staff in the human resources office to create a selection tool that helps interviewers focus on key success criteria aligned with what the leader is looking for. SCORE 6.5 AT PROFICIENT.

6.2: Eric personally leads professional development at various times throughout the school year. The leader devotes faculty meetings to professional development, not announcements. SCORE 6.2 AT PROFICIENT.

6.1: Eric creates professional development sessions that reflect the prioritized needs of the School Improvement Plan, and some effort has been made to differentiate and embed professional development to meet the needs of all principals. SCORE 6.1 AT PROFICIENT.

6.3: Eric provides formal feedback consistent with the district personnel policies and provides informal feedback to reinforce effective practices. The positive feedback is linked to organizational goals, and both the leader and employees can cite examples of where feedback is used to improve individual and organizational performance. SCORE 6.3 AT PROFICIENT.

6.4: Eric engages in coaching to improve teaching and learning. Observations are not just used for rating purposes: they are also used for coaching and professional development opportunities. Score **6.4** at Proficient.

After the principals receive their action plans, **(6.4)** Eric visits each principal to support her in implementing initiatives. During his one-hour visit, he meets with the principal for 30 minutes, allowing her to create agenda topics based on her current needs. In the last half-hour of the visit, the principal conducts classroom visits accompanied by Eric to observe what instructional strategies need further emphasis during the school's professional development time. The principals really value this time with Eric because they not only feel empowered to share their focuses in teaching and learning, but they also receive coaching from him on what new approaches they can implement based on research and data.

Scenario #43—Saffron
6.0: Faculty Development

Last year was Saffron's first year as a new assistant superintendent in the Central River School District. It was a tough year as Saffron tried to adjust to a new role and a new district. At least this year she felt a bit more comfortable and was less reliant on her roots in another district, where she had served for almost five years as a director of elementary education. Saffron enjoyed watching other educators grow and develop and believed strongly that good professional development was an important part of the professional growth process.

This year, Saffron had worked to bring forward a new initiative to ensure teachers were using effective instructional methodologies in their classrooms. The district had invested in extensive professional development last year and Saffron was now responsible for making sure that the investment paid off and classroom implementation was evident. In an effort to continue to develop the skills principals needed to effectively monitor implementation, Saffron decided that each monthly meeting with principals would include an hour dedicated to further professional development regarding instructional strategies. Saffron turned the actual professional development content and delivery over to the director of curriculum, since this seemed to be her area of expertise.

Saffron's ongoing professional development work with principals seemed well received. However, she still wasn't seeing high levels of implementation when she was out visiting schools. As she looked back on the observation forms she used during her walk-throughs, the number of strategies checked was far from impressive. When Saffron met with principals after these walk-throughs, she gave them feedback about what she had seen and asked principals to share the information they had gathered during their own visits. The two sets of results were fairly similar, which allowed Saffron to feel a bit more comfortable with principals' skill levels for evaluating what they were seeing in the classroom. However, this didn't solve the issue of what to do next about the teachers themselves. Saffron wondered about more professional development, but knew that more release days for teachers to repeat the professional development process was not a likely solution.

Instead, Saffron and the principals adopted a twofold approach. They would use the approved evaluation process to put some pressure on teachers who did not seem to be fully on board. At the same time, they would identify which teachers were using the strategies more effectively and encourage them to share ideas with their colleagues. Both of these strategies would be used and Saffron would work with the human resources department to establish new hiring criteria that would reflect the expectation that all newly hired teachers would come with a strong knowledge of the instructional strategies or would agree to professional development outside their contract day.

By the end of the year, teachers were much more aware of the expectation that obvious use of strategies would be an element of their evaluations, and some of those more resistant teachers were leaving. The new job requirements were being used throughout the hiring process and indicated that most new recruits agreed to the professional development requirement. Saffron was confident that the next year would produce an upward bump in student achievement.

CASE STUDY MATERIALS AND LEARNING EXPERIENCES

Peruse the MLP Matrix and assess Saffron's performance in Domain 6.0: Faculty Development. Make mental notes and be prepared to respond as to the reason for your score on that dimension. Please be prepared to report out in 15 minutes.

Scenario #43—Saffron
6.0: Faculty Development

PROGRESSING

Last year was Saffron's first year as a new assistant superintendent in the Central River School District. It was a tough year as Saffron tried to adjust to a new role and a new district. At least this year she felt a bit more comfortable and was less reliant on her roots in another district, where she had served for almost five years as a director of elementary education. Saffron enjoyed watching other educators grow and develop and believed strongly that good professional development was an important part of the professional growth process.

This year, Saffron had worked to bring forward a new initiative to ensure teachers were using effective instructional methodologies in their classrooms. The district had invested in extensive professional development last year and Saffron was now responsible for making sure that the investment paid off and classroom implementation was evident. In an effort to continue to develop the skills principals needed to effectively monitor implementation, **(6.1) Saffron decided that each monthly meeting with principals would include an hour dedicated to further professional development regarding instructional strategies. (6.2) Saffron turned the actual professional development content and delivery over to the director of curriculum, since this seemed to be her area of expertise.**

Saffron's ongoing professional development work with principals seemed well received. **(6.4) However, she still wasn't seeing high levels of implementation when she was out visiting schools. As she looked back on the observation forms she used during her walk-throughs, the number of strategies checked was far from impressive. (6.3) When Saffron met with principals after these walk-throughs, she gave them feedback about what she had seen and asked principals to share the information they had gathered during their own visits.** The two sets of results were fairly similar, which allowed Saffron to feel a bit more comfortable with principals' skill levels for evaluating what they were seeing in the classroom. However, this didn't solve the issue of what to do next about the teachers themselves. Saffron wondered about more professional development, but knew that more release days for teachers to repeat the professional development process was not a likely solution.

Instead, Saffron and the principals adopted a twofold approach. **(6.4) They would use the approved evaluation process to put some pressure on teachers who did not seem to be fully on board. At the same time, they would identify which teachers were using the strategies more effectively and encourage them to share ideas with their colleagues.** Both of these strategies would be used and **(6.5) Saffron would work with the human resources department to establish new hiring criteria that would reflect the expectation that all newly hired teachers would come with a strong knowledge of the instructional strategies or would agree to professional development outside their contract day.**

6.1: Saffron only embeds professional development in monthly principal meetings. SCORE **6.1** AT PROGRESSING.

6.2: Saffron relies on the director of curriculum to lead the professional development. SCORE **6.2** AT PROGRESSING.

6.4: Saffron engages in observation and relies on observational tools. SCORE **6.4** AT PROGRESSING.

6.3: Saffron provides feedback to principals that will just begin to impact organizational change through the decisions they make as a result of the data and feedback. SCORE **6.3** AT PROGRESSING.

6.4: Prescriptive assistance is not provided and the plan is not targeted. SCORE **6.4** AT PROGRESSING.

6.5: Saffron works with human resources to develop new job descriptions for posting, but does not change the hiring process in a systematic manner. SCORE **6.5** AT PROGRESSING.

By the end of the year, teachers were much more aware of the expectation that obvious use of strategies would be an element of their evaluations, and some of those more resistant teachers were leaving. The new job requirements were being used throughout the hiring process and indicated that most new recruits agreed to the professional development requirement. Saffron was confident that the next year would produce an upward bump in student achievement.

Domain 7.0:
Leadership Development

Leaders in education actively cultivate and develop other leaders within the organization. They also model trust, competency, and integrity, which positively impacts and inspires growth in other potential leaders.

Scenario #44—Raymond
7.0: Leadership Development

Bloomingdale is a large urban school district that prides itself on being able to train and hire 90 percent of their assistant principals and principals from within their school district. As part of their central office master plan, each year 15 teachers are recruited to become part of a district principal licensure cohort that spends 18 months together taking required state and district course work and interning with master principals in the district. The district's principal licensure initiative began after developing a strong partnership with a local university 12 years earlier. Practicing principals and central office staff partner with university professors to teach each course and together have developed the leadership activities that will make up each aspiring administrator's portfolio.

Raymond was a fifth-grade teacher and was seen as a leader in his school and community. Parents and students loved him and teachers highly respected his willingness to share the instructional practices he used to motivate his students to take ownership for their learning and actions. As a result, Karen, his principal, recruited Raymond to be part of the principal cohort group six years ago. It did not take the district or university teachers long to see that Raymond stood out among his peers. He was a voracious reader and was able to apply his "book learning" directly to practical uses. Raymond also took the lead in getting together the cohort team for study nights and would often post hypothetical scenarios for the group to discuss and debate.

Raymond was assigned to do his eight-week internship with Karen, the principal at Cottonwood Creek, one of the large year-round schools in the district. He was a quick learner and the district noticed his performance. While Raymond was sad to see this experience come to an end, when the cohort was finished, Raymond was offered the assistant principalship with Mary in a school in the same feeder area as Cottonwood Creek. After two years as assistant principal, Raymond was offered his own principalship. Raymond attributes his success to the excellent mentoring and support he received during the cohort and to his close work with both Karen and Mary.

Now in his third year as principal, Raymond has been asked to serve as a mentor to teachers in a new licensure cohort who are aspiring to the principalship in Bloomingdale. He has taken this role very seriously and has even identified and recruited several teachers in his own building to be part of the cohort. Mark, one of the teachers Raymond mentored, asked him if he could do his eight-week internship with Raymond at his school. Having seen many aspects of himself in this aspiring leader, Raymond was eager to support him. Over the course of the internship, their leadership styles complemented each other, creating a very trusting mutual bond. When Raymond delegated certain decision-making responsibilities to Mark, such as helping to refine the bus duty schedule, planning back-to-school night, and facilitating various professional development sessions, the staff responded favorably and with unified support. As Raymond began planning for the next school year, student enrollment was projected to grow to a point that would allow him to hire an assistant principal. Given Mark's successful internship, he was the unanimous choice of Raymond and the staff.

Peruse the MLP Matrix and assess Raymond's performance in Domain 7.0: Leadership Development. Make mental notes and be prepared to respond as to the reason for your score on that dimension. Please be prepared to report out in 15 minutes.

Scenario #44—Raymond
7.0: Leadership Development

PROFICIENT

Bloomingdale is a large urban school district that prides itself on being able to train and hire 90 percent of their assistant principals and principals from within their school district. As part of their central office master plan, each year 15 teachers are recruited to become part of a district principal licensure cohort that spends 18 months together taking required state and district course work and interning with master principals in the district. The district's principal licensure initiative began after developing a strong partnership with a local university 12 years earlier. Practicing principals and central office staff partner with university professors to teach each course and together have developed the leadership activities that will make up each aspiring administrator's portfolio.

Raymond was a fifth-grade teacher and was seen as a leader in his school and community. Parents and students loved him and teachers highly respected his willingness to share the instructional practices he used to motivate his students to take ownership for their learning and actions. As a result, Karen, his principal, recruited Raymond to be part of the principal cohort group six years ago. It did not take the district or university teachers long to see that Raymond stood out among his peers. He was a voracious reader and was able to apply his "book learning" directly to practical uses. Raymond also took the lead in getting together the cohort team for study nights and would often post hypothetical scenarios for the group to discuss and debate.

Raymond was assigned to do his eight-week internship with Karen, the principal at Cottonwood Creek, one of the large year-round schools in the district. He was a quick learner and the district noticed his performance. While Raymond was sad to see this experience come to an end, when the cohort was finished, Raymond was offered the assistant principalship with Mary in a school in the same feeder area as Cottonwood Creek. After two years as assistant principal, Raymond was offered his own principalship. Raymond attributes his success to the excellent mentoring and support he received during the cohort and to his close work with both Karen and Mary.

Now in his third year as principal, **(7.2) Raymond has been asked to serve as a mentor to teachers in a new licensure cohort who are aspiring to the principalship in Bloomingdale. He has taken this role very seriously and has even identified and recruited several teachers in his own building to be part of the cohort.** Mark, one of the teachers Raymond mentored, asked him if he could do his eight-week internship with Raymond at his school. **(7.3) Having seen many aspects of himself in this aspiring leader, Raymond was eager to support him. Over the course of the internship, their leadership styles complemented each other, creating a very trusting mutual bond. When Raymond delegated certain decision-making responsibilities to Mark, such as helping to refine the bus duty schedule, planning back-to-school night, and facilitating various professional development sessions, the staff responded favorably and with unified support. (7.1) As Raymond began planning for the next school year, student enrollment was projected to grow to a point that would allow him to hire an assistant principal. Given Mark's successful internship, he was the unanimous choice of Raymond and the staff.**

7.2: Raymond identified and recruited teacher leaders to become part of a licensure cohort. SCORE 7.2 AT PROFICIENT.

7.3: Mark and Raymond developed a close professional relationship and Raymond felt confident in delegating decision-making authority and responsibilities to Mark for the oversight of the school needs. SCORE 7.3 AT PROFICIENT.

7.1: Raymond was instrumental in personally mentoring Mark and supporting his goals of becoming a principal. SCORE 7.1 AT PROFICIENT.

Scenario #45—Frances
7.0: Leadership Development

As a primary school teacher for 12 years, Frances had always aspired to become an elementary principal. During her teaching tenure, she had been privileged to work in schools with master principals who influenced and encouraged her to take on a leadership role within the school. After finishing her principal licensure program at a local university, Frances was excited to read on the district Web site that an assistant principal position had just opened up in a neighboring district. With the support of her principal, Frances applied and was offered the position. The assistant principalship became a perfect role for Frances and, with a young family at home, this was the right amount of responsibility for her at this time in her life.

Content in her position as an assistant principal at Tuscan Elementary, Frances was determined to be as encouraging to others as her previous principals were to her, and saw supporting her teachers in pursuing their goal of becoming school leaders as part of her role. When Frances was asked to attend Data Teams (PLC) training and to select a teacher at each grade level who would become a member of the school Data Team to lead their grade-level teams, she knew this would be an opportunity for teachers to take a leadership role within the school. She wisely chose teachers who had previously demonstrated leadership qualities and who were respected by their peers. The school-level Data Team became very close and was given additional responsibilities by Frances. It was obvious that she took her role as mentor very seriously and wanted to make sure that the team was successful. While Frances trusted the teachers, oftentimes when they asked to take on a greater role, Frances was reluctant and retained her decision-making authority.

As a result of this experience, Charlotte, one of the teachers on the team, was persistent and shared with Frances that she wanted extra responsibilities as a Data Team leader and was thinking about going back to school to get a master's degree in administration. Encouraged and supported by Frances, Charlotte completed her degree in just over two years. During this time, Frances made sure that Charlotte had an opportunity to learn all aspects of leadership within the school. At the end of the following year, Charlotte applied for a principalship in a very small school in a neighboring rural community and was asked to interview for the position. When asked in her principal interview, "Who was a leader she admired and contributed to her growth as a leader?" Charlotte smiled and thought of Frances.

When Charlotte received the call offering her the position, she was thrilled and immediately called Frances to thank her for seeing leadership potential in her and for encouraging her to go back to school to become a principal. Frances was pleased to hear of the news and, for a moment, wondered if she herself needed to be applying for principal positions in the near future. Upon further thought, she knew that the role she played as assistant principal in her school/district was vital to the success of her learning community and that she was supporting other communities by encouraging aspiring teachers to leadership positions.

Peruse the MLP Matrix and assess Frances's performance in Domain 7.0: Leadership Development. Make mental notes and be prepared to respond as to the reason for your score on that dimension. Please be prepared to report out in 15 minutes.

Scenario #45—Frances
7.0: Leadership Development

PROGRESSING

As a primary school teacher for 12 years, Frances had always aspired to become an elementary principal. During her teaching tenure, she had been privileged to work in schools with master principals who influenced and encouraged her to take on a leadership role within the school. After finishing her principal licensure program at a local university, Frances was excited to read on the district Web site that an assistant principal position had just opened up in a neighboring district. With the support of her principal, Frances applied and was offered the position. The assistant principalship became a perfect role for Frances and, with a young family at home, this was the right amount of responsibility for her at this time in her life.

Content in her position as an assistant principal at Tuscan Elementary, Frances was determined to be as encouraging to others as her previous principals were to her, and saw supporting her teachers in pursuing their goal of becoming school leaders as part of her role. **(7.2) When Frances was asked to attend Data Teams (PLC) training and to select a teacher at each grade level who would become a member of the school Data Team to lead their grade-level teams, she knew this would be an opportunity for teachers to take a leadership role within the school. She wisely chose teachers who had previously demonstrated leadership qualities and who were respected by their peers.** The school-level Data Team became very close and was given additional responsibilities by Frances. It was obvious that she took her role as mentor very seriously and wanted to make sure that the team was successful. **(7.3) While Frances trusted the teachers, oftentimes when they asked to take on a greater role, Frances was reluctant and retained her decision-making authority.**

As a result of this experience, Charlotte, one of the teachers on the team, was persistent and shared with Frances that she wanted extra responsibilities as a Data Team leader and was thinking about going back to school to get a master's degree in administration. Encouraged and supported by Frances, Charlotte completed her degree in just over two years. During this time, **(7.1) Frances made sure that Charlotte had an opportunity to learn all aspects of leadership within the school.** At the end of the following year, Charlotte applied for a principalship in a very small school in a neighboring rural community and was asked to interview for the position. When asked in her principal interview, "Who was a leader she admired and contributed to her growth as a leader?" Charlotte smiled and thought of Frances.

(7.1) When Charlotte received the call offering her the position, she was thrilled and immediately called Frances to thank her for seeing leadership potential in her and for encouraging her to go back to school to become a principal. Frances was pleased to hear of the news and, for a moment, wondered if she herself needed to be applying for principal positions in the near future. Upon further thought, she knew that the role she played as assistant principal in her school/district was vital to the success of her learning community and that she was supporting other communities by encouraging aspiring teachers to leadership positions.

Scenario #46—Mary
7.0: Leadership Development

Mary is a second-year principal at Wright Middle School. She was a very successful teacher who believed that it was her responsibility to ensure the success of her students, regardless of their limitations in learning. She was the department chair at Howard High School for eight years prior to becoming an assistant principal for three years at Jefferson Middle School. Mary believes in distributed leadership and empowering others within the organization in order to create synergy among all.

Every Monday morning before students arrive, Mary meets with her leadership team, consisting of the three assistant principals, teachers, and her two counselors. Mary identifies teachers in her school who have the potential to become extraordinary leaders based on how they interact with other teachers, students, and parents. Once she identifies potential leaders, she then invites them to serve on the leadership team. The main responsibilities of the leadership team this year are to promote collaboration, lead professional learning on the Data Teams process, and to pilot the positive behavior support system. The leadership team's mission is to increase student achievement by empowering teachers to positively lead, learn, and love. By this, Mary builds relationships with her leadership team in order to demonstrate to them that she cares about who each one is as a person. Mary takes time out of every meeting to create opportunities for each leadership team member to share instructional or environmental successes from the previous week. Many of the teachers on the team would voice that Mary is not just their principal, but also their mentor and friend. They want to be future leaders because of her influence on them. Also, during the leadership team meeting, Mary presents student achievement data and teacher implementation of initiative data. After data is presented, Mary and the team plan the professional development sessions and/or reflect on the next steps for the professional learning focus. The teachers on the team feel empowered to serve as leaders because of the knowledge and support that Mary gives them. Mary regularly shares with the teachers that they were born to be the next generation of leaders. After every leadership team meeting, Mary self-reflects to assess whether she exhibited the following leadership qualities:

- building relationships based on trust
- caring about people as individuals
- valuing what others have to say
- giving them power to lead
- believing in them as leaders

Mary is proud of the work of the leadership team.

Peruse the MLP Matrix and assess Mary's performance in Domain 7.0: Leadership Development. Make mental notes and be prepared to respond as to the reason for your score on that dimension. Please be prepared to report out in 15 minutes.

Scenario #46—Mary
7.0: Leadership Development
EXEMPLARY

7.2: Mary routinely identifies and recruits new leaders. She is able to help teachers find their own leadership strengths. SCORE 7.2 AT EXEMPLARY.

7.1: Mary coaches administrators or instructional personnel who have assumed administrative positions and responsibilities. Multiple administrators throughout the system cite this leader as a mentor and a reason for their success. SCORE 7.1 AT EXEMPLARY.

7.3: Mary empowers the leadership in formal and informal ways. The leadership team participates in the facilitation of meetings and exercises leadership in professional development opportunities. Mary builds a climate of trust and delegation in this organization that contributes directly to the identification and empowerment of the next generation of leaders. SCORE 7.3 AT EXEMPLARY.

Mary is a second-year principal at Wright Middle School. She was a very successful teacher who believed that it was her responsibility to ensure the success of her students, regardless of their limitations in learning. She was the department chair at Howard High School for eight years prior to becoming an assistant principal for three years at Jefferson Middle School. Mary believes in distributed leadership and empowering others within the organization in order to create synergy among all.

Every Monday morning before students arrive, Mary meets with her leadership team, consisting of the three assistant principals, teachers, and her two counselors. **(7.2) Mary identifies teachers in her school who have the potential to become extraordinary leaders based on how they interact with other teachers, students, and parents. Once she identifies potential leaders, she then invites them to serve on the leadership team.** The main responsibilities of the leadership team this year are to promote collaboration, lead professional learning on the Data Teams process, and to pilot the positive behavior support system. **(7.1) The leadership team's mission is to increase student achievement by empowering teachers to positively lead, learn, and love. By this, Mary builds relationships with her leadership team in order to demonstrate to them that she cares about who each one is as a person. Mary takes time out of every meeting to create opportunities for each leadership team member to share instructional or environmental successes from the previous week. Many of the teachers on the team would voice that Mary is not just their principal, but also their mentor and friend. They want to be future leaders because of her influence on them.** Also, during the leadership team meeting, Mary presents student achievement data and teacher implementation of initiative data. **(7.3) After data is presented, Mary and the team plan the professional development sessions and/or reflect on the next steps for the professional learning focus. The teachers on the team feel empowered to serve as leaders because of the knowledge and support that Mary gives them. Mary regularly shares with the teachers that they were born to be the next generation of leaders.** After every leadership team meeting, Mary self-reflects to assess whether she exhibited the following leadership qualities:

- building relationships based on trust
- caring about people as individuals
- valuing what others have to say
- giving them power to lead
- believing in them as leaders

Mary is proud of the work of the leadership team.

Scenario #47—Clair
7.0: Leadership Development

Clair is a fourth-year assistant principal at Quincy 7th and 8th Grade Center. Her main responsibilities include supporting the building principal in all capacities, as well as being the lead administrator for the eighth-grade team. She is efficient in her planning and communication, but team members too often have no say in any of the decisions that are made within the building. She is well respected in the building and is considered a good listener. Clair has a reputation as being a workaholic. Her staff likes her because she is so well organized and on top of things, but she delegates very little to anyone else on her staff.

Clair always encourages staff members to take leadership roles. Some staff members who have met with her individually to share ideas state that she is supportive and, during their meetings, they have rich, meaningful conversations. Unfortunately, some have reported that oftentimes Clair takes the ideas from the discussion and creates an implementation plan on her own. When she presents it to the group, it often comes across as if she were the one who thought of the ideas and created the plan for implementation. Because of this, many of the teacher leaders in the building have backed off from giving their opinions or ideas and taking other leadership roles.

Clair has encouraged several of the department chairs to attend the district's Prospective Principal Leadership Seminar (PPLS). In fact, she sent an e-mail inviting them to the opening session. Nevertheless, she did not follow through with those she invited to see if they attended the seminar.

Clair is extremely organized and a hard worker, but she often stays at work very late and comes in early to make sure she can accomplish all of her tasks. She has entrusted some of the discipline and instructional responsibilities to the dean of students, Mrs. Kinder, and the instructional coach, Mrs. Neal. Clair believes that it is imperative for her to be involved with all the functions of the school. However, many of the tasks, such as sending out the attendance letters, collecting discipline data, and supervising lunch duty, could be delegated to secretaries, department chair heads, or other teacher leaders who are more than capable of filling a leadership role. This would encourage more teachers to take ownership in the initiatives that are set forth in the school improvement plan as well as promote growth among the teacher leaders in the building.

Peruse the MLP Matrix and assess Clair's performance in Domain 7.0: Leadership Development. Make mental notes and be prepared to respond as to the reason for your score on that dimension. Please be prepared to report out in 15 minutes.

Scenario #47—Clair
7.0: Leadership Development

PROGRESSING

Clair is a fourth-year assistant principal at Quincy 7th and 8th Grade Center. Her main responsibilities include supporting the building principal in all capacities, as well as being the lead administrator for the eighth-grade team. She is efficient in her planning and communication, but team members too often have no say in any of the decisions that are made within the building. She is well respected in the building and is considered a good listener. Clair has a reputation as being a workaholic. Her staff likes her because she is so well organized and on top of things, but she delegates very little to anyone else on her staff.

(7.1) Clair always encourages staff members to take leadership roles. Some staff members who have met with her individually to share ideas state that she is supportive and, during their meetings, they have rich, meaningful conversations. Unfortunately, some have reported that oftentimes Clair takes the ideas from the discussion and creates an implementation plan on her own. When she presents it to the group, it often comes across as if she were the one who thought of the ideas and created the plan for implementation. Because of this, many of the teacher leaders in the building have backed off from giving their opinions or ideas and taking other leadership roles.

(7.2) Clair has encouraged several of the department chairs to attend the district's Prospective Principal Leadership Seminar (PPLS). In fact, she sent an e-mail inviting them to the opening session. Nevertheless, she did not follow through with those she invited to see if they attended the seminar.

Clair is extremely organized and a hard worker, but she often stays at work very late and comes in early to make sure she can accomplish all of her tasks. **(7.3) She has entrusted some of the discipline and instructional responsibilities to the dean of students, Mrs. Kinder, and the instructional coach, Mrs. Neal. Clair believes that it is imperative for her to be involved with all the functions of the school. However, many of the tasks, such as sending out the attendance letters, collecting discipline data, and supervising lunch duty, could be delegated to secretaries, department chair heads, or other teacher leaders who are more than capable of filling a leadership role.** This would encourage more teachers to take ownership in the initiatives that are set forth in the school improvement plan as well as promote growth among the teacher leaders in the building.

Scenario #48—Max
7.0: Leadership Development

Max never felt his leadership as an assistant principal went unrecognized. Many people had encouraged him to step into the role of principal over the course of his tenure at Flaming Gorge High School, but he was content in his role. Max had seen many leaders develop their wings at Flaming Gorge, and he was proud to say that he had been a part of that legacy. Many of those people he mentored now held positions as administrators in his own district and across the state. Any of these administrators, when asked, would cite the mentoring Max provided as pivotal in their own careers. Max attributed this to his keen eye for recognizing leadership talent in others. Not everyone had this natural tendency for success as leaders.

One of the primary responsibilities Max took on each year was to facilitate department leader meetings. Many of the department leaders had aspirations for administrative positions and Max was eager to work with them to develop their leadership skills further. For some potential leaders, Max found specific duties in the building these department leaders could take on that would not only provide them with leadership experience, but would also benefit the school through additional quasi-administrative support.

This year, Max had the opportunity to work with a teacher who was not new to teaching, but certainly new to Flaming Gorge. Layla came from a district that had a much greater level of poverty than what most teachers in Max's district had experienced in the past. It was interesting to see how her background knowledge both honored and challenged the department leader group. She was quite skillful at sharing ideas for meeting the needs of students who came from more challenging backgrounds, without making her peers feel that they were unable to understand such diverse demographics. When Max began to talk with Layla one-on-one after regular department meetings, he discovered that she had intentionally moved to Flaming Gorge to position herself for entry into the district's leadership cohort. This principal licensure cohort was only open to district teaching staff, but was known across the state for the quality of instructors who served as visiting faculty for the program.

Once Max learned about Layla's plans, he made sure that he provided an easy path into the program. Given Layla's unknown status in the district, Max spoke with the coordinators of the principal cohorts to ensure that they understood Layla's potential. Max had developed an influential relationship with the coordinators over the years, given the number of developing administrators he had connected to the program.

Layla was thrilled when she learned of her entry into the next principal cohort and immediately identified administration projects she might work on at Flaming Gorge to earn her internship hours and develop her skills further as a leader. Max provided support to Layla throughout this process. One of these projects included integrating leadership development into the existing teacher evaluation tool. This revised tool helped develop a culture of distributive leadership throughout the Flaming Gorge staff. Both Layla and Max were passionate about developing leaders and were gratified by the results of the application of this new tool to teacher evaluations. After Layla completed her first year of the principal cohort, both she and Max sat down with their principal to debrief. Both were pleased to hear the praise that the principal had to offer for their work on the evaluation tool. Max was reminded once again of how much he loved his job. Even in the role of assistant principal, he knew his work developing leaders in the building had a more global impact on students.

Peruse the MLP Matrix and assess Max's performance in Domain 7.0: Leadership Development. Make mental notes and be prepared to respond as to the reason for your score on that dimension. Please be prepared to report out in 15 minutes.

Scenario #48—Max
7.0: Leadership Development

PROFICIENT

Max never felt his leadership as an assistant principal went unrecognized. Many people had encouraged him to step into the role of principal over the course of his tenure at Flaming Gorge High School, but he was content in his role. Max had seen many leaders develop their wings at Flaming Gorge, and he was proud to say that he had been a part of that legacy. **(7.1) Many of those people he mentored now held positions as administrators in his own district and across the state. Any of these administrators, when asked, would cite the mentoring Max provided as pivotal in their own careers. Max attributed this to his keen eye for recognizing leadership talent in others. Not everyone had this natural tendency for success as leaders.**

One of the primary responsibilities Max took on each year was to facilitate department leader meetings. **(7.2) Many of the department leaders had aspirations for administrative positions and Max was eager to work with them to develop their leadership skills further.** For some potential leaders, **(7.3) Max found specific duties in the building these department leaders could take on that would not only provide them with leadership experience,** but would also benefit the school through additional quasi-administrative support.

This year, Max had the opportunity to work with a teacher who was not new to teaching, but certainly new to Flaming Gorge. Layla came from a district that had a much greater level of poverty than what most teachers in Max's district had experienced in the past. It was interesting to see how her background knowledge both honored and challenged the department leader group. She was quite skillful at sharing ideas for meeting the needs of students who came from more challenging backgrounds, without making her peers feel that they were unable to understand such diverse demographics. When Max began to talk with Layla one-on-one after regular department meetings, he discovered that she had intentionally moved to Flaming Gorge to position herself for entry into the district's leadership cohort. This principal licensure cohort was only open to district teaching staff, but was known across the state for the quality of instructors who served as visiting faculty for the program.

(7.2) Once Max learned about Layla's plans, he made sure that he provided an easy path into the program. Given Layla's unknown status in the district, Max spoke with the coordinators of the principal cohorts to ensure that they understood Layla's potential. Max had developed an influential relationship with the coordinators over the years, given the number of developing administrators he had connected to the program.

Layla was thrilled when she learned of her entry into the next principal cohort and immediately identified administration projects she might work on at Flaming Gorge to earn her internship hours and develop her skills further as a leader. Max provided support to Layla throughout this process. One of these projects

7.1: Max has mentored multiple leaders who have entered into administrative positions and they cite Max's mentoring as pivotal in their careers.
SCORE **7.1** AT EXEMPLARY.

7.2: Max has recruited multiple leaders. However, he does not necessarily identify them from unexpected sources, but rather looks to those who already express an interest in leadership.
SCORE **7.2** AT PROFICIENT.

7.3: Max encourages the distribution of leadership within the organization.
SCORE **7.3** AT PROFICIENT.

7.2: Max supports and advocates for Layla once he discovers her interest in leadership.
SCORE **7.2** AT PROFICIENT.

7.3: Max contributes to the development of a new evaluation tool that focuses on distributing leadership throughout the building.
SCORE 7.3 AT PROFICIENT.

(7.3) included integrating leadership development into the existing teacher evaluation tool. This revised tool helped develop a culture of distributive leadership throughout the Flaming Gorge staff. Both Layla and Max were passionate about developing leaders and were gratified by the results of the application of this new tool to teacher evaluations. After Layla completed her first year of the principal cohort, both she and Max sat down with their principal to debrief. Both were pleased to hear the praise that the principal had to offer for their work on the evaluation tool. Max was reminded once again of how much he loved his job. Even in the role of assistant principal, he knew his work developing leaders in the building had a more global impact on students.

Scenario #49—Cordelia
7.0: Leadership Development

Cordelia started her journey as a high school principal this school year. Arriving as the new principal of Fairview High School, Cordelia knew immediately that she could make a difference. Leadership had always been second nature to her as she assumed various roles of authority throughout her life. Through her own experience, she developed a core belief that leadership was something one had or didn't have. It could be nurtured and developed, but only in those who had the basic DNA to make it happen. Cordelia knew she had this DNA.

When Cordelia first arrived at Fairview, things were clearly in a state of disarray. This was why she had been hired. Student achievement was at an all-time low, discipline was out of control, systems were nearly nonexistent, and the school seemed to simply operate under the direction of the strongest teacher voices in the building. The previous principal was not known for his ability to make decisions or to ensure that teachers were held accountable for their work with students.

One of the first steps Cordelia took was to dismantle the teacher leader group. Initially she had hoped this could stay intact so that staff would continue to feel they had a voice. But these hopes were dashed after the first two meetings of the year. It became clear to Cordelia that these sessions were being used simply to gripe, and no real problem solving was occurring. It also became clear that none of the representatives had the DNA to be a leader. Unless she hired some new talent, none of the teachers in her building seemed ready for an administrative role in the near future and none seemed to express interest or drive in this direction.

By the time October rolled around, Cordelia had gathered enough evidence about the school to determine what her next steps would be. She began by revamping the school improvement plan to reflect a lockstep plan toward improved student achievement in three years. Cordelia spent several weekends developing a document that could easily be an exemplar for other principals. When she presented the plan to the staff, she walked them through the action steps that would be required of each department to improve student achievement results in each teacher's content area. For now, Cordelia focused on the core content areas, as it was clear this was where students could show the greatest improvement on the state assessments.

Throughout the meeting, few questions were raised, which seemed to indicate that the staff clearly understood what was expected. At the end of the meeting, Cordelia let them know that she would update them throughout the year with any changes to the plan that she felt were necessary and that she would connect with each department at their November meeting to see what kind of progress each had made on the action steps.

When Cordelia visited with departments in November, she was surprised at what little progress had been made on the action steps. With the exception of a few teachers, most expressed how overwhelmed they were by the students this year and felt the school improvement plan was an added burden. In one particular meeting, Cordelia experienced quite a bit of negativity. She reminded them that implementation of the school improvement plan was a key indicator on the new teacher evaluation framework and failure to follow through with their responsibilities would result in an unsatisfactory evaluation. This seemed to create some angst in the group, which Cordelia hoped would help teachers realize that their jobs were on the line.

It took only a week for the union president to request a meeting with Cordelia and several teachers who had filed a grievance. Cordelia held her ground with the union president when he began to attack Cordelia's leadership. She explained the reason why the school improvement plan was necessary and why the school did not have time to waste. It didn't change the tone of the meeting, which ended quite abruptly. In the end, Cordelia knew she was making the right decisions for her school.

Peruse the MLP Matrix and assess Cordelia's performance in Domain 7.0: Leadership Development. Make mental notes and be prepared to respond as to the reason for your score on that dimension. Please be prepared to report out in 15 minutes.

Scenario #49—Cordelia
7.0: Leadership Development

NOT MEETING STANDARDS

Cordelia started her journey as a high school principal this school year. Arriving as the new principal of Fairview High School, Cordelia knew immediately that she could make a difference. Leadership had always been second nature to her as she assumed various roles of authority throughout her life. Through her own experience, she developed a core belief that leadership was something one had or didn't have. It could be nurtured and developed, but only in those who had the basic DNA to make it happen. Cordelia knew she had this DNA.

When Cordelia first arrived at Fairview, things were clearly in a state of disarray. This was why she had been hired. Student achievement was at an all-time low, discipline was out of control, systems were nearly nonexistent, and the school seemed to simply operate under the direction of the strongest teacher voices in the building. The previous principal was not known for his ability to make decisions or to ensure that teachers were held accountable for their work with students.

One of the first steps **(7.2, 7.3) Cordelia took was to dismantle the teacher leader group. Initially she had hoped this could stay intact so that staff would continue to feel they had a voice. But these hopes were dashed after the first two meetings of the year. It became clear to Cordelia that these sessions were being used simply to gripe, and no real problem solving was occurring. It also became clear that none of the representatives had the DNA to be a leader.** Unless she hired some new talent, none of the teachers in her building seemed ready for an administrative role in the near future and none seemed to express interest or drive in this direction.

By the time October rolled around, Cordelia had gathered enough evidence about the school to determine **(7.1, 7.2) what her next steps would be. She began by revamping the school improvement plan to reflect a lockstep plan toward improved student achievement in three years.** Cordelia spent several weekends developing a document that could easily be an exemplar for other principals. When she presented the plan to the staff, she walked them through the action steps that would be required of each department to improve student achievement results in each teacher's content area. For now, Cordelia focused on the core content areas, as it was clear this was where students could show the greatest improvement on the state assessments.

Throughout the meeting, few questions were raised, which seemed to indicate that the staff clearly understood what was expected. At the end of the meeting, Cordelia let them know that she would update them throughout the year with any changes to the plan that she felt were necessary and that she would connect with each department at their November meeting to see what kind of progress each had made on the action steps.

> **7.2 and 7.3:** Cordelia does not recognize the need for leadership in the system and dismantles the only forum that staff had to provide their input. SCORE 7.2 AND 7.3 AT NOT MEETING STANDARDS.

> **7.1 and 7.2:** Cordelia writes the school improvement plan without any input from the staff and does not afford staff the opportunity to develop their own leadership through involvement in this process. SCORE 7.1 AND 7.2 AT NOT MEETING STANDARDS.

CASE STUDY MATERIALS AND LEARNING EXPERIENCES

7.1: Staff are unwilling or believe they do not have the ability to carry out the plan or take on extra responsibilities. SCORE 7.1 AT NOT MEETING STANDARDS.

When Cordelia visited with departments in November, she was surprised at what little progress had been made on the action steps. **(7.1) With the exception of a few teachers, most expressed how overwhelmed they were by the students this year and felt the school improvement plan was an added burden. In one particular meeting, Cordelia experienced quite a bit of negativity.** She reminded them that implementation of the school improvement plan was a key indicator on the new teacher evaluation framework and failure to follow through with their responsibilities would result in an unsatisfactory evaluation. This seemed to create some angst in the group, which Cordelia hoped would help teachers realize that their jobs were on the line.

It took only a week for the union president to request a meeting with Cordelia and several teachers who had filed a grievance. Cordelia held her ground with the union president when he began to attack Cordelia's leadership. She explained the reason why the school improvement plan was necessary and why the school did not have time to waste. It didn't change the tone of the meeting, which ended quite abruptly. In the end, Cordelia knew she was making the right decisions for her school.

Scenario #50—Kenneth
7.0: Leadership Development

When Kenneth, the director of transportation for Miwauka Independent School District, arrived in his office early on Monday morning, he had a message on his desk to contact Jesus, his assistant director of transportation. Ken had a hunch he knew what Jesus wanted to talk about. Jesus had interviewed for a director of transportation position in a neighboring school district the week before. Kenneth was certain Jesus was calling to share he was offered the job. As a part of the application process, Kenneth provided a phone reference for Jesus. Kenneth had mentored him when he was a bus driver in the district, and then when his previous assistant retired he had tapped Jesus to be his assistant director. Jesus was a talented leader who had developed the knowledge and skills necessary to be a successful director.

Kenneth was right. Jesus was offered the job and would be leaving Miwauka School District in two weeks. During their conversation, Jesus thanked Kenneth for being such a great mentor to him over the past four years. Additionally, Jesus was thankful Kenneth had encouraged him as a young bus driver to be part of the "Acceleration Pool" that Kenneth had put in place in order to develop a group of individuals with high potential for executive jobs in the area of transportation.

The district supported the Acceleration Pool concept that Kenneth had put in place that identified potential future leaders and strategically gave them additional responsibilities that offered the best learning and the highest-visibility opportunities. Members in the pool had assigned mentors, received more training, attended special development experiences, such as university executive programs, and were asked to serve on district committees. They also received more individualized feedback and coaching than other staff. Moreover, Kenneth tracked pool members' development and readiness with the help of the human resources department. To date, three of the members of the pool had gone on to other central office positions in the district and two had taken leadership positions outside of the district.

In addition, Kenneth had also developed a survey that was given out to the pool members at the end of each year, and he uses the feedback to make changes for the next year. In reflecting on the survey feedback, Kenneth is aware that the pool members (which included those who were hired in central office leadership positions) are requesting additional responsibilities and greater input in the decision-making process. This next year, Kenneth will focus his goals on the delegation of leadership responsibilities and the creation of a shared decision-making model.

Kenneth has received district-level recognition for implementing the Acceleration Pool this past year and has even been asked to help other central office departments develop a similar model. He looks forward to this leadership opportunity for the upcoming school year, at which time he will be part of a central office leadership cabinet and have an opportunity to share the model with his colleagues.

While feeling both a personal and a professional loss with the departure of Jesus, Kenneth knows that he has members of his pool who are ready to step in and fill positions, and he has already put the hiring process in place with his human resources department.

Peruse the MLP Matrix and assess Kenneth's performance in Domain 7.0: Leadership Development. Make mental notes and be prepared to respond as to the reason for your score on that dimension. Please be prepared to report out in 15 minutes.

Scenario #50—Kenneth
7.0: Leadership Development

PROGRESSING

When Kenneth, the director of transportation for Miwauka Independent School District, arrived in his office early on Monday morning, he had a message on his desk to contact Jesus, his assistant director of transportation. Ken had a hunch he knew what Jesus wanted to talk about. Jesus had interviewed for a director of transportation position in a neighboring school district the week before. Kenneth was certain Jesus was calling to share he was offered the job. As a part of the application process, Kenneth provided a phone reference for Jesus. **(7.1) Kenneth had mentored him when he was a bus driver in the district, and then when his previous assistant retired he had tapped Jesus to be his assistant director. Jesus was a talented leader who had developed the knowledge and skills necessary to be a successful director.**

Kenneth was right. Jesus was offered the job and would be leaving Miwauka School District in two weeks. During their conversation, Jesus thanked Kenneth for being such a great mentor to him over the past four years. Additionally, **(7.2) Jesus was thankful Kenneth had encouraged him as a young bus driver to be part of the "Acceleration Pool" that Kenneth had put in place in order to develop a group of individuals with high potential for executive jobs in the area of transportation.**

The district supported the Acceleration Pool concept that Kenneth had put in place that identified potential future leaders and strategically gave them additional responsibilities that offered the best learning and the highest-visibility opportunities. Members in the pool had assigned mentors, received more training, attended special development experiences, such as university executive programs, and were asked to serve on district committees. They also received more individualized feedback and coaching than other staff. Moreover, Kenneth tracked pool members' development and readiness with the help of the human resources department. To date, three of the members of the pool had gone on to other central office positions in the district and two had taken leadership positions outside of the district.

In addition, **(7.3) Kenneth had also developed a survey that was given out to the pool members at the end of each year, and he uses the feedback to make changes for the next year. In reflecting on the survey feedback, Kenneth is aware that the pool members (which included those who were hired in central office leadership positions) are requesting additional responsibilities and greater input in the decision-making process. This next year, Kenneth will focus his goals on the delegation of leadership responsibilities and the creation of a shared decision-making model.**

Kenneth has received district-level recognition for implementing the Acceleration Pool this past year and has even been asked to help other central office departments develop a similar model. He looks forward to this leadership opportunity for the upcoming school year, at which time he will be part of a central office leadership cabinet and have an opportunity to share the model with his colleagues.

7.1: During the time that Kenneth mentored Jesus, he made sure he helped him develop the leadership skills necessary for becoming a future director.
SCORE **7.1** AT PROGRESSING.

7.2: Kenneth developed a system to routinely identify and mentor leaders for future leadership positions. He has identified several potential leaders, and three have moved on to central office leadership roles in the district.
SCORE **7.2** AT EXEMPLARY.

7.3: Kenneth has done an exemplary job of developing a leadership pool and of providing leadership development support. Feedback from members in the pool and even from those that have gone on to leadership positions in the district indicates he needs to delegate more of his decision-making authority.
SCORE **7.3** AT PROGRESSING.

While feeling both a personal and a professional loss with the departure of Jesus, Kenneth knows that he has members of his pool who are ready to step in and fill positions, and he has already put the hiring process in place with his human resources department.

Scenario #51—Mary Jane
7.0: Leadership Development

Mary Jane has been in the food service department of Mariposa Independent School District for the past ten years. Her first position was at her children's elementary school, where she was the head cook for three years. During this time, Mary Jane was recognized several times by her staff and the district for her outstanding leadership and her willingness to go above and beyond to ensure the success of her program. Two years ago, Mary Jane was promoted to assistant director of food service for the district. She attributes her success to the strong coaching and mentoring that she received from her supervisors and to the professional development training she received from district trainers in the areas of continuous quality improvement.

In her first year as food service director, Mary Jane worked hard to develop a broader perspective of the position and knowledge of the strengths and concerns at each of her 32 sites. In addition to visiting each site monthly, she held monthly meetings with her head cooks and was always accessible by phone or e-mail to answer questions or address their concerns.

In November at the end of her monthly meeting, one of her head cooks came up to Mary Jane and asked if she could schedule a time the following week to talk about her performance and job aspirations. Knowing that Lauren ran a quality program as measured by student, parent, and staff satisfaction feedback on the end-of-year surveys, Mary Jane welcomed the opportunity to visit with Lauren. During the visit, Lauren shared that she aspired to take on greater responsibility in her role at her school and in the district and eventually wanted to become a food service director herself. Mary Jane was pleased to be supportive of Lauren's ambitions, because she knew how much mentoring helped her to refine her leadership knowledge and skills and advance as a leader in the district. In fact, she thought about a couple of other head cooks who had shown great leadership potential and came up with an idea to develop a leadership cohort for individuals interested in additional leadership responsibilities and a greater role in food services in Mariposa.

During the meeting with Lauren, Mary Jane shared this idea and asked Lauren if she would like to help her recruit other head cooks, schedule meetings and professional development focus topics, and help facilitate portions of each session. Lauren was elated by this idea and set out to craft a letter to all lead cooks and to work with Mary Jane to schedule the meetings. Mary Jane also took it upon herself to contact three head cooks personally whom she felt would make great central office food service leaders. Both Mary Jane and Lauren were pleased to have six head cooks come forward to be part of the leadership cohort. Prior to each meeting, Mary Jane planned the agenda with Lauren and gave her the responsibility of facilitating portions of the meeting. Additionally, Mary Jane made sure that she provided additional mentoring for Lauren, and when the food service assistant director position came open, she nominated Lauren for this position. Lauren interviewed and was the unanimous choice of the central office team.

Peruse the MLP Matrix and assess Mary Jane's performance in Domain 7.0: Leadership Development. Make mental notes and be prepared to respond as to the reason for your score on that dimension. Please be prepared to report out in 15 minutes.

Scenario #51—Mary Jane
7.0: Leadership Development

PROFICIENT

7.2: Mary Jane developed a leadership cohort to help develop leadership capacity in her department.
SCORE 7.2 AT PROFICIENT.

7.3: Mary Jane has delegated decisions and authority to support Lauren in her leadership development.
SCORE 7.3 AT PROFICIENT.

7.2: Mary Jane personally identified and contacted three head cooks to become part of her leadership cohort.
SCORE 7.2 AT PROFICIENT.

7.3: Lauren was given responsibility to make decisions about the meeting and to facilitate part of the agenda.
SCORE 7.3 AT PROFICIENT.

7.1: Mary Jane personally mentored Lauren to assume an assistant food service leadership position in the district.
SCORE 7.1 AT PROFICIENT.

Mary Jane has been in the food service department of Mariposa Independent School District for the past ten years. Her first position was at her children's elementary school, where she was the head cook for three years. During this time, Mary Jane was recognized several times by her staff and the district for her outstanding leadership and her willingness to go above and beyond to ensure the success of her program. Two years ago, Mary Jane was promoted to assistant director of food service for the district. She attributes her success to the strong coaching and mentoring that she received from her supervisors and to the professional development training she received from district trainers in the areas of continuous quality improvement.

In her first year as food service director, Mary Jane worked hard to develop a broader perspective of the position and knowledge of the strengths and concerns at each of her 32 sites. In addition to visiting each site monthly, she held monthly meetings with her head cooks and was always accessible by phone or e-mail to answer questions or address their concerns.

In November at the end of her monthly meeting, one of her head cooks came up to Mary Jane and asked if she could schedule a time the following week to talk about her performance and job aspirations. Knowing that Lauren ran a quality program as measured by student, parent, and staff satisfaction feedback on the end-of-year surveys, Mary Jane welcomed the opportunity to visit with Lauren. **(7.2) During the visit, Lauren shared that she aspired to take on greater responsibility in her role at her school and in the district and eventually wanted to become a food service director herself. Mary Jane was pleased to be supportive of Lauren's ambitions, because she knew how much mentoring helped her to refine her leadership knowledge and skills and advance as a leader in the district. In fact, she thought about a couple of other head cooks who had shown great leadership potential and came up with an idea to develop a leadership cohort for individuals interested in additional leadership responsibilities and a greater role in food services in Mariposa.**

During the meeting with Lauren, **(7.3) Mary Jane shared this idea and asked Lauren if she would like to help her recruit other head cooks, schedule meetings and professional development focus topics, and help facilitate portions of each session. Lauren was elated by this idea and set out to craft a letter to all lead cooks and to work with Mary Jane to schedule the meetings. (7.2) Mary Jane also took it upon herself to contact three head cooks personally whom she felt would make great central office food service leaders.** Both Mary Jane and Lauren were pleased to have six head cooks come forward to be part of the leadership cohort. **(7.3) Prior to each meeting, Mary Jane planned the agenda with Lauren and gave her the responsibility of facilitating portions of the meeting.** Additionally, **(7.1) Mary Jane made sure that she provided additional mentoring for Lauren, and when the food service assistant director position came open, she nominated Lauren for this position. Lauren interviewed and was the unanimous choice of the central office team.**

Scenario #52—Debbie
7.0: Leadership Development

Debbie has been the director of human resources in the Washington Public School System for 10 years. She is a graduate of Lincoln University, with a degree in business administration. She was an honors student throughout high school and college, and graduated at the top of her class in undergrad and graduate school. She has received several awards recognizing her achievements in administration and leadership.

Debbie has mentored students going through the business program at Lincoln University, as well as local high school juniors and seniors. She is currently involved with training teachers and administrators to assume various leadership responsibilities and positions throughout the district. Participation in the training was part of a professional development plan that the board recommended for teachers and administrators who had demonstrated positive performance and success in their classrooms and/or schools. The selection criteria were based on the last two years' performance evaluations for each teacher and administrator. A list containing the names and e-mail addresses of the teachers and administrators who would be participating in the training was given to Debbie prior to the training date. She then e-mailed them a self-evaluation questionnaire to complete that would indicate their instructional strengths and leadership qualities. This tool assisted her in identifying potential future leaders.

Debbie has had the privilege of observing students in her mentoring program develop into leaders within the community, as well as obtain leadership positions within their career choices. She has maintained contact with most of them and often has invited them to be guest speakers in her leadership workshop series. This has provided inspiration and encouragement to training participants to become more aware of their potential and to display confidence in their ability to take on leadership roles. Most commonly, Debbie discovers that most of the participants in her training never considered themselves leaders until they assumed leadership positions.

Because of her role within the school system, Debbie believes in and supports the vision and direction of the school district and, therefore, she carefully looks for candidates who demonstrate the qualities of a leader. She understands that a leader is not always in a managerial position, but that there are student and teacher leaders. By this, she empowers the teacher leaders to facilitate meetings, spearhead committees, and assume other leadership roles in their schools. She also schedules teacher leaders to assume the role of a building leader when the principal or assistant principal is absent. Because of her knowledge and experience, the Washington School System has been able to run effectively and efficiently, holding the trust of its current employees and recruiting new leaders for the next generation.

Peruse the MLP Matrix and assess Debbie's performance in Domain 7.0: Leadership Development. Make mental notes and be prepared to respond as to the reason for your score on that dimension. Please be prepared to report out in 15 minutes.

Scenario #52—Debbie
7.0: Leadership Development

EXEMPLARY

Debbie has been the director of human resources in the Washington Public School System for 10 years. She is a graduate of Lincoln University, with a degree in business administration. She was an honors student throughout high school and college, and graduated at the top of her class in undergrad and graduate school. She has received several awards recognizing her achievements in administration and leadership.

Debbie has mentored students going through the business program at Lincoln University, as well as local high school juniors and seniors. She is currently involved with training teachers and administrators to assume various leadership responsibilities and positions throughout the district. Participation in the training was part of a professional development plan that the board recommended for teachers and administrators who had demonstrated positive performance and success in their classrooms and/or schools. **(7.2) The selection criteria were based on the last two years' performance evaluations for each teacher and administrator. A list containing the names and e-mail addresses of the teachers and administrators who would be participating in the training was given to Debbie prior to the training date. She then e-mailed them a self-evaluation questionnaire to complete that would indicate their instructional strengths and leadership qualities. This tool assisted her in identifying potential future leaders.**

(7.2) Debbie has had the privilege of observing students in her mentoring program develop into leaders within the community, as well as obtain leadership positions within their career choices. She has maintained contact with most of them and often has invited them to be guest speakers in her leadership workshop series. This has provided inspiration and encouragement to training participants to become more aware of their potential and to display confidence in their ability to take on leadership roles. Most commonly, Debbie discovers that most of the participants in her training never considered themselves leaders until they assumed leadership positions.

Because of her role within the school system, Debbie believes in and supports the vision and direction of the school district and, therefore, she carefully looks for candidates who demonstrate the qualities of a leader. **(7.3) She understands that a leader is not always in a managerial position, but that there are student and teacher leaders. By this, she empowers the teacher leaders to facilitate meetings, spearhead committees, and assume other leadership roles in their schools. She also schedules teacher leaders to assume the role of a building leader when the principal or assistant principal is absent. Because of her knowledge and experience, the Washington School System has been able to run effectively and efficiently, holding the trust of its current employees and recruiting new leaders for the next generation.**

Scenario #53—Warren
7.0: Leadership Development

Warren is a grounds and maintenance administrator in the Brown School District. He supervises the custodians and grounds workers to ensure that they carry out all duties required to create and maintain clean, safe, and aesthetically pleasing inside and outside environments.

Warren believes in fostering a work environment that nurtures employees to be effective and efficient in their jobs. Every week, Warren visits a school a day to offer support and guidance to the head custodian of each building. During his visit, he conducts walk-throughs to observe the cleanliness and safety of the school. Warren gives the head custodian immediate feedback on what he observes and ideas on improvements to make by the next school visit. He has also created video training modules that address various issues of maintaining a clean and safe environment, which he shares with the head custodians based on the results of his school visits. Many of the custodians do not like the format of the training; they would prefer coming together as a group of head custodians for hands-on trainings. The high school head custodian has even suggested having a focus topic at their monthly head custodian meetings and having a head custodian present the focus topic. But Warren did not like that idea and insisted that the videos serve their purpose as an effective training tool. Warren offered the high school custodian the job of deciding what training videos should be shown in August, December, and May. Warren appreciates the initiative and work ethic of his head custodians. He believes that they are trained well and have a strong sense of community. However, Warren is from the "old school" and believes that he is the leader and it is his responsibility to make sure the job is done. The head custodians do not appreciate his disregard for their input and suggestions; they are tired of how Warren makes decisions. Nevertheless, they highly respect Warren's tireless work ethic and his constant support of them.

The head custodians would welcome more leadership roles in developing their custodial staff. They often criticize Warren for not hiring any night-shift custodians for head custodian positions, as well as for not having a system for developing new head custodians. However, when there is a head custodian position, Warren follows the guidelines for accepting applications and interviewing within the system. Warren believes in following policies by the book.

Peruse the MLP Matrix and assess Warren's performance in Domain 7.0: Leadership Development. Make mental notes and be prepared to respond as to the reason for your score on that dimension. Please be prepared to report out in 15 minutes.

7.1: Warren provides some training for the head custodian.
SCORE 7.1 AT PROGRESSING.

7.3: Warren sometimes delegates, but also maintains decision-making authority that could be delegated to others.
SCORE 7.3 AT PROGRESSING.

7.2: Warren follows personnel guidelines for accepting applications for head custodians, but has not implemented any systematic process for identifying new head custodians.
SCORE 7.2 AT PROGRESSING.

Scenario #53—Warren
7.0: Leadership Development

PROGRESSING

Warren is a grounds and maintenance administrator in the Brown School District. He supervises the custodians and grounds workers to ensure that they carry out all duties required to create and maintain clean, safe, and aesthetically pleasing inside and outside environments.

Warren believes in fostering a work environment that nurtures employees to be effective and efficient in their jobs. Every week, Warren visits a school a day to offer support and guidance to the head custodian of each building. **(7.1) During his visit, he conducts walk-throughs to observe the cleanliness and safety of the school. Warren gives the head custodian immediate feedback on what he observes and ideas on improvements to make by the next school visit. He has also created video training modules that address various issues of maintaining a clean and safe environment, which he shares with the head custodians based on the results of his school visits. Many of the custodians do not like the format of the training; they would prefer coming together as a group of head custodians for hands-on trainings. (7.3) The high school head custodian has even suggested having a focus topic at their monthly head custodian meetings and having a head custodian present the focus topic. But Warren did not like that idea and insisted that the videos serve their purpose as an effective training tool. Warren offered the high school custodian the job of deciding what training videos should be shown in August, December, and May.** Warren appreciates the initiative and work ethic of his head custodians. He believes that they are trained well and have a strong sense of community. However, Warren is from the "old school" and believes that he is the leader and it is his responsibility to make sure the job is done. The head custodians do not appreciate his disregard for their input and suggestions; they are tired of how Warren makes decisions. Nevertheless, they highly respect Warren's tireless work ethic and his constant support of them.

(7.2) The head custodians would welcome more leadership roles in developing their custodial staff. They often criticize Warren for not hiring any night-shift custodians for head custodian positions, as well as for not having a system for developing new head custodians. However, when there is a head custodian position, Warren follows the guidelines for accepting applications and interviewing within the system. Warren believes in following policies by the book.

Scenario #54—Xander
7.0: Leadership Development

When Xander first began his career as an administrator, a very wise principal took him under his wing and offered constant support to ensure he was successful. Xander never forgot how important this was to him as a leader. Since that time, there had been many occasions for Xander to do the same for others when he served as a principal, central office administrator, and now as a superintendent. People often joked with Xander about how his school, department, or district was an "administration boot camp" because of how many leaders he had nurtured into the system.

Xander was now in his fifth year as the superintendent of Elk County School District. There was significant work to be done this year in Elk County, as the district took on a new district-wide assessment system. With a new assistant superintendent just joining the team, Xander knew that this was a great opportunity for her to build her own leadership skills, while using her expertise in assessment at the same time. Based on his reference check, the new assistant superintendent already possessed strong skills as a leader herself. His goal was to work with her to help distribute leadership responsibilities throughout the entire organization, as he knew anything less could impact the successful implementation of the new assessment system.

In the previous year, Xander had the opportunity to work closely with one high school that agreed to pilot the new assessment system. Early on he found three teachers with no leadership experience who proved to be an incredible "untapped" resource in the district. Xander discovered that their understanding of formative assessments was already improving student achievement, but their quiet natures had kept their "islands of excellence" hidden. With Xander's support, these three teachers shared their knowledge and success with other teachers and during staff meetings. Soon, these teachers became opinion leaders in their building. The new energy around their developing leadership led two of the teachers to join a principal licensure cohort in the spring. They were not only well on their way to a new career in school administration; the new assistant superintendent had recruited them to work on the district-wide implementation of the assessment system.

Xander knew that this significant need for leadership throughout the district was essential during this second-order change initiative. He looked for further ways to encourage leadership among all staff. During one conversation with the director of human resources, Xander discovered that the current evaluation documents did not reflect this value. He was surprised at the existing language that appeared in nearly every job category that promoted "subordinates following direction without question." Xander charged the director with the task of working with a team composed of representatives from each school to modify the evaluation documents to reflect an expectation that promoted the development of leadership skills at all levels of the organization.

At the end of the year, Xander sat down with his assistant superintendent and discussed what they had accomplished with regard to the rollout of the new assessment system. They both shared success stories and lessons learned,

CASE STUDY MATERIALS AND LEARNING EXPERIENCES

discovering that some of their greatest successes came unexpectedly as a result of someone other than themselves taking the initiative to bring a new idea to fruition. There was still work to be done, and the second year of implementation would certainly have some challenges, but both felt good about what had been accomplished.

Peruse the MLP Matrix and assess Xander's performance in Domain 7.0: Leadership Development. Make mental notes and be prepared to respond as to the reason for your score on that dimension. Please be prepared to report out in 15 minutes.

Scenario #54—Xander
7.0: Leadership Development

PROFICIENT

When Xander first began his career as an administrator, a very wise principal took him under his wing and offered constant support to ensure he was successful. Xander never forgot how important this was to him as a leader. **(7.2) Since that time, there had been many occasions for Xander to do the same for others when he served as a principal, central office administrator, and now as a superintendent. People often joked with Xander about how his school, department, or district was an "administration boot camp" because of how many leaders he had nurtured into the system.**

Xander was now in his fifth year as the superintendent of Elk County School District. There was significant work to be done this year in Elk County, as the district took on a new district-wide assessment system. With a new assistant superintendent just joining the team, **(7.3) Xander knew that this was a great opportunity for her to build her own leadership skills, while using her expertise in assessment at the same time.** Based on his reference check, the new assistant superintendent already possessed strong skills as a leader herself. **(7.2) His goal was to work with her to help distribute leadership responsibilities throughout the entire organization, as he knew anything less could impact the successful implementation of the new assessment system.**

In the previous year, Xander had the opportunity to work closely with one high school that agreed to pilot the new assessment system. **(7.2) Early on he found three teachers with no leadership experience who proved to be an incredible "untapped" resource in the district. Xander discovered that their understanding of formative assessments was already improving student achievement, but their quiet natures had kept their "islands of excellence" hidden. (7.1) With Xander's support, these three teachers shared their knowledge and success with other teachers and during staff meetings. Soon, these teachers became opinion leaders in their building. (7.2) The new energy around their developing leadership led two of the teachers to join a principal licensure cohort in the spring. They were not only well on their way to a new career in school administration; the new assistant superintendent had recruited them to work on the district-wide implementation of the assessment system.**

Xander knew that this significant need for leadership throughout the district was essential during this second-order change initiative. He looked for further ways to encourage leadership among all staff. During one conversation with the director of human resources, Xander discovered that the current evaluation documents did not reflect this value. He was surprised at the existing language that appeared in nearly every job category that promoted "subordinates following direction without question."

7.2: Xander has routinely identified and mentored leaders throughout his career.
SCORE 7.2 AT EXEMPLARY.

7.3: Xander delegates oversight of the implementation of the new assessment system.
SCORE 7.3 AT PROFICIENT.

7.2: Xander works with other leaders to identify and recruit others with leadership potential.
SCORE 7.2 AT EXEMPLARY.

7.2: Xander identifies potential leaders from unexpected sources.
SCORE 7.2 AT EXEMPLARY.

7.1: Xander has worked personally with others to develop their instructional leadership skills.
SCORE 7.1 AT PROFICIENT.

7.2: Two of the teacher leaders Xander identified entered into an administrative licensure program.
SCORE 7.2 AT EXEMPLARY.

7.2: Xander works with other leaders to identify and recruit new leaders.
SCORE 7.2 AT EXEMPLARY.

7.3: Xander works with the human resources director to change the language of the evaluation to reflect the expectation for leadership development across the system. This provides an example of how Xander is both delegating and distributing leadership. SCORE 7.3 AT PROFICIENT.

(7.3) Xander charged the director with the task of working with a team composed of representatives from each school to modify the evaluation documents to reflect an expectation that promoted the development of leadership skills at all levels of the organization.

At the end of the year, Xander sat down with his assistant superintendent and discussed what they had accomplished with regard to the rollout of the new assessment system. They both shared success stories and lessons learned, discovering that some of their greatest successes came unexpectedly as a result of someone other than themselves taking the initiative to bring a new idea to fruition. There was still work to be done, and the second year of implementation would certainly have some challenges, but both felt good about what had been accomplished.

Scenario #55—Eliza
7.0: Leadership Development

Eliza moved into her current position as a director of high schools after completing five successful years as a high school principal in Stonebridge School District. These years as a building leader had given Eliza a keen understanding of what it took to make a high school successful. She worked long hours, often sacrificing her own health and missing family events, to make sure that her high school was a success. Eliza had this same philosophy as she moved into her new role this school year.

When Eliza took on her new role as director of high schools, she recognized that she was filling the shoes of a beloved director who had served in his role for more than a decade. He was a legend in the minds of all who worked in the district. Eliza had liked him as well, and he even encouraged her to apply for his position when he announced his retirement. However, she knew that she had knowledge of current best practices that far exceeded his, and using this knowledge would set her apart from him in her own right. As she began the first year, Eliza set out to develop an entirely new approach to course offerings at all high schools in Stonebridge School District. This meant that some sacred cows might have to be released. But Eliza's past experience with a similar initiative in her own building proved to her that this could be done.

Eliza directed the curriculum and technology departments to work together to ensure that, as the course offerings were revamped, the student information system seamlessly reflected these changes. She did not want schools and teachers to suffer the consequences of a new course system that was not ready for prime time when course catalogs were due to be created in December. She knew all too well the kind of stress lack of readiness would create for registration at a large comprehensive high school. Eliza could have worked collaboratively with the directors from these departments who were her direct reports. However, she felt this would slow down the process even further, and time was of the essence. She let the department directors know that she was taking this one off their plates so their time could be freed up for their own initiatives. The directors made some preliminary suggestions about timeline and resources, but were quickly dismissed by Eliza. As she had told them on many occasions, she lived this course catalog as a high school principal, so her background knowledge would give her the greatest chance of success in leading the project.

Sometime in November, Eliza was making one of her weekly visits to the curriculum and technology departments to check on the progress of the new course system. She was surprised to learn that her project had been completely put on hold due to the required rework of the existing standards database. When she questioned several coordinators with whom she had been working, they simply indicated that this project was always waiting in the wings and they had planned to begin the work as soon as the state released the new standards.

Eliza was livid when they refused to promise that they would return to her project by the end of the week. In all cases, the coordinators predicted at least another month of standards work before they could get back to Eliza's course system project.

This meant that the high schools would not receive what they needed to create their catalogs and register students until sometime in January. Eliza was fuming when she headed down the hall to confront the director of curriculum and the director of technology.

Peruse the MLP Matrix and assess Eliza's performance in Domain 7.0: Leadership Development. Make mental notes and be prepared to respond as to the reason for your score on that dimension. Please be prepared to report out in 15 minutes.

Scenario #55—Eliza
7.0: Leadership Development

Not Meeting Standards

Eliza moved into her current position as a director of high schools after completing five successful years as a high school principal in Stonebridge School District. These years as a building leader had given Eliza a keen understanding of what it took to make a high school successful. She worked long hours, often sacrificing her own health and missing family events, to make sure that her high school was a success. Eliza had this same philosophy as she moved into her new role this school year.

When Eliza took on her new role as director of high schools, she recognized that she was filling the shoes of a beloved director who had served in his role for more than a decade. He was a legend in the minds of all who worked in the district. Eliza had liked him as well, and he even encouraged her to apply for his position when he announced his retirement. However, she knew that she had knowledge of current best practices that far exceeded his, and using this knowledge would set her apart from him in her own right. As she began the first year, Eliza set out to develop an entirely new approach to course offerings at all high schools in Stonebridge School District. This meant that some sacred cows might have to be released. But Eliza's past experience with a similar initiative in her own building proved to her that this could be done.

(7.2) Eliza directed the curriculum and technology departments to work together to ensure that, as the course offerings were revamped, the student information system seamlessly reflected these changes. She did not want schools and teachers to suffer the consequences of a new course system that was not ready for prime time when course catalogs were due to be created in December. She knew all too well the kind of stress lack of readiness would create for registration at a large comprehensive high school. **(7.1) Eliza could have worked collaboratively with the directors from these departments who were her direct reports. However, she felt this would slow down the process even further, and time was of the essence. She let the department directors know that she was taking this one off their plates so their time could be freed up for their own initiatives. (7.3) The directors made some preliminary suggestions about timeline and resources, but were quickly dismissed by Eliza. As she had told them on many occasions, she lived this course catalog as a high school principal, so her background knowledge would give her the greatest chance of success in leading the project.**

Sometime in November, Eliza was making one of her weekly visits to the curriculum and technology departments to check on the progress of the new course system. She was surprised to learn that her project had been completely put on hold due to the required rework of the existing standards database. **(7.1) When she questioned several coordinators with whom she had been working, they simply indicated that this project was always waiting in the wings and they had planned to begin the work as soon as the state released the new standards.**

7.2: This is just one example of how Eliza assumes the role of sole decision maker and leader and demonstrates a lack of understanding about the importance of developing leadership in others.
SCORE **7.2** AT NOT MEETING STANDARDS.

7.1: Eliza does not feel it is important to develop the two directors by including them in the project.
SCORE **7.1** AT NOT MEETING STANDARDS.

7.3: Eliza does not involve the directors and she does not allow them to exercise their own judgment or even provide input.
SCORE **7.3** AT NOT MEETING STANDARDS.

7.1: The coordinators are unwilling to work with Eliza to meet her project needs.
SCORE **7.1** AT NOT MEETING STANDARDS.

CASE STUDY MATERIALS AND LEARNING EXPERIENCES

(7.1 cont.) Eliza was livid when they refused to promise that they would return to her project by the end of the week. In all cases, the coordinators predicted at least another month of standards work before they could get back to Eliza's course system project. This meant that the high schools would not receive what they needed to create their catalogs and register students until sometime in January. Eliza was fuming when she headed down the hall to confront the director of curriculum and the director of technology.

Domain 8.0: Time/Task/ Project Management

Leaders in education manage the decision-making process, but not all decisions. They establish personal deadlines for themselves and the entire organization. Additionally, leaders understand the benefits of going deeper with fewer initiatives, as opposed to superficial coverage of everything. They also effectively manage and delegate tasks and consistently demonstrate fiscal efficiency.

CASE STUDY MATERIALS AND LEARNING EXPERIENCES

Scenario #56—Jan
8.0: Time/Task/Project Management

Several years ago, Jan, an experienced and highly recognized school principal in Mariposa School District, was asked to attend a three-day Data Teams (PLC) seminar during the summer. Held in high regard by her peers and the district, Jan was charged with implementing this new initiative the following year in her school, collecting data on its impact on student achievement, and reporting the results back to the superintendent's cabinet. The district would then use this data to determine the effectiveness of Data Teams related to student achievement gains, and to make a decision whether Data Teams would become a mandated district-wide initiative. The district appreciated Jan's accepting this assignment and communicated she should direct a request to her elementary director if additional resources were needed for subs or materials.

Jan was eager to accept this challenge and made plans to attend the seminar. At the end of the seminar, Jan felt very confident that Data Teams would align with and enhance the current work her staff was doing in her building that focused on data collection and assessing student work. Additionally, she knew that her staff would embrace the Data Teams model because, while some of the processes and vocabulary would be new, it mirrored the collaborative team processes that were already in place within the school. More importantly, Data Teams aligned with a school value and belief that the key to improved learning for students is continuous, job-embedded learning for all educators.

When Jan returned to school after her summer break and before teachers arrived for workweek, she worked diligently to develop a strategic project plan that would guide the implementation of Data Teams over the course of the next year. The nature of the plan was comprehensive, as it would impact all certified staff in her building. Jan needed to make sure that professional development reflected new Data Teams learning, but also showed the interrelationship to the work they had already done in the building. She built her plan around successful current practices such as teachers' use of common planning time and early-release days to work in their grade-level and vertical teams. By doing so, she created a stronger focus on alignment of dialogue to their school improvement SMART goals, teaching common vocabulary, and how to develop Data Team agendas and set team norms. In developing the plan, Jan created several documents outlining the Data Teams implementation plan and goals. She shared these with staff during workweek. The documents also included a vehicle for getting staff input prior to finalizing the plan, since it was important to hear multiple perspectives regarding possible changes that might need to be made to the plan.

Jan also developed several documents using multiple measures to track the success of the implementation and to what degree Data Teams were impacting student achievement. Additionally, Jan developed an implementation timeline, which outlined professional development days and Data Team meeting times, plus made sure that staff knew that Data Teams were a priority goal and that she would work hard to ensure that their time in Data Teams was honored and free from conflicting initiatives.

Prior to sharing the plan with her staff, Jan set up a meeting with her elementary director to review and ask for final suggestions and approval to proceed. The plan was approved and Jan was recognized for her willingness to support the district request that her school serve as a pilot school for implementing Data Teams and for having developed a process that redeployed her building resources and did not cost the district additional dollars.

Peruse the MLP Matrix and assess Jan's performance in Domain 8.0: Time/Task/Project Management. Make mental notes and be prepared to respond as to the reason for your score on that dimension. Please be prepared to report out in 15 minutes.

Scenario #56—Jan
8.0: Time/Task/Project Management

EXEMPLARY

Several years ago, Jan, an experienced and highly recognized school principal in Mariposa School District, was asked to attend a three-day Data Teams (PLC) seminar during the summer. Held in high regard by her peers and the district, Jan was charged with implementing this new initiative the following year in her school, collecting data on its impact on student achievement, and reporting the results back to the superintendent's cabinet. The district would then use this data to determine the effectiveness of Data Teams related to student achievement gains, and to make a decision whether Data Teams would become a mandated district-wide initiative. The district appreciated Jan's accepting this assignment and communicated she should direct a request to her elementary director if additional resources were needed for subs or materials.

Jan was eager to accept this challenge and made plans to attend the seminar. At the end of the seminar, she felt very confident that Data Teams would align with and enhance the current work her staff was doing in her building that focused on data collection and assessing student work. Additionally, she knew that her staff would embrace the Data Teams model because, while some of the processes and vocabulary would be new, it mirrored the collaborative team processes that were already in place within the school. More importantly, Data Teams aligned with a school value and belief that the key to improved learning for students is continuous, job-embedded learning for all educators.

When Jan returned to school after her summer break and before teachers arrived for workweek, **(8.3)** she worked diligently to develop a strategic project plan that would guide the implementation of Data Teams over the course of the next year. The nature of the plan was comprehensive, as it would impact all certified staff in her building. Jan needed to make sure that professional development reflected new Data Teams learning, but also showed the interrelationship to the work they had already done in the building. She built her plan around successful current practices such as teachers' use of common planning time and early-release days to work in their grade-level and vertical teams. By doing so, she created a stronger focus on alignment of dialogue to their school improvement SMART goals, teaching common vocabulary, and how to develop Data Team agendas and set team norms. In developing the plan, **(8.3)** Jan created several documents outlining the Data Teams implementation plan and goals. She shared these with staff during workweek. The documents also included a vehicle for getting staff input prior to finalizing the plan, since it was important to hear multiple perspectives regarding possible changes that might need to be made to the plan.

(8.1) Jan also developed several documents using multiple measures to track the success of the implementation and to what degree Data Teams were impacting student achievement. Additionally, Jan developed an implementation timeline, which outlined professional development days and Data Team meeting times, plus made sure that staff knew that Data Teams were a priority goal and that she would work hard to ensure that their time in Data Teams was honored and free from conflicting initiatives.

8.3: Jan developed a comprehensive strategic project plan to ensure the successful implementation of Data Teams. SCORE 8.3 AT EXEMPLARY.

8.3: Jan developed written documents outlining the Data Teams implementation plans and goals. She shared the plans with her entire staff and asked for input. SCORE 8.3 AT EXEMPLARY.

8.1: Jan is highly organized. She developed an implementation timeline that outlined the specific tasks that needed to be accomplished. She communicated with her entire staff that the successful implementation of Data Teams was a priority and personally worked to ensure this initiative was the main focus within their school. SCORE 8.1 AT EXEMPLARY.

CASE STUDY MATERIALS AND LEARNING EXPERIENCES

8.2: While Jan knew that the superintendent has shared their would-be additional resources to implement Data Teams, Jan was able to demonstrate fiscal responsibility and reallocated resources within her own building. SCORE 8.2 AT EXEMPLARY.

Prior to sharing the plan with her staff, Jan set up a meeting with her elementary director to review and ask for final suggestions and approval to proceed. The plan was approved and **(8.2) Jan was recognized for her willingness to support the district request that her school serve as a pilot school for implementing Data Teams and for having developed a process that redeployed her building resources and did not cost the district additional dollars.**

Scenario #57—Jim
8.0: Time/Task/Project Management

Jim is a third-year assistant principal for Hines Intermediate School. His main responsibility is managing special education, school-wide positive behavior supports, and scheduling. He manages his calendar using the electronic calendar on e-mail. In order to create a system-wide way of scheduling meetings and appointments, he taught his staff how to schedule and accept meetings using the e-mail scheduling system. Teachers now have access to his calendar and can now open his calendar electronically to know when he is available for conferences. He also displays his weekly agenda on a dry-erase board outside his office. At the beginning of the year, he sat down with his building principal to build the school calendar. They identified common days and times to conduct case conferences, grade-level Data Team meetings, and school improvement team meetings. The consistencies of the dates have made it much easier for the staff and administration to keep meetings balanced throughout the month.

Jim works with teacher leaders and is successful at delegating responsibilities to team members. He uses focused meeting agendas and facilitates monthly leadership team meetings to get input and make adjustments to each plan of action. His main role is to facilitate the meeting, but since the team has followed a consistent process for the last year, he can step back and watch teachers facilitate their own leadership meetings. It really has had a positive impact on the school environment. He values teacher input and has even created a reward system for teacher leadership. Teachers feel valued and believe their opinions and ideas are important to the decision-making process.

Jim's teacher leadership team is supportive and understanding when it comes to making adjustments to schedules or plans. During a Data Team meeting, the team had to make a difficult decision regarding an English language learner (ELL) who was reading below grade level but not getting direct instruction in reading to help close the achievement gap. The student's schedule made it difficult for her to receive both the ENL (English as a Non-native Language) core curriculum and an additional reading remediation course. Her oral language and listening scores were above average, while her reading and writing scores were significantly below average. Jim and the team determined that the student needed more support in reading than in language. Jim could have made the decision himself, but he let the team work it out. Doing this allowed them to make the change and adjust the timeline. When they have taken ownership in the decisions, change has been easier for them to accept.

Last week Jim attended the special education meeting. The special education staff presented him with a list of supplies they needed for the special education department and a separate list requesting items to reward students for positive behavior. Jim supports their request for supplies and rewards for the students. However, he shares with them that he needs to confirm the amount of funds in their budget. Jim meets monthly with the principal and the principal's secretary to review the school budget, so he was able to give a direct answer to them on how much and what they could purchase for school-wide behavior rewards. He gave them a list of nonmonetary rewards and offered to purchase school rubber bracelets for students who were recognized as having exemplary behavior.

CASE STUDY MATERIALS AND LEARNING EXPERIENCES

He also encouraged the team to write a proposal asking the PTA to pay for some of the items they had requested on the list. With the support of the PTA, the team was able to give each classroom teacher $25 to spend on classroom rewards for school-wide positive behavior support. Jim also had the teachers fill out an invoice to be submitted to the special education office requesting the items they needed to support students with individualized education plans.

Peruse the MLP Matrix and assess Jim's performance in Domain 8.0: Time/Task/Project Management. Make mental notes and be prepared to respond as to the reason for your score on that dimension. Please be prepared to report out in 15 minutes.

Scenario #57—Jim
8.0 Time/Task/Project Management

Proficient

Jim is a third-year assistant principal for Hines Intermediate School. His main responsibility is managing special education, school-wide positive behavior supports, and scheduling. **(8.1) He manages his calendar using the electronic calendar on e-mail. In order to create a system-wide way of scheduling meetings and appointments, he taught his staff how to schedule and accept meetings using the e-mail scheduling system. Teachers now have access to his calendar and can now open his calendar electronically to know when he is available for conferences. He also displays his weekly agenda on a dry-erase board outside his office. At the beginning of the year, he sat down with his building principal to build the school calendar.** They identified common days and times to conduct case conferences, grade-level Data Team meetings, and school improvement team meetings. The consistencies of the dates have made it much easier for the staff and administration to keep meetings balanced throughout the month.

Jim works with teacher leaders and is successful at delegating responsibilities to team members. He uses focused meeting agendas and facilitates monthly leadership team meetings to get input and make adjustments to each plan of action. His main role is to facilitate the meeting, but since the team has followed a consistent process for the last year, he can step back and watch teachers facilitate their own leadership meetings. It really has had a positive impact on the school environment. He values teacher input and has even created a reward system for teacher leadership. Teachers feel valued and believe their opinions and ideas are important to the decision-making process.

Jim's teacher leadership team is supportive and understanding when it comes to making adjustments to schedules or plans. During a Data Team meeting, the team had to make a difficult decision regarding an English language learner (ELL) who was reading below grade level but not getting direct instruction in reading to help close the achievement gap. The student's schedule made it difficult for her to receive both the ENL (English as a Non-native Language) core curriculum and an additional reading remediation course. Her oral language and listening scores were above average, while her reading and writing scores were significantly below average. **(8.3) Jim and the team determined that the student needed more support in reading than in language. Jim could have made the decision himself, but he let the team work it out. Doing this allowed them to make the change and adjust the timeline. When they have taken ownership in the decisions, change has been easier for them to accept.**

Last week Jim attended the special education meeting. The special education staff presented him with a list of supplies they needed for the special education department and a separate list requesting items to reward students for positive behavior. Jim supports their request for supplies and rewards for the students. However, he shares with them that he needs to confirm the amount of funds in their budget. Jim meets monthly with the principal and the principal's secretary to review the school budget, so he was able to give a direct answer to them on

Case Study Materials and Learning Experiences

how much and what they could purchase for school-wide behavior rewards. He gave them a list of nonmonetary rewards and offered to purchase school rubber bracelets for students who were recognized as having exemplary behavior. He also encouraged the team to write a proposal asking the PTA to pay for some of the items they had requested on the list. With the support of the PTA, the team was able to give each classroom teacher $25 to spend on classroom rewards for school-wide positive behavior support. Jim also had the teachers fill out an invoice to be submitted to the special education office requesting the items they needed to support students with individualized education plans.

Scenario #58—Eloise
8.0: Time/Task/Project Management

Eloise had a lot to look forward to as the new principal at Green Mesa High School. She felt fortunate to be stepping into the principal role in a school that she was already intimately familiar with. Having served as the assistant principal at Green Mesa for almost 10 years, she felt very comfortable with the expectations of the school and knew the people and school history. In her mind, this new role wouldn't be much of a change.

The first month of school went well for Eloise. She was enjoying the title of principal and suddenly felt empowered in a way she hadn't before. She recognized that the staff would need to learn to see her in this new role, but she knew that the personal relationships she had already developed with many would get her through the rough spots. Fortunately, she was able to continue much of what the previous principal had created, so it was just a matter of keeping things running at about the same level.

During the fourth month of school, the social studies team came to Eloise with a complaint about their budget. They felt that they had not been given a budget that was equitable and wanted things improved for the next year. Since Eloise had left budgetary issues up to the last principal, she was unclear about how the budget had been developed and was unable to help them understand the rationale behind the decision making. In an effort to appease the group, Eloise simply promised that she would increase their budget next year by whatever amount they felt was necessary to get the job done. The team left happy with the outcome of the meeting.

In December, the lead teacher for the school improvement team came to Eloise and asked when the school improvement team was going to begin developing goals for next year's plan. She stated they were already behind on examining data in the team and working through the root-cause analysis that was usually completed by November. Eloise was new to the team, so she was surprised to learn that this was the typical timeline for school improvement planning. She assumed that the group would know their own deadlines and would have mentioned this as a priority when they met monthly to share success stories. When the teacher indicated that this was usually the principal's responsibility, Eloise was surprised. She wasn't sure how she would get up to speed on working with the team around the school improvement process in time, so she asked the lead teacher to take over the process from this point forward.

Preliminary building budgets were due in February. Eloise decided to take the budget from the previous year and simply use the same figures again. Since the district said she would need to cut costs this year due to a district-wide budget shortfall, she was unsure from where to take the money. The simplest thing seemed to be to take equal amounts from every department's budget until she could get the budget to balance. Eloise turned in the budget to the district in early March, two weeks after the deadline, because her bookkeeper was on vacation and couldn't help her work through calculations of portions of the salaries for several key employees.

When Eloise presented the new budget to the staff, they were angry. She didn't expect them to not understand that budgets had to be cut district-wide. After the meeting, the social studies team confronted her about her promise to increase their budget, a promise she obviously did not fulfill. Eloise explained that she would have increased their budget, but the unexpected cuts prevented her from doing so. The team left angry and disappointed in Eloise's leadership skills. She had seemed pretty good as an assistant principal, but the job of principal was much different.

Peruse the MLP Matrix and assess Eloise's performance in Domain 8.0: Time/Task/Project Management. Make mental notes and be prepared to respond as to the reason for your score on that dimension. Please be prepared to report out in 15 minutes.

Scenario #58—Eloise
8.0: Time/Task/Project Management

NOT MEETING STANDARDS

Eloise had a lot to look forward to as the new principal at Green Mesa High School. She felt fortunate to be stepping into the principal role in a school that she was already intimately familiar with. Having served as the assistant principal at Green Mesa for almost 10 years, she felt very comfortable with the expectations of the school and knew the people and school history. In her mind, this new role wouldn't be much of a change.

The first month of school went well for Eloise. She was enjoying the title of principal and suddenly felt empowered in a way she hadn't before. She recognized that the staff would need to learn to see her in this new role, but she knew that the personal relationships she had already developed with many would get her through the rough spots. Fortunately, she was able to continue much of what the previous principal had created, so it was just a matter of keeping things running at about the same level.

During the fourth month of school, the social studies team came to Eloise with a complaint about their budget. They felt that they had not been given a budget that was equitable and wanted things improved for the next year. Since Eloise had left budgetary issues up to the last principal, she was unclear about how the budget had been developed and was unable to help them understand the rationale behind the decision making. In an effort to appease the group, Eloise simply promised that she would increase their budget next year by whatever amount they felt was necessary to get the job done. The team left happy with the outcome of the meeting.

In December, the lead teacher for the school improvement team came to Eloise and asked when the school improvement team was going to begin developing goals for next year's plan. **(8.1) She stated they were already behind on examining data in the team and working through the root-cause analysis that was usually completed by November. (8.3) Eloise was new to the team, so she was surprised to learn that this was the typical timeline for school improvement planning. She assumed that the group would know their own deadlines and would have mentioned this as a priority when they met monthly to share success stories.** When the teacher indicated that this was usually the principal's responsibility, Eloise was surprised. **(8.1) She wasn't sure how she would get up to speed on working with the team around the school improvement process in time, so she asked the lead teacher to take over the process from this point forward.**

Preliminary building budgets were due in February. Eloise decided to take the budget from the previous year and simply use the same figures again. Since the district said she would need to cut costs this year due to a district-wide budget shortfall, she was unsure from where to take the money. The simplest thing seemed to be to take equal amounts from every department's budget until she could get the budget to balance. **(8.2) Eloise turned in the budget to the district in early March, two weeks after the deadline, because her bookkeeper was on vacation and couldn't help her work through calculations of portions of the salaries for several key employees.**

8.1: Eloise seems unaware of the deadlines and lacks a plan for how to deal with this. SCORE 8.1 AT NOT MEETING STANDARDS.

8.3: Eloise does not demonstrate project management skills. SCORE 8.3 AT NOT MEETING STANDARDS.

8.1: Eloise lacks the project management skills, so turns it over to someone else. SCORE 8.1 AT NOT MEETING STANDARDS.

8.2: Eloise does not meet the district deadline for turning in the budget. SCORE 8.2 AT NOT MEETING STANDARDS.

8.2: Eloise does not follow through on her commitment to the social studies team regarding their budget. SCORE 8.2 AT NOT MEETING STANDARDS.

When Eloise presented the new budget to the staff, they were angry. She didn't expect them to not understand that budgets had to be cut district-wide. **(8.2) After the meeting, the social studies team confronted her about her promise to increase their budget, a promise she obviously did not fulfill. Eloise explained that she would have increased their budget, but the unexpected cuts prevented her from doing so.** The team left angry and disappointed in Eloise's leadership skills. She had seemed pretty good as an assistant principal, but the job of principal was much different.

Scenario #59—Lindsay
8.0: Time/Task/Project Management

Lindsay is a charismatic executive director of elementary schools in a small rural school district. As a member of the superintendent's cabinet, she was asked along with all other administrators in the district to take a leadership profile to determine her areas of strength. The superintendent truly believed (and his actions modeled this value) that each person has enduring and unique talents and that the greatest room for growth is in the areas of his or her strengths. The superintendent also uses individual signature strengths to assign individuals to certain committees and when he assigns project initiatives. The superintendent knew that Lindsay's strengths made her an excellent choice to take on the responsibility of helping schools implement their newly adopted grading system.

The superintendent knew that Lindsay had a keen ability to develop positive connections quickly with internal and external district stakeholders and, over her tenure in the district, had formed trusting personal as well as professional relationships with leaders throughout the system. The superintendent knew this strength would be one upon which Lindsay would need to rely heavily in the development of her plan, as current traditional grading practices were widely used for more than 20 years and had been a long and rich tradition that would be hard to change in the district. Lindsay's systems thinking and ability to leverage and maximize time through her strong organizational skills were additional strengths.

After accepting this project and talking at length with the superintendent, Lindsay set out to develop a comprehensive strategic plan focused on the implementation of the new grading initiative. The plan needed to be completed by the start of the new school year, which gave Lindsay the summer to complete her work.

Lindsay began by making a comprehensive list of all the tasks that needed to be completed and assigned due dates to each. She also asked for teacher and administrator volunteers from schools to serve on a planning committee task force and asked the president of the school Parent Teacher Association to serve as the community liaison. Knowing that this was the prioritized goal for the district this year, Lindsay also met with the other level directors to ensure that the implementation of the new grading practices system would be their main focus and that principals could be assured that there would be no competing initiatives.

Aware that staff development around the research and practices behind the new grading policy was critical, Lindsay first began researching state and local grants that might support the district-wide initiative. She was excited when she secured a grant from the local teaching university to fund professional development, plus university faculty buy-in to support and monitor the implementation.

Another aspect of the strategic plan that Lindsay knew was critical to ensure successful implementation was communication. The plan had to include communication systems that set up vehicles to not only share information with all stakeholders, but also set up the means to receive feedback about strengths and concerns so that the task force could address issues in a timely manner.

Lindsay met the timeline that the superintendent had given her. Upon review, the new grading practices implementation plans were accepted and made ready to be shared with building principals at their early August retreat.

As the pilot year of implementation came to a close, Lindsay knew, based on survey data from parents and staff and ongoing e-mails from principals and teachers, that the year had been a success. While there were bumps and a few bruises along the way, the district would be moving into year two feeling confident that their new grading system was one that focused on accuracy, fairness, specificity, and timeliness—qualities that parents and students all applauded. Gone was the day in the district when zeros were given and the averaging of grades determined a student's grade in class.

Peruse the MLP Matrix and assess Lindsay's performance in Domain 8.0: Time/Task/Project Management. Make mental notes and be prepared to respond as to the reason for your score on that dimension. Please be prepared to report out in 15 minutes.

Scenario #59—Lindsay
8.0: Time/Task/Project Management

EXEMPLARY

Lindsay is a charismatic executive director of elementary schools in a small rural school district. As a member of the superintendent's cabinet, she was asked along with all other administrators in the district to take a leadership profile to determine her areas of strength. The superintendent truly believed (and his actions modeled this value) that each person has enduring and unique talents and that the greatest room for growth is in the areas of his or her strengths. The superintendent also uses individual signature strengths to assign individuals to certain committees and when he assigns project initiatives. The superintendent knew that Lindsay's strengths made her an excellent choice to take on the responsibility of helping schools implement their newly adopted grading system.

The superintendent knew that Lindsay had a keen ability to develop positive connections quickly with internal and external district stakeholders and, over her tenure in the district, had formed trusting personal as well as professional relationships with leaders throughout the system. The superintendent knew this strength would be one upon which Lindsay would need to rely heavily in the development of her plan, as current traditional grading practices were widely used for more than 20 years and had been a long and rich tradition that would be hard to change in the district. **(8.1) Lindsay's systems thinking and ability to leverage and maximize time through her strong organizational skills were additional strengths.**

After accepting this project and talking at length with the superintendent, Lindsay set out to develop a comprehensive strategic plan focused on the implementation of the new grading initiative. The plan needed to be completed by the start of the new school year, which gave Lindsay the summer to complete her work.

Lindsay began by making a comprehensive list of all the tasks that needed to be completed and assigned due dates to each. She also asked for teacher and administrator volunteers from schools to serve on a planning committee task force and asked the president of the school Parent Teacher Association to serve as the community liaison. **(8.1) Knowing that this was the prioritized goal for the district this year, Lindsay also met with the other level directors to ensure that the implementation of the new grading practices system would be their main focus and that principals could be assured that there would be no competing initiatives.**

(8.2) Aware that staff development around the research and practices behind the new grading policy was critical, Lindsay first began researching state and local grants that might support the district-wide initiative. She was excited when she secured a grant from the local teaching university to fund professional development, plus university faculty buy-in to support and monitor the implementation.

8.1: Lindsay is a systematic thinker and has developed organizational skills along with personal relationships that allow her to engage in leadership activities and collaborate with individuals at all levels of the organization. The strategic plan became her main priority. Lindsay freed up her summer to accomplish her goals and developed her task list and timeline.
SCORE **8.1** AT EXEMPLARY.

8.1: Lindsay worked with other district directors to ensure that the implementation of the new grading system was a prioritized goal throughout the organization.
SCORE **8.1** AT EXEMPLARY.

8.2: Lindsay showed fiscal stewardship by researching and applying for grants to support the implementation of the new grading policy.
SCORE **8.2** AT EXEMPLARY.

8.3: Lindsay developed a comprehensive district-wide plan to share the new grading system with all schools. This incuded a feedback loop for monitoring the effectiveness of the plan. Survey feedback documented the success of the initiative. SCORE 8.3 AT EXEMPLARY.

Another aspect of the strategic plan that Lindsay knew was critical to ensure successful implementation was communication. The plan had to include communication systems that set up vehicles to not only share information with all stakeholders, but also set up the means to receive feedback about strengths and concerns so that the task force could address issues in a timely manner.

(8.3) Lindsay met the timeline that the superintendent had given her. Upon review, the new grading practices implementation plans were accepted and made ready to be shared with building principals at their early August retreat.

As the pilot year of implementation came to a close, Lindsay knew, based on survey data from parents and staff and ongoing e-mails from principals and teachers, that the year had been a success. While there were bumps and a few bruises along the way, the district would be moving into year two feeling confident that their new grading system was one that focused on accuracy, fairness, specificity, and timeliness—qualities that parents and students all applauded. Gone was the day in the district when zeros were given and the averaging of grades determined a student's grade in class.

Scenario #60—Justin
8.0: Time/Task/Project Management

Justin is the director of middle schools for the Metropolitan District of Madison Township. He was hired four years ago to help the township achieve its newly established vision of becoming a technologically driven, innovative school district. The focus of the reform was initiated at the building level, beginning at Hickory Ridge Middle School and expanding to other schools.

During the past year, Hickory Ridge faculty, staff, parents, and business partners worked toward a variety of reform initiatives, but achieved very limited success. Some of the barriers to the reform efforts included lack of trust and respect between the more experienced teachers and the younger, newly hired teachers. The veteran teachers felt that the younger teachers did not have enough experience or knowledge of the school culture, the needs of the students, or the diverse community in which the students lived. On the other hand, the younger teachers felt that the veteran teachers were out of touch with modern times and that they were too concerned about the parents and the community. In addition, the veteran teachers were close to exceeding the budget by 15 percent.

Justin realized the task ahead of him and had to adjust his schedule. He developed a prioritized task list that outlined the steps for developing the reform plan and identified the most important elements first. He presented each staff member and board member with a copy of the proposed prioritized task list. He was open to input from all parties involved, including community members who could assist with bringing outside resources to support the plan. Justin was adamant that the staff at Hickory Ridge would work together and support each other. He insisted that they have a common direction and have the time and autonomy to develop the needed reform plan.

Mr. Scott, the principal at Hickory Ridge, provided information regarding the revised budget to Justin and the board members. Justin suggested using the current budget for posting all budget changes. He shared a chart he created that outlined the sources of funding and allocations of each fund. He also developed a timeline for completing the projects and assured the board members that the current needs of the students would be met, as reflected in the document.

The initial version of the plan included examining creative ways to empower all staff throughout the school in order to improve the respect for each other and increase staff's opportunity to make a difference in the school. It also allowed Hickory teachers to participate in activities, take technology-based industry tours, and attend forums on the implementation of various pilot reform programs. As teachers began to address elements of the plan, they made revisions where needed or reported when objectives were achieved. Justin established clear objectives with regard to the reform efforts and ensured that all staff members and board members would contribute to meeting the goal. Justin communicated all aspects of the goal to all stakeholders.

Peruse the MLP Matrix and assess Justin's performance in Domain 8.0: Time/Task/Project Management. Make mental notes and be prepared to respond as to the reason for your score on that dimension. Please be prepared to report out in 15 minutes.

Scenario #60—Justin
8.0: Time/Task/Project Management

PROFICIENT

Justin is the director of middle schools for the Metropolitan District of Madison Township. He was hired four years ago to help the township achieve its newly established vision of becoming a technologically driven, innovative school district. The focus of the reform was initiated at the building level, beginning at Hickory Ridge Middle School and expanding to other schools.

During the past year, Hickory Ridge faculty, staff, parents, and business partners worked toward a variety of reform initiatives, but achieved very limited success. Some of the barriers to the reform efforts included lack of trust and respect between the more experienced teachers and the younger, newly hired teachers. The veteran teachers felt that the younger teachers did not have enough experience or knowledge of the school culture, the needs of the students, or the diverse community in which the students lived. On the other hand, the younger teachers felt that the veteran teachers were out of touch with modern times and that they were too concerned about the parents and the community. In addition, the veteran teachers were close to exceeding the budget by 15 percent.

(8.1) Justin realized the task ahead of him and had to adjust his schedule. He developed a prioritized task list that outlined the steps for developing the reform plan and identified the most important elements first. He presented each staff member and board member with a copy of the proposed prioritized task list. He was open to input from all parties involved, including community members who could assist with bringing outside resources to support the plan. Justin was adamant that the staff at Hickory Ridge would work together and support each other. He insisted that they have a common direction and have the time and autonomy to develop the needed reform plan.

Mr. Scott, the principal at Hickory Ridge, provided information regarding the revised budget to Justin and the board members. **(8.2) Justin suggested using the current budget for posting all budget changes. He shared a chart he created that outlined the sources of funding and allocations of each fund. He also developed a timeline for completing the projects and assured the board members that the current needs of the students would be met, as reflected in the document.**

The initial version of the plan included examining creative ways to empower all staff throughout the school in order to improve the respect for each other and increase staff's opportunity to make a difference in the school. It also allowed Hickory teachers to participate in activities, take technology-based industry tours, and attend forums on the implementation of various pilot reform programs. As teachers began to address elements of the plan, they made revisions where needed or reported when objectives were achieved. **(8.3) Justin established clear objectives with regard to the reform efforts and ensured that all staff members and board members would contribute to meeting the goal. Justin communicated all aspects of the goal to all stakeholders.**

Scenario #61—James
8.0: Time/Task/Project Management

James was fortunate. He moved into the role of assistant superintendent at a time when Red Rock County Schools was in good shape with regard to achievement, budget, and public support. In the past, principals often commented on James's sense of humor, understanding, and support—the hallmarks of his leadership. Eight years had passed since that time. Now the district faced a myriad of issues that created tension and discord. James often reflected with other leaders on the crumbling culture that was right in front of him every single day.

The new board of education was certainly a part of that picture. In James's mind, their goals were not about efficacy or culture, but rather a political statement about how they could control and micromanage the direction of the district and the work of district and building leaders. The new requirements for fiscal transparency had become stifling, and it seemed as if everyone questioned what James was doing with his budget, instead of trusting his experience to make sure principals had the resources they needed to feel supported. The budget crisis was making matters worse, as the flexibility that James used to have was rapidly slipping away.

This year was the year that James was going to make sure the train was set back on the tracks in the right direction. He began his call to action through private one-on-one conversations with principals, sharing ideas and concerns with staff and community, and spending time connecting with students in schools. These conversations sparked an idea for a new focus on instructional goals that were more student-based. To get these ideas off the ground, James contacted a friend who was now in the consulting business and asked if he would round up some experts to come and speak in various venues throughout the year. James had intended to schedule out these speakers so that they could all fall on principal meeting dates, but he was sidetracked when one of his directors began working on a new technology project that he was interested in.

Most of the speakers came in as planned, but some had to be canceled when conflicts with other meetings arose. James had assumed that principals would prefer to attend the speaker sessions he had planned, rather than the budget-planning workshops that finance had put on the schedule earlier in the year. Given the current budget crisis, James discovered that this wasn't true and had to cancel several speakers at the last minute due to the conflict. To add to James's frustration, several speakers still required payment because their engagements were not canceled by the deadlines in their individual contracts.

Sometime in April, James's secretary notified him that the superintendent was requesting a budget meeting with James. It seemed that James had misread his budget allocation for the year and was assuming he had an additional $100,000 that was allotted to professional development in the prior year. He was now over budget by $80,000, and the superintendent was not happy. Given the additional scrutiny that everyone was under from the board, James wasn't surprised. However, he was surprised to walk away from his meeting with the superintendent with a letter of direction regarding future budgetary actions. This seemed like just another indicator to James that the culture of Red Rock County was no longer driven by what was right for the people, but instead by compliance and rules.

Peruse the MLP Matrix and assess James's performance in Domain 8.0: Time/Task/Project Management. Make mental notes and be prepared to respond as to the reason for your score on that dimension. Please be prepared to report out in 15 minutes.

Scenario #61—James
8.0: Time/Task/Project Management

NOT MEETING STANDARDS

James was fortunate. He moved into the role of assistant superintendent at a time when Red Rock County Schools was in good shape with regard to achievement, budget, and public support. In the past, principals often commented on James's sense of humor, understanding, and support—the hallmarks of his leadership. Eight years had passed since that time. Now the district faced a myriad of issues that created tension and discord. James often reflected with other leaders on the crumbling culture that was right in front of him every single day.

The new board of education was certainly a part of that picture. In James's mind, their goals were not about efficacy or culture, but rather a political statement about how they could control and micromanage the direction of the district and the work of district and building leaders. The new requirements for fiscal transparency had become stifling, and it seemed as if everyone questioned what James was doing with his budget, instead of trusting his experience to make sure principals had the resources they needed to feel supported. The budget crisis was making matters worse, as the flexibility that James used to have was rapidly slipping away.

This year was the year that James was going to make sure the train was set back on the tracks in the right direction. He began his call to action through private one-on-one conversations with principals, sharing ideas and concerns with staff and community, and spending time connecting with students in schools. These conversations sparked an idea for a new focus on instructional goals that were more student-based. To get these ideas off the ground, James contacted a friend who was now in the consulting business and asked if he would round up some experts to come and speak in various venues throughout the year. **(8.1) James had intended to schedule out these speakers so that they could all fall on principal meeting dates, but he was sidetracked when one of his directors began working on a new technology project that he was interested in.**

Most of the speakers came in as planned, but some had to be canceled when conflicts with other meetings arose. **(8.3) James had assumed that principals would prefer to attend the speaker sessions he had planned, rather than the budget-planning workshops that finance had put on the schedule earlier in the year.** Given the current budget crisis, **(8.2) James discovered that this wasn't true and had to cancel several speakers at the last minute due to the conflict. To add to James's frustration, several speakers still required payment because their engagements were not canceled by the deadlines in their individual contracts.**

Sometime in April, James's secretary notified him that the superintendent was requesting a budget meeting with James. **(8.3) It seemed that James had misread his budget allocation for the year and was assuming he had an additional $100,000 that was allotted to professional development in the prior year. He was now over budget by $80,000, and the superintendent was not happy.** Given the additional scrutiny that everyone was under from the board, James wasn't surprised. However, he was surprised to walk away from

8.1: James's project management is haphazard, with no attention to deadlines. SCORE 8.1 AT NOT MEETING STANDARDS.

8.3: James does not plan project management based on goals or data gathered from principals regarding needs. SCORE 8.3 AT NOT MEETING STANDARDS.

8.2: James pays little attention to budget or schedule commitments. SCORE 8.2 AT NOT MEETING STANDARDS.

8.3: James manages resources and timelines poorly. SCORE 8.3 AT NOT MEETING STANDARDS.

his meeting with the superintendent with a letter of direction regarding future budgetary actions. This seemed like just another indicator to James that the culture of Red Rock County was no longer driven by what was right for the people, but instead by compliance and rules.

Scenarios 62–67

Domain 9.0: Technology

Leaders in education are savvy about technology. They process changes and capture opportunities available through social-networking tools and access and process information through a variety of online resources. To analyze school results, they incorporate data-driven decision making with effective technology integration. Furthermore, leaders develop strategies for coaching staff as they integrate technology into teaching, learning, and assessment processes.

Scenario #62—Jacob
9.0: Technology

Jacob, a fifth-year elementary principal in the Rio Grande School District, was known in the past as the technology "go-to person" by his colleagues. With double master's degrees in technology and his knowledge of dual platforms on both Mac and PC, Jacob was viewed by his peers as one who used technology to improve effectiveness, speed, depth of learning, and job performance. As a result, principals and district central office staff readily called upon Jacob for support with incorporating data-driven decision making with effective technology integration to analyze their school state achievement test results.

While Jacob had thoroughly enjoyed this role and additional responsibility in the past, he felt this year needed to be different. With a brand-new assessment system initiative being rolled out district-wide, one with which Jacob and his staff were unfamiliar, he knew his focus needed to be on ensuring a successful implementation in his own building. He needed to focus his time and energy on learning about the new system and helping his staff implement the new computerized adaptive tests assessment.

At the end of the previous year, Jacob had shared the new assessment initiative with his staff and assured them that school-wide systems were in place to support successful implementation. The staff left for the summer, trusting that it would be a smooth transition since Jacob had already taught them to use e-mail, word processing, spreadsheets, PowerPoint, databases, and district software effectively. They also had had plenty of practice in using these electronic tools during ongoing professional development. Jacob used the first 15 minutes of their weekly faculty meetings to teach and model how technology would make their jobs faster, more accurate, and fun. Jacob's day-to-day actions and leadership modeled his beliefs, as all staff were required to use and interact with each other and with parents using the technology tools they had learned. Staff endearingly referred to Jacob as "Mr. Savvy Techie."

During the summer, Jacob attended district professional development on the new assessment system and, when his staff returned, Jacob successfully implemented his plan. By the end of the year, all teachers felt comfortable and confident in having their students use the computerized adaptive tests, and they used the data collected to inform their instruction. Under Jacob's leadership, the staff truly understood the linkage between the use of technology and their organizational effectiveness.

Peruse the MLP Matrix and assess Jacob's performance in Domain 9.0: Technology. Make mental notes and be prepared to respond as to the reason for your score on that dimension. Please be prepared to report out in 15 minutes.

Scenario #62—Jacob
9.0: Technology

PROFICIENT

Jacob, a fifth-year elementary principal in the Rio Grande School District, was known in the past as the technology "go-to person" by his colleagues. With double master's degrees in technology and his knowledge of dual platforms on both Mac and PC, Jacob was viewed by his peers as one who used technology to improve effectiveness, speed, depth of learning, and job performance. **(9.1) As a result, principals and district central office staff readily called upon Jacob for support with incorporating data-driven decision making with effective technology integration to analyze their school state achievement test results.**

While Jacob had thoroughly enjoyed this role and additional responsibility in the past, he felt this year needed to be different. With a brand-new assessment system initiative being rolled out district-wide, one with which Jacob and his staff were unfamiliar, he knew his focus needed to be on ensuring a successful implementation in his own building. He needed to focus his time and energy on learning about the new system and helping his staff implement the new computerized adaptive tests assessment.

At the end of the previous year, Jacob had shared the new assessment initiative with his staff and assured them that school-wide systems were in place to support successful implementation. **(9.2) The staff left for the summer, trusting that it would be a smooth transition since Jacob had already taught them to use e-mail, word processing, spreadsheets, PowerPoint, databases, and district software effectively. They also had had plenty of practice in using these electronic tools during ongoing professional development. Jacob used the first 15 minutes of their weekly faculty meetings to teach and model how technology would make their jobs faster, more accurate, and fun. Jacob's day-to-day actions and leadership modeled his beliefs, as all staff were required to use and interact with each other and with parents using the technology tools they had learned. Staff endearingly referred to Jacob as "Mr. Savvy Techie."**

During the summer, Jacob attended district professional development on the new assessment system and, when his staff returned, Jacob successfully implemented his plan. By the end of the year, all teachers felt comfortable and confident in having their students use the computerized adaptive tests, and they used the data collected to inform their instruction. **(9.2) Under Jacob's leadership, the staff truly understood the linkage between the use of technology and their organizational effectiveness.**

Scenario #63—Judy
9.0: Technology

Judy, fifth-year principal at Harris Middle School, is one of the trailblazers in the field of instructional leadership in her district, the metropolitan Plainfield School District. She is known for her job-embedded professional development sessions, which are differentiated based on the needs of the staff.

There is a push from the director of technology for all the schools to incorporate technology in their professional development plan. Judy understands the need to include professional development on technology integration. However, she is concerned about losing momentum in her school's current professional learning initiatives that are part of the professional development plan. Judy, along with her instructional coach, facilitates job-embedded professional development every two weeks at her school. She is very uncomfortable in providing leadership in technology areas, because she does not have a clear understanding of how various programs and tools impact teaching and learning. She uses the required technology applications, like PowerPoint, Publisher, and other computer software, and understands the use of technology for simple instructional purposes.

Dr. Highland, the director of technology, is emphatic about the use of technology in classrooms. Judy agrees that the students should be exposed to technology. She is simply concerned about including this focus in the professional development plan at this time. Judy's philosophy on incorporating an effective professional development model is that the principal should take the lead in developing the knowledge, attitude, and skills that teachers will need for a focused initiative. Having this philosophy, Judy recognizes her weaknesses. She has mastered some of the programs in order to be more effective and efficient in her job, but she cannot teach teachers how to use them with students. In order to appease Dr. Highland, Judy will conduct an analysis of what the needs of the teachers are as they relate to technology integration in the classroom. She will also register for evening technology classes on using the following technology: SMART boards, Excel, and Wikis.

Peruse the MLP Matrix and assess Judy's performance in Domain 9.0: Technology. Make mental notes and be prepared to respond as to the reason for your score on that dimension. Please be prepared to report out in 15 minutes.

Scenario #63—Judy
9.0: Technology

PROGRESSING

Judy, fifth-year principal at Harris Middle School, is one of the trailblazers in the field of instructional leadership in her district, the metropolitan Plainfield School District. She is known for her job-embedded professional development sessions, which are differentiated based on the needs of the staff.

There is a push from the director of technology for all the schools to incorporate technology in their professional development plan. **(9.1) Judy understands the need to include professional development on technology integration. However, she is concerned about losing momentum in her school's current professional learning initiatives that are part of the professional development plan. Judy, along with her instructional coach, facilitates job-embedded professional development every two weeks at her school. She is very uncomfortable in providing leadership in technology areas, because she does not have a clear understanding of how various programs and tools impact teaching and learning. She uses the required technology applications, like PowerPoint, Publisher, and other computer software, and understands the use of technology for simple instructional purposes.**

Dr. Highland, the director of technology, is emphatic about the use of technology in classrooms. Judy agrees that the students should be exposed to technology. She is simply concerned about including this focus in the professional development plan at this time. Judy's philosophy on incorporating an effective professional development model is that the principal should take the lead in developing the knowledge, attitude, and skills that teachers will need for a focused initiative. Having this philosophy, Judy recognizes her weaknesses. **(9.2) She has mastered some of the programs in order to be more effective and efficient in her job, but she cannot teach teachers how to use them with students. In order to appease Dr. Highland, Judy will conduct an analysis of what the needs of the teachers are as they relate to technology integration in the classroom. She will also register for evening technology classes on using the following technology: SMART boards, Excel, and Wikis.**

Scenario #64—Kelly
9.0: Technology

Kelly had been serving as the assistant principal at Pure Creek High School for five years. She started her career in education nearly two decades ago as a high school English teacher and found each year to be another incredible learning experience. When Kelly looked back on the early years of her career, it surprised her how much she had changed as a teacher and now as an administrator. This year Kelly was excited because several of the major improvement efforts she had facilitated were finally taking hold throughout the entire building.

It had been more than three years since Kelly approached her principal and asked him to allow her to lead the school leadership team to work collaboratively on a plan to integrate the use of technology in a more integrated fashion throughout the district. Kelly's principal had agreed, but reminded her early on that many staff members were still quite fearful of technology and would need a lot of support if they were to be successful. The warnings were well intentioned but, as Kelly discovered, not as accurate as she had feared.

The initial phases of the new plan included an extensive professional development plan embedded into the overall improvement plan. In the initial stages of the plan, the team surveyed the staff and students to determine how technology was being used effectively and where improvements needed to be made. Additionally, staff comfort level with technology became a huge issue that needed to be tackled in a manner that ensured less-confident staff felt safe to admit that they needed help, without feeling that their performance as teachers would be judged. Kelly and the team were very thoughtful about how they set up the differentiated learning, so this never became an issue. Staff embraced the model and finally felt that they had an opportunity to learn at their own pace. Some teachers were surprised how quickly they learned to use their new interactive whiteboards when they did not feel self-conscious about how others would view them.

Fairly soon, staff were creating their own informal cross-department groups to share technology tools, ideas for technology integration, and troubleshooting tips. Kelly and her team were careful to consistently send the message that technology should enhance the learning, not be the learning. This caught on with all content teachers, because they felt it gave them permission to find their own way to use technology in a meaningful manner, rather than just showcase technology for its own sake.

Kelly served as a model and mentor to both the team and staff as a whole. She created "open lab" times for staff, where she would demonstrate and share the newest ideas and practical tips for technology integration. The team used a variety of online tools for planning, monitoring data, and communicating to the entire staff. The staff raved about the new online communication tool that allowed them to collaborate with each other virtually, even when department members didn't share the same planning time.

During the second year of the plan, Kelly worked with staff to provide an opportunity for students and teachers to showcase the work they had done to integrate technology during a family technology fair. Planning the event was a significant undertaking, but the results were well worth the effort. Parents and families were amazed at what they saw and were proud to know that their students were afforded the opportunity to apply technology in a meaningful way in preparation for post-graduate work or education. Several parents commented during the evening that the night was such a success that they should invite the community to drop in for "technology tours" on a regular basis. As a result of the suggestion, Kelly set up monthly open-house hours so that the community could see what was happening with technology at Pure Creek.

Within two years, leaders and teachers from across the district were coming to Pure Creek High School to witness the revolution. With the exception of a few resistant staff members, Pure Creek teachers were sharing their ideas and excitement with colleagues across the district. Kelly and her team realized that they would need a lab classroom structure to be more intentional about how they would demonstrate the work with technology at Pure Creek. Teachers within the school, some veteran teachers who Kelly thought would never embrace technology, were volunteering to serve as demonstration classrooms. They had a story to tell about their own journey and they wanted to share it with others.

This school year, Kelly and the team were implementing online monitoring systems to help track their team's use of the Decision Making for Results process (improvement planning and monitoring process). Now that use of instructional technology was common throughout the school, the staff needed to become quite savvy about using technology as a tool for monitoring student achievement. Staff found the online data and cause-effect analysis tool to be very user-friendly. Soon they were asking for a similar tool to help teams monitor their work in Data Teams (small teams that strategically improve practice through the use of data). It was clear at the end of the year that technology was no longer an unknown, but rather a way of life, and Kelly felt confident that she had had a role in this transformation.

Peruse the MLP Matrix and assess Kelly's performance in Domain 9.0: Technology. Make mental notes and be prepared to respond as to the reason for your score on that dimension. Please be prepared to report out in 15 minutes.

Scenario #64—Kelly
9.0: Technology

EXEMPLARY

Kelly had been serving as the assistant principal at Pure Creek High School for five years. She started her career in education nearly two decades ago as a high school English teacher and found each year to be another incredible learning experience. When Kelly looked back on the early years of her career, it surprised her how much she had changed as a teacher and now as an administrator. This year Kelly was excited because several of the major improvement efforts she had facilitated were finally taking hold throughout the entire building.

It had been more than three years since Kelly approached her principal and asked him to allow her to lead the school leadership team to work collaboratively on a plan to integrate the use of technology in a more integrated fashion throughout the district. Kelly's principal had agreed, but reminded her early on that many staff members were still quite fearful of technology and would need a lot of support if they were to be successful. The warnings were well intentioned but, as Kelly discovered, not as accurate as she had feared.

The initial phases of the new plan included an **(9.2) extensive professional development plan embedded into the overall improvement plan. In the initial stages of the plan, the team surveyed the staff and students to determine how technology was being used effectively and where improvements needed to be made.** Additionally, staff comfort level with technology became a huge issue that needed to be tackled in a manner that ensured less-confident staff felt safe to admit that they needed help, without feeling that their performance as teachers would be judged. Kelly and the team were very thoughtful about how they set up the differentiated learning, so this never became an issue. Staff embraced the model and finally felt that they had an opportunity to learn at their own pace. Some teachers were surprised how quickly they learned to use their new interactive whiteboards when they did not feel self-conscious about how others would view them.

Fairly soon, staff were creating their own informal cross-department groups to share technology tools, ideas for technology integration, and troubleshooting tips. Kelly and her team were careful to consistently send the message that technology should enhance the learning, not be the learning. This caught on with all content teachers, because they felt it gave them permission to find their own way to use technology in a meaningful manner, rather than just showcase technology for its own sake.

(9.2) Kelly served as a model and mentor to both the team and staff as a whole. (9.1) She created "open lab" times for staff, where she would demonstrate and share (9.2, cont.) the newest ideas and practical tips for technology integration. The team used a variety of online tools for planning, monitoring data, and communicating to the entire staff. The staff raved about the new online communication tool that allowed them to collaborate with each other virtually, even when department members didn't share the same planning time.

During the second year of the plan, Kelly worked with staff to provide an opportunity for students and teachers to showcase the work they had done to integrate technology during a family technology fair. Planning the event was a significant undertaking, but the results were well worth the effort. Parents and families were amazed at what they saw and were proud to know that their students were afforded the opportunity to apply technology in a meaningful way in preparation for post-graduate work or education. **(9.1) Several parents commented during the evening that the night was such a success that they should invite the community to drop in for "technology tours" on a regular basis.** As a result of the suggestion, Kelly set up monthly open-house hours so that the community could see what was happening with technology at Pure Creek.

(9.1) Within two years, leaders and teachers from across the district were coming to Pure Creek High School to witness the revolution. With the exception of a few resistant staff members, Pure Creek teachers were sharing their ideas and excitement with colleagues across the district. Kelly and her team realized that they would need a lab classroom structure to be more intentional about how they would demonstrate the work with technology at Pure Creek. Teachers within the school, some veteran teachers who Kelly thought would never embrace technology, were volunteering to serve as demonstration classrooms. They had a story to tell about their own journey and they wanted to share it with others.

This school year, Kelly and the team were implementing online monitoring systems to help track their team's use of the Decision Making for Results process (improvement planning and monitoring process). **(9.1) Now that use of instructional technology was common throughout the school, the staff needed to become quite savvy about using technology as a tool for monitoring student achievement.** Staff found the online data and cause-effect analysis tool to be very user-friendly. Soon they were asking for a similar tool to help teams monitor their work in Data Teams (small teams that strategically improve practice through the use of data). It was clear at the end of the year that technology was no longer an unknown, but rather a way of life, and Kelly felt confident that she had had a role in this transformation.

Scenario #65—Alma
9.0: Technology

The community in Laredo Independent School District had traditionally criticized the central office for being too "top heavy." At board meetings, parents often asked the pointed question, "What do all those people in the central office do anyway?" Armed with this information, Maxine, the new superintendent, unfolded a new comprehensive accountability system in her first address to the board and her central office leadership team that would be implemented over the next 12 months. This system would create visibility, responsibility, and accountability for all departments. She believed that it would also send a clear message to teachers and community members that the senior administrators in the district were held accountable in the same way that teachers and principals were held accountable for student learning.

During their first three months of the school year, the central office team and the accountability task force worked strategically to create common goals, which were approved by the board. Once approved, it was the task of each department to develop goals and performance indicators.

Alma, the director of transportation, applauded Maxine's leadership and created her own department task force to develop and align their goals with the common district goals. All members of the department from her leadership team, from bus drivers to mechanics, would focus on developing strategies to attain the goals, which would be monitored throughout the year. The task force met monthly, and in between meetings, Alma communicated with the team by sharing information via e-mail, via word-processing documents, and by sending out survey data on Excel spreadsheets for each member to review prior to the next meeting. After reviewing the data and the district common goals, the task force agreed to focus on student and staff safety. In reviewing safety reports from the previous three years, they noted that the data showed a high percentage of bus safety inspections that failed and a number of job-related injuries that added significant costs to their budget. All of this data gave them guidance to get on the right track in writing their new department goals.

With the goals written and plans in place, Alma was concerned about how to communicate the plan to the more than 200 employees in her department. It had been easy with her task force, because it was a small group and most members had strong technology skills. Plus, for those who needed training on the use of e-mail and Excel documents, Alma had been able to provide personal one-on-one training.

Her communication plan included sharing the goals at their district-wide transportation in-service prior to the start of school and using her 15 area transportation directors to communicate with mechanics and bus drivers assigned to their respective areas. They were to hold bimonthly meetings for ongoing in-service and continual review of their area safety data. When Alma shared with her area directors that she would communicate with them during monthly meetings at the transportation office and also weekly via e-mail, they expressed great concern. While they all had access to a computer at the main transportation office and had a district e-mail account, the majority of them had never used the system. Up to this point, they had relied on hard-copy memos and meetings with her area transportation directors to stay current on district and department updates. At their next meeting, Alma asked the director of technology to provide an in-service with her area directors so that they could all use the e-mail system to communicate. They were quick learners and, over the course of the year, asked Alma to once again provide additional training for them in word processing so that they could better communicate with their bus drivers, mechanics, and principal leaders. Alma was pleased and provided this training personally.

Peruse the MLP Matrix and assess Alma's performance in Domain 9.0: Technology. Make mental notes and be prepared to respond as to the reason for your score on that dimension. Please be prepared to report out in 15 minutes.

Scenario #65—Alma
9.0: Technology

PROFICIENT

The community in Laredo Independent School District had traditionally criticized the central office for being too "top heavy." At board meetings, parents often asked the pointed question, "What do all those people in the central office do anyway?" Armed with this information, Maxine, the new superintendent, unfolded a new comprehensive accountability system in her first address to the board and her central office leadership team that would be implemented over the next 12 months. This system would create visibility, responsibility, and accountability for all departments. She believed that it would also send a clear message to teachers and community members that the senior administrators in the district were held accountable in the same way that teachers and principals were held accountable for student learning.

During their first three months of the school year, the central office team and the accountability task force worked strategically to create common goals, which were approved by the board. Once approved, it was the task of each department to develop goals and performance indicators.

Alma, the director of transportation, applauded Maxine's leadership and created her own department task force to develop and align their goals with the common district goals. All members of the department from her leadership team, from bus drivers to mechanics, would focus on developing strategies to attain the goals, which would be monitored throughout the year. The task force met monthly, and in between meetings, **(9.2) Alma communicated with the team by sharing information via e-mail, via word-processing documents, and by sending out survey data on Excel spreadsheets for each member to review prior to the next meeting. After reviewing the data and the district common goals, the task force agreed to focus on student and staff safety. In reviewing safety reports from the previous three years, they noted that the data showed a high percentage of bus safety inspections that failed and a number of job-related injuries that added significant costs to their budget. All of this data gave them guidance to get on the right track in writing their new department goals.**

(9.1) With the goals written and plans in place, Alma was concerned about how to communicate the plan to the more than 200 employees in her department. It had been easy with her task force, because it was a small group and most members had strong technology skills. Plus, for those who needed training on the use of e-mail and Excel documents, Alma had been able to provide personal one-on-one training.

Her communication plan included sharing the goals at their district-wide transportation in-service prior to the start of school and using her 15 area transportation directors to communicate with mechanics and bus drivers assigned to their respective areas. They were to hold bimonthly meetings for ongoing in-service and continual review of their area safety data. **(9.1) When Alma shared with her area directors that she would communicate with them during monthly meetings at the transportation office and also weekly via e-mail,**

9.2: Alma personally demonstrates proficiency in using electronic communication systems to share information with her team. Reflection upon past safety reports and setting goals to improve this area of concern shows a commitment to continuous quality improvement by Alma and her team. SCORE 9.2 AT PROFICIENT.

9.1: Alma provided training for individuals on her team who had not previously acquired the skills in the areas of Excel documents and e-mail. SCORE 9.1 AT PROFICIENT.

9.1: Alma designed a model to help institutionalize effective integration of technology for improved services by providing ongoing and embedded staff development in identified areas of need. SCORE 9.1 AT PROFICIENT.

they expressed great concern. While they all had access to a computer at the main transportation office and had a district e-mail account, the majority of them had never used the system. Up to this point, they had relied on hard-copy memos and meetings with her area transportation directors to stay current on district and department updates. At their next meeting, Alma asked the director of technology to provide an in-service with her area directors so that they could all use the e-mail system to communicate. They were quick learners and, over the course of the year, asked Alma to once again provide additional training for them in word processing so that they could better communicate with their bus drivers, mechanics, and principal leaders. Alma was pleased and provided this training personally.

Scenario #66—Chris
9.0: Technology

Chris has just been hired as a manager in human resources in the Wilson Middle School District and has been charged with implementing a technology plan that will enhance job analysis and classification, staff planning, and the overall recruitment process. He feels confident he can accomplish this task with the help of other technically competent staff and key stakeholders within the school district. Chris is proficient in technology applications and is an advocate for integrating technology into education. The successful implementation of the eight-year technology plan in Wilson Middle School District will be the model for other districts within the state of Arkansas.

The initial meeting to discuss the plan was held in January, after the winter break. The superintendent, Dr. Steel, met with Chris, along with other human resource personnel and school administrators, to discuss the technology plan and steps involved for implementing the plan. Dr. Steel noted the most important part was the statement of the reason for the technology plan and how it would be measured. The school administrators raised questions regarding the impact the technology would have on their teachers and students, as well as integrating the technology with learning. Chris was able to explain that the technology plan would contribute to a more efficient way of processing, analyzing, and distributing data throughout the district, as well as provide a more effective way of communicating. However, he couldn't explain the impact integrating technology would have on teaching and learning. This is a critical component for teachers: they need to know how to develop lesson plans and activities that will ensure their students are learning the standards and they need to be able to evaluate the students' performance from these activities.

Although Chris has some knowledge of available software that the district can purchase, which can be customized to meet their instructional and administrative needs, he himself needs additional training to help him gain understanding of the relationship between technology and learning. It was apparent that he had done little or no research to learn of the effects technology in the classroom could and would have on teachers and students. Teachers gave him feedback concerning their uncertainty and anxiety about computer hardware, software selection, and which technology-supported learning activities would be useful and productive for their students. This gave Chris insight into how he needed to become more educated on this focus and how this would help him make effective decisions.

After a collaborative meeting held two weeks later with the superintendent, administrators, teachers, and school board members, the steps for implementing the technology plan were finalized, including budget planning. Once the budget was approved, implementation would start for the next academic year. Dr. Steel recommended that Chris attend a leadership technology training that would be held in the state during the spring break. Chris accepted the recommendation and registered for the training.

Peruse the MLP Matrix and assess Chris's performance in Domain 9.0: Technology. Make mental notes and be prepared to respond as to the reason for your score on that dimension. Please be prepared to report out in 15 minutes.

Scenario #66—Chris
9.0: Technology

PROGRESSING

9.1: Chris is personally proficient in required technology applications and appears to be an advocate for the use of instructional technology. But he does not have a clear understanding of its impact on teaching and learning. SCORE **9.1** AT PROGRESSING.

9.2: Chris has mastered some software programs that are required for performance. Chris will learn new technology. SCORE **9.2** AT PROGRESSING.

Chris has just been hired as a manager in human resources in the Wilson Middle School District and has been charged with implementing a technology plan that will enhance job analysis and classification, staff planning, and the overall recruitment process. He feels confident he can accomplish this task with the help of other technically competent staff and key stakeholders within the school district. Chris is proficient in technology applications and is an advocate for integrating technology into education. The successful implementation of the eight-year technology plan in Wilson Middle School District will be the model for other districts within the state of Arkansas.

The initial meeting to discuss the plan was held in January, after the winter break. The superintendent, Dr. Steel, met with Chris, along with other human resource personnel and school administrators, to discuss the technology plan and steps involved for implementing the plan. Dr. Steel noted the most important part was the statement of the reason for the technology plan and how it would be measured. The school administrators raised questions regarding the impact the technology would have on their teachers and students, as well as integrating the technology with learning. **(9.1) Chris was able to explain that the technology plan would contribute to a more efficient way of processing, analyzing, and distributing data throughout the district, as well as provide a more effective way of communicating. However, he couldn't explain the impact integrating technology would have on teaching and learning.** This is a critical component for teachers: they need to know how to develop lesson plans and activities that will ensure their students are learning the standards and they need to be able to evaluate the students' performance from these activities.

Although Chris has some knowledge of available software that the district can purchase, which can be customized to meet their instructional and administrative needs, **(9.2) he himself needs additional training to help him gain understanding of the relationship between technology and learning.** It was apparent that he had done little or no research to learn of the effects technology in the classroom could and would have on teachers and students. Teachers gave him feedback concerning their uncertainty and anxiety about computer hardware, software selection, and which technology-supported learning activities would be useful and productive for their students. This gave Chris insight into how he needed to become more educated on this focus and how this would help him make effective decisions.

After a collaborative meeting held two weeks later with the superintendent, administrators, teachers, and school board members, the steps for implementing the technology plan were finalized, including budget planning. Once the budget was approved, implementation would start for the next academic year. **(9.2, cont.) Dr. Steel recommended that Chris attend a leadership technology training that would be held in the state during the spring break. Chris accepted the recommendation and registered for the training.**

Scenario #67—Tiana
9.0 Technology

Tiana was selected to serve as superintendent of West Fork School District by the board of education three years ago. During the past several years, the face of instruction had changed significantly in West Fork. The community had pushed the board six years earlier to address the issue of lagging technology in the classrooms, a push that ultimately resulted in a successful bond measure dedicated solely to technology purchases. Technology was immediately pushed out to schools at a rapid rate. The board felt the problem had been solved, only to discover a year later that most of the technology tools were sitting unused in classrooms.

When Tiana arrived on the scene, she spent a great deal of time in schools observing in classrooms and talking with staff. She discovered early on that teachers were largely fearful of using the technology and had not received much professional development regarding its use. There were pockets of excellence, largely among the younger teachers who had a greater comfort level, but even these teachers sometimes demonstrated use of the technology that was not connected to a purpose.

It was clear to Tiana that the district needed to step back and define the purpose of technology: to support instruction through high-quality integration. This developmental process required a focused effort that included professional development and transparent use of technology at all levels of the organization. For Tiana, this was second nature. In her previous district, Tiana had overseen instructional technology and had created a teacher and administrator technology leadership cadre that grew exponentially each year. The idea was to do extensive professional development with a smaller group, which then would go on to mentor others in subsequent years. Each year, the capacity grew through this model. Tiana set out to do the same thing in West Fork.

Tiana's first hire as superintendent was an instructional technology director with experience implementing a long-range plan for technology integration. Working together, she and Tiana provided the initial professional development to the first cadre of technology leaders. Both had experiences they could share and skills they could model that helped to build the capacity of administrators, teachers, and classified staff leaders. Tiana had learned from her previous district that classified staff were an important part of this systemic change, so she intentionally included them from the start in West Fork.

In addition to a strong focus on instructional technology, Tiana worked with leaders on using technology tools to communicate more effectively with parents and community. Within the first year, the leadership cadre had investigated and helped implement entirely new Web sites for the district and individual schools using a newly emerging technology that proved to be user-friendly on both the design and user sides. During the second year of implementation of the new Web sites, West Fork won a communications award from the state association of school public relations executives.

CASE STUDY MATERIALS AND LEARNING EXPERIENCES

It was evident to the board by year three that Tiana was a good match for the district. During visits to classrooms, board members saw the use of technology blossom from no use, to tentative use, and finally to full integration. What board members complimented teachers on the most was the manner in which technology was integrated to enhance lessons, not just for show. As staff became more comfortable with instructional integration, new ideas were suddenly taking hold. Several teachers in each building were experimenting with either Web-based lessons or "flipped" classrooms. Tiana had introduced the concept of "flipped" classrooms in year three. Many of the year-one cadre members became very excited about this new concept in which homework content is introduced via the Web, thus freeing up class time for labs and project-based learning.

When the results of electronic surveys to the community, students, and staff were returned, it was clear that all saw the focus on technology in a positive light. Parents reported having better communication between home and school and felt that their students were more adequately prepared for post-secondary options. Tiana felt good about this feedback, but recognized there was still much to do to make this sustainable and truly systemic. She was excited about year four, when she would work with principals to align their work in Data Teams (small district-level teams that strategically improve practice through the use of data) more completely with the technology work they had done in the past three years.

Peruse the MLP Matrix and assess Tiana's performance in Domain 9.0: Technology. Make mental notes and be prepared to respond as to the reason for your score on that dimension. Please be prepared to report out in 15 minutes.

Scenario #67—Tiana
9.0 Technology

EXEMPLARY

Tiana was selected to serve as superintendent of West Fork School District by the board of education three years ago. During the past several years, the face of instruction had changed significantly in West Fork. The community had pushed the board six years earlier to address the issue of lagging technology in the classrooms, a push that ultimately resulted in a successful bond measure dedicated solely to technology purchases. Technology was immediately pushed out to schools at a rapid rate. The board felt the problem had been solved, only to discover a year later that most of the technology tools were sitting unused in classrooms.

When Tiana arrived on the scene, she spent a great deal of time in schools observing in classrooms and talking with staff. She discovered early on that teachers were largely fearful of using the technology and had not received much professional development regarding its use. There were pockets of excellence, largely among the younger teachers who had a greater comfort level, but even these teachers sometimes demonstrated use of the technology that was not connected to a purpose.

It was clear to Tiana that the district needed to step back and define the purpose of technology: to support instruction through high-quality integration. **(9.2) This developmental process required a focused effort that included professional development and transparent use of technology at all levels of the organization. For Tiana, this was second nature. In her previous district, Tiana had overseen instructional technology and had created a teacher and administrator technology leadership cadre that grew exponentially each year. The idea was to do extensive professional development with a smaller group, which then would go on to mentor others in subsequent years. Each year, the capacity grew through this model. Tiana set out to do the same thing in West Fork.**

Tiana's first hire as superintendent was an instructional technology director with experience implementing a long-range plan for technology integration. **(9.2) Working together, she and Tiana provided the initial professional development to the first cadre of technology leaders. Both had experiences they could share and skills they could model that helped to build the capacity of administrators, teachers, and classified staff leaders.** Tiana had learned from her previous district that classified staff were an important part of this systemic change, so she intentionally included them from the start in West Fork.

In addition to a strong focus on instructional technology, **(9.1) Tiana worked with leaders on using technology tools to communicate more effectively with parents and community. Within the first year, the leadership cadre had investigated and helped implement entirely new Web sites for the district and individual schools using a newly emerging technology that proved to be user-friendly on both the design and user sides. During the second year of implementation of the new Web sites, West Fork won a communications award from the state association of school public relations executives.**

<aside>
9.2: Tiana creates a focused professional development plan for technology that will build capacity. SCORE 9.2 AT EXEMPLARY.

9.2: Tiana serves as a model for others in her use of technology. SCORE 9.1 AT EXEMPLARY.

9.1: Tiana creates a link between technology and organizational success. There is evidence of greater efficiency and more effective communication. SCORE 9.1 AT EXEMPLARY.
</aside>

CASE STUDY MATERIALS AND LEARNING EXPERIENCES

9.1: Tiana relentlessly focuses on innovative use of technology. Implementation success is clear and public. SCORE 9.1 AT EXEMPLARY.

It was evident to the board by year three that Tiana was a good match for the district. During visits to classrooms, board members saw the use of technology blossom from no use, to tentative use, and finally to full integration. **(9.1) What board members complimented teachers on the most was the manner in which technology was integrated to enhance lessons, not just for show. As staff became more comfortable with instructional integration, new ideas were suddenly taking hold. Several teachers in each building were experimenting with either Web-based lessons or "flipped" classrooms. Tiana had introduced the concept of "flipped" classrooms in year three. Many of the year-one cadre members became very excited about this new concept in which homework content is introduced via the Web, thus freeing up class time for labs and project-based learning.**

When the results of electronic surveys to the community, students, and staff were returned, it was clear that all saw the focus on technology in a positive light. Parents reported having better communication between home and school and felt that their students were more adequately prepared for post-secondary options. Tiana felt good about this feedback, but recognized there was still much to do to make this sustainable and truly systemic. She was excited about year four, when she would work with principals to align their work in Data Teams (small district-level teams that strategically improve practice through the use of data) more completely with the technology work they had done in the past three years.

Domain 10.0: Personal Professional Learning

Leaders in education stay informed of current research in education and demonstrate their understanding. They engage in professional development opportunities that improve their personal professional practice and that align with the needs of the school system. In addition, leaders generate a professional development focus in their schools and districts that is clearly linked to the system-wide strategic objectives.

Scenario #68—Elizabeth
10.0: Personal Professional Learning

Elizabeth, a longtime resident and native of Chicago, had attended several prestigious universities in the area. During this time, she had secured her undergraduate degree in elementary education, her master's in administration, and had met the qualification for elementary certification. Until her recent divorce, Elizabeth had no desire to use her administrative license. Now single with two children still in school, plus having overwhelming financial obligations, she was forced back into the job market. After confiding in and discussing her situation with her friend Mary, who works in the same school district, she learned that an administrative position would give her the resources she needed, allow her to use her degree, and help her meet new friends.

After receiving a strong recommendation from Mary, Elizabeth was put in the administrative pool and interviewed for several positions. Reality quickly set in when she was hired for an elementary assistant principalship in an inner-city neighborhood that was riddled with poverty and crime. Soon after, Elizabeth found that her background and upbringing did not match with the surroundings in which she found herself. Because of this, she felt very uncomfortable and lacked confidence in her new role. She was reluctant to talk with her principal about her concerns because Elizabeth was afraid she would lose confidence in her and question her hiring decision. Yet, she had few personal experiences to draw from and knew that, without guidance, she would not be successful. After many restless nights, she met with Chenin, her principal, and was relieved to receive both direction and support. Chenin put her in charge of the staff development plans for the school year. Elizabeth was not a quitter and she felt confident that she could be successful in organizing and setting a schedule for professional development for her school.

First off, Elizabeth called her colleague Mary and asked about the professional development plans that were in place for her school. Elizabeth felt sure that all schools throughout the district would have similar plans and believed if she mirrored her school plan after Mary's school plan she would be successful. Mary was glad to help and sent her their professional development calendar, list of topics, and goals for the year. Elizabeth modified the calendar slightly and sent the plan out to her staff. The focus for the year would be on reading. She immediately received feedback from several teachers who shared that their focus for the year was writing based on their student achievement data that showed significant concerns and that only 38 percent of students in grades 3 through 5 were proficient. Elizabeth, once again frustrated, went back to her plan and changed the focus for the year to writing. She also asked to meet with the grade-level lead teachers to talk about suggestions and focus for the implementation plan. Once the plan was in place, Elizabeth felt confident that they would have a successful year because the professional development plan was now focused on the needs of and goals for students in her school. As the year proceeded, lead teachers and the school professional development coach took responsibility for most of the training. While Elizabeth tried to attend as many sessions as possible, her time was limited because she was spending most of her time on discipline issues. When she was able to attend, Elizabeth had difficulty focusing, since her mind was on the tasks she needed to accomplish. When she conducted her monthly classroom visits, she was able to observe these practices firsthand. Additionally, during her biweekly meetings with Mary, Elizabeth was able to reflect upon this new learning and to share how professional development was impacting their learning organization.

Peruse the MLP Matrix and assess Elizabeth's performance in Domain 10.0: Personal Professional Learning. Make mental notes and be prepared to respond as to the reason for your score on that dimension. Please be prepared to report out in 15 minutes.

Scenario #68—Elizabeth
10.0: Personal Professional Learning

NOT MEETING STANDARDS

Elizabeth, a longtime resident and native of Chicago, had attended several prestigious universities in the area. During this time, she had secured her undergraduate degree in elementary education, her master's in administration, and had met the qualification for elementary certification. Until her recent divorce, Elizabeth had no desire to use her administrative license. Now single with two children still in school, plus having overwhelming financial obligations, she was forced back into the job market. After confiding in and discussing her situation with her friend Mary, who works in the same school district, she learned that an administrative position would give her the resources she needed, allow her to use her degree, and help her meet new friends.

After receiving a strong recommendation from Mary, Elizabeth was put in the administrative pool and interviewed for several positions. Reality quickly set in when she was hired for an elementary assistant principalship in an inner-city neighborhood that was riddled with poverty and crime. Soon after, Elizabeth found that her background and upbringing did not match with the surroundings in which she found herself. Because of this, she felt very uncomfortable and lacked confidence in her new role. She was reluctant to talk with her principal about her concerns because Elizabeth was afraid she would lose confidence in her and question her hiring decision. Yet, she had few personal experiences to draw from and knew that, without guidance, she would not be successful. After many restless nights, she met with Chenin, her principal, and was relieved to receive both direction and support. Chenin put her in charge of the staff development plans for the school year. Elizabeth was not a quitter and she felt confident that she could be successful in organizing and setting a schedule for professional development for her school.

First off, **(10.3) Elizabeth called her colleague Mary and asked about the professional development plans that were in place for her school. Elizabeth felt sure that all schools throughout the district would have similar plans and believed if she mirrored her school plan after Mary's school plan she would be successful. Mary was glad to help and sent her their professional development calendar, list of topics, and goals for the year. Elizabeth modified the calendar slightly and sent the plan out to her staff. The focus for the year would be on reading. (10.1) She immediately received feedback from several teachers who shared that their focus for the year was writing based on their student achievement data that showed significant concerns and that only 38 percent of students in grades 3 through 5 were proficient. Elizabeth, once again frustrated, went back to her plan and changed the focus for the year to writing. (10.4) She also asked to meet with the grade-level lead teachers to talk about suggestions and focus for the implementation plan. Once the plan was in place, Elizabeth felt confident that they would have a successful year because the professional development plan was now focused on the needs of and goals for students in her school.** As the year proceeded, lead teachers and the school professional development coach took responsibility

10.3: Elizabeth does not have a clear understanding of how to use student data to set a professional development goal for her staff. SCORE 10.3 AT NOT MEETING STANDARDS.

10.1: As a result of Elizabeth's lack of school experience and personal learning, she struggles to develop a professional development plan for her school that reflects student needs and current research. SCORE 10.1 AT NOT MEETING STANDARDS.

10.4: Elizabeth is beginning to understand that professional development needs to be based on student and faculty needs. She models this as she asks for feedback on the plan and goals from her staff. SCORE 10.4 AT PROGRESSING.

10.2: Elizabeth struggles to attend the professional development sessions for her staff and, when she does, is unable to focus and participate. SCORE 10.2 AT NOT MEETING STANDARDS.

for most of the training. **(10.2) While Elizabeth tried to attend as many sessions as possible, her time was limited because she was spending most of her time on discipline issues. When she was able to attend, Elizabeth had difficulty focusing, since her mind was on the tasks she needed to accomplish.** When she conducted her monthly classroom visits, she was able to observe these practices firsthand. Additionally, during her biweekly meetings with Mary, Elizabeth was able to reflect upon this new learning and to share how professional development was impacting their learning organization.

Scenario #69—Scott
10.0: Personal Professional Learning

When Scott came to White Rose Elementary School as principal, he looked upon himself as an anthropologist. It was his job to dig into all the cracks and crevices of the building structures to uncover and reveal the school's culture. Scott was amazed to find out that the school did not have a mission statement, vision, or core beliefs to guide decisions. During his principal licensure program, he had learned about the importance of creating a shared vision; setting a course to align all school initiatives, policies, and practices with that mission; and establishing core beliefs that would guide decisions about school improvement goals as well as the day-to-day operation of the building. At one of Scott's first staff meetings at the beginning of the year, he shared his concern about this with his faculty. To his surprise, his new faculty were very resistant to making any changes.

Scott continued to speak and shared, "I am concerned that we are all sailing on the open seas without a compass. As teachers, you are all teaching in isolation. Individual goals may or may not be aligned with those of the school, lesson objectives appear to be more a function of favorite projects than tied to standards, and we are not assessing how our students are performing toward meeting our state and district assigned grade-level standards."

As teachers shifted in their seats, Scott could see that many of them felt very uneasy about his comments. Even so, he did not falter in his convictions and beliefs. Scott went on to share that over the course of the next year, they would move toward creating this mission/vision in their school. They would use the research-based practice of Data Teams (PLCs) to create an environment in which all educators would be committed to working collaboratively in ongoing processes of collective inquiry and action research to achieve better results for the students. He acknowledged that while the process would begin this year, he knew it was a three-year process and that their professional development would focus on the skills, knowledge, and structures needed to successfully implement the Data Teams and to create a culture with a common purpose, a shared vision, and collective commitments.

While the staff said very little during the staff meeting, the following day Scott began to receive e-mails of support and was even stopped in the hall by his staff development coach/teacher who told him that she was on board and ready to head the ship in the right direction. With her support, along with the support of many other staff members who took it upon themselves to talk with Scott personally about how they agreed with his comments, the staff reviewed student achievement data and Scott identified specific professional development offerings needed in order to move forward. A yearlong plan was set and implemented, and while Scott led many of the sessions, he also empowered individuals and teams of teachers to take a leadership role within the staff development plan. Scott attended every session and his staff began to see him as their greatest advocate and one who was totally committed to each of them personally, to their students, and to their entire learning community. With this positive energy, changes in the building happened quickly as priorities were established and their school vision, mission, and beliefs unfolded.

Peruse the MLP Matrix and assess Scott's performance in Domain 10.0: Personal Professional Learning. Make mental notes and be prepared to respond as to the reason for your score on that dimension. Please be prepared to report out in 15 minutes.

Scenario #69—Scott
10.0: Personal Professional Learning

Proficient

When Scott came to White Rose Elementary School as principal, he looked upon himself as an anthropologist. It was his job to dig into all the cracks and crevices of the building structures to uncover and reveal the school's culture. Scott was amazed to find out that the school did not have a mission statement, vision, or core beliefs to guide decisions. **(10.1) During his principal licensure program, he had learned about the importance of creating a shared vision; setting a course to align all school initiatives, policies, and practices with that mission; and establishing core beliefs that would guide decisions about school improvement goals as well as the day-to-day operation of the building.** At one of Scott's first staff meetings at the beginning of the year, he shared his concern about this with his faculty. To his surprise, his new faculty were very resistant to making any changes.

Scott continued to speak and shared, "I am concerned that we are all sailing on the open seas without a compass. **(10.3) As teachers, you are all teaching in isolation. Individual goals may or may not be aligned with those of the school, lesson objectives appear to be more a function of favorite projects than tied to standards, and we are not assessing how our students are performing toward meeting our state and district assigned grade-level standards.**"

As teachers shifted in their seats, Scott could see that many of them felt very uneasy about his comments. Even so, he did not falter in his convictions and beliefs. Scott went on to share that **(10.2) over the course of the next year, they would move toward creating this mission/vision in their school. They would use the research-based practice of Data Teams (PLCs) to create an environment in which all educators would be committed to working collaboratively in ongoing processes of collective inquiry and action research to achieve better results for the students.** He acknowledged that while the process would begin this year, he knew it was a three-year process and that their **(10.4) professional development would focus on the skills, knowledge, and structures needed to successfully implement the Data Teams and to create a culture with a common purpose, a shared vision, and collective commitments.**

While the staff said very little during the staff meeting, the following day Scott began to receive e-mails of support and was even stopped in the hall by his staff development coach/teacher who told him that she was on board and ready to head the ship in the right direction. With her support, along with the support of many other staff members who took it upon themselves to talk with Scott personally about how they agreed with his comments, **(10.2) the staff reviewed student achievement data and Scott identified specific professional development offerings needed in order to move forward. A yearlong plan was set and implemented, and while Scott led many of the sessions, he also empowered individuals and teams of teachers to take a leadership role within the staff development plan. Scott attended every session** and his staff began to see him as their greatest advocate and one who was totally committed to each of them personally, to their students, and to their entire learning community. With this positive energy, changes in the building happened quickly as priorities were established and their school vision, mission, and beliefs unfolded.

10.1: Scott takes time for personal reading and remains current on research trends. SCORE **10.1** AT PROFICIENT.

10.3: The professional development priorities are linked to the needs of the school and based on faculty-observed data. SCORE **10.3** AT PROFICIENT.

10.2: Professional development is directly linked to his school needs. SCORE **10.2** AT PROFICIENT.

10.4: There is clear evidence that Scott is using his personal learning from his principal licensure program to have a positive impact on the needs of his school. SCORE **10.4** AT PROFICIENT.

10.2: In addition to leading some of the staff development, Scott is a learner at each session. Priority is given to building on teacher personal strengths. SCORE **10.2** AT PROFICIENT.

Scenario #70—Steven
10.0: Personal Professional Learning

It is May of Steven's tenth year as a middle school principal. As he closes out the school year and begins his summer break, he has to decide what his focus for summer learning will include, based on the needs of his school, Broadway Middle School.

Steven engages in professional development every summer in order to improve his personal professional practice. Last year, he focused on best practices in instruction. Based on his analysis of cause-and-effect data, Steven saw that he needed to lead his teachers through professional development on identifying instructional strategies that included cooperative learning and nonfiction writing across the curriculum. After reading the year-end surveys that the teachers completed before leaving for the summer, Steven realizes that he needs to continue to provide professional development for the teachers in these two areas in order to build capacity and sustainability.

Upon conducting research on what professional development would align with the needs of his students and teachers, Steven decides to attend the June Power Strategies for Effective Teaching Seminar provided by The Leadership and Learning Center. He also orders two books for his summer reading. The books, *Writing Matters* and *Focus,* will be his priority readings as he prepares the professional development focus for the next school year.

Steven begins to write his professional development plan before he leaves for the summer. He includes in the plan the focus for his personal professional development. He also includes in the plan how he will participate in the Decision Making for Results professional development hosted by his district. Even though participation in this professional development is optional, Steven recognizes the need to improve his knowledge of using data to make decisions regarding organizational, instructional, programmatic, and leadership needs.

Steven also includes in the plan how he will facilitate the professional development for the teachers when they return in August. He decides to schedule weekly meetings for the teachers that will focus on either cooperative learning strategies or nonfiction writing across the curriculum. In addition to the weekly strategy meetings, Steve identifies teacher leaders who will lead the grade-level teams in a book study on *Writing Matters.* The teachers will also participate in monthly Data Team meetings in order to review the SMART goal on increased student achievement in writing and teacher implementation of nonfiction writing across the curriculum.

Steven is pleased with his personal professional development focus for the summer, because he believes that streamlining the professional development for teachers next year will lead to a greater implementation of these instructional practices, which will in turn lead to increased student achievement.

Peruse the MLP Matrix and assess Steven's performance in Domain 10.0: Personal Professional Learning. Make mental notes and be prepared to respond as to the reason for your score on that dimension. Please be prepared to report out in 15 minutes.

PROFICIENT

It is May of Steven's tenth year as a middle school principal. As he closes out the school year and begins his summer break, he has to decide what his focus for summer learning will include, based on the needs of his school, Broadway Middle School.

Steven engages in professional development every summer in order to improve his personal professional practice. Last year, he focused on best practices in instruction. **(10.3)** Based on his analysis of cause-and-effect data, Steven saw that he needed to lead his teachers through professional development on identifying instructional strategies that included cooperative learning and nonfiction writing across the curriculum. After reading the year-end surveys that the teachers completed before leaving for the summer, Steven realizes that he needs to continue to provide professional development for the teachers in these two areas in order to build capacity and sustainability.

Upon conducting research on what professional development would align with the needs of his students and teachers, **(10.1)** Steven decides to attend the June Power Strategies for Effective Teaching Seminar provided by The Leadership and Learning Center. He also orders two books for his summer reading. The books, *Writing Matters* and *Focus*, will be his priority readings as he prepares the professional development focus for the next school year.

Steven begins to write his professional development plan before he leaves for the summer. **(10.2)** He includes in the plan the focus for his personal professional development. He also includes in the plan how he will participate in the Decision Making for Results professional development hosted by his district. Even though participation in this professional development is optional, Steven recognizes the need to improve his knowledge of using data to make decisions regarding organizational, instructional, programmatic, and leadership needs.

(10.4) Steven also includes in the plan how he will facilitate the professional development for the teachers when they return in August. He decides to schedule weekly meetings for the teachers that will focus on either cooperative learning strategies or nonfiction writing across the curriculum. In addition to the weekly strategy meetings, Steve identifies teacher leaders who will lead the grade-level teams in a book study on *Writing Matters*. The teachers will also participate in monthly Data Team meetings in order to review the SMART goal on increased student achievement in writing and teacher implementation of nonfiction writing across the curriculum.

Steven is pleased with his personal professional development focus for the summer, because he believes that streamlining the professional development for teachers next year will lead to a greater implementation of these instructional practices, which will in turn lead to increased student achievement.

10.3: Steven's professional development plan is linked to the organization's strategic objectives. Steven consults student achievement data from the school year, as well as teacher data, as he decides the focus for the professional development for next year. SCORE 10.3 AT PROFICIENT.

10.1: Steven includes in his personal professional development plan readings and seminars that are based on research and his school's needs. SCORE 10.1 AT PROFICIENT.

10.2: Steven plans to attend professional development that is directly linked to his organizational needs. SCORE 10.2 AT PROFICIENT.

10.4: Steven has evidence of his application of his personal learning from the summer. He has a plan of immediate implementation from each professional development seminar. SCORE 10.4 AT PROFICIENT.

Scenario #71—Karianne
10.0: Personal Professional Learning

Karianne is a fifth-year assistant principal at Honey Creek Middle School. Her main responsibilities are to support the principal in all capacities, as well as support the initiatives in the school improvement plan. Her main duties include overseeing the special education program, facilitating Data Teams, and leading response to instruction in her building. She is heavily responsible for discipline and managing school-wide positive behavior supports for students and staff.

Recently, Karianne met with her building principal to review her individual leadership goals for the year. She had narrowed them to two goals, based on analysis of school-wide data from the previous school year. Behavior/discipline data led the administrative team to understand that the number of students receiving out-of-school suspensions was on the rise as compared to three years ago. The analysis of student behavior also showed the administrative team that most of the students serving out-of-school suspensions were minorities. Thus, for administrators and teachers both to attend the state's urban schools conference during the summer was very beneficial in learning how to combat this growing challenge. Karianne took it upon herself to read a variety of research articles and books that focused on how to improve behavior and discipline with minority students. She compiled all her findings and created a school-wide plan based on her research. Once the plan was rolled out to the staff, she would collect evidence to show whether the strategies in the plan were effective based on teacher support and implementation as compared to school-wide behavior and discipline data for the previous year. She would then use the data during data discussions to determine the effectiveness of the plan. She has truly focused on improving one area, but it directly connects to the overall vision of the school, which is to improve student achievement. This initiative is not just about improving student behavior, but also recognizes how behavior affects achievement.

Karianne recognizes the power of using a team approach to combat this growing challenge in their building and district and meets weekly with her department chairs. To gain input about what other schools are doing, she meets monthly with other assistant principals in the district to share ideas, share teacher feedback forms, and share teacher implementation checklists. She then brings that information back to the school team. The school team has a variety of members who provide multiple perspectives on the school-wide plan. The team works together to make school-wide decisions and to assist in implementing strategies to support growth. The team works diligently to modify and improve the school-wide positive behavior support plan, student achievement, and teacher implementation. They also work collaboratively to create the necessary documentation tools that are key for tracking progress toward the overall school goal of improving student achievement. Surveys, meeting notes, student data, and teacher implementation data guide the team's decision-making process. Team members then communicate with their departments to share information and get feedback from staff members. Behavior data is continuously revisited and compared to student achievement data. Quarterly, this information is shared with the whole staff. Karianne then shares their results and strategies with teachers and assistant principals in the other middle schools in the district.

Peruse the MLP Matrix and assess Karianne's performance in Domain 10.0: Personal Professional Learning. Make mental notes and be prepared to respond as to the reason for your score on that dimension. Please be prepared to report out in 15 minutes.

Scenario #71—Karianne
10.0: Personal Professional Learning

EXEMPLARY

Karianne is a fifth-year assistant principal at Honey Creek Middle School. Her main responsibilities are to support the principal in all capacities, as well as support the initiatives in the school improvement plan. Her main duties include overseeing the special education program, facilitating Data Teams, and leading response to instruction in her building. She is heavily responsible for discipline and managing school-wide positive behavior supports for students and staff.

Recently, Karianne met with her building principal to review her individual leadership goals for the year. **(10.1) She had narrowed them to two goals, based on analysis of school-wide data from the previous school year. Behavior/discipline data led the administrative team to understand that the number of students receiving out-of-school suspensions was on the rise as compared to three years ago. The analysis of student behavior also showed the administrative team that most of the students serving out-of-school suspensions were minorities. Thus, for administrators and teachers both to attend the state's urban schools conference during the summer was very beneficial in learning how to combat this growing challenge. Karianne took it upon herself to read a variety of research articles and books that focused on how to improve behavior and discipline with minority students.** She compiled all her findings and created a school-wide plan based on her research. Once the plan was rolled out to the staff, she would collect evidence to show whether the strategies in the plan were effective based on teacher support and implementation as compared to school-wide behavior and discipline data for the previous year. She would then use the data during data discussions to determine the effectiveness of the plan. **(10.3) She has truly focused on improving one area, but it directly connects to the overall vision of the school, which is to improve student achievement. This initiative is not just about improving student behavior, but also recognizes how behavior affects achievement.**

(10.2) Karianne recognizes the power of using a team approach to combat this growing challenge in their building and district and meets weekly with her department chairs. To gain input about what other schools are doing, she meets monthly with other assistant principals in the district to share ideas, share teacher feedback forms, and share teacher implementation checklists. She then brings that information back to the school team. The school team has a variety of members who provide multiple perspectives on the school-wide plan. The team works together to make school-wide decisions and to assist in implementing strategies to support growth. The team works diligently to modify and improve the school-wide positive behavior support plan, student achievement, and teacher implementation. **(10.4) They also work collaboratively to create the necessary documentation tools that are key for tracking progress toward the overall school goal of improving student achievement. Surveys, meeting notes, student data, and teacher implementation data guide the team's decision-making process. Team members then communicate with their departments to share information and get feedback from staff members. Behavior data is continuously revisited and compared**

10.1: Karianne takes it upon herself to read current research in the field of education. SCORE 10.1 AT EXEMPLARY.

10.3: Karianne has demonstrated the ability to integrate initiatives into one or two focus areas for professional development. She spends extensive time in faculty meetings, grade-level meetings, department meetings, and staff development meetings focused on intensive implementation of a few areas of learning. SCORE 10.3 AT EXEMPLARY.

10.2: Karianne meets weekly with her teachers and monthly with the assistant principals. Knowledge and skills are shared throughout the organization and with other departments, schools, and districts. SCORE 10.2 AT EXEMPLARY.

10.4: Karianne shares professional development application tools with other schools, departments, and districts in order to maximize the impact of her personal learning experience. SCORE 10.4 AT EXEMPLARY.

to student achievement data. Quarterly, this information is shared with the whole staff. Karianne then shares their results and strategies with teachers and assistant principals in the other middle schools in the district.

Scenario #72—Stewart
10.0: Personal Professional Learning

Stewart was eager to learn the ropes in his first year as assistant principal at East Rivendale High School. During the previous year, Stewart had served as the dean of students and spent most of his time dealing with student discipline. He was now looking forward to having some real involvement in the academic side of things at East Rivendale. Several of Stewart's mentors had suggested that he do some background reading so that he would become more familiar with current educational research. Stewart had intended to do this, but time got away from him and he really only was able to read one book over the summer that related to the school's major initiative for the upcoming year.

Although Stewart wasn't asked to be a part of the common formative assessment (short-cycle assessments designed to be used to inform next steps in instruction) professional development, he asked his principal if he could be involved anyway. Having been given the green light to participate, Stewart showed up to the two-day seminar ready to learn. He knew that this work was going to be very important to the organization this year, and he wanted to be fully cognizant of what it involved.

Throughout the professional development experience, Stewart asked many questions of the expert in the room and of teachers participating in the experience with him. Although he still wasn't sure what this looked like in practice, he was able to piece together a framework in his mind that showed the power these common formative assessments could have in East Rivendale's Data Teams (small teams that strategically improve practice through the use of data). Stewart also saw where he could use his own strengths to assist in successfully implementing the common formative assessments. Given his previous experience as a dean, Stewart had become quite good at developing matrices for communicating steps in behavior plans. He knew that he could adapt something similar to communicate what needed to happen throughout the school with common formative assessments.

When Stewart returned to school, he was excited about the work ahead. He decided to lead the team that would design an ongoing professional development plan to support the implementation of common formative assessments. Collaboratively, Stewart and several lead teachers fully implemented embedded professional development throughout the school year. Each month, they reviewed the evaluation data that was gathered and made adjustments to their plans accordingly.

During Stewart's end-of-year evaluation with his principal, he was praised for the work he had done with the common formative assessment professional development. However, the principal also pointed out that the planning team needed to make a more conscious effort to make the impact of this work on student achievement more visible to the school. The connections had yet to be made with the staff beyond their own Data Teams and no monitoring of school-wide common formative assessment data had occurred. Stewart made note of these suggestions for his ongoing growth and included them in his professional growth plan for the following year.

Peruse the MLP Matrix and assess Stewart's performance in Domain 10.0: Personal Professional Learning. Make mental notes and be prepared to respond as to the reason for your score on that dimension. Please be prepared to report out in 15 minutes.

Scenario #72—Stewart
10.0: Personal Professional Learning

PROGRESSING

Stewart was eager to learn the ropes in his first year as assistant principal at East Rivendale High School. During the previous year, Stewart had served as the dean of students and spent most of his time dealing with student discipline. He was now looking forward to having some real involvement in the academic side of things at East Rivendale. **(10.1) Several of Stewart's mentors had suggested that he do some background reading so that he would become more familiar with current educational research. Stewart had intended to do this, but time got away from him and he really only was able to read one book over the summer that related to the school's major initiative for the upcoming year.**

Although Stewart wasn't asked to be a part of the common formative assessment (short-cycle assessments designed to be used to inform next steps in instruction) professional development, **(10.2) he asked his principal if he could be involved anyway. Having been given the green light to participate, Stewart showed up to the two-day seminar ready to learn. He knew that this work was going to be very important to the organization this year, and he wanted to be fully cognizant of what it involved.**

Throughout the professional development experience, Stewart asked many questions of the expert in the room and of teachers participating in the experience with him. Although he still wasn't sure what this looked like in practice, he was able to piece together a framework in his mind that showed the power these common formative assessments could have in East Rivendale's Data Teams (small teams that strategically improve practice through the use of data). **(10.2) Stewart also saw where he could use his own strengths to assist in successfully implementing the common formative assessments.** Given his previous experience as a dean, Stewart had become quite good at developing matrices for communicating steps in behavior plans. He knew that he could adapt something similar to communicate what needed to happen throughout the school with common formative assessments.

When Stewart returned to school, he was excited about the work ahead. **(10.3) He decided to lead the team that would design an ongoing professional development plan to support the implementation of common formative assessments.** Collaboratively, Stewart and several lead teachers fully implemented embedded professional development throughout the school year. **(10.3) Each month, they reviewed the evaluation data that was gathered and made adjustments to their plans accordingly.**

During Stewart's end-of-year evaluation with his principal, **(10.4) he was praised for the work he had done with the common formative assessment professional development. (10.3, cont.) However, the principal also pointed out that the planning team needed to make a more conscious effort to make the impact of this work on student achievement more visible to the school. The connections had yet to be made with the staff beyond their own Data Teams and no monitoring of school-wide common formative assessment data had occurred.** Stewart made note of these suggestions for his ongoing growth and included them in his professional growth plan for the following year.

Scenario #73—Malik
10.0: Personal Professional Learning

It had been more than six years since Malik had joined the ranks of principals in his district. The first year had been a learning experience, given the unique circumstances in which he moved into the role of principal at Arching Rock High School. The principal of the school had left midyear suddenly due to health issues, and Malik had been named the interim principal until the end of the year. His learning curve from January to June was huge, but Malik felt good about where he landed at the end of the year when he was named principal of Arching Rock permanently. Malik was now in the middle of his sixth year and still considered himself to be on a learning curve—just one that was a little less steep this time.

Two of Malik's favorite activities for leadership renewal were professional reading and participating in professional development. Through research, Malik guided himself to those professional resources and activities that tied directly to the needs of his school. He found that he was more engaged in immediate application of new learning if this new learning was tied directly to his school's needs. Malik also encouraged his colleagues to join him in these opportunities so that he could share ideas informally and review research collaboratively. Malik always learned more when he could discuss the practical application of learning with others.

This past summer, Malik had taken on an extensive learning plan with other district leaders and key members of his staff that would assist his faculty with implementing the new Common Core State Standards. He knew that it was critical that he work together with a group of teachers to ensure that a well-designed implementation plan was developed and professional development supported this focused effort. Malik had used a decision-making tool that had helped him evaluate previous professional development opportunities to ensure that they were tightly aligned with the goals of the school.

An important component, cross-content writing standards, would present a new challenge to staff, and a careful implementation plan would be key to greater success. Malik wanted to avoid what had happened three years ago when the school took on a new professional development plan to integrate brain-based learning strategies into instruction. Unfortunately, when Malik analyzed the cause/effect relationship between the brain-based learning professional development and actual impact on student achievement, it seemed there was little correlation. In addition to this, the plan had not been tied to the school improvement plan strategically and ultimately was abandoned in the interest of other, higher-priority needs that were directly tied to the school's goals and student achievement results.

When Malik pulled together the team, they spent several planning sessions examining the tie between the current student achievement data and the Common Core State Standards implementation initiative. The team found that survey data from teachers indicated they were unclear about how to engage in cross-content writing that would meet the intent of the new standards. Additionally, teachers were confused about what standards they should focus on, given the number of standards cited in the new standards. Student achievement data also indicated that students could benefit from more opportunities to write in all content areas.

A comprehensive plan was developed to engage in ongoing professional development throughout the year. The full staff participated in a two-day Common Core State Standards workshop that walked staff through a prioritization process and allowed them to focus on key standards in a strategic manner. The staff worked in both like teams and cross-content teams to develop common formative writing assessments (short-cycle assessments designed to be used to inform next steps in instruction). Malik had received extensive training in common formative assessments and was able to lead department teams through professional development to expand their understanding of how to create common scoring guides. Teachers commented later in the year about how this small-group support from Malik had made them feel more comfortable with the process.

Staff surveys gathered throughout the year to monitor professional development indicated that each month the teachers were gaining greater insight and confidence in implementing the Common Core State Standards and cross-content writing. Ongoing feedback from staff helped Malik and teacher leaders adjust the professional development along the way. The final evaluation of the year attempted to summarize the professional development teachers had received all year long. There were definitely some areas for improvement for the following year. However, overall Malik was pleased with what teachers had to say about their application of this new learning to their daily practice.

Peruse the MLP Matrix and assess Malik's performance in Domain 10.0: Personal Professional Learning. Make mental notes and be prepared to respond as to the reason for your score on that dimension. Please be prepared to report out in 15 minutes.

Scenario #73—Malik
10.0: Personal Professional Learning

Proficient

It had been more than six years since Malik had joined the ranks of principals in his district. The first year had been a learning experience, given the unique circumstances in which he moved into the role of principal at Arching Rock High School. The principal of the school had left midyear suddenly due to health issues, and Malik had been named the interim principal until the end of the year. His learning curve from January to June was huge, but Malik felt good about where he landed at the end of the year when he was named principal of Arching Rock permanently. Malik was now in the middle of his sixth year and still considered himself to be on a learning curve—just one that was a little less steep this time.

(10.1) Two of Malik's favorite activities for leadership renewal were professional reading and participating in professional development. Through research, Malik guided himself to those professional resources and activities that tied directly to the needs of his school. He found that he was more engaged in immediate application of new learning if this new learning was tied directly to his school's needs. Malik also encouraged his colleagues to join him in these opportunities so that he could share ideas informally and review research collaboratively. Malik always learned more when he could discuss the practical application of learning with others.

This past summer, (10.2, 10.3) Malik had taken on an extensive learning plan with other district leaders and key members of his staff that would assist his faculty with implementing the new Common Core State Standards. He knew that it was critical that he work together with a group of teachers to ensure that a well-designed implementation plan was developed and professional development supported this focused effort. Malik had used a decision-making tool that had helped him evaluate previous professional development opportunities to ensure that they were tightly aligned with the goals of the school.

An important component, cross-content writing standards, would present a new challenge to staff, and a careful implementation plan would be key to greater success. Malik wanted to avoid what had happened three years ago when the school took on a new professional development plan to integrate brain-based learning strategies into instruction. (10.3, 10.4) Unfortunately, when Malik analyzed the cause/effect relationship between the brain-based learning professional development and actual impact on student achievement, it seemed there was little correlation. In addition to this, the plan had not been tied to the school improvement plan strategically and ultimately was abandoned in the interest of other, higher-priority needs that were directly tied to the school's goals and student achievement results.

When Malik pulled together the team, (10.3) they spent several planning sessions examining the tie between the current student achievement data and the Common Core State Standards implementation initiative. The team found that survey data from teachers indicated they were unclear about how to engage in cross-content writing that would meet the intent of the new standards. Additionally, teachers were confused about what standards they

10.1: Malik engages in regular professional reading and learning. Score 10.1 at Proficient.

10.2: Malik engages in professional development with other leaders and teachers. Professional development is tied directly to organizational needs. Score 10.2 at Proficient.

10.3: The professional development plan is focused and directly linked to organizational goals. Malik has a process for reviewing new professional development. Score 10.3 at Proficient.

10.3 and **10.4:** Malik analyzed past professional development for ties to student achievement and the school improvement plan. Based on analysis, he has abandoned the plan due to lack of alignment and positive results. Score 10.3 and 10.4 at Proficient.

10.3: The team analyzes data and ties the professional development plan to the needs identified. Score 10.3 at Proficient.

10.2: Malik uses his own strengths to enhance the professional development and builds on these strengths by connecting with the new learning for staff. SCORE 10.2 AT PROFICIENT.

10.4: Malik identifies where learning has been applied and not applied and adjusts the plan accordingly. SCORE 10.4 AT PROFICIENT.

should focus on, given the number of standards cited in the new standards. Student achievement data also indicated that students could benefit from more opportunities to write in all content areas.

A comprehensive plan was developed to engage in ongoing professional development throughout the year. The full staff participated in a two-day Common Core State Standards workshop that walked staff through a prioritization process and allowed them to focus on key standards in a strategic manner. The staff worked in both like teams and cross-content teams to develop common formative writing assessments (short-cycle assessments designed to be used to inform next steps in instruction). **(10.2) Malik had received extensive training in common formative assessments and was able to lead department teams through professional development to expand their understanding of how to create common scoring guides.** Teachers commented later in the year about how this small-group support from Malik had made them feel more comfortable with the process.

Staff surveys gathered throughout the year to monitor professional development indicated that each month the teachers were gaining greater insight and confidence in implementing the Common Core State Standards and cross-content writing. **(10.4) Ongoing feedback from staff helped Malik and teacher leaders adjust the professional development along the way. The final evaluation of the year attempted to summarize the professional development teachers had received all year long. There were definitely some areas for improvement for the following year.** However, overall Malik was pleased with what teachers had to say about their application of this new learning to their daily practice.

Scenario #74—Frank
10.0: Personal Professional Learning

Frank has been the director of food services in Pacific City Heights School District for the past 28 years. During his tenure, he has seen eight superintendents come and go and knew that Dr. Alvarez, the new superintendent for this year, would not be the last. Over the past years, Frank had little interaction with the superintendents, because they spent the majority of their time with the school board and their leadership cabinet.

At the beginning of the year, Frank attended Dr. Alvarez's first address to the central office leadership team. He immediately recognized something different about Dr. Alvarez that had not been present in any of the other superintendents. Dr. Alvarez spoke with great conviction and talked about how he would be spending time in the schools, riding school buses, and eating lunch in every cafeteria over the course of the year. Based on this statement, Frank was very concerned: in past years he had been left alone to do his work in isolation and was never held accountable in meeting his department goals. Frank could set lunch rates without consulting central office staff and neither asked for nor received customer feedback. While the majority of his students were on free and reduced lunch and ate the school lunch, he had no pressure from administration to increase the number of patrons who ate school lunches. Additionally, Frank had no pressure from parents or staff to change or vary food options and was in the "gray" area when it came to offering healthy and nutritional lunches for students.

Furthermore, school cafeteria managers, who had been hired solely by Frank, were given limited staff development and support for managing their school programs. Moreover, when staff development was provided, Frank secured outside consultants to lead the training, which he did not attend. Additionally, Frank only went out to his schools when a principal or parent had a complaint and he needed to resolve a problem.

When it came to being in compliance with federal and state regulations, Frank was pleased with each school's rating as long as it passed. When new guidelines or updates came out, he would briefly skim the reports, look for compliance mandates, and set them aside. Cafeteria manager requests were sent to Frank's secretary and routinely signed without his review. It was not until Frank received an urgent memo from Dr. Alvarez that Frank moved from being passive in his role to proactive. Frank was to work with the superintendent's secretary to set up a yearlong schedule of 90-minute blocks of time during lunch hours when the superintendent could spend time eating lunch with students and staff. Additionally, he wanted to talk with the principals about their perspective of how food service was doing in terms of providing a healthy, nutritional lunch for all students. He also wanted Frank to accompany him on each school visit. This caught Frank's attention, and after calling Dr. Alvarez's secretary, Frank called a mandatory meeting with his cafeteria managers. Frank knew that expectations in the district were going to be higher in the future than in the past.

Peruse the MLP Matrix and assess Frank's performance in Domain 10.0: Personal Professional Learning. Make mental notes and be prepared to respond as to the reason for your score on that dimension. Please be prepared to report out in 15 minutes.

10.4: When Frank provided staff development opportunities, little thought was given to his department's needs. The dollars paid to an outside consultant were an investment in constructive improvements. SCORE 10.4 AT NOT MEETING STANDARDS.

10.2: Frank did not attend the staff development sessions. SCORE 10.2 AT NOT MEETING STANDARDS.

10.1: Frank demonstrated little personal interest in learning new trends or research in his field. SCORE 10.1 AT NOT MEETING STANDARDS.

10.3: Frank routinely approved faculty requests without reviewing the needs of the school or department. SCORE 10.3 AT NOT MEETING STANDARDS.

Scenario #74—Frank
10.0: Personal Professional Learning

NOT MEETING STANDARDS

Frank has been the director of food services in Pacific City Heights School District for the past 28 years. During his tenure, he has seen eight superintendents come and go and knew that Dr. Alvarez, the new superintendent for this year, would not be the last. Over the past years, Frank had little interaction with the superintendents, because they spent the majority of their time with the school board and their leadership cabinet.

At the beginning of the year, Frank attended Dr. Alvarez's first address to the central office leadership team. He immediately recognized something different about Dr. Alvarez that had not been present in any of the other superintendents. Dr. Alvarez spoke with great conviction and talked about how he would be spending time in the schools, riding school buses, and eating lunch in every cafeteria over the course of the year. Based on this statement, Frank was very concerned: in past years he had been left alone to do his work in isolation and was never held accountable in meeting his department goals. Frank could set lunch rates without consulting central office staff and neither asked for nor received customer feedback. While the majority of his students were on free and reduced lunch and ate the school lunch, he had no pressure from administration to increase the number of patrons who ate school lunches. Additionally, Frank had no pressure from parents or staff to change or vary food options and was in the "gray " area when it came to offering healthy and nutritional lunches for students.

Furthermore, school cafeteria managers, who had been hired solely by Frank, were given limited staff development and support for managing their school programs. Moreover, **(10.4) when staff development was provided, Frank secured outside consultants to lead the training, (10.2) which he did not attend.** Additionally, Frank only went out to his schools when a principal or parent had a complaint and he needed to resolve a problem.

When it came to being in compliance with federal and state regulations, Frank was pleased with each school's rating as long as it passed. **(10.1) When new guidelines or updates came out, he would briefly skim the reports, look for compliance mandates, and set them aside. (10.3) Cafeteria manager requests were sent to Frank's secretary and routinely signed without his review.** It was not until Frank received an urgent memo from Dr. Alvarez that Frank moved from being passive in his role to proactive. Frank was to work with the superintendent's secretary to set up a yearlong schedule of 90-minute blocks of time during lunch hours when the superintendent could spend time eating lunch with students and staff. Additionally, he wanted to talk with the principals about their perspective of how food service was doing in terms of providing a healthy, nutritional lunch for all students. He also wanted Frank to accompany him on each school visit. This caught Frank's attention, and after calling Dr. Alvarez's secretary, Frank called a mandatory meeting with his cafeteria managers. Frank knew that expectations in the district were going to be higher in the future than in the past.

Scenario #75—Wendy
10.0: Personal Professional Learning

Wendy had been a successful elementary school principal for 10 years in a large suburban school district when she decided that she was ready to take on greater leadership responsibilities with the district. She loves working with teachers and knew she would miss the day-to-day interactions with students, but needed a new professional challenge. As a result, the following summer when one of three elementary director positions opened up, she was eager to apply and hopeful that this would be the perfect match for her.

Wendy was thrilled when she was hired for this position and was scheduled to begin in her new role at the end of July. After working to ensure a smooth transition for the new principal at her previous school, Wendy was ready to take on the responsibilities of being the executive director of elementary education in Cherry View School District. Now in October, nearly four months after Wendy was named director, and eight weeks after the school year began, Wendy continues to be excited about her choice of seeking a central office position. However, there are times when the excitement and enthusiasm she felt back in June and July have begun to fade. At times, Wendy thinks about her old school and wonders if she would not be happier as a principal again.

While Wendy loves visiting schools and meeting with principals, her time in schools is limited and she continually feels guilty for not being able to provide ongoing and meaningful staff development for her principals. In fact, since taking on the directorship, Wendy has struggled to keep up with her own professional reading and feels that she has not kept current with educational research. While Wendy attends district staff development offerings, she has little time to reflect upon the learning and link back to the needs of the district.

The single most frustrating feeling Wendy has is that she is becoming a manager of her schools versus a leader. The majority of her time has been spent with parents and personnel concerns. She finds herself being more reactive than proactive and is not using her strengths and talents to support principals. What she is most concerned about is the emotional toll this is taking on her and her family. While she knew there would be more parent and personnel concerns in this position, she was truly surprised at the number of issues she would deal with each day and the additional hours she would need to spend in her office.

Frustrated, Wendy knows that she needs to change this downward spiral. She is not happy and is truly concerned that the stress is having an impact on her ability to lead at the level at which she knows she is capable.

In the beginning of November, Wendy took charge of the situation by taking the time to reflect upon her time-management skills. She began by charting by school the number of parent/personnel issues. Additionally, she talked with other elementary directors about her concerns and found that they had similar feelings and were also struggling to focus their time on supporting principals in the area of student achievement. Next, Wendy scheduled a meeting with each principal and found that principals were also feeling stressed with the number of parent and personnel issues they were dealing with and the amount of time this took away from their goals. Reflecting on this data, Wendy planned a professional development session and invited all principals to attend. An outside consultant known in the educational field for helping schools and central office staffs deal with conflict and difficult situations gave a presentation. To Wendy's surprise, 90 percent of principals and central office administrators attended. Wendy received feedback from participants that they were energized, excited, and had learned new strategies to be used immediately back in their schools and the central office.

Now it is January and Wendy has settled into her new role and has been able to schedule biweekly meetings with her principals. Their dialogues have focused on their main district goal of closing the achievement gap for sub-groups in each school. While she still has parent and personnel issues that take up her time, principal leaders have been empowered by learning valuable tools to use in dealing with difficult situations. Upon reflection, Wendy knows that the focus for the staff development she set up for administrators was not directly tied to their student achievement goals, but it has freed up leaders to focus on "what matters most" in their schools.

Peruse the MLP Matrix and assess Wendy's performance in Domain 10.0: Personal Professional Learning. Make mental notes and be prepared to respond as to the reason for your score on that dimension. Please be prepared to report out in 15 minutes.

Scenario #75—Wendy
10.0: Personal Professional Learning

PROGRESSING

Wendy had been a successful elementary school principal for 10 years in a large suburban school district when she decided that she was ready to take on greater leadership responsibilities with the district. She loves working with teachers and knew she would miss the day-to-day interactions with students, but needed a new professional challenge. As a result, the following summer when one of three elementary director positions opened up, she was eager to apply and hopeful that this would be the perfect match for her.

Wendy was thrilled when she was hired for this position and was scheduled to begin in her new role at the end of July. After working to ensure a smooth transition for the new principal at her previous school, Wendy was ready to take on the responsibilities of being the executive director of elementary education in Cherry View School District. Now in October, nearly four months after Wendy was named director, and eight weeks after the school year began, Wendy continues to be excited about her choice of seeking a central office position. However, there are times when the excitement and enthusiasm she felt back in June and July have begun to fade. At times, Wendy thinks about her old school and wonders if she would not be happier as a principal again.

While Wendy loves visiting schools and meeting with principals, her time in schools is limited and she continually feels guilty for not being able to provide ongoing and meaningful staff development for her principals. In fact, since taking on the directorship, **(10.1) Wendy has struggled to keep up with her own professional reading and feels that she has not kept current with educational research. While Wendy attends district staff development offerings, she has little time to reflect upon the learning and link back to the needs of the district.**

(10.4) The single most frustrating feeling Wendy has is that she is becoming a manager of her schools versus a leader. The majority of her time has been spent with parents and personnel concerns. She finds herself being more reactive than proactive and is not using her strengths and talents to support principals. What she is most concerned about is the emotional toll this is taking on her and her family. While she knew there would be more parent and personnel concerns in this position, she was truly surprised at the number of issues she would deal with each day and the additional hours she would need to spend in her office.

Frustrated, Wendy knows that she needs to change this downward spiral. She is not happy and is truly concerned that the stress is having an impact on her ability to lead at the level at which she knows she is capable.

10.1: While Wendy has interest in leadership and educational research, she is not able to keep current or to link personal learning to her leadership actions due to time constraints.
SCORE 10.1 AT PROGRESSING.

10.4: In the first six months of her new position, Wendy spent time dealing with an important learning need for her and her principals: time management and ways to resolve difficult situations. This took the majority of her time and she was not able to address other organizational issues.
SCORE 10.4 AT PROGRESSING.

In the beginning of November, Wendy took charge of the situation by taking the time to reflect upon her time-management skills. **(10.3, 10.2)** She began by charting by school the number of parent/personnel issues. Additionally, she talked with other elementary directors about her concerns and found that they had similar feelings and were also struggling to focus their time on supporting principals in the area of student achievement. Next, Wendy scheduled a meeting with each principal and found that principals were also feeling stressed with the number of parent and personnel issues they were dealing with and the amount of time this took away from their goals. Reflecting on this data, Wendy planned a professional development session and invited all principals to attend. An outside consultant known in the educational field for helping schools and central office staffs deal with conflict and difficult situations gave a presentation. To Wendy's surprise, 90 percent of principals and central office administrators attended. Wendy received feedback from participants that they were energized, excited, and had learned new strategies to be used immediately back in their schools and the central office.

Now it is January and Wendy has settled into her new role and has been able to schedule biweekly meetings with her principals. Their dialogues have focused on their main district goal of closing the achievement gap for sub-groups in each school. While she still has parent and personnel issues that take up her time, principal leaders have been empowered by learning valuable tools to use in dealing with difficult situations. Upon reflection, Wendy knows that the focus for the staff development she set up for administrators was not directly tied to their student achievement goals, but it has freed up leaders to focus on "what matters most" in their schools.

Scenario #76—Mason
10.0: Personal Professional Learning

Mason is the grounds maintenance manager for the Iota Public School System. He is responsible for the maintenance of the Iota Board of Education facility as well as serving as the direct supervisor for workers engaged in landscaping and groundskeeping activities. He provides assistance to workers in performing duties necessary for meeting deadlines, as well as training to help his workers accomplish these tasks. Some of the administrative duties he is responsible for include hiring workers, evaluating staff performance, and maintaining personnel records.

Mason understands the importance of staying informed on current trends associated with facility management as his profession continues to mature and evolve. He has invested in reading and researching these trends in his spare time to help him identify industry patterns, skill sets, and places to allocate resources. The information he acquires provides him with better understanding of this profession and helps him to make decisions that align with the current objectives of the school district, as well as to chart a course for the future.

To help prepare and provide ongoing training for his workers, Mason engages in professional development opportunities. He is an online subscriber to Facility Management Forecast, which sends newsletters that provide information on changes and current issues within the profession. A few months ago, he attended a workshop they presented, and registered as a volunteer to facilitate a session during another workshop scheduled to occur later in the year.

The proposed agenda and topics for the next scheduled workshop were made available online for current suscribers. Mason reviewed the topics to get an idea of what sessions he would attend. He chose topics that focused on areas linked to the district's objectives, such as reducing facility costs, creating energy-efficient schools, building and sustaining effective and efficient systems to support operations and finances, and selecting and sustaining quality leaders.

It has become evident through the quality work of his staff that he has applied the training he received through professional development. However, Mason has identified other areas that need improvement within his department and is willing to provide ongoing training with his staff, as well as to participate himself in additional professional development opportunities.

Peruse the MLP Matrix and assess Mason's performance in Domain 10.0: Personal Professional Learning. Make mental notes and be prepared to respond as to the reason for your score on that dimension. Please be prepared to report out in 15 minutes.

Scenario #76—Mason
10.0: Personal Professional Learning

PROFICIENT

Mason is the grounds maintenance manager for the Iota Public School System. He is responsible for the maintenance of the Iota Board of Education facility as well as serving as the direct supervisor for workers engaged in landscaping and groundskeeping activities. He provides assistance to workers in performing duties necessary for meeting deadlines, as well as training to help his workers accomplish these tasks. Some of the administrative duties he is responsible for include hiring workers, evaluating staff performance, and maintaining personnel records.

(10.1) Mason understands the importance of staying informed on current trends associated with facility management as his profession continues to mature and evolve. He has invested in reading and researching these trends in his spare time to help him identify industry patterns, skill sets, and places to allocate resources. The information he acquires provides him with better understanding of this profession and helps him to make decisions that align with the current objectives of the school district, as well as to chart a course for the future.

(10.2) To help prepare and provide ongoing training for his workers, Mason engages in professional development opportunities. He is an online subscriber to Facility Management Forecast, which sends newsletters that provide information on changes and current issues within the profession. A few months ago, he attended a workshop they presented, and registered as a volunteer to facilitate a session during another workshop scheduled to occur later in the year.

(10.3) The proposed agenda and topics for the next scheduled workshop were made available online for current suscribers. Mason reviewed the topics to get an idea of what sessions he would attend. He chose topics that focused on areas linked to the district's objectives, such as reducing facility costs, creating energy-efficient schools, building and sustaining effective and efficient systems to support operations and finances, and selecting and sustaining quality leaders.

(10.4) It has become evident through the quality work of his staff that he has applied the training he received through professional development. However, Mason has identified other areas that need improvement within his department and is willing to provide ongoing training with his staff, as well as to participate himself in additional professional development opportunities.

Scenario #77—Paula
10.0: Personal Professional Learning

Paula is the director of middle schools in the Whiteland School District. She was a principal leader in her previous school district, one of five middle school principals in a very large, urban school system. Paula implemented the Data Teams process at every grade level and in every department during her last two years as a middle school principal. As director of middle schools, Paula's focus is to close the achievement gap for English language learners.

Paula recently attended the Accelerating Academic Achievement for English Learners Seminar hosted by The Leadership and Learning Center in Denver, Colorado. Whiteland's district data indicate there is a need for sheltered instruction in the core class for the English language learners. After analyzing the district achievement data, Paula began researching current instructional practices that increased student achievement for English language learners. Paula quickly discovered that sheltered instruction should be a professional development focus for all the middle schools. Because of her new understanding, she created monthly, job-embedded professional development that focused on teaching the five domains of language, sheltered strategies, and cooperative learning practices.

The professional development also consisted of modeled lessons and collaborative teaching. Paula created a framework of professional development to include "teachers teaching teachers," where the professional learning was ongoing and facilitated by the practitioners in the internal field. Paula identified the expert teachers who routinely incorporated best practices for English language learners and conducted monthly meetings where they discussed effective teaching practices. During their meetings, she shared with the teacher leaders what the research said and what other school districts were doing for their English language learners. Paula has also taught the team how to use the Data Teams process to identify what specific instructional strategies should be used for the English language learners. She believes in working smarter, not harder, and "killing two birds with one stone." Paula always gave the principals an update on the progress being made regarding the English language learners at the monthly principal meetings.

Not only did Paula include what was being done throughout the district during the principals' meetings, she also gave a report at the weekly cabinet meetings to her superintendent. Paula and the principals created an observation protocol for all of the teaching strategies for English language learners. To do this, Paula created data tables to show there was a direct correlation between sheltered instructional strategies and the increase in student achievement for the English language learners. Paula was very proud of her work toward closing the achievement gap for English language learners.

Peruse the MLP Matrix and assess Paula's performance in Domain 10.0: Personal Professional Learning. Make mental notes and be prepared to respond individually as to the reason for your score on that dimension. Please be prepared to report out in 15 minutes.

Scenario #77—Paula
10.0: Personal Professional Learning

EXEMPLARY

10.1: Paula takes time out to increase her personal reading, which is wide and deep in the fields of education research concerning the English language learner. SCORE 10.1 AT EXEMPLARY.

10.2: Paula approaches every professional development opportunity with a view toward multidimensional impact. She shares what other teachers and schools are doing for their English language learners. Paula has created a professional development model that is "homegrown," rather than externally generated. SCORE 10.2 AT EXEMPLARY.

10.3: Paula has demonstrated the ability to integrate initiatives into focus areas for professional development. She uses time during principal meetings to focus on intensive implementation of a few areas of learning. SCORE 10.3 AT EXEMPLARY.

10.4: Paula provides evidence of leveraging learning. This leader creates forms, checklists, self-assessments, and other tools so that concepts learned in professional development are applied in the daily lives of teachers and leaders throughout the organization. SCORE 10.4 AT EXEMPLARY.

Paula is the director of middle schools in the Whiteland School District. She was a principal leader in her previous school district, one of five middle school principals in a very large, urban school system. Paula implemented the Data Teams process at every grade level and in every department during her last two years as a middle school principal. As director of middle schools, Paula's focus is to close the achievement gap for English language learners.

Paula recently attended the Accelerating Academic Achievement for English Learners Seminar hosted by The Leadership and Learning Center in Denver, Colorado. Whiteland's district data indicate there is a need for sheltered instruction in the core class for the English language learners. **(10.1)** After analyzing the district achievement data, Paula began researching current instructional practices that increased student achievement for English language learners. Paula quickly discovered that sheltered instruction should be a professional development focus for all the middle schools. Because of her new understanding, she created monthly, job-embedded professional development that focused on teaching the five domains of language, sheltered strategies, and cooperative learning practices.

(10.2) The professional development also consisted of modeled lessons and collaborative teaching. Paula created a framework of professional development to include "teachers teaching teachers," where the professional learning was ongoing and facilitated by the practitioners in the internal field. Paula identified the expert teachers who routinely incorporated best practices for English language learners and conducted monthly meetings where they discussed effective teaching practices. During their meetings, she shared with the teacher leaders what the research said and what other school districts were doing for their English language learners. **(10.3)** Paula has also taught the team how to use the Data Teams process to identify what specific instructional strategies should be used for the English language learners. She believes in working smarter, not harder, and "killing two birds with one stone." Paula always gave the principals an update on the progress being made regarding the English language learners at the monthly principal meetings.

(10.4) Not only did Paula include what was being done throughout the district during the principals' meetings, she also gave a report at the weekly cabinet meetings to her superintendent. Paula and the principals created an observation protocol for all of the teaching strategies for English language learners. To do this, Paula created data tables to show there was a direct correlation between sheltered instructional strategies and the increase in student achievement for the English language learners. Paula was very proud of her work toward closing the achievement gap for English language learners.

Scenario #78—Roger
10.0: Personal Professional Learning

Roger had just started in his position as director of high schools for Trace County School District. He was excited to take his expertise as a high school principal to the district level, knowing that his knowledge base would further enhance the mission of the district. He recalled the conversation he had with his new supervisor, the executive director of schools, when he was first hired as easygoing and complimentary of his work.

Within the first few months of the new school year, Roger began to get a feel for his new position. In addition to applying what he already knew about running a large suburban high school, he soon discovered that he would be expected to be involved in a major initiative to bring standards-based grading practices to every high school in the district. He knew that he had some professional reading to do to even begin to understand what this meant for teachers and principals and began to keep track of the few books he was reading for his professional growth plan. He did not feel the least bit comfortable with the content, nor did he want to commit a great deal of time to this learning, because he was already up to his ears in parent complaints and other aspects of his new job. Roger resigned himself to the fact that this learning was something he would need to do to be successful in his new role.

In addition to reading, Roger would need to attend an Effective Grading Practices Summit (practical strategies for sustainable improvements in grading) with a core group of teachers and administrators throughout the district. Unfortunately, the summit came at a time when Roger was dealing with several issues back at the office. He was unable to concentrate fully on the content of the summit because, throughout it, he felt he needed to check in with his secretary and get the latest updates. These conversations always seemed to lead to the secretary letting him know about phone calls or people who had stopped by to talk with him about various issues. Roger found it easier to deal with these right away so they wouldn't pile up as a host of issues he had to deal with upon his return. Roger convinced himself that he was mostly there to demonstrate support anyway, and those who would need to implement the change were sitting tight in the summit.

The assistant superintendent approached Roger upon his return from the summit and asked if he would lead an ongoing task force for the implementation of standards-based grading practices. Given the fact that he had attended the grading practices summit, she felt Roger was highly qualified to lead the group. Roger was flattered by her confidence in his ability to lead this work and he knew that his knowledge of the content was not really necessary to make the group effective. He had led many such initiatives as a building principal, relying on his assistant principals to be the content experts.

The ongoing sessions were a mixed bag. It seemed that participants often left angry: those who were on board with the change felt their ideas were shut down by those who refused to learn more about the potential positive impact of changes on students and student achievement. After a couple of months of meetings, Roger decided to gather some feedback about how teachers would prefer to implement a new grading system. He went around to schools and asked teachers who were both involved and not involved in the initiatives what they thought. Generally, he heard that many felt that this new initiative would be too much for teachers to manage and that the district should reconsider implementation. What teachers felt they really needed was more professional development on the new grading program. The consensus was if the new program were used more effectively, they would be better prepared to engage in standards-based grading in a couple of years.

Roger always liked to guide decisions by majority opinion, so he approached the assistant superintendent to inform him of his decision to put the new standards-based grading initiative on hold. Roger was surprised by the reaction from the assistant superintendent, who reminded Roger that this was the major focus of the current district improvement plan and that they were morally obligated to implement the new grading practices.

Peruse the MLP Matrix and assess Roger's performance in Domain 10.0: Personal Professional Learning. Make mental notes and be prepared to respond as to the reason for your score on that dimension. Please be prepared to report out in 15 minutes.

Scenario #78—Roger
10.0: Personal Professional Learning

PROGRESSING

Roger had just started in his position as director of high schools for Trace County School District. He was excited to take his expertise as a high school principal to the district level, knowing that his knowledge base would further enhance the mission of the district. He recalled the conversation he had with his new supervisor, the executive director of schools, when he was first hired as easygoing and complimentary of his work.

Within the first few months of the new school year, Roger began to get a feel for his new position. In addition to applying what he already knew about running a large suburban high school, he soon discovered that he would be expected to be involved in a major initiative to bring standards-based grading practices to every high school in the district. **(10.1) He knew that he had some professional reading to do to even begin to understand what this meant for teachers and principals and began to keep track of the few books he was reading for his professional growth plan. (10.2) He did not feel the least bit comfortable with the content, nor did he want to commit a great deal of time to this learning, because he was already up to his ears in parent complaints and other aspects of his new job. Roger resigned himself to the fact that this learning was something he would need to do to be successful in his new role.**

In addition to reading, Roger would need to attend an Effective Grading Practices Summit (practical strategies for sustainable improvements in grading) with a core group of teachers and administrators throughout the district. Unfortunately, the summit came at a time when Roger was dealing with several issues back at the office. **(10.2) He was unable to concentrate fully on the content of the summit because, throughout it, he felt he needed to check in with his secretary and get the latest updates.** These conversations always seemed to lead to the secretary letting him know about phone calls or people who had stopped by to talk with him about various issues. Roger found it easier to deal with these right away so they wouldn't pile up as a host of issues he had to deal with upon his return. **(10.2) Roger convinced himself that he was mostly there to demonstrate support anyway, and those who would need to implement the change were sitting tight in the summit.**

The assistant superintendent approached Roger upon his return from the summit and asked if he would lead an ongoing task force for the implementation of standards-based grading practices. Given the fact that he had attended the grading practices summit, she felt Roger was highly qualified to lead the group. **(10.4) Roger was flattered by her confidence in his ability to lead this work and he knew that his knowledge of the content was not really necessary to make the group effective. He had led many such initiatives as a building principal, relying on his assistant principals to be the content experts.**

10.1: Roger engages in limited professional reading and some documentation of this learning exists and is linked to professional growth. SCORE 10.1 AT PROGRESSING.

10.2: Roger's participation is reflective of a personal agenda. SCORE 10.2 AT PROGRESSING.

10.2: Roger attends the professional development meetings, but is not fully engaged. SCORE 10.2 AT PROGRESSING.

10.2: Roger does not model active participation. SCORE 10.2 AT PROGRESSING.

10.4: Roger does not believe it was important for him to fully participate in the professional development opportunity to gain the appropriate knowledge about the new initiative. This demonstrates that he does not give intellectual assent to the new learning nor does he apply his own learning to the organization. SCORE 10.4 AT PROGRESSING.

10.3: Roger gathers data informally, with no real process for assessing the impact of the professional development. SCORE 10.3 AT PROGRESSING.

10.3: Roger bases his decisions on the opinions that seem most popular. SCORE 10.3 AT PROGRESSING.

(10.3) The ongoing sessions were a mixed bag. It seemed that participants often left angry: those who were on board with the change felt their ideas were shut down by those who refused to learn more about the potential positive impact of changes on students and student achievement. After a couple of months of meetings, Roger decided to gather some feedback about how teachers would prefer to implement a new grading system. **(10.3, cont.) He went around to schools and asked teachers who were both involved and not involved in the initiatives what they thought.** Generally, he heard that many felt that this new initiative would be too much for teachers to manage and that the district should reconsider implementation. **(10.3, cont.) What teachers felt they really needed was more professional development on the new grading program. The consensus was if the new program were used more effectively, they would be better prepared to engage in standards-based grading in a couple of years.**

(10.3) Roger always liked to guide decisions by majority opinion, so he approached the assistant superintendent to inform him of his decision to put the new standards-based grading initiative on hold. Roger was surprised by the reaction from the assistant superintendent, who reminded Roger that this was the major focus of the current district improvement plan and that they were morally obligated to implement the new grading practices.

Scenario #79—Gabrielle
10.0: Personal Professional Learning

Gabrielle was finally feeling that she was solid in some foundational learning that would support her success as an assistant superintendent in Tabor Falls County Schools. She had dedicated the past four years to learning as much as she could about leadership, especially district-level school leadership. She gave up a great deal of personal time to do so, but Gabrielle felt it was worth the sacrifice if it meant she could have a greater impact on student achievement throughout the district.

In order to keep on track with her own professional reading and professional development, Gabrielle created a planning document that identified her goals and a timeline for completion. This also allowed her to maintain a certain level of discipline to stay on target, even when the demands of her job became heavier. Although she created the initial plan based on her interests and her overall need to develop herself as a district leader, every few months Gabrielle reviewed and modified the plan based on the needs of the organization. Additionally, the conversations she had with colleagues not only allowed her to share her new learning, but also helped her make connections between her own learning, the organization, the learning of others, and how this new learning could be integrated with the current district improvement initiatives.

Early this year, Gabrielle attended ongoing professional development workshops that she had planned for district and school leaders to deepen their implementation of Data Teams (small district-level teams that strategically improve practice through the use of data). This series of ongoing professional development workshops would examine the role of leaders in the Data Teams process at improved levels of implementation through an ongoing model of content learning, practice, coaching, and reflective monitoring. Gabrielle was excited about her involvement in this professional development, as she felt it would be transformational in Tabor Falls' Data Teams journey.

A huge part of the long-term implementation of the Data Teams leadership training would be a monitoring plan to ensure a direct tie between adult actions (cause data) and student achievement (effect data). As Gabrielle had shared with district and building leaders on many occasions, this monitoring was important to determine the correlation between the cause and effect data. When presenting the monitoring plan for the Data Teams work, Gabrielle referred to the monitoring data for the math initiative several years ago that caused the district to abandon the professional development program due to lack of results over a five-year period.

In addition to the Data Teams leadership implementation, Gabrielle continued to work with building leaders to review the Power Strategies for Effective Teaching (instructional strategies that educators use to raise academic achievement in all subject areas) professional development that was planned for teachers throughout the district. In addition to using specific criteria for the review of professional development that Gabrielle had recently created, leaders were also examining Data Teams results from across the district that tied the implementation of specific strategies to student achievement. Through this review, it became clear that teachers wanted and needed more experience selecting high-yield instructional strategies.

All of this work was exciting, but the impact it was having on Gabrielle's own learning was what thrilled her the most. She had always been drawn to developing her own skills as a leader, even though she felt that leadership was an area of relative strength for her. This new integration of leadership and Data Teams was proving not only to expand her own view of leadership, but also to build the capacity for leadership throughout the entire organization.

Peruse the MLP Matrix and assess Gabrielle's performance in Domain 10.0: Personal Professional Learning. Make mental notes and be prepared to respond as to the reason for your score on that dimension. Please be prepared to report out in 15 minutes.

Scenario #79—Gabrielle
10.0: Personal Professional Learning

PROFICIENT

Gabrielle was finally feeling that she was solid in some foundational learning that would support her success as an assistant superintendent in Tabor Falls County Schools. She had dedicated the past four years to learning as much as she could about leadership, especially district-level school leadership. She gave up a great deal of personal time to do so, but Gabrielle felt it was worth the sacrifice if it meant she could have a greater impact on student achievement throughout the district.

(10.1) In order to keep on track with her own professional reading and professional development, Gabrielle created a planning document that identified her goals and a timeline for completion. This also allowed her to maintain a certain level of discipline to stay on target, even when the demands of her job became heavier. Although she created the initial plan based on her interests and her overall need to develop herself as a district leader, every few months **(10.2)** Gabrielle reviewed and modified the plan based on the needs of the organization. Additionally, the conversations she had with colleagues not only allowed her to share her new learning, but also helped her make connections between her own learning, the organization, the learning of others, and how this new learning could be integrated with the current district improvement initiatives.

Early this year, **(10.2)** Gabrielle attended ongoing professional development workshops that she had planned for district and school leaders to **(10.2, cont.)** deepen their implementation of Data Teams (small district-level teams that strategically improve practice through the use of data). This series of ongoing professional development workshops would examine the role of leaders in the Data Teams process at improved levels of implementation through an ongoing model of content learning, practice, coaching, and reflective monitoring. Gabrielle was excited about her involvement in this professional development, as she felt it would be transformational in Tabor Falls' Data Teams journey.

A huge part of the long-term implementation of the Data Teams leadership training would be **(10.3, 10.4)** a monitoring plan to ensure a direct tie between adult actions (cause data) and student achievement (effect data). As Gabrielle had shared with district and building leaders on many occasions, this monitoring was important to determine the correlation between the cause and effect data. When presenting the monitoring plan for the Data Teams work, **(10.3, 10.4, cont.)** Gabrielle referred to the monitoring data for the math initiative several years ago that caused the district to abandon the professional development program due to lack of results over a five-year period.

10.1: Gabrielle's professional reading and learning is evident and documented. SCORE 10.1 AT PROFICIENT.

10.2: Gabrielle ties learning to organizational goals, shares learning with others to impact the organization on a more global level, and looks for multi-dimensional impact. SCORE 10.2 AT EXEMPLARY.

10.2: In addition to planning and implementing the professional development, Gabrielle designs a professional development opportunity customized to the needs of the district. The new learning is intended to change the culture and impact of Data Teams. SCORE 10.2 AT EXEMPLARY.

10.3 and 10.4: Gabrielle ensures a monitoring plan to gauge effectiveness of professional development. SCORE 10.3 AND 10.4 AT PROFICIENT.

10.3 and 10.4: Gabrielle cites examples of professional development that were not successful and were thus discontinued. SCORE 10.3 AND 10.4 AT PROFICIENT.

> **10.4:** Gabrielle uses data linked to staff and student needs and a specific process to review potential professional development. Gabrielle also links professional development to organizational goals.
> SCORE 10.4 AT PROFICIENT.

In addition to the Data Teams leadership implementation, Gabrielle continued to work with building leaders to review the Power Strategies for Effective Teaching (instructional strategies that educators use to raise academic achievement in all subject areas) professional development that was planned for teachers throughout the district. **(10.4) In addition to using specific criteria for the review of professional development that Gabrielle had recently created, leaders were also examining Data Teams results from across the district that tied the implementation of specific strategies to student achievement.** Through this review, it became clear that teachers wanted and needed more experience selecting high-yield instructional strategies.

All of this work was exciting, but the impact it was having on Gabrielle's own learning was what thrilled her the most. She had always been drawn to developing her own skills as a leader, even though she felt that leadership was an area of relative strength for her. This new integration of leadership and Data Teams was proving not only to expand her own view of leadership, but also to build the capacity for leadership throughout the entire organization.

A Appendix A: Multidimensional Leadership Performance Domains Cross-Referenced to Contemporary Leadership Research

Multidimensional Leadership Performance Domains

1.0 Resilience: Resilience is the ability for the leader to overcome setbacks and absorb any learning offered by those setbacks quickly and at a minimal cost. Resilience includes coping well with high levels of ongoing disruptive change, sustaining energy when under constant pressure, bouncing back easily from disappointment and setbacks, overcoming adversity, changing ways of working to incorporate learning when old ways are no longer feasible, and doing all of this without acting in dysfunctional or harmful ways to others within the organization. More importantly, when leaders are practicing resilient behaviors, their actions are contagious as they model the way for others to act in similar ways *(Abbot & McKnight, 2010; Augustine, Gonzalez, Ikemoto, Russell, Zellman, Constant, ... Dembosky, 2009; Bottoms & Fry, 2009; Daly & Chrispeels, 2008; Farmer, 2010; Goldring, Cravens, Murphy, Elliott, & Carson, 2008; Hattie, 2009; Horvat, Curci, & Chaplin, 2010; Hulpia & Devos, 2010; Isaacs, 2003; Kaplan, Owings, & Nunnery, 2005; Leithwood, Day, Sammons, Harris, & Hopkins, 2006; Leithwood, Harris, & Hopkins, 2008; Leithwood & Jantzi, 2008; Lewis, 2008; Louis, Leithwood, Wahlstrom, & Anderson, 2010; Marzano, Waters, & McNulty, 2005; Mascall, Leithwood, Straus, & Sacks, 2008; Millward & Timperley, 2010; Mitchell, Ripley, Adams, & Raju, 2011; Murphy, Smylie, Mayrowetz, & Louis, 2009; Nelson & Sassi, 2005; Nettles & Herrington, 2007; Patteron & Kelleher, 2007; Patterson, Goens, & Reed, 2008; Reed & Patterson, 2007; Reeves, 2002; Reeves, 2006; Reeves, 2010; Reeves, 2011; Richards, 2008; Robinson, Lloyd, & Rowe, 2008; Robinson, 2010; Rossi, 2007; Rumley, 2010; Schulte, Slate, & Onwuegbuzie, 2010; Seashore, 2009; Schrum, Galizio, & Ledesma, 2011; Steiner & Hassel, 2011; Thoonen, Sleegers, Oort, Peetsman, & Geijsel, 2011; Wahlstrom & Louis, 2008; Wahlstrom, Louis, Leithwood, & Anderson, 2010; Waters, Marzano, & McNulty, 2003).*

2.0 Personal Behavior and Professional Ethics: Leaders in education demonstrate a high degree of personal and professional ethics, characterized by integrity, emotional self-control, tolerance, and respect. These principals establish a culture in which all stakeholders practice exemplary ethical behavior *(Abbot & McKnight, 2010; Augustine, Gonzalez, Ikemoto, Russell, Zellman, Constant, ... Dembowsky, 2009; Benham & Murakami-Ramalho, 2010; Bottoms & Fry, 2009; Daly & Chrispeels, 2008; Dufresne & McKenzie, 2009; Eyal, Berkovich, & Schwartz, 2011; Farmer, 2010; Gersti-Peipin & Aiken, 2009; Goldring, Cravens, Murphy, Elliott, & Carson, 2008; Hattie, 2009; Horvat, Curci, & Chaplin, 2010; Hulpia & Devos, 2010; Isaacs, 2003; Jean-Marie, Normore, & Brooks, 2009; Kaplan, Owings, & Nunnery, 2005; Leithwood, Day, Sammons, Harris, & Hopkins, 2006; Leithwood, Harris, & Hopkins, 2008; Leithwood & Jantzi, 2008; Lewis, 2008; Louis, Leithwood, Wahlstrom, & Anderson, 2010; Louis, Dretzke, & Wahlstrom, 2010; Marzano, Waters, & McNulty, 2005; Mascall, Leithwood, Straus, & Sacks, 2008; Millward & Timperley, 2010; Mitchell, Ripley, Adams, & Raju, 2011; Murphy, Smylie, Mayrowetz, & Louis, 2009; Nelson & Sassi, 2005; Nettles & Herrington, 2007; Oplatka, 2010; Patteron & Kelleher, 2007; Patterson, Goens, & Reed, 2008;*

Reed & Patterson, 2007; Reeves, 2002; Reeves, 2006; Reeves, 2010; Reeves, 2011; Richards, 2008; Robinson, Lloyd, & Rowe, 2008; Robinson, 2010; Rossi, 2007; Rumley, 2010; Schulte, Slate, & Onwuegbuzie, 2010; Seashore, 2009; Schrum, Galizio, & Ledesma, 2011; Steiner & Hassel, 2011; Thoonen, Sleegers, Oort, Peetsman, & Geijsel, 2011; Wahlstrom & Louis, 2008; Wahlstrom, Louis, Leithwood, & Anderson, 2010; Waters, Marzano, & McNulty, 2003).

3.0 Student Achievement: Leaders in education make student learning their top priority. They direct energy and resources toward data analysis for instructional improvement and the development and implementation of quality standards-based curricula, and evaluate, monitor, and provide feedback to staff on instructional delivery *(Augustine, Gonzalez, Ikemoto, Russell, Zellman, Constant, … Dembowsky, 2009; Benham & Murakami-Ramalbo, 2010; Bottoms & Fry, 2009; Goldring, Cravens, Murphy, Elliott, & Carson, 2008; Hallinger & Heck, 2009; Hattie, 2009; Leithwood, Day, Sammons, Harris, & Hopkins, 2006; Leithwood & Jantzi, 2008; Leithwood, Louis, Anderson, & Wahlstrom, 2004; Lewis, 2008; Loeb, Elfers, & Plecki, 2010; Louis, Leithwood, Wahlstrom, & Anderson, 2010; Marzano, Waters, & McNulty, 2005; Millward & Timperley, 2010; Nettles & Herrington, 2010; Page, 2010; Reeves, 2006; Reeves, 2010; Reeves, 2011; Robinson, 2008; Robinson, 2010; Rossi, 2007; Schrum, Galizio, & Ledesma, 2011; Silins & Mulford, 2002; Silins, Mulford, & Zarins, 2002; Steiner & Hassel, 2011; Sun & Youngs, 2009; Wahlstrom, Louis, Leithwood, & Anderson, 2010; Wahlstrom & Louis, 2008; Waters, Marzano, & McNulty, 2003).*

4.0 Decision Making: Leaders in education make decisions based on the vision and mission using facts and data. They use a transparent process for making decisions and articulate who makes which decisions. The leader uses the process to empower others and distribute leadership when appropriate *(Abbott & McKnight, 2010; Carver, 2010; Eyal, Berkovich, & Schwartz, 2011; Gronn, 2009; Hallinger & Heck, 2009; Hargreaves & Fink, 2008; Harris, 2008; Harris & Spillane, 2008; Hattie, 2009; Hulpia & Devos, 2010; Leithwood, Day, Sammons, Harris, & Hopkins, 2006; Leithwood, Harris, & Hopkins, 2008; Leithwood, Jantzi, Earl, Watson, Levin, & Fullan, 2004; Marzano, Waters, & McNulty, 2005; Mascall, Leithwood, Straus, & Sacks, 2008; Mitchell, Ripley, Adams, & Raju, 2011; Reeves, 2006; Reeves, 2011; Richards, 2008; Robinson, Lloyd, & Rowe, 2008; Robinson, 2010; Torrance, 2009; Wahlstrom, Louis, Leithwood, & Anderson, 2010; Wahlstrom & Louis, 2008; Waters, Marzano, & McNulty, 2003).*

5.0 Communication: Leaders in education understand communication as a two-way street. They seek to listen and learn from students, staff, and community. They recognize individuals for good work and maintain high visibility at school and in the community. Regular communications to staff and community keep all stakeholders engaged in the work of the school *(Abbott & McKnight, 2010; Augustine, Gonzalez, Ikemoto, Russell, Zellman, Constant, … Dembowsky, 2009; Benham & Murakami-Ramalbo, 2010; Daly & Chrispeels, 2008; Eyal, Berkovich, & Schwartz, 2011; Hallinger & Heck, 2009; Horvat, Curci, & Chaplin, 2010; Hulpia & Devos, 2010; Louis, Dretzke, & Wahlstrom, 2010; Marzano, Waters, & McNulty, 2005; Mitchell, Ripley, Adams, & Raju, 2011; Reeves, 2002; Robinson, Lloyd, & Rowe, 2008; Robinson, 2010; Rumley, 2010; Schulte, Slate, & Onwuegbuzie, 2010; Wahlstrom, Louis, Leithwood, & Anderson, 2010; Wahlstrom & Louis, 2008; Waters, Marzano, & McNulty, 2003; Wayman, Midgley, & Stringfield, 2006).*

6.0 Faculty Development: Leaders recruit, hire, and retain proficient and exemplary teachers. In their efforts to retain proficient and exemplary teachers, leaders focus on evidence, research, and classroom realities faced by teachers. They link professional practice with student achievement to demonstrate the cause-and-effect relationship. Leaders also facilitate effective professional development, monitor implementation of critical initiatives, and provide timely feedback to teachers so that feedback can be used to enhance teacher professional practice *(Augustine, Gonzalez, Ikemoto, Russell, Zellman, Constant, … Dembowsky, 2009; Benham & Murakami-Ramalbo, 2010; Hattie, 2009; Leithwood, Day, Sammons, Harris, & Hopkins, 2006; Louis, Leithwood, Wahlstrom, & Anderson, 2010; Marzano, Waters, & McNulty, 2005; Reeves, 2006; Robinson, Lloyd, & Rowe, 2008; Schrum, Galizio, & Ledesma, 2011; Steiner & Hassel, 2011; Sun & Youngs, 2009; Waters, Marzano, & McNulty, 2003).*

7.0 Leadership Development: Leaders in education actively cultivate and grow other leaders within the organization. They also model trust, competency, and integrity, which positively impacts and inspires growth in other potential leaders *(Augustine, Gonzalez, Ikemoto, Russell, Zellman, Constant, … Dembowsky, 2009; Bottoms & Fry, 2009; Finnigan, 2010; Gallimore, Ermeling, Saunders, & Goldenberg, 2009; Gronn, 2009; Hulpia & Devos, 2010; LaPointe & Davis, 2006; Leithwood, Louis, Anderson, & Wahlstrom, 2004; Leob, Elfers, & Plecki, 2010; Lima, 2008; Marzano, Waters, & McNulty, 2005; Mitchell, Ripley, Adams, & Raju, 2011; Peters, 2011; Reeves, 2002; Richards, 2008; Robinson, 2010; Saunders, Goldenberg, & Gallimore, 2009; Schulte, Slate, & Onwuegbuzie, 2010; Waters, Marzano, & McNulty, 2003; Wayman, Midgley, & Stringfield, 2006).*

8.0 Time/Task/Project Management: Leaders in education manage the decision-making process, but not all decisions. They establish deadlines for themselves and for the entire organization. Additionally, leaders understand the benefits of going deeper with fewer initiatives as opposed to covering everything superficially. They also manage and delegate tasks effectively and demonstrate fiscal efficiency consistently *(Benham & Murakami-Ramalbo, 2010; Catano & Stronge, 2007; Grissom & Loeb, 2009; Hattie, 2009; Leithwood, Day, Sammons, Harris, & Hopkins, 2006; Marzano, Waters, & McNulty, 2005; Reeves, 2002; Robinson, Lloyd, & Rowe, 2008; Robinson, 2010; Wahlstrom, Louis, Leithwood, & Anderson, 2010; Waters, Marzano, & McNulty, 2003).*

9.0 Technology: Leaders in education are technically savvy. They process changes and capture opportunities available through social-networking tools and access and process information through a variety of online resources. They combine data-driven decision making with effective technology integration to analyze school results. Furthermore, leaders develop strategies for coaching staff as they integrate technology into teaching, learning, and assessment processes *(Abbott & McKnight, 2010; Augustine, Gonzalez, Ikemoto, Russell, Zellman, Constant, … Dembowsky, 2009; Benham & Murakami-Ramalbo, 2010; Daly & Chrispeels, 2008; Eyal, Berkovich, & Schwartz, 2011; Hallinger & Heck, 2009; Horvat, Curci, & Chaplin, 2010; Hulpia & Devos, 2010; Louis, Dretzke, & Wahlstrom, 2010; Marzano, Waters, & McNulty, 2005; Mitchell, Ripley, Adams, & Raju, 2011; Reeves, 2002; Robinson, Lloyd, & Rowe, 2008; Robinson, 2010; Rumley, 2010; Schulte, Slate, & Onwuegbuzie, 2010; Wahlstrom, Louis, Leithwood, & Anderson, 2010; Wahlstrom & Louis, 2008; Waters, Marzano, & McNulty, 2003; Wayman, Midgley, & Stringfield, 2006).*

10.0 Personal Professional Learning: Leaders in education stay informed on current research in education and demonstrate their understanding. They engage in professional development opportunities that improve their personal professional practice and that align with the needs of the school system. In addition, leaders generate a professional development focus in their schools and districts that is clearly linked to the system-wide strategic objectives *(Abbot & McKnight, 2010; Augustine, Gonzalez, Ikemoto, Russell, Zellman, Constant, … Dembowsky, 2009; Bottoms & Fry, 2009; Daly & Chrispeels, 2008; Farmer, 2010; Goldring, Cravens, Murphy, Elliott, & Carson, 2008; Hattie, 2009; Horvat, Curci, & Chaplin, 2010; Hulpia & Devos, 2010; Isaacs, 2003; Kaplan, Owings, & Nunnery, 2005; Leithwood, Day, Sammons, Harris, & Hopkins, 2006; Leithwood, Harris, & Hopkins, 2008; Leithwood & Jantzi, 2008; Lewis, 2008; Louis, Leithwood, Wahlstrom, & Anderson, 2010; Marzano, Waters, & McNulty, 2005; Mascall, Leithwood, Straus, & Sacks, 2008; Millward & Timperley, 2010; Mitchell, Ripley, Adams, & Raju, 2011; Murphy, Smylie, Mayrowetz, & Louis, 2009; Nelson & Sassi, 2005; Nettles & Herrington, 2007; Patteron & Kelleher, 2007; Patterson, Goens, & Reed, 2008; Reed & Patterson, 2007; Reeves, 2002; Reeves, 2006; Reeves, 2010; Reeves, 2011; Richards, 2008; Robinson, Lloyd, & Rowe, 2008; Robinson, 2010; Rossi, 2007; Rumley, 2010; Schrum, Galizio, & Ledesma, 2011; Schulte, Slate, & Onwuegbuzie, 2010; Seashore, 2009; Steiner & Hassel, 2011; Thoonen, Sleegers, Oort, Peetsman, & Geijsel, 2011; Wahlstrom & Louis, 2008; Wahlstrom, Louis, Leithwood, & Anderson, 2010; Waters, Marzano, & McNulty, 2003).*

Multidimensional Leadership Performance
Annotated Bibliography

Abbate, F. J. (2010). Education leadership in a culture of compliance. *Phi Delta Kappan, 91*(6), 35–37.

> Leadership in education is much like leadership in business and government. Three problems in particular make education seem different: the almost constant pressure, the politics of the job, and state and federal regulations. But these are similar to problems faced by leaders in other organizations. However, education leaders must take care that blind adherence to the regulations does not erode genuine leadership and interfere with providing an excellent education to students.

Abbott, C. J., & McKnight, K. (2010). Developing instructional leadership through collaborative learning. *AASA Journal of Scholarship & Practice, 7*(2), 20–26.

> Collaborative learning teams have emerged as an effective tool for teachers to improve their instruction steadily and continuously. Evidence also suggests that a learning teams model can affect school leadership as well. We explored the impact of learning teams on leadership roles of principals and teachers in secondary schools and found that collaborative learning teams positively influenced school leadership in two ways: (1) by strengthening principals' instructional leadership, and (2) distributing leadership and instructional decision making throughout the school. These changes in instructional and distributed leadership supported implementation of collaborative learning teams and promoted three key outcomes: (1) more accurate identification of student needs and instructional strategies, (2) greater communication across grade levels, and (3) improved job satisfaction and teacher retention.

Augustine, C. H., Gonzalez, G., Ikemoto, G. S., Russell, J., Zellman, G. L., Constant, L., et al. (2009). *Improving school leadership.* (ISBN 978-0-8330-4891-2). Santa Monica, CA: Rand Corporation.

> This study had three objectives: (1) To document the actions taken by Wallace Foundation grantees to create a more cohesive set of policies and initiatives to improve instructional leadership in schools, (2) To describe how states and districts have worked together to forge more cohesive policies and initiatives around school leadership, and (3) To examine the hypothesis that more cohesive systems do in fact improve school leadership. The authors performed a cross-case analysis, using a purposive sample of 10 Wallace grantee sites, consisting of 10 states and their 17 affiliated districts. Before conducting site visits, they reviewed the literature on system building and policy coherence and developed an understanding of the indicators of cohesive systems that they used to structure, compare, and interpret their findings. They then conducted site visits during which they interviewed 300 representatives of districts, state government, and pre-service principal preparation programs. The authors also fielded a survey of more than 600 principals and collected information in an online log in which nearly 170 principals described how they spent their time every day for two weeks. They supplemented this information by interviewing 100 principals. The study found that it is possible to build more cohesive leadership systems and that such efforts appear to be a

promising approach to developing school leaders engaged in improving instruction. Perhaps the most useful result of the analysis is the authors' account of the strategies state and district actors have devised to build stronger working relationships and greater cohesion around policies and initiatives to improve education. By identifying those sites that had built more cohesive systems, they were able to compare the strategies (state and district) and historical contexts with those of sites that had not yet achieved fully cohesive systems. In this way, the authors were able to identify effective approaches to this work and local conditions that fostered success. These findings should be useful to others building statewide systems to improve education. Although they could not provide evidence that the full underlying theory behind the Wallace initiative is sound, they did find a correlation between improved conditions for principals and their engagement in instructional practices. Additionally, the study cited research that supports the findings from this study that effective principals spend more time in direct classroom supervision and support of teachers, work with teachers to coordinate the school's instructional program, help solve instructional problems collaboratively, and help teachers secure resources and professional training. Principals may also improve student learning through their control of the curriculum and their power to select and motivate skilled teachers. As "instructional leaders," principals are expected to transform schools into learning-centered organizations by focusing them on student learning, creating communities of professionals in pursuit of that goal, and interfacing with external constituents to promote learning.

Benham, M., & Murakami-Ramalho, E. (2010). Engaging in educational leadership: The generosity of spirit. *International Journal of Leadership in Education, 13*(1), 77–91.

This study presents key principles and a model of engaged leadership in indigenous communities. Engaged leadership champions children and youth, delivers learning and teaching within the context of place and spirit, and occurs in partnerships with diverse communities. Stories of educational leaders grounded in the concepts of "ha," place, relations, and collective action are included to: (1) posit the need for alternative indigenous educational settings that emerge from indigenous lifeways; (2) suggest a model of indigenous educational leadership that engages, ensures, and nurtures an ethos of collective will and supports indigenous sovereignty, culture, and language; and (3) share the reflections of educational leaders that articulate a vision for leading, learning, teaching, and living that is culturally respectful and socially just.

Blackmore, J. (2009). Leadership for social justice: A transnational dialogue. *Journal of Research on Leadership Education, 4*(1). Retrieved from http://www.eric.ed.gov/PDFS/EJ875405.pdf.

This author was asked to provide her "unique view" of social justice, presumably as an Australian, a feminist scholar, a critical policy sociologist, and an historian whose field of research has been on educational reform, leadership, and social justice for twenty years. Her "uniqueness" also lies in her centrality in feminist research within the field of educational administration and leadership and her marginality from "the mainstream." From this positioning, the author has critiqued the mainstream for its subordination to the field of business in deriving new theories and practices of educational reform and for its selective appropriation of feminist and critical sociology and history without acknowledging their origins or political intent with regard to social justice. Blackmore briefly maps the background to leadership preparation in Australia, and then develops a dialogue with Jean-Marie, et al., around social justice and leadership preparation.

Bottoms, G., & Fry, B. (2009). *The district leadership challenge: Empowering principals to improve teaching and learning.* Atlanta, GA: Southern Regional Education Board. Retrieved from http://www.wallacefoundation.org/KnowledgeCenter/KnowledgeTopics/CurrentAreasofFocus/EducationLeadership/Documents/District-Leadership-Challenge-Empowering-Principals.pdf.

Principals can profoundly influence student achievement by leading school change; but they cannot turn schools around by themselves. District leaders need to create working conditions that support and encourage change for improved achievement, rather than hindering principals' abilities to lead change. This report includes principals' perceptions of the working conditions their districts create and outlines key actions districts need to take to empower principals to improve teaching and learning. The report proposes seven specific strategies, including: establishing a clear focus and strategic plan for improving student achievement; organizing and engaging the district office in support of each school; providing instructional coherence and support; investing heavily in instruction-related professional learning for principals; providing high-quality data that link student achievement to school and classroom practices; optimizing the use of resources to support learning improvement; and using open, credible processes to involve school and community leaders in school improvement. Appendices: (1) The High Schools That Work School Reform Framework; (2) About the SREB Study of High School Principals' Working Conditions; (3) Principal Interview Protocol; and (4) Resources for an Evidence-Based Educational Approach in High Schools.

Byham, W. C., Smith, A. B., & Paese, M. J. (2002). *Grow your own leaders: How to identify, develop, and retain leadership talent.* Upper Saddle River, NJ: Financial Times Prentice Hall.

The authors, drawing on experience with more than 1,600 organizations, show exactly how to identify tomorrow's best leaders within your organization, accelerate their development and deployment, and maximize their value to your organization. The authors cover every phase of executive development and succession, introducing high-impact, no-bureaucracy techniques that work. Readers will discover how to align executive development with corporate strategy; take full advantage of short-term assignments, professional coaching, and other approaches; and ensure accountability and measure results. Moreover, the authors introduce a flexible, high-speed approach and show readers how to implement it from start to finish.

Carver, C. L. (2010). Mentors coaching principals in instructional leadership: The case of Rebecca and Ramon. *Journal of Cases in Educational Leadership, 13*(2), 39–46.

This case is told from the perspective of Rebecca, a highly skilled mentor teacher, who struggles to work effectively with Ramon, the school principal.

This case focuses on the supports and resources that instructional teacher leaders can provide to their school administrators. As the case suggests, the presence of well-trained mentors presents the field with an opportunity to reconceive traditional views of leadership practice. Ultimately, the case challenges the notion that principals alone are responsible for providing instructional leadership.

Catano, N., & Stronge, J. H. (2007). What do we expect of school principals? Congruence between principal evaluation and performance standards. *International Journal of Leadership in Education, 10*(4), 379–399.

This study used both quantitative and qualitative methods of content analysis to examine principal evaluation instruments and state and professional standards for principals in school districts located in a mid-Atlantic state in the United States. The purposes of this study were to (1) determine the degrees of emphasis that are placed upon leadership and management behaviors expected of school principals, (2) explore the congruence of principal evaluation instruments with instructional leadership and management attributes, and (3) explore the congruence of principal evaluation instruments with state and professional standards. Findings revealed that a school district focus on instructional leadership, organizational management, and community relations in principal evaluation instruments reflected common expectations of principals among school districts and state and professional standards.

Connelly, S., Allen, M. T., & Waples, E. (2007). A case-based approach to developing leadership skills. *International Journal of Learning and Change, 2*(3), 218–249.

Case studies are frequently used in a number of organizational training settings. However, there has been little empirical study of how these cases can be most effective for developing leadership skills. The present study tests the impact of case content and structural features on the acquisition and transfer of leadership skills. Content features include explanations for failure, lessons learned, and making forecasts. Structural features include chunking information, advanced organizers, and presenting related types of information together. Results suggest that training using case studies is most effective when both case content and structural features are either present or absent. Having content without structure can hinder performance. Furthermore, participants in the case-based training conditions outperformed participants in the principle-based training conditions on a learning task. The implications for the development of Tacit Knowledge and leadership skills are discussed.

Daly, A. J., & Chrispeels, J. (2008). A question of trust: Predictive conditions for adaptive and technical leadership in educational contexts. *Leadership and Policy in Schools, 7*(1), 30–63.

Recent studies have suggested that educational leaders enacting a balance of technical and adaptive leadership have an effect on increasing student achievement. Technical leadership focuses on problem solving or first-order changes within existing structures and paradigms. Adaptive leadership involves deep or second-order changes that alter existing values and norms in an organization. Empirical evidence has also shown that several aspects of trust—benevolence, reliability, competence, integrity, openness, and

respect—are strongly connected with school performance and student outcomes. However, the connections between trust and leadership are areas that
are ripe for deeper study. In this article, we present the hypothesis that the
multifaceted construct of trust has a predictive relationship with both adaptive and technical leadership. We tested this hypothesis by using an originally
designed instrument that measures each facet of trust and the leadership
behaviors of school and district central office administrators. A total of 292
site and district administrators and teachers were surveyed in four school
districts in California to learn their perceptions of their site and district
leaders. Results of multiple linear regression models indicate that trust,
particularly the specific aspects of respect, risk, and competence, are
significant predictors of adaptive and technical leadership.

Eacott, S. (2010). Bourdieu's "strategies" and the challenge for educational leadership. *International Journal of Leadership in Education, 13*(3), 265–281.

The quality of scholarship in educational leadership has frequently been
questioned both within and beyond the field. Much of the work in the field is
limited to the analysis of either individual or structural influences on practice.
The resulting lists of traits, behaviors, and organizational structures provide
little to further our understanding of leadership. Theoretically informed by
the work of Pierre Bourdieu and building on a previous special issue edited
by Lingard and Christie, in this paper the author contends that insufficient
attention has been devoted to the temporal features of leadership actions.
Analogies provided by practicing principals are used to highlight the directly
unobservable features of school leadership. The central argument of this paper
is that heightened attention to temporal elements of leadership as a social
action has the prospect of elucidating that which is not directly observable
and consequently to move scholarship beyond the superficial measurement
of what is directly observable to a thick description of educational leadership.

Eyal, O., Berkovich, I., & Schwartz, T. (2011). Making the right choices: Ethical
judgments among educational leaders. *Journal of Educational Administration,
49*(4), 396–413.

Scholars have adopted a multiple ethical paradigms approach in an attempt
to better understand the bases upon which everyday ethical dilemmas are
resolved by educational leaders. The aim of this study is to examine the
ethical considerations in ethical judgments of aspiring principals. To examine
the ethical considerations involved in school leadership decision making, a
specially designed ethical perspective instrument was developed that draws
on the multiple ethical paradigms. This exploratory instrument was pretested
for validity and reliability among school principals and students of educational administration. The research sample consisted of 52 participants in
principal training programs in Israel. Findings: Negative correlations were
found between choices reflecting values of fairness and those reflecting
utilitarianism and care. In addition, negative correlations were found between
choices reflecting values of community and those reflecting care, critique,
and profession. Critique turned out to be the value most widely adopted
by educational leaders to solve ethical dilemmas, followed by care and
profession. The common notion in the literature is that the various ethics
complement one another. There is, however, little empirical work on ethical

judgments of educational practitioners. The importance of this exploratory research is twofold: first, it examines the extent to which multiple ethical considerations can be taken into account simultaneously; and second, it identifies the prevailing values that come into play most often.

Farmer, T. A. (2010). *Overcoming adversity: Resilience development strategies for educational leaders.* Paper presented at the annual meeting of the Georgia Educational Research Association, Savannah, GA, October 23, 2010. (ERIC Document Reproduction Service No. ED512453).

The purpose of the paper is to address, in the author's view, a national problem that finds current school leaders facing a variety of difficulties that make sustaining school reform efforts exceedingly difficult. Collectively, these modern-day challenges have the capacity to form the perfect storm. School leaders need effective strategies to cope with these difficult circumstances and to continue the thrust toward school reform. Effective coping mechanisms and resiliency development strategies that can be used by educational leaders to overcome adversity include a routine of exercise and healthy diet, a positive life view, a sustained focus on building bridges between stakeholders, spiritual renewal, a focus on one's personal mission, a determination to model resilience, and the utilization of supportive professional networks. Resilience development strategies can be effective in helping school leaders to overcome adversity and accomplish organizational objectives.

Fernandez, K. E. (2006). Clark county school district study of the effectiveness of school improvement plans (SESIP). Unpublished manuscript, University of Nevada, Las Vegas.

The purpose of this study is to examine the relationship between the quality of a school's improvement plan and student achievement. The Clark County School District (CCSD) Study of the Effectiveness of School Improvement Plans (SESIP) purpose is to develop valid and reliable measures of the quality of School Improvement Plans (SIPs) and school performance in order to examine the relationship between SIPs and student achievement. To address the question of whether SIPs were effective in increasing school performance, data was collected from 309 public schools in Clark County School District in Nevada from 2005 and 2006. This report uses two primary sources for the data analysis: The Center for Performance Assessment report on SIP quality, which includes a content analysis of each school's SIP; and CCSD Database, which includes data on student scores on standardized examinations, as well as school demographics and resources. The breadth and quality of the data allow for a rigorous examination of the relationship between SIP and school performance. The results are quite consistent: SIP quality is positively and significantly related to school performance. This holds true even when controlling for various other factors, or whether one uses various measures of school performance. Some practitioners and scholars have expressed concern that strategic planning creates rigidity, or at best wastes valuable resources. Others have been more optimistic about planning, but are unable to show empirically a relationship between planning and performance. The results in this study provide strong evidence that there is a direct relationship between the quality of strategic planning and performance in the education field.

Finnigan, K. S. (2010). Principal leadership and teacher motivation under high-stakes accountability policies. *Leadership and Policy in Schools, 9*(2), 161–189.

This article examines principal leadership and teacher motivation in schools under accountability sanctions. The conceptual framework is grounded in research on expectancy theory and transformational leadership. The study involves a survey of Chicago teachers and indicates that principal instructional leadership and support for change are associated with teacher expectancy. In addition, teacher experience, advanced education, and race, as well as the school's performance level, are associated with teacher expectancy. Finally, teacher expectancy is associated with a school's ability to move off of probation status. These findings have important implications in the current policy context.

Gallimore, R., Ermeling, B. A., Saunders, W. M., & Goldenberg (2009, May). Moving the learning of teachers closer to practice: Teacher education implication of school-based inquiry teams. *Elementary School Journal, 109*(5), 537–553.

A five-year prospective, quasiexperimental investigation demonstrated that grade-level teams in nine Title 1 schools significantly increased achievement by using an inquiry-focused protocol to solve instructional problems. Teachers applying the inquiry protocol shifted attribution of improved student performance to their teaching rather than external causes. This shift was achieved by focusing on an academic problem long enough to develop an instructional solution. Seeing causal connections fosters acquisition of key teaching skills and knowledge, such as identifying student needs, formulating instructional plans, and using evidence to refine instruction. These outcomes are more likely when teams are teaching similar content, led by a trained peer-facilitator, using an inquiry-focused protocol, and have stable settings in which to engage in continuous improvement.

Goldring, E., Cravens, X. C., Murphy, J., Elliott, S. N., & Carson, B. (2008, March). *The evaluation of principals: What and how do states and districts assess leadership?* Paper presented at the annual meeting of American Educational Research Association, New York. Article downloaded on September, 12, 2011, from http://www.valed.com/documents/6_ESJ_Goldring%20et%20al_Published%20version.pdf.

The purpose of this paper is to present the results of a comprehensive review of current principal leadership assessment practices in the United States. Analyses of both the general content and the usage of 65 actual instruments used by districts and states provide an in-depth look of what and how districts evaluate their school principals. Using the Learning-Centered Leadership Framework (Porter, et al., 2006), the paper focuses on identifying the congruency (or lack thereof) between current evaluation practices and the research-based criteria for effective leadership that are associated with school performance. Using an iterative and deductive process for instrument content analysis, the review revealed that districts focus on a variety of performance areas when evaluating their principals, with different formats at various levels of specificity. It also found very limited coverage on leadership behaviors ensuring rigorous curriculum and quality instruction, which are linked with school-wide improvement for the ultimate purpose of enhanced student learning. In seeking information on how principals are evaluated, researchers found that, in most cases, the practices of leadership assessment lack justification and documentation in terms of the utility, psychometric properties, and accuracy of the instruments.

Grissom, J. A., & Loeb, S. (2009). Triangulating principal effectiveness: How perspectives of parents, teachers, and assistant principals identify the central importance of managerial skills. Working Paper 35. National Center for Analysis of Longitudinal Data in Education Research. (ERIC Document Reproduction Service No. ED509691).

While the importance of effective principals is undisputed, few studies have addressed what specific skills principals need to promote school success. This study draws on unique data pairing survey responses from principals, assistant principals, teachers, and parents with rich administrative data to identify which principal skills matter most for school outcomes. Factor analysis of a 42-item task inventory distinguishes five skill categories. Yet only one of them, the principals' organization management skills, consistently predicts student achievement growth and other success measures. Analysis of evaluations of principals by assistant principals confirms this central result. The authors' analysis argues for a broad view of instructional leadership that includes general organizational management skills as a key complement to the work of supporting curriculum and instruction. Two appendices are included: (1) Factor Loadings Matrix for Principal Effectiveness Factors; and (2) Factor Loadings Matrix for Assistant Principal Effectiveness Factors. (Contains 3 figures, 5 tables and 6 footnotes.) [This paper was supported by the Stanford University K–12 Initiative.]

Gronn, P. (2009). Hybrid leadership. In K. Leithwood, B. Mascall, & T. Strauss (Eds.), *Distributed leadership according to the evidence* (pp. 17–40). New York, NY: Routledge.

This chapter attempts to answer the key question, "With the recent emergence of distributed leadership, what happens next?" By employing data from a case study, the author explains why various patterns (e.g., distributed versus traditional individualistic leadership approaches or the polarization of the field around reassertions from individualism and proponents of distribution or accommodation between distributed and individualistic approaches, or hybridity) arise and how hybrid leadership operates. The author also identifies some of the problems and possibilities opened up by a hybrid view of leadership, and the significance of this perspective for the future of the field.

Hallinger, P. (2003). Leading educational change: Reflections on the practice of instructional and transformational leadership. *Cambridge Journal of Education, 33*(3), 329–351.

Over the past two decades, debate over the most suitable leadership role for principals has been dominated by two conceptual models: instructional leadership and transformational leadership. This article reviews the conceptual and empirical development of these two leadership models. The author concludes that the suitability or effectiveness of a particular leadership model is linked to factors in the external environment and the local context of a school. Moreover, the paper argues that the definitions of the two models are also evolving in response to the changing needs of schools in the context of global educational reforms.

Hallinger, P., & Heck, R. P. (2009). Leadership for learning: Does collaborative learning make a difference in school improvement? Article published by Sage. PDF downloaded from http://ema.sagepub.com/content/38/6/654 .full.pdf+html on November 18, 2010.

Although there has been a sizable growth spurt in empirical studies of shared forms of leadership over the past decade, the bulk of this research has been descriptive. Relatively few published studies have investigated the impact of shared leadership on school improvement, and even fewer have studied effects on student learning. This longitudinal study examines the effects of collaborative leadership on school improvement and student reading achievement in 192 elementary schools in one state in the United States over a four-year period. Using latent change analysis, the research found significant direct effects of collaborative leadership on change in the schools' academic capacity and indirect effects on rates of growth in student reading achievement. In addition, the study was also able to identify three different growth trajectories among schools, each characterized by variations in associated school improvement processes. The study supports a perspective on leadership for learning that aims at building the academic capacity of schools as a means of improving student learning outcomes.

Hargreaves, A., & Fink, D. (2008). Distributed leadership: Democracy or delivery? *Journal of Educational Administration, 46*(2), 229–240.

This paper discusses the nature and benefits of lateral approaches to educational change, especially in the form of distributed leadership, that treat schools, localities, states, or nations as "living systems" interconnected by mutual influence. The paper presents a conceptual discussion of the interrelated ideas of living systems, communities of practice, and networks. Research examples from England, North America, and Finland are used to underscore the article's argument. The paper underlines how, within this conception, distributed leadership operates as a network of strong cells organized through cohesive diversity and emergent development rather than mechanical alignment and predictable delivery. However, more deeply and more critically, the paper also investigates whether, in practice, these lateral strategies are being used to extend democratic public and professional involvement in developing the goals and purposes of education or whether they are being primarily used as motivational devices to reenergize a dispirited profession into producing more effective and enthusiastic delivery of imposed government performance targets. The paper provides useful information on developments in distributed leadership.

Harris, A. (2008). Distributed leadership: According to the evidence. *Journal of Educational Administration, 46*(2), 172–188.

This paper aims to provide an overview of the literature concerning distributed leadership and organizational change. The main purpose of the paper is to consider the empirical evidence that highlights a relationship between distributed leadership and organizational outcomes. Design/methodological approach: The paper draws on several fields of enquiry, including organizational change, school effectiveness, school improvement, and leadership. It systematically analyzes the evidence in each field and presents a synthesis of key findings. Findings: The evidence shows: first, that there is a relationship between distributed leadership and organizational change; second, that there is evidence to suggest that this relationship is positive; and third, that different patterns of distribution affect organizational outcomes. Originality/value: The significance and originality of this paper lies in the fact that it: takes a normative position on distributed leadership and is chiefly concerned with the question of organizational impact; demonstrates the importance and necessity of further research about the way in which distributed leadership influences organizational outcomes; and acknowledges the methodological challenges in conducting research on distributed leadership, but argues that such research will make a significant contribution to knowledge and theory generation in the leadership field.

Harris, A., & Spillane, J. (2008). Distributed leadership through the looking glass. *Management in Education, 22*(1), 31–34.

Distributed leadership is an idea that is growing in popularity. There is widespread interest in the notion of distributing leadership, although interpretations of the term vary. A distributed leadership perspective recognizes that there are multiple leaders and that leadership activities are widely shared within and between organizations. A distributed model of leadership focuses upon the interactions, rather than the actions, of those in formal and informal leadership roles. It is primarily concerned with "leadership practice" and how leadership influences organizational and instructional improvement. A distributed perspective on leadership acknowledges the work of all individuals who contribute to leadership practice, whether or not they are formally designated or defined as leaders. Distributed leadership is also central to system reconfiguration and organizational redesign, which necessitates lateral, flatter decision-making processes. Despite the growing enthusiasm for distributed leadership within the research community, it is clear people need to know much more about its effects and influences. Leithwood, et al. (2004) suggest that there is an "urgent need to enrich the concept with systematic evidence." A number of research projects are currently underway that are gathering this systematic evidence. However, if distributed leadership is not to join the large pile of redundant leadership theories, it must engage teachers, head teachers, support staff, and other professionals. It must be put to the test of practice. This can only be achieved with the cooperation of those keen to explore a different world-view of leadership and with the enthusiasm to redesign and reconfigure schooling.

Distributed leadership is not a panacea or a blueprint or a recipe. It is a way of getting under the skin of leadership practice, of seeing leadership practice differently and illuminating the possibilities for organizational transformation. This is not without its risks, as it inevitably means holding up the looking glass to schools and being prepared to abandon old leadership practices. For those genuinely seeking transformation and self-renewal, this is a risk well worth taking.

Hattie, J. (2009). *Visible learning: A synthesis of over 800 meta-analyses relating to achievement.* London, UK: Routledge.

This book is the result of 15 years' research and synthesizes over 800 meta-analyses relating to the influences on achievement in school-aged students. The author presents research involving many millions of students and represents the largest ever collection of evidence-based research into what actually works in schools to improve learning. Areas covered include the influences of the student, home, and school, based on the notion of visible teaching and visible learning. A major message within the book is that what works best for students is similar to what works best for teachers. This includes attention to setting challenging learning intentions, being clear about what success means, and attention to learning strategies for developing conceptual understanding about what teachers and students know and understand. This book is about using evidence to build and defend a model of teaching and learning.

Hattie, J. (2012). *Visible learning for teachers: Maximizing impact on learning.* New York: Routledge.

This book follows Professor Hattie's earlier work in which he synthesized the results of more than 15 years' research involving millions of students, representing the largest to date collection of evidence-based research into what actually works in schools to improve learning, and takes the next step by bringing these ground-breaking concepts to teachers. It explains how to apply the principles from *Visible Learning* to any classroom anywhere in the world. The author offers concise and user-friendly summaries of the most successful implementation of visible learning and visible teaching in the classroom. Included within the book are checklists, exercises, case studies, and best practice scenarios to assist in raising student achievement, incorporates whole school checklists and advice for school leaders on facilitating visible learning in their institution, and adds additional meta-analyses bring the total cited within the research base to over 900 meta-analyses.

Hulpia, H., & Devos, G. (2010). How distributed leadership can make a difference in teachers' organizational commitment. A qualitative study. *Teaching and Teacher Education: An International Journal of Research and Studies, 26*(3), 565-575.

The present study explores the relation between distributed leadership and teachers' organizational commitment. Semi-structured interviews with teachers and school leaders of secondary schools were conducted. A comparative analysis of four schools with high and four schools with low committed teachers was carried out. Findings revealed differences in the leadership practices, which influenced organizational commitment. The leadership practices include the quality and distribution of leadership functions, social interaction, cooperation of the leadership team, and participative decision making. Teachers reported being more strongly committed to the school if the leaders were highly accessible, tackled problems efficiently or empowered teachers to participate, and frequently monitored teachers' daily practices.

Isaacs, A. J. (2003). *An investigation of attributes of school principals in relation to resilience and leadership practices.* Unpublished doctoral dissertation, Florida State University, Tallahassee, Florida. Retrieved September 13, 2011, from http://etd.lib.fsu.edu/theses_1/available/etd-09212003-212500/unrestricted/Dissertation_Isaacs_full.pdf.

The purpose of this investigation was to determine relationships among the dimensions of resilience, leadership practices, and individual demographics of high school principals toward strengthening the leadership abilities of principals. This quantitative study employed the survey method in its research design. Those surveyed included 68 high school principals, 136 assistant principals, and 340 teachers selected from 6 school districts in the State of Florida. The investigation used three online questionnaires to collect data on the dimensions of resilience, leadership practices, and demographics of these principals. The data were analyzed by using three statistical methods: Pearson-Product Moment Correlation, T-test, and Analysis of Variance (ANOVA). Hypothesis testing was introduced to determine statistical significance. The investigation found significant relationships among the resilience dimensions of Positive: The World, Focused, Flexible: Thoughts, Organized and Proactive, and the leadership practices of challenging the process, inspiring a shared vision, enabling others to act, modeling the way, and encouraging the heart of high school principals. Thus, the researcher concluded that high school principals who have a higher percentage of resilience dimensions of Positive: The World, Focused, Flexible: Thoughts, Organized and Proactive are better able to employ the leadership practices of challenging the process, inspiring a shared vision, enabling others to act, modeling the way, and encouraging the heart to become more effective high school principals. The implications of the investigation suggested a base of knowledge from which school principals could assess their leadership strengths and weaknesses and improve their leadership performance. It also provided a basis for the selection of materials for enhancing in-service components in school leadership for school districts and for pre-service courses in educational leadership for universities charged with training principals. Further research was recommended on resiliency in education because it is a critical component to successfully managing change.

Jean-Marie, G., Normore, A. H., & Brooks, J. S. (2009). Leadership for social justice: Preparing 21st-century school leaders for a new social order. *Journal of Research on Leadership Education, 4*(1), 1–31.

At the dawn of the 21st century, there has been an increased focus on social justice and educational leadership (Bogotch, Beachum, Blount, Brooks, & English, 2008; Marshall & Oliva, 2006; Shoho, Merchang, & Lugg, 2005). This paper explores and extends themes in contemporary educational research on leadership preparation in terms of social justice and its importance for both research and practice on a national and international level. In particular, it examines various considerations in the literature regarding whether or not leadership preparation programs are committed to, and capable of, preparing school leaders to think globally and act courageously about social justice for a new social order.

Jonsson, A., & Svingby, G. (2007). The use of scoring rubrics: Reliability, validity, and educational consequences [Electronic version]. *Educational Research Review, 2,* 130–144.

Several benefits of using scoring rubrics in performance assessments have been proposed, such as increased consistency of scoring, the possibility to facilitate valid judgment of complex competencies, and promotion of learning. This paper investigates whether evidence for these claims can be found in the research literature. Several databases were searched for empirical research on rubrics, resulting in a total of 75 studies relevant for this review. Conclusions are that: (1) the reliable scoring of performance assessments can be enhanced by the use of rubrics, especially if they are analytic, topic-specific, and complemented with exemplars and/or rater training; (2) rubrics do not facilitate valid judgment of performance assessments per se. However, valid assessment could be facilitated by using a more comprehensive framework of validity when validating the rubric; (3) rubrics seem to have the potential of promoting learning and/or improving instruction. The main reason for this potential lies in the fact that rubrics make explicit expectations and criteria, which also facilitates feedback and self-assessment.

Kaplan, L. S., Owings, W. A., & Nunnery, J. (2005). Principal quality: A Virginia study connecting interstate school leaders licensure consortium standards with student achievement. *NASSP Bulletin, 89*(643), 28–44.

Investigators randomly selected principals from Virginia's public schools to investigate the significant relationship that exists between principal quality and student achievement. Two persons supervising each principal were asked to complete the Interstate School Leaders Licensure Consortium (ISLLC)–based questionnaire about the principal. State achievement test data were entered for each principal's school. Those principals who had been in their schools fewer than five years were dropped from the study to better control for principals' effect on student achievement. Results find that principals who were rated higher on school leadership standards have schools with higher student achievement than comparable schools headed by lower-rated principals. Implications for increasing student achievement, professional development, and evaluation are discussed.

LaPointe, M., & Davis, S. H. (2006). Effective schools require effective principals. *Leadership, 36*(1), 16–19.

At long last, scholars and policy makers have come to realize what most school administrators have known for years—-that effective schools require both outstanding teachers and strong leaders. Although there is considerable research about the characteristics of effective school leaders and the strategies principals can use to help manage increasingly diverse roles, comparatively little is known about how to design programs that can develop and sustain effective leadership practices. In an effort to increase the knowledge about professional development programs, the Wallace Foundation recently commissioned a study of innovative principal professional development programs and the policy and funding mechanisms that support them. In fall 2003, a team of researchers from the Stanford School of Education was awarded a Wallace grant and proceeded to design and embark upon a nationwide study of both the pre- and in-service professional development of school principals. This article discusses the findings about the qualities and impact of strong programs from a study of professional development for principals.

Leithwood, K., Day, C., Sammons, P., Harris, A., & Hopkins, D. (2006). *Successful school leadership: What it is and how it influences pupil learning.* PDF article retrieved from http://illinoisschoolleader.org/research_compendium/documents/successful_school_leadership.pdf on September 26, 2012.

This research report provides a state-of-the-evidence description of what is already known about successful leadership. In doing so, it considers definitions of leadership, the nature of successful leadership practices, the effects of distributed leadership, and the characteristics of successful leaders. It also examines how successful leaders can influence their immediate colleagues and have an impact upon pupil learning. The authors describe three leadership practices, which (based on their summative, qualitative judgments or impressions arrived at after carefully reading the substantial quantity of literature cited in their review) have a strong relationship to improved student achievement: (1) Direction setting—vision, goals, and expectations, (2) Developing people—individual support, intellectual stimulation, modeling, and (3) Redesigning the organization—culture, structure, partnership, family, outside connections.

Leithwood, K., Harris, A., & Hopkins, D. (2008). Seven strong claims about successful school leadership. *School Leadership and Management, 28*(1), 27–42.

This article provides an overview of the literature concerning successful school leadership. It draws on the international literature and is derived from a more extensive review of the literature completed in the early stage of the authors' project. The prime purpose of this review is to summarize the main findings from the wealth of empirical studies undertaken in the leadership field. These claims are as follows:

1. School leadership is second only to classroom teaching as an influence on pupil learning.

2. Almost all successful leaders draw on the same repertoire of basic leadership practices.

3. The ways in which leaders apply these basic leadership practices—not the practices themselves—demonstrate responsiveness to, rather than dictation by, the contexts in which they work.

4. School leaders improve teaching and learning indirectly and most powerfully through their influence on staff motivation, commitment, and working conditions.

5. School leadership has a greater influence on schools and students when it is widely distributed.

6. Some patterns of distribution are more effective than others.

7. A small handful of personal traits explain a high proportion of the variation in leadership effectiveness. For example, "… the most successful school leaders are open-minded and ready to learn from others. They are also flexible rather than dogmatic in their thinking within a system of core values, persistent (e.g., in pursuit of high expectations of staff motivation, commitment, learning and achievement for all), resilient and optimistic."

Leithwood, K., & Jantzi, D. (2008). Linking leadership to student learning: The role of collective efficacy. *Educational Administration Quarterly, 44*(4), 496–528.

This study aimed to improve our understanding of the nature, causes, and consequence of school leader efficacy, including indirect influences on student learning. Authors asked about district contributions to school leader efficacy, whether leader self- and collective efficacy responded to the same or different district conditions, and the effects of leader efficacy on conditions in the school and the learning of students. Evidence for the study was provided by 96 principal and 2,764 teacher respondents to two separate surveys, along with student achievement data in language and math averaged over three years. Path analytic techniques were used to address the objectives for the study. In this study, school leaders' collective efficacy was an important link between district conditions and both the conditions found in schools and their effects on student achievement. School leaders' sense of collective efficacy also had a strong, positive relationship with leadership practices found to be effective in earlier studies. These results suggest that district leaders are most likely to build the confidence and sense of collective efficacy among principals by emphasizing the priority they attach to achievement and instruction, providing targeted and phased focus for school improvement efforts, and by building cooperative working relationships with schools.

Leithwood, K., Jantzi, D., Earl, L., Watson, N., Levin, B., & Fullan, M. (2004). Strategic leadership for large-scale reform: The case of England's National Literacy and Numeracy Strategies. *Journal of School Leadership and Management, 24*(1), 57–80.

Both "strategic" and "distributed" forms of leadership are considered promising responses to the demands placed on school systems by large-scale reform initiatives. Using observation, interview, and survey data collected as part of a larger evaluation of England's National Literacy and Numeracy Strategies, this study inquired about sources of leadership, the distribution of leadership functions across roles, and how such distribution could also provide the strategic coordination necessary for successful implementation of such an ambitious reform agenda.

Leithwood, K., Louis, K. S., Anderson, S., & Wahlstrom, K. (2004). *How leadership influences student learning. Review of research.* New York: The Wallace Foundation. Retrieved from http://www.cehd.umn.edu/carei/publications/documents/ReviewofResearch.pdf.

This report by researchers from the Universities of Minnesota and Toronto examines the available evidence and offers educators, policymakers, and all citizens interested in promoting successful schools some answers to these vitally important questions. It is the first in a series of such publications commissioned by The Wallace Foundation that will probe the role of leadership in improving learning. As the first step in a major research project aimed at further building the knowledge base about effective educational leadership, available evidence in response to five questions was reviewed. They are: (1) What effects does successful leadership have on student learning? (2) How should the competing forms of leadership visible in the literature be reconciled? (3) Is there a common set of "basic" leadership practices used by successful leaders in most circumstances? (4) What else, beyond the basics, is required for successful leadership? and (5) How does successful leadership exercise its influence on the learning of students? This review of the evidence suggests that successful leadership can play a highly significant—and frequently underestimated—role in improving student learning. This evidence also supports the present widespread interest in improving leadership as a key to the successful implementation of large-scale reform.

Lewis, M. (2008). Community connection and change: A different conceptualization of school leadership. *Improving Schools, 11*(3), 227–237.

Many of our schools are situated in communities characterized by high levels of disadvantage, presenting a range of challenges. One possible response is to acknowledge this disadvantage and to try to address some of the problems it raises for students. Another is for the school to be proactive, recognizing the challenges faced by the community and taking a lead in bringing about change. Part of a larger research project, this article explores the extraordinary leadership role of Prospect Road State School (a pseudonym) in bringing change to a multiply disadvantaged community though collaborative action with other agencies and creative approaches to bringing people together. This school's experiences and achievement illustrate what may be possible when school leadership proactively sets out to improve a community described by the principal as being "in crisis." The experiences explored indicate ways of rethinking the relationship between school and disadvantaged community—of working synergistically with others to make a significant difference.

Lima, J. A. (2008). Department networks and distributed leadership in schools. *School Leadership & Management, 28*(2), 159–187.

Many schools are organized into departments, which function as contexts that frame teachers' professional experiences in important ways. Some educational systems have adopted distributed forms of leadership within schools that rely strongly on the departmental structure and on the role of the department coordinator as teacher leader. This paper reports a study of department networks and distributed leadership in two schools. The study collected two types of data on teacher networks in the schools: attributions of the influence of colleagues on one another's professional development and joint professional practice. Measures included actor centrality and network density. The study identified distinct leadership configurations in different departments. The implications for the study of distributed leadership and for the distribution of leadership roles in educational organizations are discussed.

Loeb, H., Elfers, A. M., & Plecki, M. L. (2010). Possibilities and potential for improving instructional leadership: Examining the views of national board teachers. *Theory into Practice, 49*(3), 223–232.

The expectation for schools to continually improve outcomes for students underscores the importance of tapping teacher leaders' contributions in school improvement and renewal efforts. As National Board (NB) certification has become a common feature of state and district policies to improve teaching and learning, it is worthwhile to explore how this effort has shaped the context and contributions of teacher leadership. Both recent research and a statewide survey of National Board Certified Teachers (NBCTs) suggest that NBCTs may be in a strong position to help support school improvement initiatives. Echoing other studies, findings indicate that NBCTs bring considerable leadership experience to their work and are willing to be engaged in activities necessary to improve teaching and learning. The authors discuss perceived barriers in assuming leadership roles and conclude with approaches that schools, districts, and the National Board for Professional Teaching Standards may take to better tap the leadership potential of accomplished teachers.

Louis, K. S., Leithwood, K., Wahlstrom, K. L., & Anderson, S. E. (2010). *Investigating the links to improved student learning: Final report of research findings.* St. Paul, MN: University of Minnesota. Retrieved from http://www.cehd.umn.edu/carei/ publications/documents/LearningFromLeadershipFinal.pdf.

The final report on the results of a study designed to identify and describe successful educational leadership and to explain how such leadership at the school, district, and state levels can foster changes in professional practice that yield improvements in student learning. The report, commissioned by The Wallace Foundation and issued by the University of Minnesota Center for Applied Research and Educational Improvement and the University of Toronto Ontario Institute for Studies in Education, draws on research conducted over a five-year period.

Marzano, R. J., Waters, T., & McNulty, B. A. (2005). *School leadership that works: From research to results.* Alexandria, VA: Association for Supervision and Curriculum Development.

The authors synthesize 35 years of research on leadership using a quantitative, meta-analysis approach as they felt it provided the most objective means to answer their research question, "What does the research tell us about school leadership?" Utilizing this process, they examined 69 studies involving 2,802 schools, approximately 1.4 million students, and 14,000 teachers. The authors concluded that a highly effective school leader could have a dramatic influence on the overall academic achievement of students. Given the fact that their meta-analysis was based on principal leadership defined in very general terms, they further analyzed the 69 studies in their meta-analysis looking for specific behaviors related to principal leadership. The authors identified 21 "responsibilities" (some of which included situational awareness, flexibility, discipline, monitoring/evaluating, outreach, knowledge of curriculum, instruction, and assessment, order, resources, input, and change agent) of school leaders, which all yield a statistically significant relationship to increases in student achievement.

Mascall, B., Leithwood, K., Straus, T., & Sacks, R. (2008). The relationship between distributed leadership and teachers' academic optimism. *Journal of Educational Administration, 46*(2), 214–228.

The goal of this study was to examine the relationship between four patterns of distributed leadership and a modified version of a variable Hoy, et al. have labeled "teachers' academic optimism." The distributed leadership patterns reflect the extent to which the performance of leadership functions is consciously aligned across the sources of leadership, and the degree to which the approach is either planned or spontaneous. Design/methodology/approach: Data for the study were the responses of 1,640 elementary and secondary teachers in one Ontario school district to two forms of an online survey, xx items in form 1 and yy items in form 2. Two forms were used to reduce the response time required for completion and each form measured both overlapping and separate variables. Findings: The paper finds that high levels of academic optimism were positively and significantly associated with planned approaches to leadership distribution, and conversely, low levels of academic optimism were negatively and significantly associated with unplanned and unaligned approaches to leadership distribution. This study provides as-yet rare empirical evidence about the relationship between distributed leadership and other important school characteristics. It also adds support to arguments for the value of more coordinated forms of leadership distribution.

Millward, P., & Timperley, H. (2010). Organizational learning facilitated by instructional leadership, tight coupling and boundary spanning practices. *Journal of Educational Change, 11*(2), 139–155.

Three organizational learning mediation processes are proposed as mechanisms for organizational change in this article. These include instructional leadership, tight coupling, and boundary spanning. While each of these processes has received attention in the research literature, the authors propose that their power arises from their particular combination rather than the occurrence of each in isolation. The authors illustrate the ways in which these processes might combine to create an organizational learning environment required for the kind of changes needed to raise student achievement. They do this by referring to a case study of a New Zealand school that dramatically improved the learning outcomes of students in reading. They describe the practices of a new principal, who was relatively inexperienced in school management but experienced in curriculum leadership. The case study illustrates how through her instructional leadership the principal was able to span the boundaries of her organization so that within a relatively short space of time the school became a more tightly coupled system that learned how to improve the learning outcomes of its students.

Mitchell, R. M., Ripley, J. Adams, C., & Raju, D. (2011). Trust an essential ingredient in collaborative decision making. *Journal of School Public Relations, 32*(2), 145–170.

This study explored the relationship between trust and collaboration in one Northeastern suburban district. In sum, 122 teachers responded to a trust and a collaboration survey. The authors hypothesized that the level of trust would be correlated with the level of collaboration. Bivariate and canonical correlations were used to analyze the findings. This study confirmed that trust in the principal was correlated with collaboration with the principal and that trust in colleagues was correlated with collaboration with colleagues. However, trust in clients (students and parents) was not correlated with collaboration with parents. The set of trust variables together explained 71 percent of the variance in the collaboration variables, with trust in clients being the most significant variable in predicting teacher–teacher collaboration. Collaboration with colleagues was the most potent of the collaboration variables. These findings suggest the importance of establishing a culture of trust in fostering collaboration between teachers. More research is needed to understand the complexities involved with parent collaboration.

Murphy, J., Smylie, M., Mayrowetz, D., & Louis, K. S. (2009). The role of the principal in fostering the development of distributed leadership. *School Leadership & Management, 29*(2), 181–214.

This article explores the role that formal leaders play in helping distributed leadership take root and flourish in schools. The focus of the study is an urban middle school, one of six cases in a larger three-year investigation of distributed leadership in two mid-Atlantic states. Using interview and document-based data, the authors illustrate ways in which the principal of Glencoe Middle School worked to overcome cultural, structural, and professional barriers to create a leadership-dense organization.

Nelson, B., & Sassi, A. (2005). *The effective principal: Instructional leadership for high quality learning.* New York, NY: Teachers College Press.

This volume examines how effective instructional leadership by principals and other school administrators is affected by their own knowledge and beliefs about learning, teaching, and subject matter. Using mathematics as a subject focus, the authors examine several specific aspects of instructional leadership, such as teacher supervision and classroom observation, curriculum selection, and student assessment. Nelson and Sassi provide detailed portraits of administrators at work, illuminating key decision-making situations and the actions they choose to take. This volume: (1) Looks at a new image of the school principal, one that is tied more closely to learning and teaching; (2) Discusses what instructional leaders need to know about subject matter in order to discharge their responsibility effectively in the current climate of standards and accountability; (3) Presents the voices of elementary school principals as they develop new ideas and work to connect these ideas to their administrative practice; (4) Examines how principals view themselves as on-the-job learners, how they work with teachers, and how they perceive their role within the broader organizational and political context; and (5) Offers important implications for mathematics education, educational policy, and school improvement.

Nettles, S. M., & Herrington, C. (2007). Revisiting the importance of the direct effects of school leadership on student achievement: The implications for school improvement policy. *Peabody Journal of Education, 82*(4), 724–736.

Much is left to be known regarding the impact of school principals on student achievement. This is because much of the research on school leadership focuses not on actual student outcomes but rather on other peripheral results of principal practices. In the research that has been done in this area, significant relationships have been identified between selected school leadership practices and student learning, indicating that evidence existed for certain principal behaviors to produce a direct relationship with student achievement. Further, although these relationships typically account for a small proportion of the total student achievement variability, they are of sufficient magnitude to be of interest and additional investigation. Actions taken to better understand and improve the impact of principals on the achievement of students in their schools have the potential for widespread benefit, as individual improvements in principal practice can impact thousands of students. It is in this light that potential direct effects of principal practices should be revisited.

Page, D. (2010). Systemic efforts in Georgia to improve education leadership. *Performance Improvement, 49*(3), 11–16.

Research points to links between school and school district leadership and student achievement. Local and national education reform has created rising expectations for student performance. Education leadership is both complex and high stakes. Key stakeholders in Georgia have developed a solution to improve factors in the work, workplace, and therefore workers' performance in education leadership using human performance technology standards and practices blended from business and education to improve education leadership in Georgia and beyond.

Patteron, J. F., & Kelleher, P. (2007). Resilience in the midst of the storm. *Principal Leadership, 7*(8), 16–20.

Resilience is a trait that can help school leaders use their energy wisely when faced with adversity. But why do some leaders emerge from adversity with a balance in their account and others with a deficit? To explore this question, the authors conducted a case study with a single focus: "How do resilient school leaders move ahead in the face of adversity?" They identified six specific strengths that contribute to increased resilience. This case study illustrates the dynamics of how one principal demonstrated the six strengths of resilient leaders as he led a task force effort in his school district. He drew upon these strengths to form a strong foundation for moving ahead in the face of adversity. Equally important, he created the quiet, reflective time to examine how he performed and assessed how he could build on these strengths in the future. In summary, he modeled what it takes to be a resilient leader in the midst of a storm.

Patterson, J. L., Goens, G. A., & Reed, D. E. (2008). Joy & resilience: Strange bedfellows. *School Administrator, 65*(11), 28–29.

Joy does not come easily to superintendents. The path is often strewn with conflict, adversity, and crises. In their own experience supporting superintendents across the country, the authors have learned that joy in the face of adversity accrues primarily to superintendents who demonstrate the elements of resilience. Resilient superintendents possess the ability to recover, learn, and grow stronger when confronted by chronic or crisis adversity. In this article, the authors suggest that in the face of adversity, superintendents must call upon three broad skill sets to be resilient: (1) resilience thinking skills; (2) resilience capacity skills; and (3) resilience action skills. Examples of superintendents who have developed these skill sets serve as models for others.

Peters, A. (2011). (Un)planned failure: Unsuccessful succession planning in an urban district. *Journal of School Leadership, 21*(1), 64–86.

Leader succession is often the result of a broken system, resulting in the loss of leadership gains from the exiting leader and leaving the incoming leader without proper support for success. The author contends that this system needs to be replaced with a system of dynamic succession planning that is carefully planned and an integral part of a school's improvement plan. To examine and understand these challenges in successful succession planning, the author undertook a qualitative instrumental case study of a founding high school principal and her successor in an urban district engaged in small school reform. The findings suggest that these leaders' lack of sustainability was influenced by a lack of district support and mentoring. These supports (or their lack thereof) affected the school's and district's effectiveness in transitioning the successor, planning for new leadership, and anticipating the supports needed for the school and its leaders.

Reed, D., & Patterson, J. L. (2007). Voices of resilience from successful female superintendents. *Journal of Women in Educational Leadership, 5*(2), 89–100.

School superintendents work in increasingly high-stakes environments full of adversity. The purpose of this study was to examine how female superintendents apply strategies to confront adversity and become more resilient in the process. Fifteen female superintendents in New York State were interviewed. The findings about resilient leadership are reflected in five action themes that emerged from the data: (a) remain value-driven, not event-driven; (b) comprehensively assess past and current reality; (c) stay positive about future possibilities; (d) maintain a base of caring and support; and (e) act on the courage of your convictions. The study also reports on participant comments about the distinction between resilient female superintendents and male superintendents.

Reeves, D. B. (2002). *The daily disciplines of leadership: How to improve student achievement, staff motivation, and personal organization.* San Francisco, CA: Jossey-Bass.

In this book, the author offers educational leaders a practical primer for meeting the daily challenges of school leadership, including a discussion on the purpose of leadership. He presents four leadership archetypes and suggests effective strategies for action. More importantly, the author demonstrates how to include leadership in an integrated system of educational accountability, teaching, and curriculum for student achievement; clear your desk of activities that are ineffective, obsolete, and unnecessary; and develop the skills leaders need to evaluate, coach, and groom new leaders.

Reeves, D. B. (2006). *The learning leader: How to focus school improvement for better results.* Alexandria, VA: Association for Supervision and Curriculum Development.

The book describes the PIM™ (Planning, Implementation, and Monitoring) Study involving more than 280,000 students and almost 300 schools in Nevada's Clark County School District. Clark County School District is one of the nation's largest school systems that is considered a "majority–minority" district, with a majority of its students who are members of ethnic minorities. Clark County includes schools that have some of the nation's highest-performing students and schools in challenging urban settings that contain profoundly disadvantaged students. Each of the school improvement plans were scored on 17 separate indicators using a rubric that was subjected to an internal assessment of inter-rater reliability, with a double-blind check for consistency. This study sought to answer the following question: "When the external variables—governance, budget, union agreements, policies, and planning requirements—are constant, then which variables are most related to improvements in student achievement and educational equity?" The study found that there are correlations between specific elements of building plans and student achievement that can give school leaders insight into how to focus their efforts as they revise and improve their school improvement plans. More importantly, the study identified two variables, implementation and frequent monitoring, as being particularly important variables influencing student achievement and equity.

Reeves, D. B. (2010). *Transforming professional development into student results.* Alexandria, VA: Association for Supervision and Curriculum Development.

This book addresses the question, "How can we create and sustain professional learning programs that actually lead to improved student achievement?" The author presents an informative guide for teachers, administrators, and policymakers. First, the author casts a critical eye on professional learning that is inconsistent, unfocused, and ultimately ineffective and explains why elaborate planning documents and "brand-name" programs are not enough to achieve desired outcomes. Then the author outlines how educators at all levels can improve the situation by (1) taking specific steps to move from vision to implementation, (2) focusing on four essentials—teaching, curriculum, assessment, and leadership, (3) making action research work, (4) moving beyond the "train the trainer" model, and (5) using performance assessment systems for teachers and administrators.

Reeves, D. B. (2011). *Finding your leadership focus: What matters most for student results.* New York: Teachers College Press.

This book identifies three essential clusters of leadership practices that positively impact student achievement: focus, monitoring, and efficacy. Reeves' evaluation of 15 leadership practices revealed that a combination of high scores in these three practices yielded strikingly positive results for all schools and all subjects for which he was able to gather student achievement results: reading, writing, math, and science. The author's research is carefully documented (in the Appendices) and clearly argued throughout the book.

Richards, P. (2008). A competency approach to developing leaders—is this approach effective? *Australian Journal of Adult Learning, 48*(1), 131–144.

This paper examines the underlying assumptions that competency-based frameworks are based upon in relation to leadership development. It examines the impetus for this framework becoming the prevailing theoretical base for developing leaders and tracks the historical path to this phenomenon. Research suggests that a competency-based framework may not be the most appropriate tool in leadership development across many organizations, despite the existence of these tools in those organizations, and reasons for this are offered. Varying approaches to developing effective leaders are considered and it is suggested that leading is complex as it requires both competencies and qualities in order for a person to be an effective leader. It is argued that behaviorally based competencies only cater to a specific part of the equation when they relate to leadership development.

Robinson, V. (2011). *Student-centered leadership.* San Francisco, CA: Jossey-Bass.

Instructional leadership has been a much talked about topic in educational research for a number of years. Robinson finally helps educators understand what school leaders would be doing if they are operating as instructional leaders. This book offers a timely and thoughtful resource for school leaders who want to turn their ideals into action. Written by an educational leadership expert from the University of Aukland in New Zealand, Viviane Robinson, the book identifies five dimensions of instructional leadership that are strongly related to increases in student achievement and provides practical examples of how leaders can make a bigger difference to the quality of teaching and learning in their school and ultimately improve their students' performance. This book is based not on fad or fashion, but on the best available evidence about the impact of instructional leadership on student outcomes. The book includes examples of five types of leadership practice as well as rich accounts of the knowledge and skills that leaders need to employ them with confidence.

Filled with practical lessons for practicing leaders, clear information, and much inspiration, the author encourages leaders to experiment with changing how they lead so they can transform their schools for the better.

Robinson, V. M. J. (2010). From instructional leadership to leadership capabilities: Empirical findings and methodological challenges. *Leadership and Policy in Schools, 9*(1), 1–26.

While there is considerable evidence about the impact of instructional leadership on student outcomes, there is far less known about the leadership capabilities that are required to confidently engage in the practices involved. This article uses the limited available evidence, combined with relevant theoretical analyses, to propose a tentative model of the leadership capabilities required to engage in effective instructional leadership. Research is suggestive of the importance of three interrelated capabilities: (1) using deep leadership content knowledge to (2) solve complex school-based problems, while (3) building relational trust with staff, parents, and students. It is argued that there is considerable interdependence between these three capabilities, and fine-grained specification of each is less important than developing leadership frameworks, standards, and curricula that develop their skillful integration.

Robinson, V. M. J., Lloyd, C. A., & Rowe, K. J. (2008). The impact of leadership on student outcomes: An analysis of the differential effects of leadership types. *Education Quarterly, 44*(5), 635–674. Retrieved on April 6, 2009, from http://eaq.sagepub.com at Regent University Library.

The purpose of this study was to examine the relative impact of different types of leadership on students' academic and nonacademic outcomes. The methodology involved an analysis of findings from 27 published studies of the relationship between leadership and student outcomes. The first meta-analysis, including 22 of the 27 studies, involved a comparison of the effects of transformational and instructional leadership on student outcomes. The second meta-analysis involved a comparison of the effects of five inductively derived sets of leadership practices on student outcomes. Twelve of the studies contributed to this second analysis. The first meta-analysis indicated that the average effect of instructional leadership on student outcomes was three to four times that of transformational leadership. Inspection of the survey items used to measure school leadership revealed five sets of leadership practices or dimensions: establishing goals and expectations; resourcing strategically; planning, coordinating, and evaluating teaching and the curriculum; promoting and participating in teacher learning and development; and ensuring an orderly and supportive environment. The second meta-analysis revealed strong average effects for the leadership dimension involving promoting and participating in teacher learning and development and moderate effects for the dimensions concerned with goal setting and planning, coordinating, and evaluating teaching and the curriculum.

Rossi, G. A. (2007). *The classroom walkthrough: The perceptions of elementary school principals on its impact on student achievement.* Unpublished doctoral dissertation, University of Pittsburgh.

The purpose of this qualitative study was to focus on elementary school principals using the walkthrough model and to evaluate how the walkthrough model improves student learning. The goal was to identify the key indicators of success from elementary principals who used the Walkthrough Observation Tool from the Principals Academy of Western Pennsylvania. The research questions investigated elementary school principals' perceptions of the impact of the classroom walkthrough model. Participants were selected because of their involvement and experiences with the walkthrough model developed by Joseph Werlinich and Otto Graf, co-directors of the Principals Academy of Western Pennsylvania. Methods of data collection were face-to-face semistructured interviews. The interviews were transcribed verbatim and content analysis was used to identify consensus comments, supported, and individual themes. Key findings of this study indicate that the classroom walkthrough did affect instructional practices and student achievement from the perspective of the elementary school principals. The study showed that teachers are sharing and more aware of best practices, principals are more aware of what is occurring in the classrooms, principals have meaningful data to share with teachers, and principals are better-informed instructional leaders.

Saunders, W. M., Goldenberg, C. N., & Gallimore, R. (2009). Increasing achievement by focusing grade-level teams on improving classroom learning: A prospective, quasi-experimental study of title I schools. *American Educational Research Journal, 46*(4), 1006–1033.

The authors conducted a quasi-experimental investigation of effects on achievement by grade-level teams focused on improving learning. For two years (Phase 1), principals-only training was provided. During the final three years (Phase 2), school-based training was provided for principals and teacher leaders on stabilizing team settings and using explicit protocols for grade-level meetings. Phase 1 produced no differences in achievement between experimental and comparable schools. During Phase 2, experimental group scores improved at a faster rate than at comparable schools and exhibited greater achievement growth over three years on state-mandated tests and an achievement index. Stable school-based settings, distributed leadership, and explicit protocols are key to effective teacher teams. The long-term sustainability of teacher teams depends on coherent and aligned district policies and practices. (Contains 6 tables and 2 figures.)

Schrum, L., Galizio, L. M., & Ledesma, P. (2011). Educational leadership and technology integration: An investigation into preparation, experiences, and roles. *Journal of School Leadership, 21*(2), 241–261.

This research, looking through the lens of Fullan (1991) regarding the complexity of implementing school-wide change, sought to explore preparation and requirements of new administrators with respect to the integration of technology by first gathering data regarding licensure and course requirements from state departments of education and educational institutions. Overall, most states and institutions do not require any formal preparation in understanding or implementing technology for instructional purposes, and likely their graduates are not prepared to implement technology systemically in their school. Given that these data were remarkably uniform, next researchers sought to gather experiences, training, and perspectives of technology-savvy administrators as to how they learned what they know and how they lead their schools in the 21st century. The research found that administrators do learn on their own, have a dedication to these changes, and promote their staff members' implementation through professional development, by modeling its use, and by purposefully setting goals for their school.

Schulte, D. P., Slate, J. R., & Onwuegbuzie, A. J. (2010). Characteristics of effective school principals: A mixed-research study. *Alberta Journal of Educational Research, 56*(2), 172–195.

In this multi-stage mixed analysis study, the views of 615 college students enrolled at two Hispanic-serving institutions in the Southwest were obtained concerning characteristics of effective school principals. Through the method of constant comparison (qualitative phase), 29 dominant themes were determined to be present in respondent-identified characteristics of effective school principals: Leader, Communication, Caring, Understanding, Knowledgeable, Fair, Works Well with Others, Listening, Service, Organized, Disciplinarian, Good Attitude, Patience, Respectful, Helping, Open-Mindedness, Motivating,

Professional, Flexible, Being Visible, Honest, Good Role Model, Responsible, Builds Relationships, Involving, Consistent, Friendly, Focus on Schools, and Experience in the Classroom. An exploratory factor analysis revealed that these 29 themes represented five meta-themes. Then these themes (quantitative phase) were converted into numbers (i.e., quantitized) into an interrespondent matrix that consisted of a series of 1s and 0s and were analyzed to determine whether participants' themes differed as a function of sex, ethnicity, college status, and first-generation/non-first-generation status. Statistically significant differences were present between undergraduate and graduate students, between males and females, between Hispanics and Whites, and between first-generation and non-first-generation college students. Implications are discussed.

Seashore, K. R. (2009). Leadership and change in schools: Personal reflections over the last 30 years. *Journal of Educational Change, 10*(2–3), 129–140.

The two fields of leadership studies and school change have increasingly converged over the last 30 years. This paper reviews the origins of the intersection and the development of research themes in three areas: The role of leaders in shaping and using organizational culture, the agency of teachers in the change process, and the importance of leadership in knowledge use. The conclusion suggests some arenas for further research and areas of policy application.

Silins, H., & Mulford, W. (2002). Schools as learning organizations: The case for system, teacher and student learning. *Journal of Educational Administration, 40*, 425–446.

An Australian government–funded four-year research project involving 96 secondary schools, more than 5,000 students, and 3,700 teachers and their principals has provided a rich source of information on schools conceptualized as learning organizations. The LOLSO project focused on three aspects of high school functioning: leadership, organizational learning, and the impact of both on student outcomes. This research has established a relationship between the system factors of leadership and organizational learning and student outcomes as measured by student levels of participation in and engagement with school. This paper summarizes this research and reports on a study that empirically tests the relationship between students' participation in and engagement with school and student achievement using model building and path analysis. The importance of learning at the system, teacher, and student level is discussed in the context of school restructuring.

Silins, H. C., Mulford, W. R., & Zarins, S. (2002). Organizational learning and school change. *Educational Administration Quarterly, 38*(5), 613–642.

This article examines the nature of organizational learning and the leadership practices and processes that foster organizational learning in Australian high schools. A path model is used to test the relationships between school-level factors and school outcome measures in terms of students' participation in and engagement with school. The importance of re-conceptualizing schools as learning organizations to promote successful school change is discussed.

Smith, R. L. (2011). *Advanced decision making for results* (training manual). Englewood, CO: Lead + Learn Press.

Advanced Decision Making for Results (ADMR): Helping Leaders Create and Sustain A Culture of Collaborative Inquiry is a professional development program that targets central office and building leaders, builds upon the knowledge and skills clients have learned in our Decision Making for Results and Data Teams Seminars, and introduces participants to the specific knowledge, skills, and practices required to create and support a culture of collaborative inquiry. Simply put, ADMR is concerned with the actions and activities assigned to or required/expected of central office and building leaders in this increasingly complex, competitive, and fast-paced world to help groups become more effective at their work.

Spillane, J. P. (2009). Managing to lead: Reframing school leadership and management. *Phi Delta Kappan, 91*(3), 70–73.

By concentrating on the formal school organization, researchers can miss the informal relationships that are fundamental to leadership. Distributed Leadership Studies (DLS) provides a framework for examining school leadership and management that considers the interactions of leaders, followers, and aspects of the context. The framework involves two core aspects: principal plus and practice. The principal plus aspect acknowledges that multiple individuals are involved in leading and managing schools. The practice aspect prioritizes the "practice" of leading and managing and frames this practice as emerging from "interactions" among school leaders and followers, mediated by the situation in which the work occurs.

Steiner, L., & Hassel, E. A. (2011). *Using competencies to improve school turnaround principal success.* Charlottesville, VA: University of Virginia's Darden/Curry Partnership for Leaders in Education. Retrieved from http://www.darden.virginia.edu/web/uploadedFiles/Darden/Darden _Curry_PLE/UVA_School_Turnaround/School_Principal_Turnaround _Competencies.pdf.

This paper, produced for the University of Virginia's School Turnaround Specialist Program, describes how using competencies that predict performance can improve turnaround principal selection, evaluation, and development. Although the term "competency" often describes any work-related skill, in this context competencies are the underlying motives and habits—patterns of thinking, feeling, acting, and speaking—that cause a person to be successful in a specific job or role. The primary critical competencies for school turnaround leader are "achievement" and "impact and influence." Achievement is having the drive and taking actions to set challenging goals and reach a high standard of performance despite barriers. Impact and influence is acting with the purpose of affecting the perceptions, thinking, and actions of others. This report provides guidance for organizations on how to use competencies to select, evaluate, and develop effective school turnaround leaders.

Sun, M., & Youngs, P. (2009). How does district principal evaluation affect learning-centered principal leadership? Evidence from Michigan school districts. *Leadership and Policy in Schools, 8*(4), 411–445.

This study used Hierarchical Multivariate Linear models to investigate relationships between principals' behaviors and district principal evaluation purpose, focus, and assessed leadership activities in 13 school districts in Michigan. The study found that principals were more likely to engage in learning-centered leadership behaviors when the purposes of evaluation included principal professional development, school restructuring, and accountability; when the focus of evaluation was related to instructional leadership; and when evaluation addressed leadership in school goal setting, curriculum design, teacher professional development and evaluation, and monitoring student learning. The findings from this study have implications for improving district evaluation policies and practices.

Torrance, D. (2009). Distributed leadership in Scottish schools: Perspectives from participants recently completing the revised Scottish qualification for headship programme. *Management in Education, 23*(2), 63–70.

The Scottish Qualification for Headship (SQH) was established in 1998 and is organized and delivered by two (previously three) consortia comprising a partnership model with universities and local authorities. SQH participants are encouraged to adopt a distributed style of leadership in taking forward their School Improvement Project. Currently, SQH participants are exposed to some of the "big ideas" within the distributed leadership literature, but there is an expectation that participants ground theory in their own practice and in the contextual practice of their schools. This article describes research that explores the experiences of the first cohort of participants graduating from the revised SQH programme at the University of Edinburgh. Findings of this study imply that SQH participants encounter a range of tensions in trying to take forward a "distributed leadership perspective" in leading school improvement initiatives.

Wahlstrom, K. L., Louis, K. S., Leithwood, K., & Anderson, S. A. (2010). *Investigating the links to improved student learning: Executive summary of research findings.* St. Paul, MN: University of Minnesota. Retrieved from http://www.cehd.umn.edu/carei/publications/documents/learning-from-leadership-exec-summary.pdf.

The executive summary of research findings from a study designed to identify and describe successful educational leadership and to explain how such leadership at the school, district, and state levels can foster changes in professional practice that yield improvements in student learning. The report, commissioned by The Wallace Foundation and issued by the University of Minnesota Center for Applied Research and Educational Improvement and the University of Toronto Ontario Institute for Studies in Education, draws on research conducted over a five-year period.

Waters, T., Marzano, R. J., & McNulty, B. (2003). *Balanced leadership: What 30 years of research tells us about the effect of leadership on pupil achievement. A working paper.* Denver, CO: Mid-continent Research for Education and Learning (McREL).

Research report detailing the outcomes of a meta-analysis of research on the effects of principal leadership practices on student achievement. The authors conclude that: (1) Leadership matters. A significant, positive correlation exists between effective school leadership and student achievement; (2) Effective leadership can be empirically defined. Contrary to misperceptions that leadership is more art than science, the authors have identified 21 key leadership responsibilities that are significantly correlated with higher student achievement; and (3) Effective leaders not only know what to do, but when, how, and why to do it. This is the essence of balanced leadership—knowing not only which school changes are most likely to improve student achievement, but also understanding staff and community members' dispositions to change and tailoring leadership practices accordingly.

Wayman, J. C., Midgley, S., & Stringfield, S. (2006). *Leadership for data-based decision making: Collaborative educator teams.* Paper presented at the annual meeting of the American Educational Research Association in San Francisco.

The use of student data to inform school improvement is increasing in popularity and importance, but is unfamiliar territory to most educators. The formation of collaborative Data Teams offers a positive environment for faculties to learn together and build an initiative they can call their own. Principals and other school administrators serve an essential role in leading, guiding, and organizing the work of collaborative Data Teams.

In this paper, the authors discuss four contexts that are important for school leaders in the establishment of collaborative Data Teams: (1) "Calibration," (2) Focus on student data, (3) Engagement of educators, and (4) Technology to support data use. Four districts partnering in school reform with the Stupski Foundation served as a backdrop for this discussion, lending practical illustrations for the discussion. The discussion set forth in this paper highlights the potential that lies in collaboration around student data for school improvement, but has also highlighted the fact that educator collaboration and student data investigation are difficult endeavors to perform efficiently.

White, S. H., & Smith, R. L. (2011). *School Improvement for the next generation.* Bloomington, IN: Solution Tree Press.

The authors review school improvement planning efforts that have, for decades, been met with disappointing results. The authors contend that to ignite positive change, educators must adopt next-generation processes. The book expands the planning, implementation, and monitoring framework of first-generation school improvement into a focused cycle that combines collaboration, accountability, planning, implementation, monitoring, and evaluation. The results of this next-generation process are lasting gains in student achievement and systemic changes in educational practices. The authors explain the fundamental shifts in thinking and practice of school improvement, include concrete examples from schools across North America, provide specific strategies and best practices for each phase in the cycle, emphasize the importance of improving both teaching and learning, and focus on the importance of leadership with the school improvement process.

B Appendix B: Multidimensional Leadership Performance Implementation Rubric

Leadership Competencies	4 Deep Implementation (System-wide Impact)	3 Proficient Implementation (Local Impact)	2 Partial Implementation (Leadership Potential)	1 Minimal Implementation
1.1 Develops, articulates, and communicates a shared vision of the MLP System.	*In addition to meeting the requirements for proficient performance, central office and building leaders…* • Share throughout the organization and with other departments, schools, and districts the knowledge and skills they are learning (both successes and failures) from their efforts to help staff to visualize the successfully implemented practices associated with the MLP System.	There is clear evidence central office and building leaders… • Have clearly defined the components of the MLP System, which enables staff to understand its related parts. • Use multiple opportunities to describe and share with staff mental images of what the MLP System practices look like within each of its components when implemented at "proficient" or higher levels. • Have used a variety of means (e.g., spoken word, text, graphics, etc.) to remind staff of the vision of the MLP System and where the district/school is in relationship to realizing it. • Vigorously work at meaning-making with staff; help staff see how the MLP System connects with other initiatives being implemented within the organization.	There is clear evidence central office and building leaders… • Have only partially defined the components of the MLP System. As a result, the undefined parts contribute to staff confusion. • Talk with staff about the MLP processes, but are not confident as to what it is supposed to look like. Consequently, staff receives vague descriptions of the expected practices within its related elements. • Tend to rely on one primary means (e.g., spoken word, text, graphics, etc.) to reinforce with staff the MLP System and where the district/school is in relationship to implementing this change. • Address staff questions about how the MLP System connects to prior initiatives when they ask, but do not proactively seek out areas of staff confusion nor do they have a plan for helping staff make meaning of the initiative relative to other ongoing initiatives.	There is clear evidence central office and building leaders… • Spend little if any energy creating mental images for staff of what the vision of the MLP System looks like when fully implemented. Consequently, staff is left to develop their own idiosyncratic descriptions of what the expected practices are or are not. • Rarely, if ever, talk with staff as to where they are in relationship to the implementation of the MLP System. • Indiscriminately take on every innovation that comes along. Consequently, staff may feel overwhelmed with yet one more initiative that appears to be unconnected to other ongoing change efforts within the organization.

Leadership Competencies	4 Deep Implementation (System-wide Impact)	3 Proficient Implementation (Local Impact)	2 Partial Implementation (Leadership Potential)	1 Minimal Implementation
1.2 Plans and provides resources to support deep implementation of the MLP System.	*In addition to meeting the requirements for proficient performance, central office and building leaders…* • Use the MLP System implementation plan as a teaching device, helping others in the organization understand the interrelationship of milestones reached. • Make sure that the MLP System implementation plan is visible in heavily trafficked areas of the organization so that accomplishments are publicly celebrated and implementation challenges are open for input from a wide variety of sources. • Share knowledge and skills as a result of the implementation of all state legislative and Department of Education requirements throughout the organization and with other departments, schools, and districts.	There is clear evidence central office and building leaders… • Have developed an MLP System implementation plan including, state legislative requirements, goals, specific, measurable adult practices, along with corresponding improvements in student achievement, deadlines, and persons responsible. • Use the MLP System implementation plan to build systems thinking (e.g., how the MLP practices connect with other systems) throughout the district/school. • Have infused the implementation plan with adequate resources (time, money, ongoing training, on-site coaching) to sustain implementation efforts. • See to it that the MLP System implementation plan is frequently revised and updated as milestones are achieved or deadlines are changed. • Have developed specific MLP System facilitator interventions (e.g., observation, formal and informal feedback) to assist with monitoring implementation efforts.	There is clear evidence central office and building leaders… • Have developed an MLP System implementation plan. However, the plan may look like a task analysis of steps that are not measurable nor are they directly connected to anticipated increases in student achievement results. • The implementation MLP System plan and its processes may not necessarily be related to other district/school systems (curriculum, instruction, assessment). • Have politicized the allocation of resources (dollars and materials) making certain that they give a little something to each level within the organization. • Provide staff updates on the MLP System implementation plans but rarely document the impact it's having on the organization. • Make limited use of MLP System implementation interventions to assist with monitoring practices.	There is clear evidence central office and building leaders… • Have not developed an MLP System implementation plan. • Tend to allocate resources based on the pressures of the moment without regard to long-term implementation needs of the MLP System or other high-priority initiatives. • Have little to no awareness of the impact the practices of the MLP System are having on student achievement. • Are not aware of what specific MLP System implementation interventions are available to assist with monitoring practices.

Leadership Competencies	4 Deep Implementation (System-wide Impact)	3 Proficient Implementation (Local Impact)	2 Partial Implementation (Leadership Potential)	1 Minimal Implementation
1.3 Invests in professional learning to support deep implementation of the MLP System.	*In addition to meeting the requirements for proficient performance, central office and building leaders…* • Choose one or two focus areas within the MLP System for professional development, with extensive time in faculty, grade-level, department, and professional development meetings all focused on intensive implementation of a few elements of the MLP System. • Share throughout the organization and with other departments, schools, and districts the knowledge and skills they are learning (both successes and failures) from their efforts to implement the MLP System to spread best practices and build the professional knowledge opportunities of the entire community.	There is clear evidence central office and building leaders… • Afford staff formal, ongoing professional development and other forms of staff and personal development relative to staff needs and the implementation of the MLP System. • Schedule training and development sessions across time as the staff move from novice toward expert (provide information about the MLP System; teaching the skills required of the process; developing positive attitudes about the use of the process; holding workshops; modeling and demonstrating how the MLS System is being used; clarifying misconceptions) in their levels of use of the MLP System. • Are personally engaged in and apply the learning from professional development that is directly linked to the implementation of the MLP System.	There is clear evidence central office and building leaders… • Have provided professional development, but only at the beginning of the MLP System implementation. • Assume that the initial professional development provided staff is sufficient. Consequently, leaders may or may not understand the unique learning needs of their staff relative to deep implementation of the MLP System. • Personally attend the MLP System training but may not systematically apply the concepts to their practice.	There is clear evidence central office and building leaders… • Expect the staff to implement the MLP System. However, the leaders assume individual staff will secure their own training in order to implement the MLP System. • Introduce a professional development program for the MLP System, but quickly leave the room or sit in the room attending to matters other than the professional development content, sending the signal to colleagues that "This really is not worth my time."

Leadership Competencies	4 Deep Implementation (System-wide Impact)	3 Proficient Implementation (Local Impact)	2 Partial Implementation (Leadership Potential)	1 Minimal Implementation
1.4 Monitoring—Checks on progress of those educators implementing the MLP System.	*In addition to meeting the requirements for proficient performance, central office and building leaders…* • Can cite specific examples of practices that have been changed, discontinued, and initiated based on data analysis of the implementation of the MLP System. • Use a variety of data sources, including qualitative and quantitative measures, to help determine the degree to which the MLP System is being implemented compared to gains in student achievement. • Inferences from data collected are shared widely outside of the district/school community in order to share the analysis and replicate their personal and collective successes.	There is clear evidence central office and building leaders… • Are continuously (at least monthly) assessing and monitoring the implementation of the MLP System relative to the impact on student achievement. • Routinely check the progress of each staff member (gather and chart data about the staff needs; collect information about the knowledge and skills of the staff; collect feedback at the end of workshops and provide feedback on the feedback; talk informally with users about their progress) and their level of use of the MLP System. • Use multiple intervention strategies (e.g., observation, formal and informal feedback, etc.) that help them understand staff concerns associated with their attempted use of the MLP System.	There is clear evidence central office and building leaders… • Monitor the implementation of the MLP System fewer than seven (7) times during the school year. Furthermore, the leaders do not compare how adult practices are impacting student achievement. • May or may not know the importance of checking on the progress of each staff member as they implement the MLP System processes. Consequently, they may check the progress of some staff, but not all. Data that is collected is most likely anecdotal and rarely shared with staff. • Utilize mostly informal, casual conversation as their means of understanding staff issues related to implementation efforts.	There is clear evidence central office and building leaders… • Rarely (fewer than four times per year) or never check on the implementation of the MLP System. • Do not collect data on adult practices associated with the implementation of the MLP System or how they are impacting student achievement.

Leadership Competencies	4 Deep Implementation (System-wide Impact)	3 Proficient Implementation (Local Impact)	2 Partial Implementation (Leadership Potential)	1 Minimal Implementation
1.5 Provides continuous assistance to those implementing the MLP System.	*In addition to meeting the requirements for proficient performance, central office and building leaders…* • Create specific adaptations to staff needs relative to their levels of use of the MLP System, rather than merely adopting the tools of external assistance, so that learning tools become part of the culture of the district/school and are "homegrown." • Share knowledge and skills as a result of the implementation of the MLP System throughout the organization and with other departments, schools, and districts.	There is clear evidence central office and building leaders… • Systematically identify staff needs and/or problems and respond (supplying additional materials; providing formal or informal learning activities; teaming with staff to demonstrate refinement of practice relative to the implementation of the MLP System; coaching; assisting single and small-group staff in problem solving; celebrating successes and failures both large and small) in order to support their implementation efforts; in other words, assisting is directly coupled with assessing.	There is clear evidence central office and building leaders… • Respond to staff needs and/or problems when they arise, but tend to rely upon external resources to provide additional professional development or support to meet those needs or solve problems of those implementing the MLP System.	There is clear evidence central office and building leaders… • Are out of touch with the needs of staff relative to their implementation of the MLP System. Consequently, staff is left to their own devices to problem solve and figure out the unique processes associated with the MLP System.

Leadership Competencies	4 Deep Implementation (System-wide Impact)	3 Proficient Implementation (Local Impact)	2 Partial Implementation (Leadership Potential)	1 Minimal Implementation
1.6 Creates a context supportive of the MLP System.	*In addition to meeting the requirements for proficient performance, central office and building leaders...* • Share throughout the organization and with other departments, schools, and districts the creative ways they have overcome specific **physical and people aspects** of the district/school that may be perceived as barriers to implementing the MLP System. • Hire new staff that come with strong values that support the purpose of the MLP System. • Identify and support the acquisition of additional skills and models that focus on deepening the implementation of the MLP System throughout the organization.	There is clear evidence central office and building leaders... • Are supporting the implementation of the MLP System by routinely addressing any **physical** (non-organic) **aspects** of the district/school (schedules, policies, building facilities) that may be perceived as barriers to implementing the MLP System to high levels. • Are supporting the implementation of the MLP System by routinely addressing the **people aspects** of the district/school (the beliefs and values held by the members; norms that guide their behavior, relationships, and attitudes) that could be negatively impacting successful implementation of the MLP System.	There is clear evidence central office and building leaders... • Are supporting the implementation of the MLP System by addressing the **physical** (nonorganic) **aspects** of the school (schedules, policies, building facilities) that may be perceived as barriers to implementing the evaluation framework. • Have yet to adequately address the **people aspects** of the district/school that could be negatively impacting successful implementation of the MLP System, which may be resulting in feelings of confusion and frustration.	There is clear evidence central office and building leaders... • Support for the implementation of the MLP System relative to changes in the **physical** (non-organic) **aspects** or the **people aspects** of the school that may be perceived as barriers to implementing the MLP System is not apparent.

References

Besser, L., Almeida, L., Anderson-Davis, D. M., Flach, T., Kamm, C., & White, S. (2008). *Decision making for results: Data-driven decision making* (2nd ed.). (Training Manual). Englewood, CO: Lead + Learn Press.

Besser, L., Flach, T., Gregg, L., Nagel, D., Syrja, R. C., et al. (2010). *Data teams* (3rd ed.). (Training Manual). Englewood, CO: Lead + Learn Press.

Burns, J. M. (1978). *Leadership.* New York: Harper & Row.

Bryson, J., & Roering, W. D. (1987). Applying private-sector strategic planning in the public sector. *Journal of the American Planning Association, 53:* 9–22.

Byham, W. C., Smith, A. B., & Paese, M. J. (2002). *Grow your own leaders: How to identify, develop, and retain leadership talent.* Upper Saddle River, NJ: Financial Times Prentice Hall.

Connelly, S., Allen, M. T., & Waples, E. (2007). The impact of content and structure on a case-based approach to developing leadership skills. *International Journal of Learning and Change, 2*(3), 218–249.

Covey, S. (1991). *Principle-centered leadership.* New York: Summit Books.

Fullan, M. (1997). *What's worth fighting for in the principalship.* New York: Teachers College Press.

Fullan, M. (2005). *Leadership & sustainability: System thinkers in action.* Thousand Oaks, CA: Corwin Press.

Fullan, M., & Hargreaves, A. (1996). *What's worth fighting for in your school?* New York: Teachers College Press.

Fullan, M., Hill, P., & Crévola, C. (2006). *Breakthrough.* Thousand Oaks, CA: Corwin Press.

Garmston, R. J., & Wellman, B. M. (1999). *The adaptive school: A sourcebook for developing collaborative groups.* Norwood, MA: Christopher-Gordon.

Halachmi, A. (1986). Strategic planning and management: Not necessarily. *Public Productivity Review, 40:* 35–50.

Hattie, J. (2009). *Visible learning. A synthesis of over 800 meta-analyses relating to achievement.* New York: Routledge.

Hattie, J. (2012). *Visible learning for teachers: Maximizing impact on learning.* New York: Routledge.

Heifetz, R. A. (1994). *Leadership without easy answers.* Cambridge, MA: Harvard University Press.

Heifetz, R. A., & Linsky, M. (2002). *Leadership on the line: Staying alive through the dangers of leading.* Boston, MA: Harvard Business School Press.

Jonsson, A., & Svingby, G. (2007). *The use of scoring rubrics: Reliability, validity and educational consequences.* Retrieved January 12, 2012, from http://uncw.edu/cas/documents/JonssonandSvingby2007.pdf

Kannapel, P. J., Clements, S. K., Taylor, D., & Hibpshman, T. (2005, February). *Inside the black box of high-performing high-poverty schools*. Lexington, KY: The Prichard Committee.

Kouzes, J. M., & Posner, B. Z. (1987). *The leadership challenge: How to get extraordinary things done in organizations*. San Francisco, CA: Jossey-Bass.

Kouzes, J. M., & Posner, B. Z. (1993). *Credibility: How leaders gain and lose it, why people demand it*. San Francisco, CA: Jossey-Bass.

Kouzes, J. M., & Posner, B. Z. (2010). *The truth about leadership: The no-fads, heart-of-the-matter facts you need to know*. San Francisco, CA: Jossey-Bass.

Leithwood, K., Jantzi, D., & Steinbach, R. (1999). *Changing leadership for changing times*. Philadelphia, PA: Open University Press.

Lipton, L., Wellman, B., & Humbard, C. (2003). *Mentoring matters: A practical guide to learning-focused relationships* (2nd ed.). Sherman, CT: MiraVia, LLC.

Louis, K. S., Leithwood, K., Wahlstrom, K. L., & Anderson, S. E. (2010). *Investigating the links to improved student learning: Final report of research findings*. St. Paul, MN: University of Minnesota. Retrieved January 26, 2011, from http://www.cehd.umn.edu/carei/publications/documents/LearningFromLeadershipFinal.pdf

Marzano, R. J., Waters, T., & McNulty, B. A. (2005). *School leadership that works: From research to results*. Alexandria, VA: Association for Supervision and Curriculum Development.

Mintzberg, H. (1994). The fall and rise of strategic planning. *Harvard Business Review* (Reprint No. 94107). Retrieved from hbr.org/1994/01/the-fall-and-rise-of-strategic-planning/ar/1

National Research Council. (2000). *How people learn: Brain, mind, experience, and school*. Washington: National Academy Press.

Peters, T. J. (1985). *A passion for excellence: The leadership difference*. New York: Random House.

Peters, T. J., & Waterman, R. H. (1982). *In search of excellence: Lessons from America's best-run companies*. New York: Harper & Row.

Pezdek, K., & Miceli, L. (1982, May). Life-span differences in memory integration as a function of processing time. *Developmental Psychology, 18*(3), 485–490.

Popham, W. J. (2003). *Test better, teach better: The instructional role of assessment*. Alexandria, Va.: Association for Supervision and Curriculum Development.

Reeves, D. B. (2002). *The leader's guide to standards: A blueprint for educational equity and excellence*. San Francisco: Jossey-Bass.

Reeves, D. B. (2004). *Assessing educational leaders: Evaluating performance for improved individual and organizational results*. Thousand Oaks, CA: Corwin Press.

Reeves, D. B. (2006). *The learning leader: How to focus school improvement for better results*. Alexandria, VA: Association for Supervision and Curriculum Development.

Reeves, D. B. (2009). *Assessing educational leaders: Evaluating performance for improved individual and organizational results* (2nd ed.). Thousand Oaks, CA: Corwin Press.

Reeves, D. B. (2010). *Transforming professional development into student results.* Alexandria, VA: Association for Supervision and Curriculum Development.

Reeves, D. B. (2011). *Finding your leadership focus: What matters most for student results.* New York: Teachers College Press.

Robinson, V. (2011). *Student-centered leadership.* San Francisco, CA: Jossey-Bass.

Rowe, M. B. (1972). *Wait-time and rewards as instructional variables: Their influence on language, logic, and fate control.* Paper presented at the National Association for Research in Science Teaching, Chicago, Illinois. (ERIC Document Reproduction Service No. ED 061103).

Rowe, M. B. (1987). Wait time: Slowing down may be a way of speeding up. *American Educator, 11,* 38–43.

Schön, D. A. (1983). *The reflective practitioner.* New York: Basic Books.

Schön, D. A. (1987). *Educating the reflective practitioner.* San Francisco, CA: Jossey-Bass.

Senge, P., Cambron-McCabe, N., Lucas, T., Smith, B., Dutton, J., & Kleiner, A. (2000). *Schools that learn: A fifth discipline fieldbook for educators, parents, and everyone who cares about education.* New York: Doubleday.

Smith, R. L. (2011). *Advanced decision making for results.* (Training Manual). Englewood, CO: Lead + Learn Press.

Stahl, R. J. (1994). *Using "think-time" and "wait-time" skillfully in the classroom.* (ERIC Document Reproduction Service No. 370885).

Tobin, K. (1987). The role of wait time in higher cognitive level learning. *Review of Educational Research, 57,* 69–95.

Wahlstrom, K. L., Louis, K. S., Leithwood, K., & Anderson, S. A. (2010). *Investigating the links to improved student learning: Executive summary of research findings.* St. Paul, MN: University of Minnesota. Retrieved September 25, 2010, from http://www.cehd.umn.edu/carei/publications/documents/learning-from-leadership-exec-summary.pdf

Wheatley, M., & Frieze, D. (2010). Leadership in the age of complexity: *From hero to host.* Retrieved December 1, 2010, from http://www.margaretwheatley.com/writing.html

Index

Curriculum, 197, 199, 221, 222, 235, 236, 237, 238, 267, 325, 326, 327, 328
  adopting, 223, 225, 247
  ENL, 335, 337
  instruction and, 269
  mapping, 201, 202, 255, 256
  monitoring, 223, 225
  standards-based, 187
  writing, 285, 287
Custodians, 265, 266, 319, 320

Data, 8, 360, 362
  academic, 155, 157, 285, 287
  analyzing, 197, 199, 205, 211, 213, 217, 233, 241, 248
  assessment, 132, 200, 202, 215, 217, 234
  behavior, 383, 385
  cause-and-effect, 82, 189, 245, 247, 285, 287, 381, 382, 407, 409
  charts, 275, 276
  collecting, 10, 13–14, 71, 147, 148, 230, 232, 241, 242, 331, 333
  decision making and, xvi, 191, 198, 199, 200, 215, 217, 227, 231, 243, 244, 353, 355, 356
  discipline, 155, 157, 285, 287, 383, 385
  district, 221, 222
  feedback and, 239, 241, 291
  formative, 196, 197, 199
  goals and, 195, 213
  growth, 143, 144
  mathematics, 183, 185
  monitoring, 118, 121, 223, 226
  objective, 229, 231
  personnel, 261, 263
  questions about, 223, 225
  sources of, 205, 247
  strategies and, 213, 221, 222
  student achievement, 189, 191, 193, 195, 216, 217, 218, 273, 274, 275, 276, 285, 287, 331, 333, 375, 377, 379, 380, 382, 383, 386, 389, 392
  success, 190, 192
  survey, 159, 161, 211, 213, 268, 270
  trends with, 235, 237

  using, 159, 195, 197, 199, 213, 245, 247, 377, 381, 382, 383, 385
Data-Driven Decision Making, 99
Data Teams, 19, 99, 118, 132, 159, 160, 161, 162, 189, 190, 191, 192, 203, 216, 218, 221, 297, 298, 299, 300, 370, 372, 381, 382, 401, 402, 408
  impact of, 409
  instructional strategies and, 235, 237
  leadership and, 410
  meetings of, 281, 283, 331, 333, 335, 337
  monitoring plan for, 407, 409
  research-based practice of, 379, 380
  student achievement and, 195, 331, 333
  using, 193, 195, 201, 202, 205, 215, 217, 229, 231, 285, 287, 332, 333, 334, 383, 385, 387, 388, 407, 409
Decision making, xv, 4, 15, 58, 65, 67, 77, 92, 131, 145, 152, 227, 229–248, 254, 295, 301, 311, 313, 335, 337, 412
  achievement and, 225, 243, 244
  authority for, 302, 320
  collaborative, 189
  data and, xvi, 191, 198, 199, 200, 215, 217, 227, 231, 243, 244, 353, 355, 356
  delegating, 296, 298, 316
  effective, 26, 27, 242, 367, 368
  feedback and, 214
  framework for, 153, 154, 193, 195
  leadership and, 220, 234
  learning and, 243, 244
  managing, 329
  matrix, 175, 177, 235, 237
  models for, 229, 231
  opinions and, 406
  process of, 246, 248, 383, 385
  reflecting on/reevaluating, 234
  role of, 327
  understanding, 339, 341

Decision Making for Results, 99, 229, 231, 245–246, 247–248, 275, 276, 285, 287, 360, 362, 381, 382
Decision-Making for Results 6+1 Process, The (Smith), 99
Decision-Making Structure, 58, 92
Decisions Evaluated for Effectiveness, 58, 92
Decisions Linked to Vision, 58, 92
Delayed response, 77–78, 79, 82, 84
Demographics, 223, 225
  student, 203, 205, 226
  understanding, 303, 305
Desired benefits, 117, 118
  instructional example of, 117 (fig.), 119 (fig.)
  noninstructional example of, 117 (fig.)
Discipline problems, 16, 170, 173, 174, 251, 253, 301, 302, 375, 378, 387, 388
  data on, 155, 157, 285, 287, 383, 385
Dissent, 20, 41, 55, 87, 161, 162, 165
  handling, 44, 149, 151, 152, 157
District Crisis Team, 251, 253
District Improvement Plans, 245–246, 247–248, 285, 287, 404
Domain monitoring schedule, sample, 46 (fig.)
Domain Weighted Score, calculating, 51 (table)
Domains, 8, 73, 86
  leadership, 4, 15, 16, 17, 18 (fig.), 131
  MLP, 87–98, 411–415
  rating, 47, 50, 50 (table)

Educating the Reflective Practitioner, 112
Education, 181, 182, 243, 244
  character, 277, 279
  elementary, 281, 283
Effective Grading Practices Summit, 403, 405
ELLs. *See* English Language Learners
Empowerment, 4, 207, 209, 299, 300

English Language Learners (ELLs), 106, 335, 337
  achievement gap for, 401, 402
Ethical and Legal Compliance with Employees, 56, 89
Evaluatee, 9–10
  evaluator meeting with, 13, 14
Evaluation, xvi, 16, 41, 45, 5, 71, 145, 171, 172, 277
  classroom, 278, 280
  implementing, 181, 182
  leadership, 1, 2, 4, 6, 15
  objectivity/consistency in, 17
  performance, 317, 318
  principals and, 289, 291
  process, 9–10, 11, 12, 13, 14, 53, 123, 124, 161
  summative, 9, 123, 124
  system of, 278, 279, 280
  teacher, 304, 306
  tools, 303, 304, 306
  unsatisfactory, 308, 310
Evaluator, 10
  evaluatee meeting with, 13, 14
Excel, 357, 358, 363, 365
Exemplary, 3, 4, 9, 15, 46, 47
  described, 5, 41–42
Expulsion rates, 155, 157

Facility management, 219, 220, 399, 400
Facility Management Forecast, 399, 400
Factual Basis for Decisions, 58, 92
Faculty development, 4, 15, 30, 31, 32, 33, 60, 65, 68, 73, 94–95, 135, 271, 273–292, 413
Faculty Proficiencies and Needs, 60, 94
Feedback, 3, 8, 72, 109, 112, 147, 163, 165, 183, 185, 186, 211, 213, 236, 238, 240, 242, 257, 271, 275, 319, 320, 346
  accepting, 154, 253
  analysis of, 29
  asking for, 232, 252, 254, 261, 262, 263, 264, 377
  constructive, 274, 284
  data and, 239, 241, 291
  decision making and, 214
  electronic, 268, 270
  formal/informal, 31, 276, 287
  formative, 45